Francis A. Drexel
LIBRARY

Books For College Libraries
Third Edition

Core Collection

SAINT JOSEPH'S UNIVERSITY

THE GUIDANCE OF
EXCEPTIONAL CHILDREN

THE GUIDANCE OF
EXCEPTIONAL CHILDREN

A BOOK OF READINGS

Edited by

JOHN CURTIS GOWAN

*Professor of Education and
Chairman of the Guidance Department
San Fernando Valley State College
Northridge, California*

and

GEORGE D. DEMOS

*Associate Dean of Counseling and Testing
and Associate Professor
California State College at Long Beach
Long Beach, California*

DAVID McKAY COMPANY INC.

New York, 1965

THE GUIDANCE OF EXCEPTIONAL CHILDREN: A BOOK OF READINGS

LIBRARY OF CONGRESS CATALOG CARD NUMBER: 65–12639

MANUFACTURED IN THE UNITED STATES OF AMERICA

Foreword

It is remarkable to realize that guidance of exceptional children is a subject just now coming of age. Many of us who have worked in this field have looked forward to the day when guidance would take its place as a full-fledged team member in diagnosis and therapy along with medicine, psychology, social work, education, and administration. That day is now at hand, and those of us who have taught the new and developing courses on the guidance of exceptional children in training institutions now have in this volume a book of readings to serve as a text or supplement.

Professor Gowan and Dean Demos have performed a valuable and highly useful service in bringing together such material for general use. To a wise and perceptive selection of material they have added their own offerings, reflecting a profound guidance emphasis and considerable professional competency in at least several section areas. They have not excluded bibliographies, and have often added their own annotations at the end of chapters, evidencing scholarship in so doing and thereby enhancing the quality of the book. But in the larger sense, it is to be hoped that neither they nor others will delay, now that this first book of readings is out, in attempting to give guidance in this area the philosophical structure and the professional status which it has lately won in other areas. All of us who work with exceptional children will profit from these efforts, and, more importantly, so will those children we refer to as exceptional.

JAMES O. SMITH
Associate Professor of Special Education
The University of Kansas
Lawrence, Kansas

Contents

THE GUIDANCE of exceptional children is one of the last areas of guidance to be developed. Consequently, guidance theory and practice in this area are, in many instances, in a rather primitive state. Typical of this situation is a view which regards guidance as equivalent to vocational information or involved only in the identification of the exceptional child. It is true that testing, on the one hand, and occupational rehabilitation, on the other, are two legitimate functions of pupil personnel services, but between these two extremes stretches a whole continuum of other guidance functions whose delineation becomes plain only with the full development of the art. In this unfoldment, the counselor's function in dealing with the normal and abnormal problems of exceptional children becomes especially important. And it is this process whose description has been particularly prized in the papers selected for this chapter.

The overview opens with a statement by the senior compiler. Then follows Cutter's definitive article regarding the importance of self-concept. Eskridge and Partridge next report on the vocational rehabilitation of exceptional children. This is followed by Muthard and Jaques's wise analysis of counselor opinion in this process. Porter defines the nature of the counselor's job. Rhodes reviews some of the psychological techniques applied to behavior modification. Strang shows how guidance of several different groups of exceptional children has common characteristics. Finally, Switzer concludes with a discussion of the work of the Office of Vocational Rehabilitation. The emphasis of the chapter is on the social and vocational competence of the exceptional child and methods of counselor interaction to change the child's self-concept in that direction.

1. The Guidance of Exceptional Children

JOHN CURTIS GOWAN

C ONCERN for the qualities of exceptional human beings arises out of an exceptional concern for the qualities of all human beings. Thus, a good guidance program for exceptional children is an outgrowth of a good general guidance program, just as the latter in turn is an outcome of an intelligent and democratically oriented school administration.

But concern without knowledge of procedure can be sentimental at best and dangerous at worst; what is needed is the carrying over of the principles and objectives of guidance to fit the special cases involved in the education of exceptional children. It is certainly appropriate to reiterate these principles briefly.

1. School guidance seeks to help children solve their developmental tasks on schedule.

2. School guidance seeks to individualize the curriculum according to the child's needs and capacities.

3. School guidance recognizes the primacy of cognitive competence in influencing emotional health and over-all orientation to reality.

4. School guidance is also concerned with the promotion, establishment, and maintenance of sound social relationships.

5. School guidance seeks to be permissive rather than directive, non-punitive rather than punitive, listening rather than talking, and ameliorative rather than threatening.

6. School guidance seeks first the child's welfare.

It remains only to assess how these principles need to be modified in procedures carried out for the guidance of the exceptional child. Obviously, the major modification in the principles is that of adapting to the capacities of the child and the timing of guidance procedures. We cannot, for example, expect that the retarded child will accomplish all his developmental tasks on schedule. We can, however, begin to help him, very early, and with a wider assortment of people to assist the task.

This brings us to two major departures in the guidance of exceptional children: (1) guidance is distributed over a wider temporal span, starting earlier and extending later in the lifetime of the individual; and (2) guidance is distributed over a wider personnel span, embracing not just the ordinary guidance workers but literally all persons who come in contact with the exceptional child, from his parents onward. It should come as no great

2

surprise to us to find that the guidance of all types of exceptional children follows these general guidelines: whether children are delinquent, potential dropouts, emotionally disturbed, mentally handicapped, or physically handicapped, *the remedy for their problems is to start as early and involve them with as many types of guidance workers as possible, enlisting the home whenever feasible.* It is certainly easier to involve guidance in preschool, school, and vocational training of these unfortunates than to neglect them until they become public charges and then try vainly to rehabilitate them when it is too late. In medicine, we would never think of allowing children to become infected with disease and then try to cure them years later, when we could have prevented the infection in the first place.

The broadened function of guidance may be divided into six areas: (1) parental, (2) preschool, (3) personality and self-concept, (4) cognitive, (5) emotional and social, (6) vocational. These will be treated briefly in turn.

In most cases involving exceptional children, the parents are the most important guidance influence; yet they may be the most unwholesome and unco-operative. Often immobilized by guilt about the exceptional child, coupled with rejection of him, and frequently having problems of their own, their influence is generally negative and usually magnifies whatever problem exists. It is therefore very important that parents be reached and that every effort be made to help them understand and cope with the problem. One of the best ways of handling this is through group guidance sessions with parents who have children with similar problems.

Preschool guidance is very important for the exceptional child, since it accomplishes two important things: it involves a professional worker early in the child's life who can take some of the strain off the parents and the child, and it involves the child early in making a start to cope with his problems. The child hence gets into the habit of open co-operation with others and of looking outside family figures for approval. Such guidance also helps the child in his first efforts to socialize.

In working with exceptional children, a great part of the counselor's job centers around changing their self-concept. This task involves helping the student over a "discontinuity" or transition from one aspect of role function to another in which the student's self-concept is changed from seeing himself in a nonperformance role to seeing himself in a competent performance role. The student who sees himself on the side lines needs to see himself as someone who can and does perform. The following suggestions are pertinent for effecting this change.

1. Give regard and attention to the student's problem; show sympathetic understanding; make him feel that you are interested personally; listen. In many instances, just listening to a student's problem helps him to talk about it and so handle it. To be a person whose problems can be listened to may itself start to change the student's valuation of himself.

2. Get the student to talk about his problem; get it out on the table where it can be looked at. No problem ever seems so bad when it can be discussed, for that which is not possible to talk about is the most fearsome. Merely to be able to state a problem and discuss it may help a student to change his feeling about himself in relation to it.

3. Isolate and specify the fear. Many times a student's self-concept suffers from some vague fear or anxiety blown up out of all proportion to its base. If we can get the student to the specific root of his troubles, we may help him to see that he is not handicapped in all ways—only in a certain number. The isolation and specification of fears allows change in self-concept because it gives the student a larger free area in which to maneuver and he comes to see himself as not completely blocked but still able to operate in a restricted area.

4. Get him to see that others have similar problems. Nothing does as much good to self-concept as to realize that others labor with the same difficulties; and if they can succeed, so can we. Nothing does so much harm as to feel that we are uniquely bad and have a problem totally unlike anyone else's. Here, of course, lies one of the freeing aspects of group therapy. The discovery that others are like himself in their problems is a powerful stimulus to self-concept change.

5. Act as a type of corrective mirror in getting him to see himself as others see him. This step may not always be necessary, but it is often salutary. Good self-concept depends upon objective analysis of feed-back information from one's peers, and we need to help the student to assess properly this intake and insulate himself from the social insensitivity which he has built up around him to preserve his miserable truce in the face of the outside world.

6. Get him to accept himself as he is and to begin to compensate for it. If, as Sullivan suggests, personality is a function of our interactions with the outside world, then we can change self and self-concept by changing the interactions. It seems much easier to a student to change his interactions with others than to change himself. To change his self-concept, we need to help him to take the pressure off himself and place it more on the nature of his outside relationships.

7. Find strengths and build on them. Competence in operation and func-

tion is the key to a healthy self-concept, so we must find some area in which the student is competent and build and enlarge from there. This may be athletics, leadership, aggressiveness, energy, or some special skill. We may have to help others in his circle come to value more his particular skills, and we must use those skills to help alleviate his poor self-concept.

8. Invest confidence and encouragement at the right moment. There comes a crisis time in the treatment of most counseling situations when the counselor has to put his trust and belief in the student on the line and inspire the student to make a large gain in self-concept and do something because the counselor believes he can do it! This operation is something analogous to using a new helper battery to turn over the car whose old battery is insufficiently powerful. The counselor must be careful in picking the right moment for this step because to fail in it is disastrous for both the client and the counseling relationship. However, there will usually come a time when this powerful step can be taken safely and when, as a result of the counselor's belief in him, the student will go out and perform in a way that he did not believe he could. At this point the change in self-concept on the part of the student is often so dramatic that the case is virtually completed.

Change in self-concept is at the basis of effective counseling. We can help students to better and more viable self-concepts as we make easy for them the process of self-concept change. This process, often not well thought out by the counselor, is one of the most important to his general effectiveness.

The process of self-concept change requires changes in attitudes about the self, and many exceptional children will cling to older feelings about self, even though these offer them only a miserable truce in the face of their outlook, because they feel change in themselves as a threat and a further mutilation of personality. We can make this process of change easier for them by focusing on the change in personal relationships with others instead of the change in themselves. Osgood's semantic differential method provides clear suggestions here. Briefly, he found that of all the adjectives used to describe persons, things, and events, three grand clusters were evident: (1) those relating to value (goodness-badness), (2) those relating to potency (weak-strong), and (3) those relating to action (active-passive). Using this cue, we can encourage the exceptional child in his relationships with others to appear better, not worse, than he was yesterday, stronger, not weaker, than he was yesterday, and more active and less passive than he was yesterday. He will see it as possible to make such daily changes in his relationships to others; but actually we are making changes in self-concept and personality as well, though in a much less threatening manner. Of such quiet accretion is the stuff of a healthy self-concept made.

The development of cognitive competence requires a wider view of abilities than we have held heretofore, for education, rightly considered, involves stimulation of all the abilities of man, not just the narrow verbal ones. It is easy to blame failure in school on the fact that the child is exceptional; it is much more difficult to accommodate the school program to the stimulation of the abilities he presents. But this is what we must do to solve the intellectual problems of exceptional children, whether they are potential dropouts, retarded, handicapped, or others. There is no reason why the curriculum program for exceptional children should be tied to academic college requirements: we should find out what abilities these youngsters possess and stimulate them through appropriate curriculum alterations.

The encouragement of emotional needs of children who are exceptional is most important. Not infrequently, such children feel baffled in the expression of their emotional and social feelings and tend to deny them or bottle them up altogether. The arranging of informal and nonthreatening social situations within and without the classroom, the easy availability of small animals, especially those a child can pet and lavish affection on, and opportunity to discuss such problems with a teacher-counselor are all useful devices. Adolescence, partly because of its heterosexual demands, presents especial threat to the exceptional child, and he may try in various ways to keep from growing up. Special help is often needed here. In particular, the school, and especially the guidance function, should be seen by the exceptional child as an agency which ameliorates rather than exacerbates the growing problems of this period.

For the exceptional child, vocational guidance should become a long-term process entwined with the whole educational effort rather than a one-shot incident or an adult-rehabilitation effort. The child should early have some opportunity at vocational exploration, and there should be both discussion and some activity about various methods of making a living. Here, especially, is where a healthy self-concept becomes so important. Children tend to think of handicapped workers as marginal; whereas experience in veteran's rehabilitation work shows that, given an emotionally healthy adult, there is practically no handicap that cannot be tolerated in some occupation.

Since the professional worker who comes in contact with the exceptional child, including the teacher, the physician, the nurse, the social worker, and others, has major responsibilities for dealing with his guidance problems—even more so than with normal children—it is evident that those who work with exceptional children should have thorough guidance training. Yet very often this is not the case. We can only hope that as the importance of longitudinal guidance for exceptional children becomes more evident, there will be more disposition to involve these workers in preservice guidance courses and in in-service guidance techniques. Guidance is often the missing part in the current team approach to the problems of the exceptional child. We can accomplish a great deal more by prevention than by cure. The individualization of education, which is so important for exceptional children, is in essence a guidance problem. The education of exceptional children of all varieties will profit immensely by more thorough application of guidance principles and practices. Then our concern for exceptional children will be supplemented by sound knowledge of techniques to give them the equality of opportunity which they deserve.

2. The Place of Self-Concept in the Education of the Physically Different Child *

ALBERT V. CUTTER, M.D., *Formerly Medical Director of Psychiatric Clinic, Inc., Buffalo, New York; now at 74 Linwood Ave., Buffalo 9, New York*

I'M STUPID, I can't learn in school." This was Tommy's response to the question of why he had come to my office. Helped to reflect on this, he amplified: "Yes, my father calls me stupid, the kids tease me about schoolwork, and they won't play with me. My teacher calls me dumb and gets mad at me because I can't remember what I'm supposed to. I guess I must be stupid."

The material to be presented represents my initial understanding of a

* Reprinted by permission of the author and *Exceptional Children*, 28:343–350; March, 1962.

behavioral and verbal language expressed by children who have a poor self-concept and who have had consistently negative experiences at home and in school. The children studied were nine to ten years of age and in the third to fifth grades in normal classrooms. They fit the general definition of the exceptional child; namely, one who deviates markedly in growth and development from what is considered normal and who, because of physical, intellectual, emotional, or social differences, or combinations of these, cannot learn like other children and requires special educational services. Excluded from consideration were the gifted children and those with severe mental handicaps (mentally retarded). Thus, the child to be discussed had physical differences and emotional and social problems which affected the learning process.

Basic Theoretical Principles

A brief digression is necessary at this point to consider some basic theoretical principles.

1. Conception initiates the process of development of a genetically determined biological individual. The primordial physical equipment for learning and performance is formed by the end of the first trimester of fetal life. Registry of sensory perceptions begins *in utero*. These, along with action and regulatory (secretory) functions, develop and mature at a biologically individualized pace but in a sequence that is characteristic of man. The functions are autonomous and automatic during gestation and in the early months after birth. As millions upon millions of nerve cell interconnections develop, the first purely reflex reactions to percepts are, for the most part, altered into purposeful functions through regulatory control. All the gradations of feeling and action of which the child is capable are provided by variation in the frequency of nerve impulses and the number of nerve cells stimulated. Through the correlation of percepts over a vast sensory association network, through the projection of these correlated sensory percepts to motor cell areas and a vast motor association area, and through interconnections with organs (visceral reflexes) evoking physical awareness (feeling) of percepts, the brain stores in memory learned patterns available for recall in the appropriate functioning of the individual.

2. The infant is born with a genetically determined potential for physical, intellectual, and emotional development. He is born of parents who create a parental milieu which from the advent of birth will, in part, determine the pattern of development of the child's potentials. Many, many studies have shown the importance of the mother–child relationship. It has been shown

that "mothering" is not only meeting the raw physical needs of the child but in addition supplying stimulation of perceptual organs (cutaneous, hearing, vision, proprioception, and so forth) and providing feelings of safety, security, love, and acceptance. Again, speaking in adultomorphic terms, the child's most important early perception of his environment is dependent upon qualitative and quantitative aspects of mothering. These aspects of mothering are dependent upon the personality of the father and mother, the strength of the relationship between the parents and the child. It is within the framework of the varied relationships that the developing child differentiates himself as an individual, develops a physical percept of himself (body image) and a psychological image (self-concept).

3. The parental milieu into which the child has been born can be thrown into disequilibrium by many factors, and both the quality and quantity of mothering may be impaired. Specifically for the physically different child, I quote from a previous writing.

A generalization that can be made is that parents intuitively sense that their child is mentally or physically different or severely emotionally disturbed. They develop intense feelings of failure and personal inadequacy. The presence of the child in the home furthers these feelings. The parents react in accordance with their individual and collective security and maturity. Mature parents, though hurt, are able adequately to accept the child and meet his physical and emotional needs. Less mature parents, or parents who have conflicts in their relationship, react quite differently. They have normal parental feelings for the child but feel guilty because of incomplete or ambivalent acceptance of the child's condition. The child may appear to be normal in specific respects and deviant in others. The parents have difficulty in equating the differences of functioning. They are confused by this and by hollow reassurances of relatives and well-meaning friends. They witness failure of their many efforts to meet the needs of the child. The repeated frustrations lead to mounting negative feelings and to a parent's giving up in some situations. The guilt, anxiety and confusion call forth self-protective defenses which partially block him from giving freely of himself to the child or to the other parent. One parent may play down observed signs of deviation in attempting to make things easier for the spouse and for himself. However, the similarly upset spouse may interpret this as indifference, callousness or lack of concern, and react strongly. One parent may claim complete blame for the condition and bear the burden in masochistic fashion. He may so dote on the child that the other parent reacts by feeling shut out of his own family. The child in turn reacts as if he interprets as rejection the well-intentioned but inadequate supply of love, acceptance and understanding. Thus the stage is set for conflicts in the relationships in the family.

4. Learning is an ego function, and its impairment or breakdown can

be a sensitive indicator of more extensive maladjustment. Anxiety, fear of achieving, fear of failure, unhappiness or depression, dammed-back motivation, negativism, or personality disorganization can impair learning. With many children who have physical differences, the total learning maladjustment picture is greater than can be accounted for on the basis of the physical limitations present. The learning problem frequently is in part or wholly a secondary process and due to emotional factors.

A sensitive "listening" to the verbal, behavioral, and feeling communication of parents, child, and teacher brings to light many dynamic factors in the "why" of the child's poor school learning performance.

The following brief case presentations will reveal how the child's self-concept derives from impairment in his relationship with his parents and from his experiences in early schooling; how an understanding of the child can be gained through direct interviewing and physical examination; how parental attitudes toward the child with his physical difference are uncovered; and how, with the understandings gained, the teacher plays a vital role in helping the child.

Brief Case Presentations

TOMMY—AGE NINE AND A HALF YEARS

Tommy was referred because of "depression," periods of being "withdrawn," and nonparticipation in school learning or school activities.

A tall boy, he was passed from grade to grade, the teacher said, "because he would stand out if we kept him back with the smaller children." He had not participated in achievement testing and was an enigma to his teachers. When seen by the school psychologist, Tommy claimed that he could not write, read, spell, nor do arithmetic. Not only did he claim that he could not, but he even refused to try. He had been diagnosed as a child with "asymbolia" and "cerebral dysgenesis."

Tommy's parents reported that the boy had always been "different." He was slow to walk (eighteen to twenty months), slow to learn to feed himself, and clumsy. Frankly, the father admitted, he had been extremely disappointed in his son. "Who wouldn't be? He can't do anything like other boys his age. He gets into fights, but is beaten up. He can't play baseball and he can't do things I ask him to." The other children in the family were "rewarding," but "Tommy sticks out like a sore thumb." This, the father said, was because of the boy's awkwardness—always knocking things over and spilling things and messing things up—and his "acting like an infant" when out socially. Other children of his age refused to play with Tommy because of this. It grieved both the father and the mother that the boy played with five- and six-year-old children.

A review of school cumulative records and a conference with the teacher revealed that Tommy sat quietly in class—often with his head on his desk. Each teacher had accepted Tommy as a challenge but had given up after a few months of school. One of the teachers said, "Tommy was no problem in class. He seemed to be 'brain-damaged' or mentally retarded. I hadn't had experience in teaching such children so I left him pretty much alone. Oh, at first when it looked as if he was bored and about to fall asleep, I'd shake him and try to wake him up."

Seen in four interviews for neuropsychiatric appraisal, Tommy demonstrated that he could read, write, spell, and do simple arithmetic at a late first-grade or starting second-grade level. In revealing this, Tommy began to talk about himself and why he refused to do schoolwork. He spoke of his awkwardness and of his poor motor co-ordination, of his light and dark and gray spells (it had been noted that Tommy had frequent petit mal seizures and frequent mild subliminal lapses in attention), and of how no one, not even his parents, had ever understood his problem or accepted or liked him. Of school he said, "My teacher in the first grade slapped me in the face because I couldn't remember what she just told me. I've hated school ever since first grade. They [teachers] don't understand me. No one has." When asked what people should understand about him, Tommy said, "Oh, things like the light and dark spells I get. They make reading awfully bad. I lose my place and forget what I read. I sometimes— (Tommy has seizure)—When I get dark spells I can't remember what you said. Tell me again." Tommy was asked in what ways he would like to be different than he now was. He replied, "Be able to play and throw a ball like the other boys and be able to learn in school. Then my father would like me and my teachers wouldn't get angry with me."

The physical and neurological examinations revealed difficulty with gross motor co-ordination, a mild visuomotor perceptual problem, and the petit mal epilepsy. Tommy had potential for average intellectual functioning but was severely educationally retarded.

The physical (neurological) problems which Tommy had were compounded by felt parental rejection and felt rejection by teachers and the peer group. He reacted to this with discouragement and depression. His opening statement (see first paragraph of this article) summarizes Tommy's interpretation of the feelings of others toward him and indicates why he had given up in school learning and in life generally.

.   .   .   .

[1] Two case histories were omitted at the ellipsis above. *Ed.*

Children Recognize Their Self-Concept

Many exceptional children are able to put their plight into words. They can express their awareness of physical difference from other children and can reveal their self-concept and some of the factors which have contributed to their life problems. In this the children talk of the primary importance of parental attitude, the attitude of siblings and the peer group, and teacher attitude.

Each of the three children mentioned knew that he had normal abilities for learning. Each wanted to learn and in this to be like other children. However, their physical appearance caused adverse reactions which the children interpreted as rejection. The use of symptoms and behavior in the face of anxiety and fearfulness or as protection against their own hostile expression was self-protective defense. Sensitive and constantly on the defensive, they so tenaciously protected their feelings about themselves (self-concept) that they dared not participate.

Energy is contained or expended in their defensive effort, and little if any is free for learning per se. They have tried their best at times but have been hurt by criticism, teasing, failure, and so forth. Tommy, for example, in talking about his first-grade teacher, said, "I was trying my best, but she was too mad to see it. She hit me when I didn't answer. Those black spells made me forget what she'd asked. Finally, I quit. I hoped she wouldn't call on me. After a while she didn't."

The most important hurt is that of felt rejection by the parents. This rejection is not conscious or purposeful but is based on parental feelings evoked by having produced a child who, in their eyes, is not perfect or the image of their expectation. The parents try extremely hard to meet the needs of the child, but, finding themselves psychologically blocked from accepting him, they set up their line of defense. Such parents, in describing their child as "normal," do so in a superficial and intellectual way. They give the feeling that something is missing from their recitation, namely, the child. Similarly, parents who describe their children accurately and as if they accept his difference often do so in a dispassionate way and give the impression that they are living with a group of symptoms rather than the child. It is this quality of parental self-protectiveness and distortion that the child reacts to as if he were rejected. In relation to their child, parents are emotionally ill, with energies so completely tied up within themselves that they are unable to meet the emotional needs of the child.

Concomitantly, the child has learned to make an adjustment in his family that is fairly protective of himself. This is interrupted by the advent of schooling and all that it implies. For example, from the relative security of the home the child enters a program which demands group conformity, the disciplined attention to training and learning, and all under the leadership of a strange adult "parental" figure. The child unconsciously looks for psychological and physical safety, i.e., positive mothering qualities, in the teacher. In the stressful situation, he will act and react according to previously learned patterns in attempting to achieve comfort and relative safety. There is no economy in these patterns. Rather, they are pathological in that he becomes insulated and isolated from learning. The problem for the child is further compounded by negative reactions of the teacher and pupils. The vicious cycle in which the child is caught continues and expands. Soon the physical differences become minor, and the child is predominantly emotionally and attitudinally handicapped.

Seeking to Better Themselves

It was of interest to find that these children want things to be better and can spell out how the school and the home can provide the needed security. They show some confusion in this because of the reaction of others to them. They have a good awareness of physical difference, of their potential for learning, and feel in many respects like other children. Many of the children question their self-concept because it is now incompatible with the negative attitudes of others. To protect what he had, Tommy defended himself by complete withdrawal from the hurtful learning situation. To outward appearance, he was so well insulated that there was a grave question regarding his ego strengths. Bob escaped into the rationalization that he did not need an education to work for Dad. Sandra used crying and physical symptoms to avoid the pain of participation and possible failure.

It has been found—and this is under further investigation—that children who have been "different" from birth and whose parents have reacted adversely have an acceptance of their physical self. They have found that they can learn and that they can do things to their own satisfaction, close to their potential. There is recognition that generally they cannot do as well as their peers. They ask only to be understood and accepted as they are.

By contrast, the child who was born "normal" and who developed a normal self-concept but then reached an ego blow (paralytic poliomyelitis, meningoencephalitis, physical injury, and so forth) wants to be returned to his original physical self. The acquired "difference" has broken down a previously adequate physical and psychological image of the self. In this, the child reacts to the reactions of parents and others, but mainly on the basis of the personal narcissistic blow.

Summary

In the foregoing case examples, the school representatives in their own ways expressed the conviction that the children were brain-damaged and/or mentally retarded. Mistakenly, they assumed that this alone was the basis of the learning deficit. They felt that such children could be helped only through specialized approaches to teaching. Their preoccupation with organic factors, namely, "brain damage," caused them to lose focus in trying to treat the symptom. In doing so, they lost the child. The teacher's use of a limiting diagnostic label represented a defense against her failure to understand and teach the child. Sometimes the child's physical difference stirs up a personal subconscious problem in the teacher. For example, Sandra's athetosis was repulsive to her teacher, whose sister died during an epileptic seizure. The teacher lived in dread of marriage and the possibility of having children. She found herself psychologically blocked to teaching children with physical differences.

When parents, teachers, and others discover the real child behind the physical difference and behavioral symptoms, the emotionally determined learning difficulties can be overcome. For example, Tommy was hostile and challenged the teacher to reach him. He told me, "She is big and fat and I hate her. If she tells me to stay in my seat and work, I'll beat her up. She'll see." The teacher, a firm and motherly person, did reach out to Tommy. As his behavior required it, she disciplined him. Tommy did not fight back but instead gradually settled into learning. He had found a person who understood him and accepted him and with whom he could feel safe and secure.

I have tried in this article to convey the feelings of inadequacy, unworthiness, and confusion that the physically different child has about himself and the underlying theoretical and dynamic considerations. The child's confused self-concept derives from the lack of understanding and consequent negative feelings of the parents, teachers, children, and others. Of key importance is the help given the parents toward an understanding of themselves and their child and the close collaborative working relationship with the school and teacher.

3. Vocational Rehabilitation for Exceptional Children through Special Education *

CHARLES S. ESKRIDGE, *Assistant Commissioner of Education for Vocational Rehabilitation and Special Education*

DON L. PARTRIDGE, *Director, Division of Special Education, Texas Education Agency*

THE PORTAL ENTRY into the field of special education, particularly the area of mental retardation, has been dimly lighted. Progress has been made by feeling our way along. One thing that has been learned through this braille system is that we cannot have a random cafeteria-type preparation program for the educable mentally retarded enrolled in our special education classes. Instead of "just another class" offering a scattering of unrelated activities, we must have a well-organized state-wide program.

The program must have a sequential preparation of materials which will lead to an orderly outcome of employment for its students in the community. Such a program now exists in Texas. It is designed to assist each local school district in making its total program for the educable mentally retarded consistent with programs in other districts.

The educable mentally retarded program began in 1951 with a few scattered classes over the state. For the most part, the curriculum was a watered-down version of the regular curriculum, a "baby sitting" class, or a random cafeteria-type preparation program.

In 1954, a committee was authorized to develop a state-wide curriculum guide for the educable mentally retarded. This committee produced *Curriculum Guide, Special Education, Volume 1,* which is the basic guide throughout the state. Curriculum for the educable mentally retarded is based on the philosophy of individual difference in pupil growth and development. The program is so structured that each pupil may progress at his own rate of development without comparison to the theoretical norms or other pupils in his group. It is free of grade level stigmas and expected annual promotions. A skilled teacher is most essential in planning, guiding,

* Reprinted by permission of the authors and *Exceptional Children,* 29:452–459; May, 1963.

and developing learning experiences. He has a placement committee for support and the community for resources for his classroom.

The program for the educable mentally retarded is a separate and distinct curriculum tract. Seven sequential levels of development are utilized in lieu of the traditional twelve grades for the public schools. A child becomes eligible for public school attendance at the age of six and may progress through the program until graduation. The first three levels are considered the elementary school setting (chronological ages six to twelve inclusive).

Levels of Development

In Level I, or preprimary level, activities are structured to allow the child to react according to the environmental attraction of the moment. Activities are centered around prereadiness materials, motor and sensory training, personal hygiene, habit training, speech improvement, emotional control, and simple tasks in the school which will have carry-over value in the home and community. Formal instruction in the tool subjects is omitted.

Level II, or the primary level activities, is for children older chronologically but still having a mental age of below six and not yet ready for formal instruction in reading, writing, and arithmetic. This level is more structured than Level I.

Level III consists of intermediate level activities which are primarily instructional in basic tool subjects. Emphasis is placed on developing skills in communicative arts and arithmetic. The children are given a chance to make progress in these fields in keeping with their ability, without sacrifice of the much more important social values. Field trips, audiovisual materials, and community resources are used generously in the three levels in an elementary school setting. Socially, it is most essential that these boys and girls be taught in a school setting that has a similar chronological age grouping for those of their normal peers, friends, and neighbors.

At the junior high setting we have two levels which are Level IV and Level V (chronological ages thirteen to fifteen inclusive). In Level IV, introduction to vocations, students are ready for instruction in areas of occupational education, social relationships, and homemaking as they relate to vocational proficiency in life situations. Art and craft activities are continued as an essential part of the program. The academic subjects become functional rather than traditional in nature. For social reasons, it is most important that in his early teen-age period the special education student participate in at least one class with regular students. This class may be physical education, music, art, industrial arts, homemaking, or some other similar class.

Level V, exploring vocations, is the other level of the junior high school program. At this level activities are similar to the activities of Level IV but broader in scope. Occupational education and vocational proficiency become the most important areas of the curriculum. Emphasis is given to exploring work stations within the school environment or on-campus job-training experiences. These work stations are established on the school campus and are designed to give the student the chance to explore possible vocations, gain work experience, and have an opportunity for vocational evaluations. Students are rotated from job to job in keeping with the policies outlined in the local plan for exploring vocations. These work stations are essentially laboratory experiences for the students. In addition to the experience gained, the student is expected to develop dependability, work tolerance, and good working relationships with fellow employees and learn to follow directions from persons other than the teacher. The art and craft activities at this level should be such that the student has the major part of planning, performing, and self-evaluation with a minimum of supervision by the teacher. Association with regular students is most essential for the educable student, and integration into at least one regular class should be continued.

Levels VI and VII are considered high school levels (chronological ages sixteen to twenty-one) and should be located on the high school campus. Level VI, on-the-job training, emphasizes learning a job. The job-training station may be for part of the day or the full day. The special education class becomes a vocational adjustment facility and the teacher a vocational adjustment co-ordinator. Emphasis is given to vocational evaluation, planning, and suitable training through on-the-job training in the community. All efforts are made to help the student adjust to the work world, to learn a particular job, and to develop skills so that he may become an employee. Training stations are a part of the student's curriculum; so are counseling by the vocational adjustment co-ordinator in personal and social adjustment, both on and off the job, and assistance in functional and academic skills related to specific job areas.

When a student progresses from on-the-job training to employment, he moves into Level VII, employment. Emphasis is placed on getting and holding a job, maintaining acceptable adult behavior patterns, and becoming a more productive employee. The vocational adjustment co-ordinator continues working with the individual student. Curriculum items such as how to become a more productive employee and problems encountered on the job and during leisure time are essential parts of the program. When the student has made the adjustment from the protective school environment to the work world and demonstrated acceptable adult behavior patterns, he has completed the seven levels of development in the curriculum and is eligible for school graduation.

In Level VIII, postschool, a vocational rehabilitation counselor may continue to carry a student for a time after graduation for the purpose of follow-up before closing the client's case.

Vocational Rehabilitation Assistance

As this curriculum was implemented, the workers in special education realized that an additional or final step was needed. Assistance was needed in such areas as vocational diagnosis, evaluation of employee potential, developing a feasible vocational plan, making actual arrangements and contracts for job training, and providing for such services as the Division of Vocational Rehabilitation normally provides under its traditional program. With these shortcomings, it was realized on the part of special education that additional help would be needed from the Division of Vocational Rehabilitation.

Studies and reports further indicated that mentally handicapped were losing jobs more often by their failure to adjust to a work situation than by their inability to perform the job assigned. Studies also indicated that failure in job training and employment was primarily due to lack of supervision in the initial training and/or employment periods. There seemed to be a pressing need to supplement current available services to provide the handicapped student with the kind of vocational experiences and supervision which would help him past these pitfalls.

Vocational rehabilitation became actively interested in the older mentally retarded youth in 1957 when the legislature earmarked funds to be used in the rehabilitation of these youths. Since that time, the Division of Vocational Rehabilitation has given increased emphasis to providing appropriate and needed services designed to assist physically and mentally handicapped youths in making a more effective transition from a protective school or institutional environment to a work world. The methods and approaches employed have consisted primarily of the following.

1. Assigning counselors to work with the state schools for the mentally retarded.

2. Establishing a specialized residential and day facility for training, evaluating, and social adjustment, together with some work experiences.

3. Establishing a special training facility in the large vocational school.

4. Making use of "halfway houses" for supervising living arrangements of employed older mentally retarded.

5. Assigning special counselors to work in co-operation with special education in large school districts.

6. Providing services through the traditional approaches.

All these efforts have met with a degree of success. However, two things become apparent in vocational rehabilitation work. First, large numbers of youths were being terminated from special education programs and were not being picked up as vocational rehabilitation clients for three or four years or longer. These years were deteriorative to the retarded and were very costly to vocational rehabilitation. Second, it became apparent that one of the most effective and economical ways of preparing substantial numbers of retarded youths for suitable and productive work was through co-operative working arrangements with special education at the state and local levels. The soundness of this was substantiated by the results of the two-year pilot project, in which approximately 60 per cent of the youths were successfully rehabilitated and made the transition from school to the work world.

The Texas Education Agency is charged by law with the responsibility for a state program of education and vocational rehabilitation of disabled youths from the time they enter school until they are placed on the job. With the exception of the residential schools for the blind and the deaf, this responsibility is discharged through the Division of Special Education, which works with local school districts in the education of disabled youths between the ages of six and twenty-one, and the Division of Vocational Rehabilitation, which provides authorized services to eligible disabled youths sixteen years of age and older. The agency has long felt there is no segment of its program more important than the training and rehabilitation of disabled young people who have before them the possibility, with adequate services, of a full and productive life. Major attention was, therefore, directed toward affecting a comprehensive and co-ordinated program between special education and vocational rehabilitation which has many strong common bonds and objectives with the view of bridging the gap between special education and the work world.

The Texas Plan

The Commissioner of Education, through the State Board of Education, named a state-wide advisory committee to work with the Texas Education Agency staff to co-ordinate the activities of vocational rehabilitation and special education. The committee, after careful study, recommended that certain steps be taken to develop a total and comprehensive plan of services for disabled children and youths from the beginning of their school experience to suitable employment in the community, making full use of the facilities and services of special education and rehabilitation. They directed that the plan give special attention to providing continuous and uninterrupted service from school to work. Pursuant to the committee's recommendation, the Texas Education Agency staff, along with school administrators, rehabilitation counselors, and special education personnel of independent school districts, developed the co-operative program of special education and vocational rehabilitation designed to bridge the gap from school to employment. To augment further this program and to assure its success, the position of an Assistant Commissioner of Education for vocational rehabilitation and special education was created.

The co-operative program is a formal agreement between independent school districts, the Division of Vocational Rehabilitation, and the Division of Special Education to operate co-operatively a vocational adjustment facility for handicapped boys and girls. The independent school district, in its local written plan for operation and administration of special education programs, shows that there is an organized and well-developed program for the educable mentally retarded and that the required number of pupils are enrolled to warrant a vocational adjustment facility and agrees, in signing the formal agreement, that such a facility will be established and a vocational adjustment co-ordinator will be designated.

Approved units in special education are financed through the Minimum Foundation School Program. An eligible school district receives minimum state teacher's salary plus $600 for maintenance and operation of each approved vocational adjustment unit. In addition, the Division of Special Education provides leadership and consultant services in developing the total special education program. The Division of Vocational Rehabilitation in turn, after approving the program and the teacher designated as the vocational adjustment co-ordinator, assigns a vocational rehabilitation counselor to the co-operating school district. The rehabilitation counselor, whose entire case load consists of student-clients in the co-operative schoolwork program, works in the assigned school district one day each week.

The vocational adjustment facility is designed for those students sixteen years of age and older who are in their final phase of completing the curriculum for the educable mentally retarded. The development and continued operation of special education programs in accordance with the revised curriculum, which includes the actual establishment of the vocational facility, is the primary responsibility of the Division of Special Education and the co-operating school district. The operational aspect of the plan as it relates to phases of the program, which currently, traditionally, and legally are functions of rehabilitation, is the continued responsibility of that division. Authorized rehabilitation services are provided when indicated under the conditions and limitations stipulated in the State Plan for Vocational Rehabilitation. Specifically, the rehabilitation division has the following responsibilities: (1) determination of eligibility for all clients accepted for services, (2) determination of the nature and scope of all vocational rehabilitation services to be provided rehabilitation clients, and (3) direct supervision of all personnel assigned to the rehabilitation part of the program.

In a program of this type and scope, it was recognized that certain services to mentally retarded youths can legally be the responsibility of both special education and vocational rehabilitation. The very nature of the problem and the common objectives make this so. This program is proving a continuous and uninterrupted service to disabled youths while still in a school setting through common areas without duplication or encroachment of one division upon the legal responsibility of the other. This is a means of enrichment of the separate programs of each division and a saving of substantial sums of public money.

Two key staff members involved in the operation of the program are the vocational rehabilitation counselor and the vocational adjustment co-ordinator. The counselor is an employee of the Division of Vocational Rehabilitation and is assigned to the co-operating independent school district. The general practice is to assign one vocational rehabilitation counselor for every four vocational adjustment co-ordinators.

THE VOCATIONAL ADJUSTMENT CO-ORDINATOR

The vocational adjustment co-ordinator is a certified teacher for retarded children employed by the co-operating school district and assigned to work full time in the co-operative program. His duties, in addition to the special education responsibility, are (1) administering vocational rehabilitation functions under the direction of the rehabilitation counselor assigned to the local school district, (2) preparing and maintaining class records and reports, (3) participating in joint conferences with the counselor and the school staff regarding the students referred to the unit, (4) responsibility for the supervision of job training under the direction of the counselor and as liaison person between the community and vocational rehabilitation division, (5) supervising, under the direction of the counselor, those individuals in on-the-job training, (6) making reports of individual progress of clients, (7) formulating, along with the counselor, reports of success and failure, and (8) acting as a consultant to the vocational rehabilitation counselor in all instances concerning the special education student-client.

The vocational rehabilitation counselor assigned to the school district has the following duties: (1) certify all trainees for vocational rehabilitation services, (2) consult with school officials on training arrangements within the participating school district, (3) provide vocational rehabilitation services not offered within the unit to additional trainees when extended services are needed, (4) receive and evaluate from public schools all records pertaining to those individuals referred for rehabilitation services, (5) initiate and conduct joint conferences with the vocational adjustment co-ordinator, (6) approve all job-training stations, evaluate training facilities, make training arrangements and agreements, advise with trainee and vocational adjustment co-ordinator, (7) approve all expenditures for client's services, (8) approve all individual vocational rehabilitation plans for clients accepted for vocational rehabilitation services, (9) supervise the co-ordinator's work with rehabilitation clients, and (10) maintain individual case records on vocational rehabilitation clients.

The vocational adjustment co-ordinator, in working with the vocational rehabilitation counselor in the new co-operative arrangement, has a responsibility that cannot, by any stretch of the imagination, be directed or governed by strict rules and regulations. It is to be, in effect, a sincere effort on the part of the rehabilitation counselor and the adjustment co-ordinator that must be controlled only by strict adherence to the word "co-operation" in all dealings with special education teachers, co-ordinators, directors, principals, and superintendents in any given area or school district in the state. School districts with an established vocational adjustment facility will have made the necessary adjustments in administration, organization, and curriculum, with emphasis on attaining vocational proficiency, since this area is paramount in the program for the educable mentally retarded.

School Principal's Role

Another very important member of the co-operative team is the high school building principal. He has the administrative responsibility of professional leadership, in its broadest terms, for the successful operation of this program. In addition to providing the routine school services, he must also co-ordinate this program as it relates to the total educational program in his building.

As we move into the second year of the Texas Plan, we now have sixty-one independent school districts participating in the special education and vocational rehabilitation schoolwork program, with seventy vocational adjustment co-ordinators and twenty-two vocational rehabilitation counselors assigned directly to the program. More than 1,800 educable mentally retarded and physically handicapped boys and girls sixteen years of age and older are in job-training stations in the community either on a half-day or full-day basis, which will help them make the transition from school to work and earn graduation from the special education program. Special education in Texas has developed into an integral part of the total public education program through the development of a direct and meaningful approach to bridging the gap from a public school setting to employment in the community for all educable mentally retarded and some physically handicapped youths.

Results of the Program

The Division of Vocational Rehabilitation, too, is feeling the impact of the co-operative program. It is receiving a larger number of more sophisticated clients at an earlier age with some vocational orientation. The rehabilitation counselor now has an opportunity of evaluating and planning with a client for a longer period of time and has more time to spend with a client in on-the-job training. Through this program the Division of Vocational Rehabilitation has an opportunity to identify larger numbers of potential clients long before they become of employable age.

We definitely feel that our thinking and projected plan is sound. This has been demonstrated by the interest and wholehearted acceptance the program has received from independent school districts, special education personnel, rehabilitation personnel, individuals, and organizations interested in rehabilitation services to the mentally retarded and physically handicapped.

4. Barriers to Effective Rehabilitation: Counselor Opinion *

JOHN E. MUTHARD, *Professor of Education and Co-ordinator of Rehabilitation Training Program, State University of Iowa*

MARCELINE E. JAQUES, *Director of Rehabilitation Counseling, University of Buffalo*

THIS STUDY investigates counselor thinking about the barriers to improving client services in rehabilitation settings. In effect, it points to those deficiencies or present circumstances which counselors believe need reexamination and possibly modification. It presumes that counselors, as a group which has primary responsibility for client services, have understandings and knowledge which can contribute to improving both the quality of rehabilitation services and the number served. No studies of this type have been reported in the literature of rehabilitation.

Sample

The sample of rehabilitation counselors for this study is essentially the same as that described by Jaques. It includes 282 state DVR counselors and 54 counselors who work in other rehabilitation settings, including VA hospitals, VA regional offices, Jewish Vocational Service, and other private agencies. The characteristics of this population are described in detail by Jaques. The sample represents about 10 per cent of the estimated total population of counselors in the United States. Since they come from twenty different states and in a number of instances represent all or most of the counselors of the states which participated, there is reason to believe that this group is a representative sample of the rehabilitation counseling profession.

Procedures

The data were collected between June, 1957, and March, 1958, in conjunction with the securing of critical incidents. Each counselor responded

* Reprinted by permission of the authors and *Personnel and Guidance Journal,* 39:710–716; May, 1961.

in a group interview session to the question, "What in your opinion are some of the factors that stand in the way of doing the best kind of rehabilitation job with clients?" This question was part of the booklet in which counselors wrote the critical incidents and their personal data. Subsequent to the group interviews, there was an opportunity in individual sessions, ranging from 15 to 45 minutes, to clarify any statements which the respondent had made. In most instances this was done for the question which is the focus of this study.

The statements were taken from the booklets and placed on cards. The counselor responses were divided into idea units. That is, when the counselors' statements dealt with a separate thought, they were listed on individual cards; in those instances in which the counselor merely amplified a thought, this was incorporated with the thought to which it was related. Some examples of idea units are "lack of any training facilities," "too large an area geographically," and "too many duties not pertaining to counseling." To bring order and meaning to the 1,142 statements which were taken from the counselor responses, it was necessary to develop a systematic procedure of content analysis.

The development of the category system used to classify a counselor's opinion went through several stages. Items were first grouped on a common-sense basis. Examination of these groupings suggested that a useful and comprehensive rationale for studying the counselor responses would be to analyze them in terms of the locus of the difficulty as seen by the counselor. The categories developed are listed and described by Table 1. The subcategories were, by and large, suggested by the data, but the labels and organization reflect the psychological frame of reference of the investigators whose major concern is training. The system developed had a total of seventy-two headings.

To test the degree of reliability with which counselor statements could be classified within this system, the investigators judged a random sample of 224 counselor statements. There was 83.5 per cent complete agreement between the two judges and 4.9 per cent total disagreement in the classification of idea units. This was deemed a high enough level of reliability to justify application of the system to the entire set of statements.

The investigators made independent classifications of each card to assign the remaining statements to categories. In those instances in which there was partial or total disagreement, the judges discussed the item and arrived at a pooled rating. A similar procedure was used with the statements in the reliability sample.

After each item was classified, the results were prepared for tabulation and analysis by IBM procedures. Each counselor was recorded as either expressing or not expressing ideas classifiable under each of the seventy-two categories and subcategories. When a counselor made two or more statements which belonged in the same category, they were counted as one item. This was done to permit discussion of the findings in terms of the proportion of counselors expressing concerns in each classification.

The results were tabulated for all counselors on each of the seventy-two classifications and were also recorded for three counselor characteristics—counselor type, experience, and training—on the five major categories. The two counselor types were State DVR Counselors and Other Counselors. The former were the vocational rehabilitation counselors employed by state agencies. The latter included counselors from VA hospitals and regional offices, Jewish Vocational Service agencies, and other private agencies. In the two experience groups, those having five or more years of counseling experience were the Experienced; the Inexperienced were those with four years or less of experience. Trained counselors included persons with the M.A. degree in rehabilitation counseling, counseling and guidance, psychology, and social work as well as all persons with Ph.D. or Ed.D. degrees in education, psychology, or counseling and guidance. The Somewhat Trained counselor group comprised those counselors with M.A. degrees in education, sociology, or anthropology, school administration, and personnel or public administration. The Untrained group included all other counselors. For the most part, this group was made up of persons with college degrees or with some graduate training. Further descriptions of these classes can be found in the Jaques monograph.

Results

The number of idea units contributed by each counselor ranged from one to ten with a mean of 3.40 units. More idea units were listed by State DVR Counselors (3.50) than Other Counselors (2.87). There were no marked differences between the mean number of responses by different training or experience subgroups.

From Table 1 the reader can see how the responses of the total counselor population were distributed.

Comparisons of the responses of Trained and Untrained counselors are summarized in Table 2. In addition to analyzing these differences, comparisons were made between the DVR counselor and Other Counselor groups and the Experienced and Inexperienced subgroups. In reading Table 2, the first entry reads as follows: Of the 83 trained counselors in our

TABLE 1—THE CLASSIFICATIONS USED TO ORDER REHABILITATION COUNSELOR
OPINIONS REGARDING BARRIERS TO EFFECTIVE REHABILITATION AND THE
PERCENTAGE OF COUNSELORS CITING IDEAS WITHIN EACH CLASS
(NUMBER OF COUNSELORS—336)

Per cent	Classification
33.0	I. Self (counselor)
11.3	A. Lack of education or training
0.6	1. Graduate education
3.9	2. In-service training
8.5	3. Unspecified
19.3	B. Lack of knowledge and skill
5.6	1. Vocational information (includes training facilities and opportunities, job possibilities, and job placement)
3.7	2. Social-psychological aspects of disability (personality theory, individual differences, behavior disorders, CNS disorders, speech disorders, etc.)
3.0	3. Testing and evaluation (psychological and other, except medical)
1.5	4. Physical aspects of disability (includes medical information and reports)
1.2	5. Community resources
4.2	6. Counseling theory and technique
4.2	7. Lack of skills and knowledge (nonspecific, case-load management, general)
1.5	C. Lack of experience
6.0	D. Personal inadequacies
2.1	1. Inadequate relationship with client
3.3	2. Personality inadequacies
0.9	3. Philosophy of rehabilitation
0.3	4. Other
10.4	II. Client
4.2	A. Lack of motivation (includes all types of apathy, resistance, unwillingness, or inability to change life situation, e.g., hospitalitis)
1.8	B. Personal maladjustment
1.8	C. Lack of education
4.5	D. Other deficiencies
10.1	III. Supervisor
4.2	A. Lack of supervision
5.3	B. Quality of supervision
1.5	C. Counselor-supervisor relationship
81.2	IV. Employing agency
19.3	A. Lack of funds and facilities
14.0	1. Funds for services
6.5	2. Facilities for counseling (inadequate space and lack of privacy)
41.4	B. Administrative policy and procedures
2.7	1. Administrative practices and behavior (those items attributed to administrators as individuals)
39.3	2. Agency regulations and policies
8.6	a. General
12.2	b. Personnel

(Continued)

TABLE 1 (*Continued*)

Per cent	Classification
2.1	(1) General (dissatisfaction with "working conditions")
2.7	(2) Salaries
3.6	(3) Too few counselors
1.2	(4) Selection (deficiencies in staff training or experience)
4.2	(5) Lack of clerical and secretarial help
6.2	c. Client services (difficulty in initiating, giving, and completing services to clients) (restrictions imposed regarding who should receive services and what these services should be)
22.0	d. Emphasis on reports and records (red tape and paper work)
2.7	e. Other (research, follow-up, nonspecific)
64.9	C. Counselor assignments and work expectancies
26.2	1. Case load too large
5.4	2. Territory size limits frequency of client-counselor meetings
22.0	3. Lack of time
13.4	a. For counseling activities (include all aspects of counseling process)
6.8	b. For developing employer and community relations
1.5	c. For self-improvement as a counselor
2.1	d. Nonspecific
27.1	4. Agency emphasis on numbers of rehabilitations (quota, numbers, closures, quantity vs. quality)
14.0	5. Definition of counselor role (too many diverse duties and work demands)
46.4	V. Community resources
29.2	A. Lack of facilities, services, or professional workers (availability and quality)
2.7	1. Psychiatric, psychological, or social services or workers
10.4	2. Training facilities (schools or facilities for education and vocational preparation of clients—including on-the-job training)
4.8	3. Rehabilitation centers and sheltered workshops (include pre-vocational and work adjustment program)
10.4	4. Employment opportunities (lack of job openings)
9.8	5. General (when use two or more of above)
13.7	B. Relationship problems (co-operation, co-ordination, and integration)
8.3	1. Between agencies or professions
2.1	2. Between individual rehabilitation workers (inappropriate role behavior)
2.1	3. Lack of understanding of DVR (agency) role by other agencies
2.7	4. Referral problem (inappropriate or ineffective referral by other agency)
15.8	C. Attitude toward handicapped and rehabilitation services
4.8	1. General community
8.3	2. Employer
5.1	3. Inadequate public education and public relations this area
1.8	D. Legislation barriers

sample, 34.9 per cent cited ideas which mention self-deficiencies of the counselor as barriers to effective rehabilitation. The results for Somewhat Trained were 25.7 per cent and for Untrained 35.0 per cent. One reads Table 3 in a similar fashion. The statistical test used for studying the differences discussed below was Chi-Square. The 0.05 level of confidence was accepted in rejecting the null hypothesis.

As Table 2 shows, the two major categories on which the Trained and Untrained rehabilitation counselors differ were Client and Supervisor.

TABLE 2—THE PERCENTAGE OF TRAINED, SOMEWHAT TRAINED, AND UNTRAINED COUNSELORS CITING IDEAS WITHIN THE FIVE MAJOR CATEGORIES USED TO CLASSIFY OPINIONS REGARDING BARRIERS TO EFFECTIVE REHABILITATION

| | All Counselors Studied | | |
	Trained (N = 83)	Somewhat Trained (N = 70)	Untrained (N = 183)
Self (Counselor)	34.9	25.7	35.0
Client *	33.7	8.6	11.5
Supervisor *	0.0	12.9	13.7
Employing Agency	80.7	84.3	80.3
Community Resources	47.0	50.0	44.8

| | State DVR Counselors | | |
	Trained (N = 53)	Somewhat Trained (N = 57)	Untrained (N = 172)
Self (Counselor)	32.0	28.1	34.9
Client	9.5	7.0	11.6
Supervisor †	0.0	12.3	14.0
Employing Agency	90.6	87.7	80.2
Community Resources	37.8	45.6	44.2

| | Other Counselors | | |
	Trained (N = 30)	Somewhat Trained (N = 13)	Untrained (N = 11)
Self (Counselor)	40.0	15.4	36.4
Client *	76.7	15.4	9.1
Supervisor	0.0	15.4	9.1
Employing Agency	63.3	39.2	81.8
Community Resources	63.3	69.2	54.5

* Difference significant at the 0.01 level of confidence.
† Difference significant at the 0.05 level of confidence.

Trained counselors listed deficiencies of the client as barriers more often than Untrained. Further analysis showed that this was a function of the proportion of non-DVR counselor responses in this category. The differences between Trained and Untrained for this category were not significant within other subgroups, i.e., DVR counselors and Experienced-Inexperienced. The percentage difference between Trained and Untrained with regard to the deficiencies of the supervisor was not large; however, it is noteworthy not only because it was statistically significant but also because no Trained counselor cited barriers in this category. Although the Trained and Untrained did not differ on the major category Employing agency, there was a significant difference between these groups on its subcategory, counselor assignment and work expectancies, and the subdivision, case load too large.

When Experienced counselors were compared with Inexperienced on the 24 classifications which include the five major categories (See Table 3), the highest-level subcategories, and those subdivisions which accounted for large numbers of counselor responses, there were no significant differences. This lack of difference between counselors classified as Experienced and Inexperienced remained when training was controlled; that is, when the Trained, Somewhat Trained, and Untrained counselor groups were divided into Experienced and Inexperienced groups, the analysis showed no differences.

Comparisons of DVR counselors with other counselors showed a significantly larger portion of the DVR counselors mentioning the employing agency as a barrier than counselors from other rehabilitation agencies. As can be seen from Table 3, five out of six DVR counselors see some aspect of their agencies' practices and procedures as being barriers to effective rehabilitation, while the same ratio is about two out of three for Other Counselors. The Other Counselor group, more often than the DVR Counselor, regards the lack of community resources as a serious barrier to effective rehabilitation. Both of these differences are statistically significant. The two groups do not differ in the proportion of counselors which attribute deficiencies or lacks to self, client, and supervisor categories.

Further examination of the subcategories under the employing agency showed that significantly more DVR counselors than other counselors were concerned with the following areas: lack of funds and facilities; emphasis on reports and records; counselor assignments and work expectancies; too large case loads; and the emphasis on numbers of rehabilitations. Analysis of the subcategories under community resources showed only one in which the proportion of counselors responding was significantly different. Some 26 per cent of the Other Counselors reported items classified under the relationship problem heading, while only 11.3 per cent of the DVR group mentioned such items. This may be a function of the more intimate working

TABLE 3—THE PERCENTAGE OF COUNSELORS CITING IDEAS WITHIN THE FIVE MAJOR
CATEGORIES USED TO CLASSIFY OPINIONS REGARDING BARRIERS
TO EFFECTIVE REHABILITATION

	By Counselor Type †		
	State DVR Counselors (N = 282)	Other Counselors (N = 54)	All Counselors (N = 336)
Self (Counselor)	33.0	33.3	33.0
Client	10.3	11.1	10.4
Supervisor	11.0	5.6	10.1
Employing Agency *	83.7	68.5	81.2
Community Resources *	43.3	63.0	46.4
	By Amount of Experience		
	Experienced (N = 149)	Inexperienced (N = 187)	
Self (Counselor)	28.9	38.3	
Client	8.6	12.8	
Supervisor	12.3	7.4	
Employing Agency	81.3	81.2	
Community Resources	49.7	42.3	

* Difference significant at the 0.01 level of confidence.
† The Chi-Square statistic was used to compare DVR and other counselors and did not include the total group.

relationship involved in hospital and rehabilitation center work; that is, working together in one facility may intensify any possible differences arising from roles ascribed and assumed by particular disciplines and workers.

To understand better the results above, it seems desirable to complement the statistical findings with some impressions based on observations made during the data-collection process. The participants seemed to have a great need to talk about the question posed by this study. Once rapport was established, it was frequently difficult to terminate discussion. They expressed a sense of frustration in not being able to do more for their clients. The perceived barrier was the impersonal demands and limits of their agency and the interpretations given procedures and policies by supervisors and administrators. They seemed to feel "squeezed between the needs of their clients and the demands of their agency," as one respondent put it. The counselors expressed, with marked feeling, the belief that they should be consulted by their agencies on questions concerned with improving services and ameliorating the frustrations associated with rehabilitation counseling. Associated with this was a lack of feeling of reward for effort; they expressed the belief that the agency heads had little interest in "how well" the counselor was doing his job but were much interested in "how many" he processed.

Discussion

The analysis of counselors' statements describing barriers to effective rehabilitation shows that counselors report a wide range of lacks in their work setting. The deficiencies listed within the five major categories all suggest possible areas needing further study and amelioration. The barriers associated with the Employing agency represent a problem area which merits much more consideration and thought. Both administrative action and training programs may be needed to avert the deficiencies subsumed under Self and Community resources categories. The fairly low frequency for Supervisor as a barrier suggests that the need may not be to enhance their supervision skill but rather to increase their effectiveness in the training function and as liaison between (1) counselors and administrative heads and (2) counselors and other professions and agencies.

The substantial counselor opinion which links barriers to effective rehabilitation to the activities of the Employing agency suggests a need for a careful reappraisal of agency policies, procedures, and practices. There seem to be two principal ways to interpret this information. Counselors may project the blame for their frustrations upon higher administrative levels or lack sufficient understanding of the pressures with which the administrator must cope. We might ask, if projection was the mechanism, why counselors mentioned ideas associated with the agency rather than Self, Client, Supervisor, or Community resources. If lack of counselor understanding of the realities of agency pressures is the problem, it would still seem that the initiative for creating greater understanding must repose upon the professional leaders in rehabilitation: administrators, supervisors, and teachers. Another reasonable interpretation might be that agency policies, regulations, and practices do, in fact, work as barriers to the counselor's rehabilitation efforts. The data of this study do not permit a resolution of the causal factors. We might well assume that both major interpretations are in part true and are inextricably bound together. Whether the origins of these dissatisfactions were primarily in the distorted perceptions of the counselor or a function of administrative inadequacies, they should be of concern to the profession of rehabilitation counseling and especially to administrators and teachers.

Our data and observations suggest that some of the reasons for the counselor opinion may include: (1) He perceives the agency's professed goals and philosophy as being in conflict with its practices; e.g., he is continually reminded of the need for professional-quality services but even more frequently admonished to meet his quota. (2) He perceives his work as guided not by his professional judgments but by forms and regulations. (3) He sees himself as a part of a depersonalized bureaucratic machine which imposes regulations and procedures with little regard for his views or the needs of his clients. Considered in the light of industrial studies such as Roethlisberger and Dickson, Coch and French, and Fleishman, the interpretations above seem reasonable.

The substantial proportion of counselors who think that the lack of community resources is a barrier suggests two main interpretations. One of these may be that counselors are not well informed about the community resources, while the other may arise from the absence of such resources. There seems to be some justification for the first view for at least part of the counselor group. If we keep in mind that the Other Counselors of this study are located in urban centers and that such centers are the established loci of rehabilitation services and facilities, it is difficult to understand the greater concern of Other Counselors than of DVR Counselors for this lack. It would appear that some Other Counselors either do not know about these services or have not established a relationship with the other community resources, especially training facilities and employment opportunities. Probably a larger portion of all counselors with items in this category have had problems arising from the absence of suitable training and employment facilities.

Summary

A study of rehabilitation counselor responses to the question, "What in your opinion are some of the factors that stand in the way of doing the best kind of rehabilitation job with clients?" was made. The opinions of the 336 counselors from both state-federal and other agencies were classified in a system which included five major categories and a total of seventy-two headings. The reliability of this procedure was found adequate, and pooled ratings were used to resolve any differences in classification. The results were reported for the entire set of categories and analyzed by counselor type, level of experience, and training for the five major categories.

The findings show that rehabilitation counselors think that their agencies' policies, procedures, and practices stand in the way of their doing the best kind of job with clients. The results suggest that improved communications between counselor and agency leadership and an increased opportunity for the counselor to see himself as a professional person whose opinions and judgments are wanted and considered may be needed in rehabilitation work. There also may be a need to re-examine the work of rehabilitation agencies with these stated concerns in mind. The data also suggest some concern about community resources and the counselor's own competencies. The supervisor's competencies and client deficiencies were seldom reported as barriers to effective rehabilitation.

5. Structure of the Vocational Rehabilitation Program and Nature of the Counselor's Job *

E D G A R   B .   P O R T E R ,   *Director of Training, American Hearing Society, Washington, D.C.*

TURNING from a discussion of various concepts of rehabilitation to the role of rehabilitation counselor, we find that as the "needs of the individual" concept becomes practice in our agencies, so does the role of the counselor change and become more complex and professional.

No one can be so unrealistic as to suggest or approve a procedure by which the handicapped individual is compelled to "shop around" from agency to agency and from profession to profession to find the help he needs to overcome his handicaps. He may not be aware of the nature and extent of his handicaps. His problems may require study and analysis. He may need interpretation. He may require assistance in planning the help he needs. Resources for help must be located and then made known and available to him. Finally, it must be made clear that no one agency or professional group has the knowledge, skill, or facilities to render all the help needed in solving the sometimes complex problems associated with handicaps.

The procedure described requires teamwork. Its effect upon the elimina-

* Excerpted from address delivered by Mr. Porter at the Workshop on Vocational Rehabilitation Services for Executive Directors of Hearing and Speech Centers, Washington, D.C., January 26, 1961.

tion of handicaps depends upon a realistic integration of the skills of several professions. Continuity of services must be assured from onset of disability to maximum adjustment.

To bring about such integration of functions and continuity of service requires a person specially trained to understand the handicap and to adapt the services for meeting it—one integrating force: the rehabilitation counselor. The more highly specialized the various team members become, the more necessary is this service of integration. To the degree that he possesses sound professional preparation will the rehabilitation counselor be recognized as the logical co-ordinator of resources in the rehabilitation of disabled persons, at least to those whose objective is remunerative employment.

What can we say regarding the abilities the counselor requires to carry out his responsibilities in an efficient, professional manner? Authorities in the field have listed twenty-four abilities, some of which are noted here as illustrative.

1. An understanding of human anatomy and physiology, the effects of disease or injury on body structure, functions, behavior, and personality.

2. An understanding of mental and emotional conditions affecting social and vocational adjustment.

3. Familiarity with medical information, therapies, prostheses, services, and equipment designed to remove or minimize the effects of disability.

4. The ability to establish and maintain a satisfactory counseling relationship.

5. The ability to analyze occupations in terms of skills, physical demands, training requirements, and working conditions.

6. An understanding of community organizations and of the facilities and procedures, policies and limitations, under which services are made available.

7. Ability to analyze the rehabilitation needs of a community and to organize resources to meet these needs.

8. The ability to use consultative services, both within and outside the rehabilitation agency staff.

9. The ability to orient employers to the employment of disabled persons.

10. And many more.

What of the type of individual who can be expected to perform the duties required? Some of the characteristics of the ideal rehabilitation counselor are contained in the following words and phrases.

1. Strong interest in people and their welfare.

2. Optimism concerning the potentialities and motivation of disabled persons.

3. Creative, imaginative, persevering nature.

4. Soundness of judgment, emotional maturity.

5. Capacity to organize effectively and to follow plans to their conclusion.

6. An uncommon measure of common sense.

7. Ability to inspire others.

8. View of his professional development in a dynamic sense, giving constant attention to new growth opportunities.

9. Finally, a keen sense of humor, so that he can retain a reasonable measure of sanity.

Who will say that with these demands on knowledge, skill, and personal characteristics the rehabilitation counselor has not attained a level of professional recognition equal to that accorded other professional persons to whom he is constantly relating? On the other hand, we have described the *ideal* of a rehabilitation counselor to which all should aspire but few will reach. For if such a person were in existence, he would probably make some of us mortals who would be required to work with him rather uncomfortable and possibly insecure.

6. Psychological Techniques and Theory Applied to Behavior Modification *

WILLIAM C. RHODES, *Professor of Psychology,*
George Peabody Teachers College

A N INCREASING NUMBER of special classes and other educationally focused programs are being developed for emotionally disturbed children. There will probably be a growing demand for knowledge of behavior modification which might be applied in a classroom situation. There are many

* Reprinted by permission of the author and *Exceptional Children*, 28:333–337; February, 1962.

possible sources of accumulated knowledge in this area. One resource which has not been fully utilized is the body of theory and laboratory findings of psychology, which does not require training in psychotherapy.

A review of the psychological literature reveals two types of possible contributions: one is primarily theoretical and/or experimental, with implications for approaches to behavior development and modification, while the other consists of concrete laboratory-derived operations which have already been applied to modification of emotionally maladjusted behavior. In the theoretical or experimental category, there are those references which deal only with the medium of the interpersonal relationship and others which do not depend upon this medium but are concerned with ways in which the environment can be prepared or manipulated to help produce learning of new behaviors.

Theoretical and Experimental Literature

EXAMPLES OF USE OF RELATIONSHIP

During the nineteen-thirties there were several attempts to integrate psychoanalysis with behaviorism or "condition reflex" theory. Clark Hull (1939) restated the definitions of such concepts as id, libido, object cathexis, ego, superego, fixation, and symptom formation in learning terms.

Thomas French (1932–33) saw the psychoanalytic concept of adjustment to reality to be based on Pavlovian conditioning and differentiating processes. A trauma was an experience calling forth a conflict of such intensity that the individual had no energy left to turn to neutral differential stimuli. As a result, the traumatic experience was withdrawn from the learning process. The solution was: (1) reinstate the conflict to permit a reliving of the traumatic experience and (2) handle the transference relationship to reduce the intensity of this new edition of the conflict so that energy is free to be turned to other stimuli and the process of conditioning differentiation can then take place. This is the only way the traumatic experience can be made accessible to learning.

As applied to the classroom, for instance, this would mean that a child with a "reading block" must be handled so that the original traumatic experiences can be reinstated in the presence of a warm, understanding, nonpunitive teacher and classroom environment. The block can be dissolved, and the child can be freed to go on with learning to read.

A number of other theorists made early attempts at integration between analysis and behavioral theory. R. R. Sears (1936) wrote on the relationship of stimulus response theory to abnormalities of memory, with special reference to amnesia and repression. Kubie (1934) wrote on the relation of the conditioned reflex to psychoanalytic technique. Krasnogarski (1925) wrote on the conditioned reflex and children's neuroses. All of these are important because they deal essentially with the learning process. They are, however, technical and require interpretation by a person trained in both psychoanalysis and learning theory before their teaching implications are apparent.

In the nineteen-forties and nineteen-fifties there were a number of attempts to reinterpret maladjusted behavior and behavior modification in terms of principles derived from the experimental laboratory. This is particularly true of learning principles.

Shoben (1949) said that the primary motivation in all emotional disturbance is anxiety. To modify anxiety one must (1) reinstate, in symbolic form, the stimuli which triggered off the anxiety originally, (2) use counter-conditioning by attaching these symbolic stimuli for anxiety to comfort reactions made to the helping person, and (3) re-educate the disturbed individual by helping him formulate rational goals and behavioral methods to attain them.

Ann Magaret (1950) said that the emotionally disturbed individual must learn how to learn a certain variety of interpersonal problems in the presence of the person helping him.

Shaffer (1947) said the goals of working with an emotionally disturbed person are, first, to help him learn words for the cues he needs for normal behavior and, second, to reward appropriate responses to these words. He said that normal persons control their own behavior by using language signals. The maladjusted individual must learn to speak to himself in appropriate ways to control his own behavior.

F. J. Shaw (1948) postulated that the problems dealt with in emotional disturbance are behaviors which have immediate rewarding consequences but long-term punishing consequences. In the context of a growth-producing relationship, one must teach him the cues to the long-term punishing consequences of these particular behaviors, minimize his ego involvement, and provide opportunity for him to take active steps to help himself.

Among others who have, in limited or nonsystematic reports, suggested the integration of formal propositions of clinic and laboratory are Mowrer (1950), Miller (1951), Meignant (1948), and Hofstatter (1954).

More systematic integrations of the formal propositions of the laboratory and clinic are Dollard and Miller (1950), Cameron and Magaret (1951), Rotter (1954), and Shaffer and Shoben (1956).

EXAMPLES OF USE OF ENVIRONMENT

J. B. Watson (1921) conditioned Albert to show fear responses to the rabbit and other white furry objects on a stimulus generalization gradient. M. C. Jones (1924), in the well-known case of Peter, found a child with similar fears and demonstrated a method of changing the fear. Her first step was to present the rabbit to Peter in the presence of three other children who had no fear of the rabbit. Then, she moved directly to "unconditioning." The rabbit was introduced in their periphery of the room at the time the child was hungry and sitting in a high chair being fed. Over a period of many days, the rabbit was gradually moved closer and closer until the child would pet it and show other positive reactions to this stimulus. M. C. Jones reports that this unconditioning did generalize to other white objects.

Knight Dunlap (1928) was concerned with the correction of habits. His method was "negative practice." By deliberately massed repetitions of long-standing errors in typing, for instance, he was able to correct the errors. He announces applications of this method to stuttering, thumb sucking, tics, and even reports: "It has already been applied to a case of homosexuality with astonishingly rapid results."

A. T. Jersild and F. B. Holmes (1935) reported a study of methods of overcoming a child's fears. They conclude that among the most helpful techniques are (1) prompting the child to acquire skills that specifically aid in coping with the feared situation, (2) leading the child by degrees into activity with and participation in the situation feared—presenting the stimulus first in less intense form or without some of its frightening features and then gradually introducing all the conditions that provoke fear, and (3) giving the child the opportunity to become acquainted with the feared stimulus on his own accord by making it readily accessible to him in his normal environment and under circumstances that permit him to inspect or ignore it, approach or avoid it, as he sees fit.

Holmes (1936) went on to an experimental investigation of a method of overcoming children's fears. Working with nursery children, he attempted to overcome fears of a high place and a dark room. For fear of high places, he had the child walk across a board whose height was raised only slightly after each performance. For coping with the dark room, he helped the child to learn ways of orienting himself and finding his way through the dark to turn on a light at the back of the room.

Guthrie (1938) said that inability to forget is often one of the outstanding difficulties in emotional disturbance. A phobia is a special type of fear in which the victim has learned to avoid the fearsome stimulus and cannot unlearn his fear because unlearning requires that the stimulus be present and that some other response be attached to it. He believes that breaking one habit always means establishing another that interferes with the old one in a particular situation. He suggests three ways in which a given stimulus can be prevented from eliciting a given response: (1) introducing the stimulus at such weak strengths that it will not cause the response and then gradually increasing the intensity of the stimulus, always taking care that it is below the threshold of response; (2) introducing the stimulus at its regular intensity, but controlling the situation so the customary response is prevented from occurring; (3) presenting the stimuli for an act at a time when some of the instruments necessary for carrying out the act are not present.

Jules Masserman (1943) suggests human applications of his animal experimentations. Behavior can be modified by:

1. Reducing the intensity of one of the conflicting drives in a situation.

2. Environmental press. This application might imply gently pressuring a child into a situation he may want to take part in but tries to avoid.

3. Social example. An example could be observing other children.

4. Working through. The teacher might give the child some means of controlling the situation, like the Holmes experiment with learning to flip a switch in a dark room.

5. Reassurance, persuasion, and suggestion.

Joseph Wolpe (1958) defines neurotic behavior as "any persistent habit of unadaptive behavior acquired by learning in a physiologically normal organism." Wolpe has developed a general principle of behavioral modification: "If a response antagonistic to anxiety can be made to occur in the presence of anxiety-evoking stimuli so that it is accompanied by a complete or partial suppression of the anxiety responses, the bond between these stimuli and the anxiety responses will be weakened." He has devised a number of ingenious applications of this principle.

H. G. Jones also sees anxiety as a central component of neurosis and neuroses as behavioral disturbances. He analyzes the behavioral disturbance into two types of response: (1) the anxiety response itself, with visceral, skeletal, and central nervous components; (2) the various responses which are instrumental in preventing the individual from coming in contact with or having to deal with the stimuli which have been conditioned to the anxiety response. The conditioned stimuli may come from the punishing agent itself, the incidental environmental stimuli at the time of stress, or the stimuli stemming from the individual's behavior at the time of stress. He believes that the individual must "unlearn" both the instrumental response and the anxiety. Eliminating or decreasing these can be accomplished through punishment, removal of the conditioned or unconditioned stimuli, massed evocation of the response without reinforcement, modification of expectation for punishment, and strengthening incompatible responses.

Learning Laboratory Operations Which Have Been Applied to Emotional Disturbance

There have been a number of applications of specific operations transferred directly from the learning laboratory to a variety of emotional and behavior disorders.

Lehner (1954) reports on multiapplications of negative practice, and Wolpe (1958) and Eysenck (1960) report on various applications of learning techniques. In one of the most serious disorders—psychosis—very concrete and easily duplicated learning techniques have been applied and reported by Ayllon and Michael (1959), Robertson (1958), Peters and Jenkins (1954), King, Armitage, and Tilton (1960), Skinner (1954), Issacs, Thomas, and Goldiamond (1960).

In conditions of psychoneurosis, anxiety, and phobic reactions, Rachman (1959), Meyer (1957), and Jones (1956) describe the use of desensitization and other learning operations. Application of specific learning methods to sexual problems is reported by Max (1935), Dunlap (1930), and Raymond (1956). Learning procedures, very carefully described, have been used in stuttering by Wichner (1959), Fishman (1937), Sheehan (1950), and Rutherford (1940).

Fingernail biting, tantrums, enuresis, tics, and writer's cramps have been extinguished through learning by Leshan (1942), Yates (1958), Mowrer and Mowrer (1938), Morgan and Witmer (1939), Davidson and Douglas (1950), Williams (1959), and Liversedge and Sylvester (1955).

Summary

Learning theory and techniques suggested for modification of behavior in emotional disturbance have included:

Symbolic reinstatement of an original trauma and relearning.

Symbolic reinstatement of cues or environmental aspects tied to anxiety while pairing them with comfort reactions in the new interpersonal situation.

Helping the individual to learn how to learn to solve his interpersonal problems in the interaction with the teacher.

Teaching the individual the right words to control his own behavior and reinforce these until they are learned and used.

Teaching the long-term punishing consequences of undesirable behavior which is rewarding only in the immediate situation.

Extinguishing fear of necessary situations which are avoided, by slowly and gradually working into the feared situation, at the same time giving positive reinforcements.

Teaching skills which will give control of feared situations.

Exposing to feared conditions but arranging the situation so that the undesirable behaviors cannot occur.

Reducing the intensity of one of the conflicting motivations.

Gentle pressuring into the feared or avoided situation.

Using negative practice or deliberate practice of the undesirable behavior.

Inducing a response antagonistic to anxiety in an anxiety-provoking situation.

Building habits that interfere with the old, undesirable habits.

Having the undesirable behavior repeated over and over in a short period of time with neither positive nor negative reinforcement.

Using negative reinforcements applied immediately after the occurrence of the undesirable behavior.

Using recorded negative suggestion repeated over and over in sleep (or, perhaps, while occupied in some other task).

7. The Counselor's Contribution to the Guidance of the Gifted, the Underachiever, and the Retarded *

RUTH STRANG, *Professor of Education, University of Arizona*

WHEN A YOUNG rural teacher was asked to list the gifted children in her classes she said, "All my children are gifted." This would be an ideal attitude for deans and counselors to take. If they look for the special gifts

* Reprinted by permission of the author and *Personnel and Guidance Journal*, 34:494–497; April, 1946.

and potentialities of every individual, they will focus their attention on opportunities rather than on "problems." The gifted, the underachiever, and the mentally retarded all offer a challenge to the counselor.

Whom Are We Talking About?

In recent years the definition of "the gifted" has been broadened to include not only the verbally gifted with IQ's above 130 or 135. We now tend to think of the gifted as "individuals whose performance in any line of socially useful endeavor is consistently superior."

The underachiever is one whose performance is below his ability to achieve. In this category, the ratio of boys to girls is usually two to one. Many gifted students are underachievers, though they may be achieving above the average for their grade. In one suburban senior high school almost half (49 per cent) of the forty-five students with IQ's of 130 or more on the California Test of Mental Maturity were underachievers; in an independent boarding school only 9 per cent of the fifty-seven with IQ's of 130 or more were underachievers. Apparently the percentage of underachievers among gifted students varies with the nature of the school's program and the quality of its instruction as well as with the individual students' interests and motivations. Gowan defined underachievers among the gifted as those in the middle third of their group in academic work and severe underachievers as those in the lowest third. He observed that the gifted underachiever tends to be unsocial, to feel insecure and fearful, to refrain from identifying himself with his parents or his teachers, and to develop few skills that would aid him in gaining economic independence from his family. Their problems center around home situations. According to Gowan, if the percentage of underachievers in a school is higher than 15, it is probable that something is wrong with the morale and social climate of the school. These students often need to be socially successful in athletics, music, a hobby, a part-time job, or some other activity. They often need effective counseling to help relieve their anxieties about sex, choice of vocation, relations with parents, and ways to earn money enough to gain some independence from a domineering or possessive parent.

The mentally retarded child is one whose mental age is considerably below his chronological age. In terms of IQ, students with IQ's from 75 to 90 are considered somewhat retarded though able to profit by a school program that is adjusted to them. Those below 70 IQ are usually assigned, in both elementary school and, more recently, high school, to special classes for children of retarded mental development.

What Is the Counselor's Responsibility?

The counselor who serves as the only full-time guidance worker in a school has four main functions:

1. To be helpful to teachers in their guidance while teaching and to teacher-counselors in their small guidance units such as the home room or group guidance class or core curriculum.

2. To work with complex cases for which teachers have neither the time nor skill.

3. To advise on policies of marking, promotion, discipline, curriculum, etc.

4. To discover and use the guidance resources of the school and community.

These four functions the counselor performs to some extent with all students and to a greater extent with the gifted, the underachievers, and the retarded.

More specifically, the counselor has seven main responsibilities for these exceptional children: (1) to identify them, (2) to help teachers provide the experiences they need in classes and extraclass activities, (3) to assist teacher-counselors in helping these students to accept and make the most of themselves, (4) to hold interviews as needed with these students and their parents, (5) to open up community resources and educational opportunities for them, (6) to call case conferences as needed to further the best development of these students as well as to explore complex and baffling problems, (7) to advise administrators and curriculum committees about changes in the school program that will meet their needs. Fortunately, all the students usually benefit by the efforts which the counselor makes on behalf of these individuals.

How to Identify Them

The counselor should periodically go over the cumulative records with a view to identifying these kinds of exceptional children. In Long Beach, California, the school counselors located all the students with IQ's of 120 or over and also those whose records gave some indication of special talent in science, mathematics, art, music, mechanical ability, or social skill. Then they interviewed each of these students, with his parents if possible. In the interview they obtained additional information about educational and vocational plans, interests and hobbies, purposes and goals. This information they recorded on a form which was added to the student's cumulative record folder.

The counselors also tried to help these students gain a sense of direction and of responsibility for profiting by the lucky combination of heredity and environment which had made them gifted in some respect. They were careful, however, not to use the words *gifted* or *superior* with the students or their parents, but rather to emphasize the social responsibility of able learners—of persons with exceptional potentialities. After each interview, the counselor made a few helpful memoranda for the student's teachers, suggesting certain class or extraclass experiences that would enrich his program.

In a similar manner, counselors can identify the underachievers and the mentally retarded students. Underachievers are readily identified by discrepancies between their scores on intelligence tests and their over-all school marks or marks in certain subjects.

The counselor should be very cautious about designating an individual as mentally retarded before making a thorough study of the case. Many factors may prevent an individual from demonstrating his true mental ability; these factors operate to depress the IQ. Teachers' observation of the way such an individual functions in the classroom is an important supplement to the cumulative record data.

The memoranda on each student which the counselor sends to teachers contain helpful suggestions. It is even better if the counselor can hold a short, informal conversation with the teacher, suggesting ways to meet the needs of different kinds of students in the classroom—projects, special library or free reading periods, discussions, interest groups, or opportunities to be of service to the class as a whole. Such suggestions often stimulate teachers to enrich their classroom work.

Voluntary study groups or workshops may be formed to deal with each type of exceptional child. In these groups, the members gain a deeper understanding of the needs of these students and share their most successful methods of helping them to realize their potentialities. Occasionally faculty meetings and departmental meetings may be devoted to this kind of sharing of experience.

Teachers especially appreciate the counselor who gives them materials they need—books and other instructional material for both gifted and retarded students. If the School Board cannot be persuaded to purchase such materials, PTA's and social and civic clubs sometimes will. This is where the counselor's community contacts come in handy.

It is most important that the counselor take the attitude that it is his function to show and help teachers rather than merely to tell them. Teachers sometimes resent the guidance person who comes in and tells them what to do. But they are grateful to the one who will demonstrate techniques, provide books, pamphlets, and information which they need, and talk over difficult cases from their point of view.

How to Help Teacher-Counselors

In a large school, even a large staff of guidance workers cannot have adequate individual contacts with all the students. A small guidance unit is necessary. Here the teacher-counselor has responsibility for a relatively small number of students, usually thirty to thirty-five. If these teacher-counselors are to meet the needs of all the students in their group, they must have help from the specially prepared full-time guidance person. Sometimes they can arrange to meet at lunch if they have the noon hour free. Otherwise the guidance co-ordinator may meet with them once a week in their free periods. In these meetings they will deal with their immediate practical problems: how to help the students plan a long-term educational and recreational program, how to interview gifted students, underachievers, and retarded students about the things that most concern them, how to give information about scholarship opportunities, how to use the group as an instrument of guidance.

Interviews on More Complex Problems

There will be cases which the teacher-counselor cannot handle. These he will refer to the more fully trained guidance worker or specialist, who may use other resources of the school and the community. Here expert skill in interviewing and case work is needed. Gifted individuals sometimes show serious maladjustment, though this is not so common among them as among the population in general. Some have problems of social adjustment and family relations. These students are usually rewarding to work with because of their keener insights and greater ability to see relations. A few gifted children have reading problems. If a gifted student is retarded in reading, the counselor should try to find out whether the student is using the reading retardation to serve some purpose; how the student feels about it; what immediate conditions in the present or unrecognized influences in the past are preventing the potentially able student from putting his mind on his reading; and what procedures will be most effective in helping him to release his fettered psychological energy.

The multiple causes of underachievement must be uncovered, if possible, in order to help these students to make progress. Underachievement may stem from earlier educational deprivation and poor reading ability, from a lack of purpose or goal, from a general feeling of inadequacy and hope-lessness, or from feelings of hostility and resistance directed at parents who have deprived them of the love they need. Given a chance to think through their situation, these individuals will often be able to help them-selves.

The counselor's method of interviewing mentally retarded students is not different in principle from that used with the gifted. A basic factor is respect for each individual and for the resources he has within himself. The mentally retarded will not be able to talk about themselves so fluently as the gifted; they will need more help in relating the ideas they express. However, within the limits of their experience and with the counselor's help, they can gain understanding and acceptance of themselves and acquire a clearer vision of realistic educational and vocational goals and the meth-ods of making progress toward them.

How to Open Up Community Opportunities and Resources

In Hartford, Connecticut, the Director of Guidance made a useful direc-tory of all the guidance resources in the city, classified under headings such as health, mental hygiene, recreational opportunities, etc. This directory was very helpful to deans and counselors in meeting the needs of individuals. The resources in a rural county can be similarly canvassed. Some state and national facilities will also be available for individual cases and for local in-service education programs.

The Case Conference

If time can be found in an unassigned period at the beginning or at the end of a school day, during teachers' free periods, or even at the noon hour, a case conference on individual students is most helpful. It not only clarifies the needs of the individual being discussed but also contributes to the growth of all who attend—nurse, physician, psychologist, guidance worker, teacher-counselor, teachers, and others who may have contact with the individual. Everyone learns. What kinds of information are most significant, what this information means, how to synthesize it, and what to do about it—these are some of the learnings that take place.

The case conference usually consists of four parts: (1) the co-ordinator of the case—the person who has requested the case conference—presents all the information he has been able to collect, (2) those present pool any additional information they may have, (3) all the participants try to interpret and relate the information now available and to formulate tentative hypotheses as to the nature and causes of the individual's failure to realize his potentialities, and (4) they make recommendations as to the next steps to be taken. Each person present may assume some specific responsibility in order to initiate immediate action.

By talking with the administrators and by sitting in at departmental meetings and with curriculum committees, counselors may bring the guidance point of view to bear on policy and practice. In their close contacts with teachers and students they become aware of needs; they can then suggest how these needs may be met in the school program as a whole.

Counseling the gifted, the underachievers, and the mentally retarded involves knowing the characteristics and special needs of these students. It also involves having a repertory of enrichment activities to suggest for the gifted and of appropriate practical experiences for the mentally retarded in which they can succeed with reasonable effort and from which they will get social satisfactions. Of course, the counselor's general approaches and techniques for understanding and for working with all students, teachers, administrators, parents, and community agencies are also applicable to these special areas of guidance. Other prerequisites for successful work with the gifted, the underachievers, and the mentally retarded are the counselor's own evaluated experience and sensitivity to each individual.

Permeating the whole process are the counselor's values and standards which he often unconsciously shares with the student. Dr. Albert Schweitzer well expressed the point of view which counselors should hope to share with their counselees, all of whom have some gift which they can develop and use for social purposes. He wrote:

"What ever you have received more than others in health, in talents, in ability, in success, in a pleasant childhood, in harmonious conditions of home life, all this you must not take to yourself as a matter of course. You must pay a price for it. You must render in return an unusually great sacrifice of your life for other life."

8. The Present Vocational Rehabilitation Program *

MARY E. SWITZER, *Commissioner of Vocational Rehabilitation, U.S. Department of Health, Education, and Welfare*

IN 1963, the federal-state rehabilitation program rehabilitated more than 110,000 disabled persons. Around 22,000 of them were under age twenty-one, of whom 40 per cent had been referred for rehabilitation services by educational institutions: 34 per cent from public schools, 4 per cent from schools for the handicapped, and 2 per cent from other schools.

And we know from experience that of an estimated 27,000 young people who will receive rehabilitation services in 1964, about 36 per cent will have orthopedic disabilities; about 7 per cent will have defects in speech and hearing, including deafness; 10 per cent will be blind or have serious visual defects; 6 per cent will be mentally retarded; 9 per cent will have some form of mental illness; 2 per cent will be epileptics; and the remainder will have various disabilities in smaller percentages of the total.

It must be apparent, therefore, that special education and rehabilitation have made more than just a start at the co-operative task of helping handicapped youngsters to become active and useful adults. Our job, then, is to broaden our programs together until we can say with confidence that handicapped young people in this country are receiving the services they need to become responsible and self-sufficient adults.

The public program of vocational rehabilitation is forty-four years old. In the last ten years, however, the strides it has made have been enormous in comparison to the earlier years. This progress came after passage of new legislation in 1954. This gave the nationwide program a sounder financial structure and provided the Vocational Rehabilitation Administration (VRA) with authority to launch strong research and training activities. Both of them are of great significance to all of the disabled and to all of us who are concerned with their welfare.

* Excerpted from a speech, "Assessment: Capacity for Useful Living," at the 1962 CEC Convention, as revised to appear in *Exceptional Children,* May, 1962. Reprinted by permission of the author and *Exceptional Children.*

Aid for Teacher Training and Research

The strength of both the public and private rehabilitation programs is heavily dependent on the number of people who enter its professional phases. Consequently, we are constantly expanding the support we give to educational and training institutions that are qualified to teach and train in subjects close to rehabilitation.

In 1963 we expended more than $13 million dollars in grants for training. This will help us to catch up with the great shortages of rehabilitation personnel that have existed for several years.

We have about seventy-seven schools involved in our training program. We hope for a considerable increase in physical medicine and rehabilitation. Another increase is in rehabilitation counseling, where the shortage is acute. Still another shortage area is in speech pathology and audiology. And we need more trained workers in prosthetics and orthotics as well as occupational therapy, physical therapy, and psychology.

We have also increased short-term training, the courses that last from a few days to a month. These are designed to orient professional personnel in rehabilitation philosophy and practices, teach new concepts, and refresh those in practice.

Since 1954 the VRA has approved more than six hundred research and demonstration projects in rehabilitation. To the end of June, 1963, about $46 million in federal funds were expended or obligated for these purposes. Grants are made to state rehabilitation agencies, colleges, and universities or to public and private nonprofit groups in support of those proposals that seem worthy to a National Advisory Council that meets three times a year.

The projects bring a wealth of talent and imagination to rehabilitation, either for research per se into matters that will benefit the program as a whole or for demonstrations of ideas or techniques and their application to a given situation or set of conditions.

In addition, the VRA has given special sponsorship for demonstration projects in selected, severe disabilities. The purpose of these projects is to put a mass of new information about severe disabilities to practical and rapid use, and on a national scale. The response has been strong, particularly for mental retardation.

Research in Mental Retardation

One of the first grants awarded for rehabilitation research was to a group in New York City for development of an occupational training center for the mentally retarded on new principles. Its avowed purpose was to demonstrate that mentally retarded young adults whose employment had been considered virtually impossible could be rehabilitated into various jobs through carefully planned workshop training.

Even before the project was complete, its methods were so firmly accepted that project after project was proposed for other areas, so that the new principles could be applied on a massive basis.

Now there are forty-one of these projects in thirty-one states. They are continuously proving that many mental retardates, with proper evaluation of their capabilities and appropriate training, can be taught to do useful work. Many of them are in competitive jobs, and many more are working in sheltered employment under conditions compatible with their social and work adjustments.

These centers bolster the insistence of the National Association for Retarded Children that public inertia was the great obstacle to help for the retarded child. Since our centers began to prove their point and the association has successfully turned the national spotlight on mental retardation, we have learned much more about the disability, and the public attitude has changed greatly.

We are continuing to learn, and there is great support from the public in the educational and training projects that are building bridges across gaps that occur in the lives of mentally retarded youths when they enter the period where educational and vocational processes begin to merge.

The Georgia Division of Vocational Rehabilitation has a fine demonstration project to assist the state's secondary schools in meeting the needs of retarded children with the co-ordination of educational, rehabilitation, and community resources, to smooth the pathway of transition in this period.

In Minneapolis the public school system and in Milwaukee the Jewish Vocational Service have programs that are investigating the practicality of integrating academic schooling with job experience for mentally retarded youths in their high school senior year. And two of our state universities are making studies and demonstrations at their level. The University of Alabama is developing vocational rehabilitation procedures for mentally retarded youths that can be used by rehabilitation facilities in co-operation with local systems to teach and train retarded youths. The University of Colorado has a project to study the effects of special vocational training procedures on the retarded.

When new knowledge out of these and other programs reaches the applicable stage, then we can feel that special education and the vocational processes will be much more effectively joined to give the retarded youth a greater equality of opportunity for useful living.

The situation of the mentally retarded was brought to the greater attention of the nation when the late President Kennedy evinced his great interest. He named a panel of outstanding physicians, scientists, educators, lawyers, psychologists, and specialists in the field to prescribe a new and vigorous plan of action. His directive to the panel was to explore possibilities and paths to prevent and cure mental retardation. The report has been made and outlines a national plan for action.

Projects in Speech and Hearing Disabilities

Another area of great mutual interest is that of children and youths who have problems in hearing and speech.

There has been a great surge of interest in this field in the past few years, and it has brought these disabilities into sharper focus in the total picture of rehabilitation. Many school systems have taken cognizance of the situation and are responding with more special classes for children with hearing difficulties. All the way up the age and education scales there are new concepts of how to prepare these children for usefulness in their productive years.

A project for which a grant has been made will, we hope, be of value in bringing established facilities to more persons who have hearing difficulties. The American Hearing Society has a long-range program of helping to establish new, smaller speech and hearing centers supervised and guided by large, well-established speech and hearing centers within a radius of a hundred miles.

These satellite facilities have a dual purpose: to teach persons with speech and hearing difficulties who are not aware of or unable to get to the larger facility and to screen and refer difficult cases to the larger facility.

Two such centers are in operation; one in Mansfield, Ohio, in liaison with the Hearing and Speech Center of Columbus, and another in Macon, Georgia, in liaison with the Atlanta Speech School, Inc.

But there are more than fifty projects relating to speech and hearing. They include studies of aphasia, cleft palate, esophageal speech, stuttering, lip reading, and mental health of the deaf. Their translation into services is a current activity.

The renewed interest in hearing and speech difficulties has deeply touched the two agencies in the Department of Health, Education, and Welfare that are most concerned: the Office of Education and the Vocational Rehabilitation Administration.

Perhaps one of the most significant activities of the Office of Education in this area is administration of a grant system authorized by the Congress not long ago. It is helping to solve a long-time shortage of personnel, for it provides additional funds to schools that prepare selected persons as instructors of the deaf.

This new era is already beginning to produce fresh thought and direction. We in VRA sense new influences in vocational training for the deaf. We agree with those who advocate broad shop training which fosters adaptability in the individual. He is then better able to cope with the demands of modern living and the employment needs of a world changing rapidly in economic and technological concepts.

Although some schools persist in providing vocational training for very young deaf persons, there is a growing concept which holds that schools for deaf children should make the earliest possible tests for interests and aptitudes and introduce them to business and industrial practices and environments.

It is inefficient to try the relatively impossible task of turning out artisans of tender years. Moreover, it is not good educational psychology to immerse immature children in educational practices that are necessarily involved with mature minds and bodies, as is generally true of vocational education.

We share the view that schools for the deaf should concentrate on building the fundamentals for a useful life. In the early years there should be instillment of good personal habits, good work habits, development of favorable personality traits, the abilities to take instructions and to get along with others.

But they should do more. In addition to raising communications skills to the highest levels, the schools should assume an obligation to hold up a mirror of achievement before them so that they may have the inspiration and incentives to rise to their true capabilities and dreams through pursuit of enlarging opportunities in highly skilled and professional work.

There are two projects in particular in our research that tie into the transitional period for the deaf. Both are under direction of the Clarke School for the Deaf, in Massachusetts. One, now reaching the completion stage, is investigating the effects of deafness on the learning process and the relation of learning deficiencies to the vocational and social adjustment of the deaf. The second is studying the effects of school experience on the intellectual capacity and personal adjustment of deaf adolescents in preparation for adult vocational life.

A visitor from the rehabilitation agency of one of our most progressive states once discussed some aspects of this question with us and used as a practical illustration the experience of a large and successful private vocational school in his state that admitted a few deaf students.

The initial effort, he said, showed up some extremely difficult problems. They are far from insurmountable, but they do point out some of the special attributes that a deaf person should bring to a training course and some of the obstacles that appear when standard courses of vocational training are offered to them.

The principal need, he says, is for improved teaching methods and for personal evaluation. The usual instruction methods are too slow. There is intense need for faster and more highly comprehensible methods of imparting information to deaf students, more use of demonstrations and sign language. He believes there is need for research into such matters as the known success that some teachers have had in the field and into the personal factors and teaching techniques that tend to make some deaf students more receptive to instruction than others.

Projects for Children with Visual Disabilities

Another area where the VRA is providing a measure of aid for the handicapped child is that of optical aids for those with low visual acuity.

The selected demonstration activities within VRA research embrace a number of optical aids clinics over the country, to which supporting grants are made. The clinics utilize the services of highly skilled ophthalmologists to diagnose and correct the vision of persons whose sight may in some cases be so low as to classify them as legally blind.

There are now twenty-three of these clinics in twenty-one states. One of the states, with a fine record in rehabilitation, has reported an increasing use of its clinic by children, though the original purpose was to improve the vision of persons of working age.

In this one clinic, operated by the state vocational rehabilitation agency in Georgia, prescriptions for optical aids of various kinds were written for 406 adults in three years, and a follow-up study reveals that their sight was improved by an average of 82 per cent. In the same report, the optical services provided to children are reported to have improved their vision by an average of some 30 per cent, an immense help for a child who is looking forward to a useful life.

VRA-Supported Programs on Other Disabilities

There are other disabilities in which special education, the vocational rehabilitation process, and the work of other groups are joined.

The number of cerebral-palsied persons rehabilitated in 1963 through the public program of vocational rehabilitation was about 850. A small but still impressive number of them are youths who have the courage to attend college. In recognition of the growing number, the College of Education of the State University of Iowa has in operation an intensive study of the social, psychological, physical, and environmental problems encountered by the young cerebral-palsied person in college.

It is demonstrably certain that cerebral palsy is not well enough identified in the public consciousness as a severe disability. Consequently, we were glad in VRA for a project to support United Cerebral Palsy in a demonstration program to develop ways to meet the vocational rehabilitation needs of multiply handicapped young people. We hope there will be enough warmth generated to motivate a great deal more activity on behalf of the cerebral-palsied.

The United Epilepsy Association also has a grant to help with development of informational and educational material aimed at sparking community action to provide greater consideration of the problems of the epileptic.

These are some of the research activities in which we are engaged in relation to specific disabilities. We are, however, also attacking disability in young persons on a broader scale.

In a study at the University of Florida, it was conclusively shown that college training was a definite factor in vocational success and personal adjustment of the young disabled person.

While this is not a startling conclusion, it confirms the belief that higher education for the young disabled must be offered in our program. Based on that belief, several highly interesting projects are under way to provide more information and to demonstrate methods to give disabled youths greater educational opportunities in high school and college.

One of the most helpful high school projects is in Detroit, under the leadership of Dr. Samuel Brownell, former Commissioner of the U.S. Office of Education and now head of the Detroit school system. It is conducted by the Department of Special Education and combines the efforts of school personnel, counselors, and placement personnel of the Michigan state vocational rehabilitation agency to study educational and vocational techniques for helping handicapped youths.

The youngsters served are mentally retarded. Detroit's huge metropolitan and industrial area is a choice site for the study, out of which are expected guidelines for curricula for handicapped school-age youths and better ways to place them in employment.

Other projects are studying various aspects of high school education for handicapped youth. Oklahoma's state agency is demonstrating a co-ordinated plan of educational and rehabilitation services in meeting needs of handicapped youths, a project highly successful in its initial stages and one which has captured the intense interest of state educators.

Another project of uncommon interest is that of the Vocational Counseling Service of St. Louis, demonstrating the value of intensive counseling for physically handicapped high school students. And in Maryland, a county board of education is making a study of the feasibility of a four-year program of supervised out-of-school experience in job training.

At the college level, the University of Missouri is developing ways to establish a regional university facility to meet the needs of severely handicapped college students. And at Georgetown University, in Washington, D.C., blind young persons are studying the Russian language to prepare them for transcribing and translating recorded materials. The program has been enlarged to include the German language and thus give additional sources of employment for blind persons.

VRA-supported research in behalf of disabled youth is not always bound to formal education. Some disabled youths are homebound, for instance, and the Federation of the Handicapped of New York City is studying the effectiveness of prevocational services to help these persons find and attain vocational usefulness. We are supporting, too, a project in New York which we hope will show that vocational rehabilitation services can help to meet the vocational and social needs of emotionally disturbed adolescents who have exhibited tendencies toward delinquency.

Aims and Responsibilities of VRA

All of us who work with and for the disabled have a fundamental working premise, whether or not we realize it. The basic needs of life are common to everyone, but capacities vary for their attainment. We have before us the goal of balancing these needs with provision of opportunity, with services, with understanding, and with hard work.

We in vocational rehabilitation work under law—a wise and flexible law that gives the federal office and the state rehabilitation agencies the eans and the proper attitudes to deal in humanistic terms with the lives f disabled persons.

The VRA was given an appropriation of $88.7 million for the year ending June 30, 1964, to meet obligations in matching funds with the states. he sum of $34.8 million was approved for research and demonstration rojects, for grants to educational institutions to support curriculums and aff in teaching rehabilitation subjects, and for special research and training centers being established.

It is the task of VRA to administer these funds as wisely as we can, lways bearing in mind the true function of the law: to convert dependency to independence.

Suggested Reading

eview of Educational Research, 33:1; February, 1963. This issue on the education of exceptional children contains chapters on Organization of Special Education, The Speech Handicapped, The Visually Handicapped, The Deaf and Hard of Hearing, The Mentally Retarded, The Gifted, Children with Crippling Conditions and Special Health Problems, The Emotionally and Socially Handicapped, and Programmed Instruction for the Mentally Retarded. Previous reviews of research on this subject appeared in 1941, 1944, 1953, and 1959.

CHAPTER ||| GIFTED CHILDREN

THE EMERGING STATUS of guidance in the area of exceptional children finds guidance at different positions in the different areas. At the present time, guidance of the gifted is somewhat more accepted than guidance in some other areas, but this was not true as little as a decade ago. Most of the articles in this section reflect the change which has taken place since then—a change aided by sputnik, NDEA, and a growing awareness of the importance of talent. It is interesting to report that the first group to be aware of the need of guidance for bright students was the bright students themselves. Some of the reasons for the need of special guidance procedures for the gifted are discussed in separate articles by each of the compilers. They have expanded similar material into another book, *The Education and Guidance of the Ablest* (Springfield, Ill.: Charles C Thomas and Co., 1964).

The chapter starts with a vocational exploration of the aspirations of gifted children by Barbe and Chambers. It continues with Barrett's perceptive study of the developmental problems of the gifted. Beals and Simmons discuss high school counseling problems. Two papers by the editors then follow. Torrance concludes by widening our horizons in an illuminating discussion of the guidance of creative children. Thus the chapter presents in miniature a capsule history of the gifted-child movement during the past decade, as it has moved from vocational and educational planning through developmental problems and counseling to a consideration of the guidance of creative children.

9. Career Requirements of Gifted Elementary Children and Their Parents *

WALTER B. BARBE, *Professor of Special Education and Department Head, Kent State University*
NORMAN S. CHAMBERS, *Intern Psychologist, Oberlin City Schools*

L ITTLE ATTENTION has been directed toward the requirements of a career which make it attractive to elementary school children. This is undoubtedly a result of the belief that because of their immaturity, there is reason to believe that choice of career is not yet a serious concern for them. With gifted children, however, there is mounting evidence that the selection of a career is of major concern for them much earlier than had previously been thought.

The importance of the parents' attitude toward the essentials of a career choice for their child has received only limited attention. It is well accepted that many of the attitudes toward the attractiveness or unattractiveness of certain careers are gained in the home. It would be expected that when young children were studied, the influence of home attitudes would be even greater than it would be with high school students.

There can be no question but that more information is needed about the requirements of a career in order for it to be chosen by a young person. Such questions as "When in the student's growing up are such requirements about a career formulated?" "What is the influence of a child's parents in formulating such requirements?" and "Does intellectual level of the student determine when and what requirements are formulated?" cannot be answered by the results of any one study. It is clear, however, that attention must be directed toward finding answers to these questions.

Purpose of Study

The purpose of the present study was to seek information about the career choice requirements of a group of gifted elementary school children and compare these with the career choice requirements which the parents

* Reprinted by permission of the authors and *Vocational Guidance Quarterly*, 11:137–139; Winter, 1963.

of these children had for them. Specifically, answers were sought to the following questions.

1. What are the career choice requirements of gifted elementary school children?

2. What are the career choice requirements for their gifted children of the parents of the gifted?

3. How do the career choice requirements of gifted children differ from those which their parents have for them?

4. Is there a difference between the mothers' and the fathers' career choice requirements for their gifted children?

Procedure

As part of the Portage County Gifted Child Project, which was supported by the Division of Special Education of the State Department of Education, special classes for gifted elementary school children were established. One hundred fifty-six gifted children in special classes, who had received an IQ above 120 on group and individual tests of intelligence, in grades 3 through 6, and 263 parents of these gifted children were included in this study.

Morris Rosenberg, in *Occupations and Values* (Glencoe: The Free Press, 1957), listed "Requirements for Ideal Job or Career" which ranked the requirements of a large group of college students. This list was adapted for use with elementary school gifted children and their parents. Ten statements were presented to the children and their parents. The children were asked to rank "How a job or career would have to satisfy each of these requirements before you could consider it ideal." The parents were asked to rank "How a job or career would have to satisfy each of these requirements before you could consider it ideal for your child."

Results

The group of children included an even number of boys and girls. There was found to be no significant difference in the responses of boys and girls, so no separation of the data was made. Reports were received from 142 mothers and 121 fathers. There was no significant difference in their responses, so the study was confined to a comparison of the responses of parents, both mothers and fathers, and the responses of the children.

The mothers and fathers of gifted elementary school children in this study selected the statement "Provide an opportunity to use my special

TABLE I—CAREER CHOICE REQUIREMENTS OF GIFTED ELEMENTARY CHILDREN
AND THEIR PARENTS

Job Requirement Before You Could Consider It Ideal	Ranked by Children as "Most Important" (Percentage)	Ranked by Parents as "Most Important" (Percentage)
1. Provide an opportunity to use my special abilities or aptitudes	15	51
2. Provide me with a chance to earn a great deal of money	10	2
3. Permit me to be creative and original	3	4
4. Give me social status and prestige	2	0
5. Give me an opportunity to work with people rather than with things	6	2
6. Allow me to look forward to a stable, secure future	21	26
7. Leave me fairly free of supervision by others	1	0
8. Give me a chance at leadership	2	1
9. Provide me with adventure	2	1
10. Give me an opportunity to be helpful to others	37	13

abilities or aptitudes" as the most important requirement of a job for their child before they would consider the job ideal. More than half of the parents made this selection as being most important. About half of the remaining parents, or slightly more than a quarter of the total group of parents, selected the statement "Allow me to look forward to a stable, secure future" as the most important requirement of a job for their child before they would consider the job ideal. Again, half of this number (about 13 per cent) selected the statement "Give me an opportunity to be helpful to others" as the most important requirement of a job for their child before they would consider the job ideal. None of the seven remaining areas was selected by more than an insignificant number of parents.

The largest number of gifted children in this study (37 per cent) selected the statement "Give me an opportunity to be helpful to others" as the most important requirement of a job before they would consider the job ideal. Twenty-one per cent selected the statement "Allow me to look forward to a stable, secure future," 15 per cent selected the statement "Provide an opportunity to use my special abilities or aptitudes," and 10 per cent selected the statement "Provide me with a chance to earn a great deal of money."

Interestingly, parents of gifted children and the gifted children themselves included the same requirements in the three highest. The order was not the same, however. The parents clearly selected only three requirements, and each of the three requirements was clearly selected by more parents than the next highest. This was not so true of the gifted children. The spread over the characteristics was greater, and there was less agreement as to the most important characteristic.

The most important characteristic to the parents (providing an opportunity to use his special abilities) was chosen by only 15 per cent of the children as being most important. Conversely, having an opportunity to be helpful to others was chosen by the largest number of children as the most important, but was chosen by only 13 per cent of the parents. The characteristic dealing with a "stable, secure future" was chosen as most important by 21 per cent of the children and 26 per cent of the parents.

An attempt to explain some of these differences by noting the relative youth of these children necessitates a few notes of caution. The children are relatively young, but their mental ages are in every instance considerably above their chronological ages. Even though the children are less interested in a job which provides an opportunity to use their special abilities than in a job which gives an opportunity to be helpful to others, it must be noted that the very placement in a special class necessitated some counseling, either direct or indirect, concerning their special abilities. The fact that, in spite of this awareness of their abilities, more of them nevertheless listed the more altruistic answer would be interpreted by this author not as a sign of immaturity but as a direct benefit resulting from placement in a class where social responsibility is being taught.

Summary and Conclusions

One hundred fifty-six children in grades 3 through 6 attending special classes for gifted children in the Portage County Schools were asked to select from a list the most important characteristic for job satisfaction. Two hundred sixty-three of their parents were asked to make the same selection for job satisfaction for their children. The children listed having an opportunity to be helpful to others as the most important, while their parents listed having an opportunity to use their special abilities as most important. There was no difference between the mothers' and the fathers' choices for their children, nor was there a difference between the gifted boys' and gifted girls' responses. The requirements were adapted from a list in Rosenberg's book, *Occupations and Values*.

With elementary school guidance becoming more important, it is necessary that an attempt be made to understand the vocational aspirations of elementary school children. So little attention has been given to this particular area of study that the training of guidance counselors for the elementary school has often neglected to mention that gifted students in particular, and perhaps all students, determine early career choice requirements which greatly affect their later decisions. Attention must be directed to the differences which appear to exist between the children and their parents with respect to requirements for an ideal job.

Only through more research on the elementary school child can the elementary school guidance worker truly play a part in the child's growing up. What is the role of the guidance worker at the elementary level? The answer must be, in part, that of a researcher seeking information about the needs of elementary school children. It will not be surprising if such research uncovers a greater need for the specialized guidance worker at the elementary school than has ever been suspected.

10. An Intensive Study of Thirty-Two Gifted Children *

HARRY O. BARRETT, *Associate Professor of Educational Psychology, Ontario College of Education, University of Toronto*

UNDERACHIEVEMENT among gifted children has engaged the attention of most school counselors. In their close contact with individual students counselors are well aware that a large number of pupils in our secondary schools who have ability are not using it.

The heads of the guidance departments of the Toronto secondary schools have undertaken two studies of the problem and are at present laying plans for a comprehensive long-term project covering eight hundred pupils. A preliminary survey of superior pupils was carried out in Toronto secondary

* Reprinted by permission of the author and *Personnel and Guidance Journal,* 36:192–194; November, 1957.

schools in 1953 in an attempt to find some of the underlying causes of underachievement. This study indicated that there was no apparent relationship between the severity of the problem and the type of school. There was as large a percentage of underachievers in the technical and the commercial schools as in the collegiate institutes (academic, college entrance). Too many outside interests did not seem to interfere seriously with the academic achievement of superior-ability pupils. The preliminary survey raised so many questions and provided so few answers that counselors decided that a further, more intensive study should be undertaken. The study was planned to include qualitative as well as quantitative data—a clinical evaluation as well as a statistical one. It was hoped that the dual approach would disclose some of the underlying reasons why pupils with outstanding ability were not doing better work.

For the purposes of the intensive study, the superior child was defined as one having an IQ of 130 or higher on the Henmon-Nelson Advanced Test (Grades 7 to 12). The guidance head in each school was asked to make a very thorough study of two pupils in the superior group in his school—the two who made the highest standing and the lowest standing respectively on the Christmas examination of December, 1953. This meant the assembling of information about thirty-two students, sixteen achieving a standing commensurate with their capacity and sixteen definitely underachieving. It was realized that the sample was very small, but it was hoped that the intensity of the study would reveal real difference between the two groups and thus serve as a basis for new experiments by guidance personnel directed toward improving the performance of underachievers. Although some of the data were of a strictly factual, objective nature, a considerable amount involved subjective evaluation. Since each of the evaluators, however, had had ten or more years of work in guidance, their ratings had at least the merit of experience.

A Team Approach

For the clinical side of the study, the guidance counselors enlisted the help of the chief of the Child Adjustment Services of the Toronto Board of Education. It was believed that the projective techniques of the clinical psychologists of his department would add greatly to an understanding of the pupils being studied. An additional benefit resulting from his co-operation was, of course, the ability to profit by his years of service as a psychiatrist.

This report, then, is the result of a co-operative effort made by persons trained in a number of disciplines: the psychiatrist, the psychologist, the school counselor, the teacher, and the public health nurse.

General information and home background were investigated by reference to elementary school records, secondary school records, pupil interviews, home visits, and autobiographies written by the students as part of regular class activity. An assessment, admittedly subjective, was made by the school counselor of the nature and degree of home encouragement given to the student. The projective tests, in addition, provided information concerning the family emotional atmosphere as assessed by the child.

A medical history was provided by the public health nurse, using data from the elementary school records and from examinations made by the school doctor.

Intellectual ability was measured by the Henmon-Nelson Advanced Test and by the Differential Aptitude Tests. The latter gave verbal, numerical, abstract, spatial relations, and mechanical reasoning scores. Again, the projective tests provided additional information.

An attempt was made to determine the pupils' personality pattern by the use of ratings on a five-point scale by individual teachers; by the use of a sociometric scale; by student autobiographies; by figure drawings; and by Rorschach and TAT responses. Individual intelligence testing was not done, as the committee felt that the available time of the clinical psychologists should be spent on projective tests.

Study Characteristics

Before looking at the results which were obtained, let us consider briefly the characteristics of the study. These are as follows.

1. The use of such a small number of cases makes it unwise to draw general conclusions applicable to all gifted children on this evidence alone. The findings, strictly speaking, apply to these thirty-two students only.

2. Because of the small number of cases studied, no attempt was made to investigate the interrelationships of the various factors. Such an investigation with a large number of cases might indicate definite patterns.

3. The value of the study is highly dependent on the validity of the initial premises or criteria. When, for instance, the research committee selected the four "basic" and the six "desirable" criteria by which to set up positive and negative categories of school attitudes, they did so arbitrarily, before seeing the data to be judged by those criteria. This deductive approach was based on the assumption that they, as teachers, knew from experience what constitutes acceptable attitudes.

4. In a co-operative study of this nature, it was necessary to divide the work evenly among the sixteen heads of guidance. Therefore, two students were chosen from each school, although it was recognized that the sampling did not give truly representative groups of achievers and underachievers in the secondary schools. If an accurate sampling of all the gifted Grade 9 students had been taken, there would have been several students from some secondary schools and none from others. Such a plan, although desirable, was impracticable.

5. In the selection, the guidance heads relied entirely on group test results. It would have been desirable to verify the accuracy of the group test results by individual tests. This was difficult because of lack of time and staff.

6. The study commenced at the Grade 5 level because that was the first grade at which the elementary school records were adequate for research purposes.

Conclusions

Bearing in mind the characteristics of this study, it is possible to discern certain patterns.

Pattern of Intellectual Achievement and Ability

1. The pattern of underachievement is apparent by Grade 5.
2. The gifted children with high achievement in the elementary school maintain that standard in the secondary school.
3. The children with weak performance in the elementary school do even more poorly in the secondary school.
4. When using standardized achievement tests instead of subject examinations, the gap between the achievers and the underachievers tends to narrow except in the case of arithmetic.
5. The low achievers tend to be less gifted in numerical and abstract reasoning as measured by the Differential Aptitude Tests.

Pattern of Home Background

The pattern of the home background is less distinct than in other areas. Nevertheless, although existing in varying degrees in the two groups, there are discernible patterns.

1. Parents of the underachiever tend to exhibit a neutral or uninterested attitude toward education.

2. Parents of the underachiever are likely to be overanxious, over-solicitous, or inconsistent in their attitude toward the child.

3. The lack of co-operative spirit in the family, as evidenced by conflict, authoritarianism by the parent, or domination by the child, and the lack of co-operation in church participation are present in about the same degree.

Pattern of School Attitudes

It should be noted that the pattern of school attitudes is the pattern as seen by the teacher in the classroom situation.

1. The underachievers exhibit a predominantly negative attitude toward school.

2. Achievers and underachievers are equally courteous, co-operative, and self-sufficient.

3. Classmates show considerably greater acceptance of the achievers than of the underachievers.

4. On the whole, the achievers show a greater interest in reading than the underachievers.

Pattern of Personality

1. There are emotional disturbances among both achievers and under-achievers. It should be pointed out that adolescence is a period of adjustment in which the child is struggling toward maturity. The achievers, however, tend to be more aware of the nature of their disturbances and to be more constructive in their efforts to cope with them.

2. As seen in the school situation, the achievers come considerably closer to the guidance heads' conception of the well-integrated personality than do the underachievers.

3. On three personality criteria—feeling of worth as an individual, the ability to persist in face of difficulty, and the amount of interest or energy devoted to leisure-time activities—there is considerable overlapping in individual cases, but on the average the achievers excel.

4. The achievers appear to have a more rational approach to the problem of solving difficulties than the underachievers.

5. Good academic achievement is not incompatible with a high degree of acceptance by classmates.

6. Both groups suffer from feelings of inadequacy. Among the achievers, this tends to act as a motivating force. The achievers want to prove to the world that they are adequate and worthy. Among the underachievers the feelings of inadequacy act as depressors. The underachievers withdraw and refuse to compete.

General Conclusion

Only by a careful and thorough study of each individual personality can we find the reasons for underachievement. If the individual is underachieving, it is because he cannot adequately utilize his inner resources or because he chooses not to. In either case, he needs help from professionally trained counselors.

11. Counseling Needs of Gifted High School Students *

LESTER BEALS, *Associate Dean of Students and Professor of Education, Orange County State College, Fullerton, California*

PATRICIA SIMMONS, *Director of Research and Statistics, Orange County Schools, Santa Ana, California*

MANY STUDIES have been made of the characteristics of the gifted student and the type of school program needed. Comparatively little study, on the other hand, has been made of the counseling needs of these students as related to vocational and personal decisions. Studies so far have been more concerned with the curricular needs of the gifted student than with his personal needs, with his academic potential rather than with his leadership potential. In a sense, it would seem that our public concern has been that of directing the gifted student into careers valuable in our national defense or our economic well-being. Perhaps more emphasis should be

* Reprinted by permission of the authors and *Personnel and Guidance Journal,* 40:712–716; April, 1962.

given to guiding the gifted toward making diversified contributions to society. Counseling has generally followed the premise that society will benefit most as each person achieves self-realization.

America needs people who will contribute solutions to problems of science and technology and to civic, social, and moral problems. The able person is often able to be both a scientist and an educational statesman, a physician and a humanitarian, or an artist and a physicist—a Conant or a Schweitzer, for example. There is a multitude of people in America today who could make a much larger social contribution if they had been given better guidance. Ernest Ligon has done much study along these lines. He says in *A Greater Generation* (New York: Macmillan, 1948) that there are a million and a half people today who are more highly endowed intellectually than Lincoln or Washington! The question seems, then, why are there not more people with a sense of social responsibility and dedication? Counseling may play an important role in helping develop this social conscience.

The Present Study

A study was undertaken in Orange County, California, under the sponsorship of the County School Office with the co-operation of the high schools and financed by Title V of the National Defense Education Act. The purpose was to determine the counseling needs and the kind of counseling being given a selected group of gifted high school students. This study required, initially, that the group to be studied be defined and described.

To select the students called "gifted," scores on the California Test of Mental Maturity were used. All eighth- or ninth-grade students are given this test as pre-enrollment to high school in the various school districts of Orange County. A minimum score of 140 on either the Language or Non-Language section of the CTMM was set to define the lower limits of the group to be studied.

An analysis of the test scores for the four years prior to the study yielded the names of 310 students from thirty schools who became the sample studied. The test had been administered during the eighth grade, and some diminution of the sample occurred. Complete information was secured on 247 students placed in Grades 9 through 12.

After identification, student achievement was examined. This was considered to be revealed by scores on standardized achievement tests and scholastic grades earned. Student participation in leadership activities and clubs was also examined. Furthermore, study was made to discover the kind of future planning these students were doing, their life goals and values, and the extent to which they were guided in achieving these goals. Hence, parents, teachers, and counselors needed to be contacted. Terman and others had shown earlier that the gifted students are not the stereotype so popularly pictured and that they tend in fact to be very well adjusted.

During the summer of 1959, letters were sent to all student participants. Interviews followed. The interviews were structured to ensure securing the same basic information from each student. These informal interviews were conducted in each student's school and varied in length from 25 to 35 minutes.

Later, a three-page questionnaire was sent to the parents of the students participating in the study. Information requested included parental opinions regarding the counseling received by their son or daughter, the extent of parental involvement in the decision making by the student, and ways in which the home and school might work together better.

Finally, a brief opinionaire was sent to all high school counselors regarding the students involved in the study. The opinionaire supplemented informal interviews made with the counselors prior to the student interview.

Findings

An analysis of all scholastic grades earned indicated that about 70 per cent of these students were making a 3.00 point or above grade-point average on a 4.00 scale, or a B. Another 20 per cent were making between a C and a B average. The rest, about 10 per cent, were making less than a C, including one student making less than a D average. Many of these students were in accelerated groups. It would appear that the majority were doing quite well academically. An analysis of the students making less than a C average indicated that many had personal problems or were not highly motivated.

On the average, girls earned higher grades than boys. Boys, on the other hand, had higher intelligence scores. The grades of both boys and girls tended to improve a bit as they progressed in school. A study of the relationship of intelligence scores to grade-point averages, using the Pierson Product Moment Formula, was made but yielded very low correlations, especially on the Non-Language section of the CTMM and grade correlations. The correlation for the Language score on the CTMM and grade-point average was .340; the relation between the Non-Language section of the CTMM and grades was .028. The publishers of the CTMM corroborated these findings, as this is a truncated sample drawn from the upper portion of the normal distribution range. A correlation with grades is influenced by the fact that each person in the sample seems to have the potential of an A student.

Much information was secured from the interviews. Additional information was secured from the student questionnaire and combined with the material from the interviews. A study of this information, in general, reveals that these students came from homes economically and socially in the middle or upper middle class. Nearly 90 per cent of the students were living with both their natural father and mother. Students from unbroken homes tended to make better grades than those from broken homes. In view of the fact that Orange County is a changing and rapidly growing county, it is interesting to note that 65 per cent of the students had lived in the county or in the adjoining Los Angeles County all of their lives. Ten per cent came from other regions of California, while the other 25 per cent had migrated to California.

The occupations of fathers and mothers, when placed in job classifications given in the *Dictionary of Occupational Titles,* revealed a large percentage of highly trained personnel. Fifty-two per cent of the parents were employed in managerial or professional positions; 13 per cent, in clerical and sales; 9 per cent were skilled workers; 7 per cent were in service occupations; the remainder were scattered among other major groups. The 52 per cent engaged in managerial and professional occupations is very considerably higher than the national proportion of 10 per cent in these occupations. It may be assumed that children whose fathers are in professional and managerial occupations may have greater opportunities at home to practice academic skills and understandings that will enable them to succeed better in a typical academic high school.

A large percentage of the mothers (65 per cent) were not employed outside the home. Of the mothers employed, most were in professional, managerial, clerical, or sales occupations.

All the students planned to finish high school, and approximately 96 per cent planned to go to some kind of college. About half of them did not have a specific college in mind. A named college was more frequently given by those students about to be graduated. About half of all these participants stated that they were encouraged by their counselors to consider college. Most had also been encouraged by their parents.

In terms of present and future educational planning, a large majority, or 63 per cent, said that their parents gave them the most help; 17 per cent said counselors; and 11 per cent mentioned teachers.

Vocational objectives for 80 per cent of these students tended to be in the professional and managerial areas. The most popular vocational choices were mathematics, science, teaching on all levels, engineering, medicine, and law. Again, parents seemed to have supplied the primary information and incentive to these young people.

An analysis of vocational choices in terms of test scores, grades, and stated interests tended to indicate realistic planning. A majority of these students seemed to have made their vocational decisions on the basis of personal interests and aptitudes without parental pressures. During the student interview and on the parent questionnaire, little evidence existed that parents coerced their offspring relative to specific occupations.

When questioned about their counselor, the students' answers revealed great variance, depending for the most part on the kind and length of time that a counseling program had been operating in the school plus the length of time the student had been in school. A large number knew that there was someone to whom they could go for help; this might be the counselor, vice-principal, or dean. A large number indicated that they saw their counselor twice a year; presumably these visits were for program planning. A large number said they felt free to talk with a counselor or a dean about an educational or vocational problem; however, they did not say they felt as free in discussing their personal problems. It may be that these students had fewer personal problems than other students or that they went to their parents for such help. In interview, students stated that they received nearly as much educational and occupational information from teachers as from counselors.

In addition, the interviews revealed that the participants took an active part in community and school events. Nearly all of them, boys and girls alike, were interested and active in sports. While not many of this group were represented on the first team of a major sport, most of them had attained skill and participated in minor sports. Further, these students said that they took part in some kind of an interest club. They also were actively engaged in community groups, e.g., church organizations, Scouts, YMCA, YWCA, and recreation groups. Their interests seemed to be most varied.

Very few of the participants had important leadership positions. There were a few student body officers or organization officers among these students. For the most part these able students did not take leadership roles. They were responsible participants but not very active in leadership roles. The lack of leadership responsibilities raises questions. Could it be that this kind of student does not want to take the time to prepare for leadership positions?

The students, for the most part, indicated that their counseling had not included guidance in the selection of activities. Parents stated that they felt this was an area of need in the counseling program.

An attempt was made during the interviews to determine the basic life motivation or philosophy of the individual. Certain questions and discussions gave some clue. A summary of the data from this part of the interview indicates that three-fourths seemed to lack a well-defined philosophy. For example, when asked this question, "What do you hope to get out of life?" a majority stated that they did not know. Many young people seemed to be groping for more definite life goals and values to which they might tie their educational and vocational plans. A small number, however, reflected in a very mature fashion and had definite life goals or plans for attaining these goals.

A large majority of the parents were found to be college-educated, and many held advanced degrees. Since much of the educational and occupational guidance comes from parents, the parental education level becomes significant. The parents said also that they wanted to work more closely with the school in providing information and guidance. Parents said they would like to have more information on standardized tests. Parents further stated that although they felt moral and spiritual guidance to be primarily their responsibility, they did appreciate all the help that the school could give them in reinforcing such guidance. A large number of parents expressed an opinion that counselors and teachers should give more guidance in aiding young people develop a life philosophy and in establishing the values needed in a democratic society.

Implications

The high schools in the county have a variety of counseling programs, and multiple services are offered. Most of the large high schools tend to have a staff of well-trained, experienced counselors. The counseling program is organized so that each student has some individual counseling. In addition to counseling, the counselors spend some time working with teachers and administrators. Most of the counselors surveyed said that these students should be counseled as are all students. However, counselors said they would like to give more time to the parents. Counseling programs seemed to lack time for much parent conference work. Some counselors indicated that they felt that they should spend more time with teachers in order to provide the teacher with information and understanding. While counselors said they believed guidance in the moral and spiritual areas was important, they were not sure how to offer such service. Counselors said they had so many clerical duties to perform that they did not have the time to do what they felt should be done.

It seems clear that academic underachievers among the able students should be identified as early as possible. The reasons for the lack of top achievement by these students need to be analyzed carefully. A diagnosis might be possible early in the elementary school. If such an early diagnosis could be made, perhaps corrective action could be taken. Assistance needs to be given to the underachiever from the time a diagnosis is made until his schooling ends. In some cases financial assistance to the student and his family may be necessary.

It appears that counselors need to guide students so that they also achieve outside of class activities. Counseling may be in order so that the able student might be helped to enter and achieve in those activities that would seem best to fit his needs and interests.

The data indicated that counselors and teachers should work much more closely with the home. The parents of the gifted exercise much influence in both educational and vocational decisions. Such decision making implies that counselors are important assistants to the parents. Nearly all parents indicated that they wanted to work much more closely with the counselors in matters related to the progress of their sons and daughters. Counselors, teachers, and administrators, therefore, should spend more of their time with parents. Counselors might profitably spend one-fourth to one-third of their time in individual and group contacts with parents. Perhaps time could be used during the summer for counseling with parents and students. What has been said in terms of working with these parents may well be applied to all parents.

The findings seem to point to the teachers' role of providing educational and vocational information to students. Therefore, counselors may well spend more time in providing information of many kinds to teachers, who in turn could pass it along to their students. Such information might well include the educational and vocational requirements of the various occupations, college admission requirements, training facilities available, and employment opportunities. Teachers need to be given more information about the student, along with interpretation of this information. Guiding all students, including the gifted, can be much more effective if a team approach is used, with the teacher, counselor, and parents working together to help the student. Such teamwork may mean that counselors, through periodic group meetings, written reports, and materials, provide parents and teachers with the information each needs to help each student.

This study revealed that counselors need more time to spend with students in exploring life goals and values in terms of their own needs and those of the democratic society in which the school operates. Perhaps too much of the counselor's time is spent in program making and other clerical chores that could be done in part by others.

Juniors and seniors receive additional counselor time when they request help in checking admissions requirements for college and securing scholarship information. These are important services; but could such services be simplified?

All students have a social contribution they can make. The gifted need to be encouraged and helped to make social and civic achievements in keeping with their abilities. Many social scientists do not accept the premise of Plato's *Republic*. At the same time, many of these leaders would agree that America and the world must look to intelligent leadership for a solution to the problems of the world. Needed are people who see the social significance of their actions and who have more concern for others than these leaders do themselves. Needed today are people who are willing to dedicate their lives to serving humanity and themselves well.

12. Guidance and Counseling with the Ablest *

GEORGE D. DEMOS

GUIDANCE AND COUNSELING for the ablest students conformt to the general principles of good practice in the pupil personnel services. The necessary and sufficient conditions for useful helping relationships have been stated by Carl Rogers many times (1957, 1959, 1961, 1962). These conditions are presumably applicable in relationships with individuals of

* Printed by permission of the author.

virtually all levels of intelligence. It was originally felt that the therapeutic conditions necessary for growth in a counseling relationship hypothesized by Rogers were most applicable to individuals with average or above-average intelligence. This position has been altered to assume that the conditions are essentially the same regardless of the problem, the intelligence levels of the individuals, etc. They are essentially:

1. *Empathic understanding* (counselor is experiencing an accurate understanding of the client's private world).

2. *Unconditional positive regard* (counselor cares for the client in a nonpossessive way, as a person with human potentialities).

3. *Congruence* (genuineness—counselor is without a façade).

In a study by Demos (1962) in which gifted students of secondary school age were counseled primarily for educational and vocational purposes, it was hypothesized that in working with these youngsters two additional characteristics were necessary for maximum growth. They were:

1. *Comfort:* The counselor expressed to the client a feeling of being at ease, with lack of stress.

2. *Respect for the client:* The counselor showed in his reactions to the client's remarks that he respected his judgments, attitudes, values, and viewpoints. The counselor did not place himself in the position of knowing all the answers.

It was hypothesized that these two additional characteristics played an integral part in effective counseling and, furthermore, were particularly important ingredients in counseling with able secondary school students. In this particular study, it was found that the most effective counselors (using multiple subjective and objective criteria) were in fact exhibiting two of the three qualities postulated by Rogers at the .01 level of confidence: namely, *empathic understanding* and *unconditional positive regard*. Of the two additional hypothesized conditions (Demos 1962), *respect for the client* was also found to be significant at the .01 level of confidence. *Comfort* and *congruence* were not found to be significant, but in both cases the most successful counselors received better ratings on these scales than did the least successful counselors. Despite the fact that these two characteristics were considered to be exceedingly important in working with gifted youngsters but were found to be not significant, this did not lead to dismay on the part of both supervisors and researcher in that it was also found that these two qualities were exceedingly difficult to measure, rate, and judge.

It is also postulated by many workers in the field of counseling and guidance with able students that the ablest, by virtue of their giftedness, are more likely to be sensitive to façades, to lack of genuineness, to uncomfortableness, and to lack of warmth and understanding than most individuals. The ability to detect sham and hypocrisy are also likely to be accentuated in the ablest.

An additional aspect was the hypothesis that when able youngsters positively perceived the above-mentioned five characteristics of helping relationships, as judged by the clients themselves through a rating scale which they completed subsequent to the interviews, it was more likely that the counseling relationship was a fruitful one. In general, this hypothesis was tenable; but in view of the relatively small sample, additional research is needed for further corroboration of this seemingly apparent conclusion. In other words, it is not enough for the counselor to feel as though he is understanding the client, that he likes him, that he is congruent with him, is comfortable, and respects him, but, more important, does the client perceive these characteristics to be prevalent in the counseling situation? Even though the counselor may feel that these qualities are present, by other subliminal or unconscious cues is he projecting another image which the able youngster is acquiring? Does this not frequently occur on an unconscious level? This phenomenon may account for the fact that when youngsters were questioned as to their reactions to their counselor, they would generally give evasive responses such as, "He was all right," "Okay," "I guess," "I don't know"—all of which seemed to indicate client reservations about the counselor. When the student was asked to clarify his feelings further, he usually had considerable difficulty pinpointing operational occurrences which accounted for his decision. No doubt many confusing, and sometimes contradictory, stimuli were screened by the client, but in some cases the balance happened to fall on one side or the other of the scale. This proved to be somewhat tautological but at the same time one of the most fruitful findings of the study. In addition, it was virtually unanimous in the opinions of the counselors who worked with these gifted youngsters that they were much more perceptive than the average with regard to the counselor's strengths and shortcomings in the counseling relationship. It was concluded by the counselors that the differences they felt in counseling with gifted youngsters in comparison with the norm were quantitative rather than qualitative; that is, the characteristics of helping and helpful relationships appear to be important for success with all youngsters, but exceptionally important with the ablest—not a different kind necessarily, but a greater amount of the same.

These researches could have particular meaning for secondary school counselors who feel a propensity for client-centered counseling. On the basis of these studies, it appears that counselors who are rated as being most successful do, in fact, possess the conditions hypothesized by Carl R. Rogers.

Too prevalent at all levels from elementary school through college is the assumption that able students do not need the guidance and counseling that are necessary for average or below-average individuals. It is assumed that these youngsters are bright enough to handle their own problems without the help of an adult and, furthermore, that it is desirable for them to work through their own problems with as little help as possible.

Several writers have rejected this assumption; for example, Dement (1957), in studying bright students, found that they felt a definite lack of counseling. Passow and others (1955) found that gifted students expressed a need for curriculum adjustments, and the NEA Project on the Academically Talented (1960) corroborated these findings. Demos (1962) also found that gifted college students expressed a genuine need for counseling, both in high school and in college.

Finally, guidance for the able involves the realization that counseling is not just the solving of problems but a positive process promoting high mental health. This is important for all students, but it is vital for the bright ones. For in order to deal with more complex aspects of problems and to bring into concert and focus more kinds of abilities, in longer process sequences, for more creative endeavors, under conditions of less external reward, the able youth needs a higher level of mental health than the average. He needs this so that he can handle without disabling stress, and keep longer in tension, the problems that he alone can cope with. We can condition learning in psychotics; we can train for creativity and causal thinking only those who are highly able cognitively, and highly sound emotionally.

13. The Organization of Guidance for Gifted Children *

JOHN CURTIS GOWAN

THEORETICALLY and practically, education for the ablest students is best viewed as a natural outcome of good guidance services which stress individualization of education. Yet, because the pupil personnel area has been the last major educational area to develop maturity and status, there is a tendency, even among adherents of education for the gifted, to view guidance as an afterthought. Since the beginnings of the guidance movement some fifty years ago, development in guidance has shown the trends of (1) extending the scope of guidance far beyond vocational concepts to include all aspects of childhood and developmental tasks; (2) proliferating the counselor's tools, especially in testing; and (3) moving toward a more global and clinical analysis of people and their problems.

Special Problems of the Gifted

Side by side with these developments has come a growing consciousness of the importance of guidance for the gifted. Just as it was once thought that the able needed no curriculum modifications, so it has been said that they are bright enough to find their way unaided by guidance services. What is conveniently forgotten is that the able may have special problems, which it takes individual guidance to handle. Some of these may be:

1. They may be faced with an embarrassment of riches in trying to make wise occupational and educational choices.

2. There may be problems attendant upon upward social mobility.

3. They may become aware of developmental tasks before they have the physical resources to solve them.

4. They may have more need than usual to develop the specialized interests which go with certain professional occupations.

5. There may be problems connected with the lack of adult model figures.

One of the problems which many gifted youngsters face in connection with guidance has been expressed with some humor by a gifted student as

* Reprinted by permission of the author and *Personnel and Guidance Journal*, 39:275–279; December, 1960.

the perennial question of "How far out beyond the safety railing can I lean without going over the cliff?" Gifted students are bright enough to know that they deviate in characteristics considerably from the norms and to see that, in consequence, many generalizations that apply to the average student do not apply to them. The problem for them is to discriminate between those situations which apply equally to all persons, regardless of ability, and those which apply to them only with diminished force. For example, the gifted student frequently finds that he can take one or two courses in excess of the requirements and that he does not need this or that prerequisite. It takes a wise counselor to help him discriminate between those experiences he can safely telescope and those that he should undertake in as full measure as the next student.

A comprehensive statement about guidance for the gifted has yet to be written. Practically nothing exists about guidance for the able where (1) the word *guidance* is used in its specific and not in its generic sense and (2) the article has been written by a practicing expert in the field. Often the term *guidance* is used generically to include the whole of education, and a series of generalities results. Another difficulty is that few guidance people have had specific experiences with the able, and as a result there are few articles on guidance for the gifted written from a professional point of view.

Burnside, in a thoughtful article, noted five points in a guidance program for able children as follows: (1) early recognition; (2) a challenging educational program; (3) individual counseling; (4) guidance for parents; and (5) community co-operation. Bowman and others describe the Quincy Project in a booklet called *Studying Children and Training Counselors in a Community Program,* which has guidance value. Passow, in an article regarding counseling on the college level, has discussed the problem and application of guidance for the gifted in higher education. The guidance implications of the J.H.S. 43 Project in New York City, where massive guidance procedures are being used to upgrade motivation in a culturally deprived area, are reported by Wrightstone. Strang is the only writer who has provided guidance materials to be given directly to the gifted child himself.

Probably the best over-all view of guidance for the able, and one of the few exceptions to the strictures noted earlier in that it is written by a guidance expert and is also specific, is the Rothney and Koopman chapter in the *National Society for the Study of Education Yearbook.* In many respects this is the best statement to be found anywhere at the present time. The authors declare:

Guidance for the gifted varies from the usual primarily in these respects:

1. Educational and occupational opportunities for the gifted are usually of greater proportion than for others.

2. Gifted pupils become ready for self-appraisal and self-conceptualization at higher levels and at earlier ages.

3. Gifted children may be subject to unusual pressures by parents, teachers, peers, and others.

A Part of a Total Program

Despite the lack of guidance for the able, a large number of writers are on record in favor of it. Passow, Goldberg, and Tannenbaum point out the need of adequate guidance in any curriculum adjustments for the gifted. Dement finds in a follow-up study that highly endowed students feel the lack of counseling, especially in the areas of self-assessment, vocational information, human relations, and personal philosophy. Traxler notes that pupil personnel services become more and more important as our schools grow larger. The National Education Association Conference on the Academically Talented Student states, "Guidance in the broadest and deepest sense of the term is essential for the adequate development of the academically talented." The writer, after a careful survey of programs for gifted children, has yet to find a program that is not the outcome of a strong guidance group in the system or a strongly guidance-minded individual. Good programs for gifted children grow out of (1) good school systems well supported by the public with (2) good administrators who foster democratic relationships and (3) good guidance practices. The former (gifted-child programs) is always the effect, never the cause, of the latter.

Just as a good program for the able is a natural outcome of a good guidance program in general, a good guidance program in turn is a natural outcome of an intelligent and democratically oriented school administration. It is impossible to reverse the process. *Concern for the qualities of exceptional human beings arises out of an exceptional concern for the qualities of all human beings.*

The function of guidance workers at the different grade levels will differ somewhat as being more concerned with identification in the grades and more concerned with placement in the senior high school. What is not sufficiently appreciated at present is that guidance must be integrated throughout the system and that guidance in the grades is as valuable as guidance in the high school. No elementary school should be without the services of a full-time counselor. The gifted in elementary school face special problems in not being challenged by the curriculum and in failing to find friends who are agemates. Thus twin developmental tasks of industry and socialization, plus problems of identification, home, and environmental difficulties, can be cleared away with minimal difficulty if counseling help is available. But if allowed to run unchecked, another gifted underachiever is too likely to be delivered to the high school.

The major function of the guidance person working with the able youth is twofold: first, to assist in personality development and the removal of emotional or environmental handicaps; and second, to aid and advise in the maximizing of achievement and college placement which will facilitate his progress to a professional career. Both of these matters are complex enough to require separate analysis and hence will not be developed here. It should be emphasized, however, that these tasks should be prosecuted with positive, aggressive action in place of the all too current passivity about able youth which infects many guidance offices. It is not enough to measure the function of the guidance office against the comparison of the mental health and scholastic achievement of these able youngsters with the norms; instead, we should strive to prepare these outstanding representatives for the really grueling task ahead of them. If our intellectual leaders are to keep pace and be found in the frequencies demanded by modern conditions, we need not only to deliver a much higher percentage of our able youth to the door of the university but to ensure that they have the motivation and mental health to graduate. This means a program of college-going for able youth involving the encouragement, the motivation, the strengthening of curriculum, and the upbuilding of achievement on a level not approached by our high schools at present. It means a change of attitudes in students, teachers, parents, and the public regarding the importance of high school scholarship, the desirability of taking more than four "solids" per year, the need for new prestige symbols in adolescent groups, the decrease of community anti-intellectualism, the fostering of the conservation principle in young human talent—all matters of social values with which the guidance worker is concerned. While these issues are matters of community concern, they can be raised and fought for if professional educators are truly social leaders. A program for scholarship in the senior high school extending through the three years—not just the senior year—with prestige and other rewards for the participants and with good publicity regarding effective college placement and the various scholarships and awards which come to students is one way of starting such a program. Needless to say, such a job is a full-time task in the average high school and can scarcely be accomplished if the counselor is so burdened with the problems of the lower 10 per cent that he has no time for the able.

The Counselor's Role

Characteristics of the counselor for the gifted youngster may be briefly summarized. Wide cultural background with superior scholarship may be taken for granted. In addition to successful teaching experience and an absorbing interest in children, the counselor should have professional training, being well grounded in testing, statistics, education of the able, psychology, and interviewing techniques. The counselor, compared to the teacher of the gifted, should be even more permissive, intraceptive, nondirective, and nonauthoritarian and should be eminently capable of playing the adult figure model role for these bright charges.

What kind of counseling works best with the gifted? Obviously, not the directive variety. The able are independent-minded and want to figure out problems for themselves. This is not to say that they will not need and even demand information. They are usually more effective than the average in evaluation of their own position. The counselor, therefore, should distinguish between providing information and providing decisions. It is not directive to provide the former, but it is directive to provide the latter.

The able student is often more able to profit much more from the inspection of his own test results than the average youth, and the counselor need feel few qualms about giving him considerable test information. It will come as no shock to the bright child to find that he is able, nor is it likely to make him boastful or vainglorious. The counselor can do the youth a valuable service by pointing out specific, relative weaknesses as clues either for remedial work or for college or career planning. A gifted child who is at the 75th percentile of his grade in reading skill needs remediation; another who has A's in all senior subjects, but with an ACE score on the 99th percentile in linguistic areas and the 88th percentile in numerical areas, needs to be apprized of his problem before he elects M.I.T. or C.I.T.

Counselors working with the able will need to take special precautions against counselor involvement. It is very easy to identify with these youngsters, and resultant countertransference phenomena may obscure detailed consideration of the youngster's real problems. In such a situation the counselor is very apt to push the youth toward his occupational or educational bias, forgetting that a counselor, unlike a teacher, is not looking for disciples. Another easy mistake to make in counseling with the gifted is to be misled by the general halo effect of good grades, sound attitude and other positive aspects. It is important to remember that these youngsters are preparing for top-level competition against far more difficult college and graduate standards than they are ever likely to meet in high school. The counselor who does not provide the gifted student with some prognosis of the problems which he may face in the future is doing him no service. Another special difficulty often encountered with the able is that of keeping grades and morale up until the gifted and sometimes temperamental youth can get away to college. With some of these talented underachievers, it is almost a race to see if they can make college before their environmental frustrations sidetrack them completely. Sometimes, the form book of grades and deportment needs to be thrown away and a college encouraged to take a chance on the wild talents of some fiery nonconformist.

While guidance should be a continuous process throughout school, there are some critical junction points where lack of guidance may shunt the gifted onto the wrong track. Especially at the ninth and twelfth grades, the efforts (or lack of them) of the guidance worker to locate all the able youths, despite poor grades and lower socioeconomic status, is crucial. In the ninth grade all these youngsters should be strongly encouraged to take an academic college preparatory program, and at the twelfth grade all of them should be encouraged to go on to college.

The importance of guidance generally and its integration of the school system is nowhere better illustrated than by Conant in *The American High School Today,* a volume destined to become an educational bible. It is significant that nearly half his recommendations concern guidance matters directly, and over a quarter pertain to the progress of the academically talented.

Counselor and Faculty

While the counselor for the able has the major responsibility for their guidance, he cannot be expected to function alone. He needs co-operation from the principal, staff members, and teachers. On the part of the teachers, this co-operation includes, besides consultation with counselors, the ability, skill, and presence of mind to make referrals promptly when able students are not performing properly. On the part of other staff members, such co-operation includes communication, so that the co-ordination of the special program may blend harmoniously with that of general education. Co-operation with curriculum personnel is especially important. The principal can help by understanding and supporting the guidance role and by not confusing this function with that of errand boy, disciplinary assistant, stool pigeon, or substitute teacher. The proper relationship between administrator and personnel worker is somewhat like that between the commander of a military unit and its chaplain. The counselor should have "noncombatant" status. Other needs which the administrator can help supply include office space with privacy for interviewing, a budget and work load which are realistic, tests and supplies, an information library, and the appreciation that pupil personnel work embraces something more than programing.

It goes without saying that every guidance program should have the funds and staff to conduct a continuous follow-up of its able students. In the first place, no other group can acquaint the administration so well with the benefits and weaknesses of the program. Second, the community deserves and needs to have an accounting of how well its able graduates are doing in college. Proper publicity on this score will do much to ensure that public support for guidance will be forthcoming. Finally, no other group is so likely in later years to bring credit to the school and the community, and these youngsters should not be lost.

The feed-back process from able students constitutes probably the most important and intelligent evaluation a school can make of its services. The administrator who is able to employ this procedure will find that the feedback from these youngsters even while in school will be helpful. The administrator who makes it a policy to find out "how guidance feels" about a school problem can save himself many headaches and gain a reputation for ideas which are likely to make his administration highly successful.

Proper guidance for the able is not a luxury but a necessity of American cultural life. The organization of adequate programs of guidance for the academically talented awaits only the demands of the districts and the efforts of educational personnel. It is time for us all to come to a realistic appraisal of the importance of guidance programs for all youth in the procedures of general education and in the specific problems of the able. In no other way shall we meet the problem of achievement and productivity which appears to be in the process of becoming the central educational issue of the mid-twentieth century.

14. Understanding Creativity in Talented Students *

E. PAUL TORRANCE, *Director, Bureau of Educational Research, University of Minnesota*

Counseling Problems of Highly Creative Individuals

ISOLATION AND ESTRANGEMENT FROM PEERS AND TEACHERS

ON THE BASIS of information developed through our research with children in the early school years and by Getzels and Jackson in the high school years, I would suspect that a large share of the highly creative individual's personal problems are likely to be centered in his psychological isolation and estrangement from his peers and teachers. It will be no news to counselors that peer groups exercise rather severe sanctions against their most creative members. In no group thus far studied has the author failed to find relatively clear evidence of the operation of these pressures. Both sociometric studies and small-group experiments have thus far been used. Both types of study have yielded many clues for helping youngsters avoid some of the severity of peer sanctions without sacrificing their creativity. Since the results of the experimental study are simpler and more straightforward, only this study will be described.

In this study (Torrance, 1959a), we formed groups of five children, and in each we placed one of the most creative children in the class, as identified by tests administered earlier. We then placed each group in a situation requiring creative thinking and involving competition among groups. This situation permitted the group to experiment for 25 minutes trying to discover all the things which could be done with a box of science toys and the principles whereby they worked. After a period of 5 minutes for planning demonstrations and explanations, each group was given 25 minutes in which to present their demonstrations and explanations. The focus of observation was upon the techniques used by the groups to control the most creative member and the strategies of the most creative member in coping with these pressures. Much of the behavior observed suggests that in many cases the highly creative individual may be responsible for his own woes.

At the second-grade level, the most highly creative individuals were gen-

* Excerpt from paper prepared for Summer Guidance Institute Lecture, July, 1959.

erally quite unpleasant, showing little consideration for the group, little or no goal orientation, little or no identification with the group, and little or no heed to the leadership attempts of their less creative peers. In the third grade, the most creative subjects tended to work independently and were ignored for the most part. This tendency persisted into the fourth grade, where the most creative members assumed little responsibility for leadership and were given little credit in the final ratings for the important contributions which they actually made to the group's success. The highly creative subjects in the fifth grade manifested more leadership attempts and were more dominant than in the fourth grade but brought upon themselves open criticism and attack for "being too scientific," "being too greedy," and the like. These tendencies became more pronounced in the sixth-grade groups.

An examination of almost any of the many lists of personality characteristics of highly creative individuals suggests a number of quite valid reasons why such individuals alienate their peers and elders. In our studies it has certainly become quite obvious that many of the highly creative individuals are disturbing elements in classroom groups in elementary schools. The problem of teachers and guidance workers resolves itself into one of helping highly creative individuals maintain those characteristics which seem essential to the development of creative talent and at the same time helping them acquire skills for avoiding or reducing to a tolerable level the peer sanctions.

Stein (1956) has offered a set of interesting suggestions concerning the social role of the creative industrial researcher. If we translate Stein's principles to teachers and guidance workers, the objective in helping highly creative youngsters would run something like the following: Help the highly creative child to maintain his assertiveness without being hostile and aggressive. He must be aware of his superiors, peers, and subordinates as persons. He may work alone, but he must not be isolated, withdrawn, or uncommunicative. He must "know his place" without being timid, submissive, or acquiescent and must "speak his mind" without being domineering. As he tries to gain a point, he can be subtle but not cunning or manipulative. In all relationships, he must be sincere, honest, purposeful, and diplomatic but not unwilling to accept "short cuts." In the intellectual area, he must learn to be broad without spreading himself too thin, deep without being "bookish" or "too scientific," and "sharp" without being overcritical.

The model above obviously asks much of the child, but at least it provides a model which the highly creative child apparently needs to achieve, and it should challenge the imaginative counselor.

"UNREALISTIC" CAREER CHOICES

The career aspirations of highly creative students are sure to puzzle the counselor and to seem unrealistic. Getzels and Jackson's data throw some light upon this problem. When their highly intelligent and highly creative subjects were asked (Getzels and Jackson, 1959), on sentence-completion type questionnaires, to state the kinds of occupations they would like to have, the Creatives gave a significantly greater variety of occupations than did the highly intelligent group. When the occupations reported were divided into conventional and unconventional categories (e.g., doctor, engineer, businessman, etc., were classified as conventional; inventor, artist, spaceman, disk jockey, as unconventional), 18 per cent of the highly intelligent group gave unconventional career aspirations; 67 per cent of the high Creatives gave such aspirations.

I would also like to mention another problem regarding career choice, which has been discussed in detail by Anne Roe (1959). This problem concerns the highly creative and talented individual from the lower socioeconomic class. Even in the grade school, such an individual is likely to suffer as a consequence of the differences in the value structure of the home and those built into the educational career required for a full-fledged career as a creative scientist. Roe particularly emphasizes some of the hazards inherent in current national testing programs and efforts to urge talented youngsters to go to college and to prepare for careers in science. Counselors should be aware of the conflicts such youngsters are likely to experience. Both the lower and higher socioeconomic classes tend to devaluate scientific careers. She maintains that many scholarship students are likely to drop out in college because they do not become members of any in-group in college. She suggests that personnel workers give consideration to establishing the kinds of in-groups in which such individuals can obtain support.

Another career choice problem quite likely to exist among highly creative individuals concerns the choice made because it provides a technique for handling a particular personal problem. Their curiosity and their searching is for a solution to a personality problem. Roe (1959) maintains that in such cases all may go well as long as the individual is still climbing in his career and still has hopes of solving his problem. When the apex is reached, however, he may experience depression and become unproductive. Individuals so motivated in their career choices may be blocked in finding the solution to problems; they "just can't see the answer." Some such individuals are noted for their compulsive repetitions of experiments and inability to complete a task. Counselors could probably assist here by helping them to understand the nature of their creative processes and to seek psychotherapy. Successful psychotherapy is more likely to unlock greater powers of creativity than to destroy creative genius.

VALUES AND ATTITUDES

The counselor should also recognize that the values and attitudes of the highly creative student are likely to be different from those of other students. The very fact that he is capable of divergent thinking, has unusual ideas, and is independent in his thinking in itself is likely to make his values and attitudes different from the norms of his group. Some of these differences are highlighted in the Getzels and Jackson (1959) study. They found that for the high IQ group, the rank-order correlation between the qualities they would like for themselves and the qualities making for adult success was .81; for the high Creativity group it was .10. Among the highly intelligent, the correlation between the qualities they desire and the qualities they believe teachers favor was .67; for the highly creative group, it was minus .25. In other words, the highly creative student desires personal qualities having little relationship to those which he believes make for adult success and which are in some ways the opposite of those he believes his teachers favor. Thus, counselors should recognize that the desire to emulate the teacher is absent or weak among creative students.

Getzels and Jackson (1959) also found a certain mocking attitude on the part of the Creatives toward what they call the "All-American Boy"—a theme almost totally lacking in the stories of the highly intelligent group. Again, this highlights the counselor's problem in helping the highly creative student to learn to be independent without being obnoxious.

Helping Teachers Understand the Creative Student

In closing, I would like to discuss briefly the problem of the counselor in helping teachers understand the highly creative student. In attempting to do this, the counselor should recognize that highly creative students think up many things which are difficult for teachers to cope with. Many of the most highly creative subjects in our studies in the early school years are almost famous for their skill in thinking up ideas for being naughty as well as for their wild or silly ideas. Few teachers are likely to respond as did one of the third-grade teachers in our study, who commented to me: "Even if you do not learn anything from the data you have collected, the study has changed the school and the way we teachers look at our students. For example, we no longer look upon them as being naughty but as creating ideas for being naughty." This difference at first glance might seem too subtle, but I think it is an important one.

As I have discussed the matter at length in another paper (1959c), I shall only list what I think the counselor can do to help the teacher to understand the highly creative student and help him develop his creative thinking to its fullest degree. I believe that the counselor can help the teacher to:

1. Learn to value creative thinking and to forge an environment which places value on creative activity so that the highly creative student will not have to exist as a miserable deviate in the shadow of his more socially successful peers.

2. Find ways of assisting children to be more sensitive to environmental stimuli and to trust their own perception of reality.

3. Permit and encourage manipulation of objects and ideas.

4. Lead students to test systematically each new idea.

5. Develop tolerance of new ideas.

6. Beware of forcing a set pattern.

7. Develop a creative classroom atmosphere.

8. Teach the child to value his own creative thinking.

9. Teach skills for avoiding peer sanctions.

10. Understand the creative process and share this understanding with pupils.

11. Dispel the sense of awe of masterpieces.

12. Encourage and evaluate self-initiated learning.

13. Create "thorns in the flesh," to be sensitive to defects, to recognize the disturbing element.

14. Create necessities for creative thinking.

15. Provide for both active and quiet times for the production of ideas.

16. Make available resources for working out ideas.

17. Encourage the habit of working out the full implication of ideas.

18. Develop constructive criticism—not just criticism.

19. Encourage acquisition of knowledge in a variety of fields.

20. Become more adventurous-spirited.

Summary

In summary, I would maintain that counselors and guidance workers should be concerned about understanding creativity in talented students. Such an understanding is important from the standpoint of personality development and mental health, the acquisition of knowledge and understanding, vocational success, and social welfare. A variety of materials are being developed and tested for identifying creative thinking at all educational levels and for guiding its fuller development. New directions have been toward the development of procedures for identifying creative talent at an early age and for understanding its development during the important early school years. The direction has been toward materials which can be manipulated and which yield such measures as Inventivlevel, Spontaneous Flexibility, and Constructiveness; materials which permit exploration through "asking" and "guessing" (formulating hypotheses) concerning the causes and consequences of behavior; and the like.

Both measures of IQ and measures of creativity appear to be essential in identifying giftedness. In spite of large differences in mean IQ (23 to 26 IQ points), elementary and secondary school pupils high on creativity but not high on IQ achieve as well as those high on IQ but not on creativity, as measured by standardized achievement tests. Children high on measures of creativity appear to become alienated from peers and teachers and manifest behaviors which elicit pressures from their peers.

Counselors need to understand the special blockages to the development of creative thinking. Among those which appear most prominent and obvious are the following: premature attempts on the part of parents and teachers to eliminate fantasy, restrictions on manipulativeness and curiosity, overemphasis on prevention, overemphasis on sex roles, fear and timidity, emphasis in education on verbal skills, and limitations of resources for working out ideas.

Major counseling problems presented by the highly creative student are likely to center around his isolation and estrangement from his peers and teachers, what appear to be "unrealistic" career choices, divergent values and attitudes, and the like. Counselors can possibly do much by working with teachers to help them understand the creativity in talented students and to use procedures which will implement the greater development of creative thinking in all students.

Suggested Reading

Broedel, J., and others. "The Effects of Group Counseling on Gifted Adolescent Underachievers," *Journal of Counseling Psychology,* 7:163–170; Fall, 1960. Group counseling improved mental health of underachiever to the extent it was felt that other school help would be of value. Factors found related to underachievement were hostility, rebellious attitudes, conflicts in values, frustrated emotional needs, intense personal problems, remoteness of goals.

Buhler, E. O., and Guirl, E. N. "The More Able Student Described and Rated," *Vocational Guidance Quarterly,* 8:217–219; Summer, 1960. A thirteen-item check list described.

Forrest, Aubrey. "Counseling Talented Students on College Choice," *Personnel and Guidance Journal,* 40:42–47; September, 1961. Practical tips for the college counselor include suggestions that (1) college size, sex, cost, religion, location, curriculum, and prestige are important, (2) change and growth of interests and maturity of the brightest students while in college should be expected, and (3) there is no best college for all talented students; each placement must be individual.

French, J. L. "Interests of the Gifted," *Vocational Guidance Quarterly,* 7:14–15; Autumn, 1958. Top 25 per cent on ACE (98 males and 183 females) of teachers college freshmen showed more Kuder elevations (over 75th percentile) than random group.

Gowan, J. C. *An Annotated Bibliography on the Academically Talented Student.* Washington: National Education Association, Project on the Academically Talented Student, 1961. Cross-indexed, annotated bibliography of 800 references on gifted children, about fifty of them on guidance. (*Note:* The compiler is now engaged in a Cooperative Research Grant updating this effort. The new bibliography should be available by the summer of 1965. Write J. C. Gowan, Education, State College, Northridge, California, 91326.)

Gowan, J. C., and Demos, G. D. *The Education and Guidance of the Ablest.* Springfield, Ill.: Charles C Thomas, 1964. Handbook of 500 pages and 2,000 references on the gifted contains extensive material on guidance. Chapters include lengthy ones on guidance, identification, achievement, scholarships, college and vocational guidance, administration, research, evaluation, the teacher of the gifted, and a dozen others including creativity. Topics in the guidance chapter include: administration of guidance, general functions of the guidance program, counseling with the gifted child, counseling with the parents of the gifted, and emotionally maladjusted gifted children.

Harrison, Edna. "The Counselor's Role in the Early Identification of Gifted Children," *Personnel and Guidance Journal,* 39:735–737; May, 1961. General hortatory article on characteristics, identification, objectives, and responsibilities for parental counseling.

——. "The Elementary School Counselor and the Gifted Underachiever," *Personnel and Guidance Journal,* 41:716–719; April, 1963. A general discussion of counselor's responsibilities with child, parents, and teachers. In counselor's work with teachers it points out need to (1) gain rapport, (2) accept teachers needs for elevating children of lesser ability to top, (3) tactfully point out differences between giftedness and high average achievement, (4) place before teachers articles as needed, and (5) help solve problems encountered with children of high capacity.

Hayes, D. G., and Rothney, J. W. M. "Educational Decision-Making by Superior Secondary School Students and Their Parents," *Personnel and Guidance Jour-*

nal, 38:26–30; September, 1960. Ninth-grade superior students prefer to make their own decisions on educational matters, but their fathers prefer to make these choices themselves. Conferences between teachers, counselors, parents, and pupils appear necessary.

Hoedt, K. H., and Rothney, J. W. M. "Guidance for Superior Student," *Vocational Guidance Quarterly,* 11:199–201; Spring, 1963. Indicates need for more guidance.

Katz, Evelyn; Ohlsen, M.; and Proff, F. C. *An Analysis of the Interpersonal Behavior of Adolescents in Group Counseling.* Urbana: University of Illinois, 1959. (Mimeo.) A study of the interpersonal behavior of eight gifted underachievers involving "approach, withdrawal and attack" in sixteen counseling sessions.

Klausmeier, H. J. "Effects of Accelerating Bright Older Elementary Pupils: A Follow Up," *Journal of Educational Psychology,* 54:165–171; 1963. A follow-up study was completed toward the end of the fifth grade to determine the effects of accelerating bright older pupils from second to fourth grade after a five-week summer session. The Ss were one group of ten boys and ten girls, above the median CA of second-graders prior to being accelerated; two groups of twenty nonaccelerated fifth-graders of superior abilities, one above and one below the median CA of nonaccelerated fifth-graders; and two groups of twenty nonaccelerated fifth-graders of average abilities, one above and one below the median CA of nonaccelerated fifth-graders. No unfavorable academic, social, emotional, or physical correlates of acceleration were found. A comparison of these results with other research on acceleration without skipping of content suggests that pupils of superior abilities should complete the baccalaureate degree no older than age twenty-one.

Koeppe, R. P., and Rothney, J. W. M. "Evaluation of First Steps in the Counseling of Superior Students," *Personnel and Guidance Journal,* 42:35–38; September, 1963. A one-day guidance clinic had no effect on students' self-concept as adequate students.

Laycock, S. "Counseling Parents of Gifted Children," *Exceptional Children,* 23:108–110, 134; December, 1956. Makes the point that parents of gifted children often need counseling. Parents need to know the uneven development these children show in social, emotional, and intellectual growth. A high degree of parental acceptance, understanding, and guidance is necessary to guarantee full development of these children.

Leichman, N. S. "Counseling the Parents of Gifted Children," *California Guidance Newsletter,* 11:9–10; May, 1957. An analysis of recorded interviews with parents of fifty gifted children. Suggestions are given, as a result, to counselors who meet parents of gifted children. Problems of the children, as well as parental attitudes, discussed.

Orr, D. B. "Project Talent: A National Inventory of Aptitudes and Abilities," *Phi Delta Kappan,* 13:237–243; March, 1961. Explanation of the longitudinal project of J. C. Flanagan.

Passow, A. H. "Identifying and Counseling the Gifted College Student," *Journal of Higher Education*, 28:21–30; January, 1957. Thoughtful article by person experienced with gifted students will be helpful to college and high school counselors of the gifted. Attention suggested to following areas: financial and educational planning before college, sharpening vocational goals, orientation to the rigors of academic life, development of systematic work habits, development of scholastic excellence, modification of college programs for gifted, possibility of underachievement, emotional and social insecurities, need to explore unusual range of vocational possibilities, stimulation of extracurricular activities, special attention to the special needs of gifted women students, encouragement of teaching as a career.

Rothney, J. W. M., and Koopman, N. "Guidance of the Gifted," in N. B. Henry (ed.), *Education for the Gifted*. Fifty-Seventh Yearbook, Part II, National Society for the Study of Education. Chicago: The University of Chicago Press, 1958, pp. 347–361. (Cf. *School and Society*, 85:340; November 9, 1957.) A good statement on some problems in guidance of the gifted.

Smith, L. M., and Wientge, K. M. "Some Observations on the Vocational Interests of Gifted Adolescents in an Intensive Academic Experience," *Personnel and Guidance Journal*, 42:15–19; September, 1963. Expressed interest and inventoried interest (SVIB) was not generally significant for sixty male seniors and juniors in a summer school program of vocational exploration. Little change evident. Implications of this definitive article are that gifted students need careful vocational guidance.

A LOT OF WORK has been done on underachievement, and we are apparently not much closer to a solution. One of the reasons is that we have never bothered to define the issue with enough clarity. (In this connection the definition of "underachievement" in the first article should be noted.) There is certainly considerable difference between underachievement defined as the discrepancy between an IQ and an achievement test and that defined as the discrepancy between an IQ test and school marks. It is also important to note that the component of intelligence measured by a traditional IQ test excludes the more exotic factors often subsumed under the rubric of "creativity." Since creativity is important, even in convergent-conformity type achievement, underachievement markwise may simply indicate lack of creativity in conventionally bright students. One might go farther and suggest that this differential attrition or loss in creativity, as opposed to cognitive-memory factors, is due to the effects of authoritarian personality factors and similar cultural pressures.

The first three articles have been placed here for historical reference, as they give a fairly good introduction to the subject. Lodato and Sokaloff then follow with an essay on group counseling. Patterson's masterly statement on the counseling problems with underachievers details some of the difficulties counselors face in attempting to change self-concept in this area. The chapter closes with a theoretical formulation by Roth and Meyersburg, a summary of a survey by Stern, and a review of the state of the art by Taylor.

15. The Underachieving Gifted Child— A Problem for Everyone *

JOHN CURTIS GOWAN

O NE OF THE GREATEST social wastes in our culture is that presented by the gifted child or young person who either cannot or will not work up to his ability. Moreover, this situation often leads to undesirable social or personal behavior as an outward indication of the power within which is seeking some outlet. Counseling and rehabilitating these young people present challenging and important problems for teachers and personnel workers.

Definitions and Population

The present study uses "gifted child" to mean a youngster two or more standard deviations from the mean in general intelligence, within approximately the top 2 per cent of the population, equivalent to an intelligence quotient above 129 on the Stanford Binet. Recognizing that practically all gifted children are underachievers to some extent, we define "underachievement" in general as performance which places the individual 30 percentiles or more below his ability standing in the same group. Applying this concept to gifted children, we shall call them "underachievers" when they fall in the middle third in scholastic rank and "severe underachievers" when they fall in the lowest third.

Some of the best work in surveying the problems of gifted underachievers has been done by teachers, counselors, supervisors, and principals in the field. All of the research referred to in this article presents unpublished projects undertaken by experienced school personnel in the writer's classes.

First, let us see what percentage of gifted children are underachievers as represented by the previous definitions. Alter found that in a high socioeconomic area, one suburban high school enrolling 1,162 students had 74, or 7 per cent, of students with intelligence quotients of 130 or more on the California Test of Mental Maturity. Among the 45 of these who were in senior high school, 19, or 42 per cent, were underachievers and 3, or 6 per cent, were severe underachievers. In similar research in an independent

* Reprinted by permission of the author and *Exceptional Children,* 21:247–249, 270; April, 1955.

boarding school enrolling 485 boys of whom 57, or 12 per cent, showed 130 IQ or above on the Terman-McNemar, the writer found that only 5 of the 57, or 9 per cent, were underachievers and none were severe underachievers. This lower number of underachievers probably reflects greater 24-hour control as well as differential attrition factors. Wilbar discovered that in a representative suburban high school, 31, or 9 per cent, of the students had intelligence quotients of over 130 on the California Test of Mental Maturity, and of these 5, or 16 per cent, were underachievers and 1, or 3 per cent, was a severe underachiever.

It seems evident that while the percentage of underachievers and severe underachievers is a function of the program of the school, its location, the control it has over its students, and student interests, there are in all cases significant numbers of underachievers among the highly gifted. These students merit special attention.

Studies of Underachievers

Robert found that of 587 cases of maladjusted youngsters handled by a clinic in a large metropolitan area, 38, or 6.5 per cent, had intelligence quotients of 130 or above on the Stanford Binet, almost evenly divided between boys and girls. The majority of these children liked school, and their problems centered around the home situation. Those who were school problems stated their reasons as follows:

Not interested.
Didn't like the teacher.
Work was too easy.
Didn't have any friends and couldn't make any.
Liked to stay home with mother.

Only one child was proud of her school record, and only one had been accelerated. All indicated that they could do better work if they tried.

The major disturbances characteristic of the group (some children, of course, had more than one) were noted in clinic records as follows.

27 felt insecure.
17 had poor social adjustment.
15 had enuresis.
14 were intolerant of parental authority.
13 were fearful.
7 were jealous.
9 had no identification with parents.
6 were poor sleepers.

5 were nail biters.

5 were poor eaters.

9 had miscellaneous behavior disturbances.

The basic causes for the children's behavior as diagnosed by the clinic staff were:

1. Disagreement between the parents, and of the parents with their parents, over methods of rearing the child.

2. Transference of problems of parents to the child.

3. Overanxiety or overprotectiveness on the part of parent.

4. Fears of parents regarding child's health or safety.

5. Divorces or separations of parents.

6. Parents' failure to prepare child for the birth of a new baby.

Landstrom and Natvig conducted a provocative survey of four groups of 25 students each in a metropolitan senior high school. All were scored on the California Test of Mental Maturity. Group I consisted of gifted students who were high achievers having IQ's ranging from 125 to 150 with a median of 131. Group II consisted of gifted students who were underachievers ranging similarly from 125 to 150 in IQ with a median of 130. Group III consisted of overachieving students who were not gifted, whose school marks matched those for Group I but whose IQ's ranged from 86 to 112 with a median at 103. General biographical data including material concerning home relationships were then secured from each individual.

Table I indicates that the gifted achievers and underachievers in this study differed significantly (at the 5 per cent level of confidence or better) in that the underachievers were predominantly boys, had parents who took little part in church activities, had fewer books in their homes, had less often received private lessons, and expressed a desire in choosing a vocation for working away from the parental family. In general, the pattern that emerges is one of indifference and rejection on the part of the parent, or at least of behavior which is significantly more often interpreted in this manner by the underachiever. In addition, it is interesting to note that while the underachiever does less studying, he also has less time for other activities. Clearly, one of his problems is the use of time. He seems to lack ability to handle himself well in social interaction and to make easy adjustments to the societal structure.

In an earlier study the writer found that when a secondary school population of 485 boys was analyzed for underachievement and overachievement as previously defined, 16 per cent of the *total* group were

TABLE I—HOME BACKGROUND AND EXTRACURRICULAR ACTIVITIES OF HIGH SCHOOL
STUDENTS BY CATEGORIES OF ABILITY AND ACHIEVEMENT

	I Gifted Achievers	II Gifted Nonachievers	III Over- achievers	IV Average Controls
Number in group	25	25	25	25
Scholarship grades	A	C	A	C
Median IQ	131	130	107	103
Number of boys	12	19*	3**	6
Number of parents deceased	1	3	5	0
Father in professions	11	8	5	5
Mother a housewife	12	13	17	20
Parents divorced	2	3	4	6
Family attends church	14	6*	15	10
Foreign language in home	11	12	6	8
Favorite subject, Mathematics	13	7*	1**	0
High school major is Mathematics	16	15	4**	1
Skipped grades	15	10	4	4
Hours per week homework	8.4†	5.5	11.0	6.9
Number with time for other work	21	11*	16	14
Private lessons, training	20	12*	16	14
Total number of awards	50†	20	42	20
Activities or offices	134†	65	145	50
Number with 100 books or more	15	6*	6	7
Part-time job	13	7	9	15
Vocational choice, profession	25	21	13**	5
Preference for working with people	20	16	18	21
Preference for working near family	19	10*	11	11

The minimal difference between columns to make the activity discriminate at the
5 per cent level is seven.

† Means the response is in units as given, but the significance of the difference was
not computed.

* Indicates a difference between columns I and II significant at the 5 per cent
level.

** Indicates a difference between both columns I and II and column III at the
5 per cent level.

underachievers and 11 per cent were overachievers. The overachievers asserted much more leadership than did the underachievers. The underachievers were significantly less sociable, as measured by the sociability scale of the Bernreuter. The conclusion was that the genesis of underachievement lay in self-sufficiency and that, in general, underachievement in academic work and underachievement in leadership tended to appear together and to be connected with high unsociability ratings.

Research Findings

Summing up the experience of these and other researchers, it may be said that counseling gifted underachievers offers a number of problems.

1. The gifted underachiever tends to be *self-sufficient* and unsociable. He is, therefore, harder to reach and harder to interest in social activities. He learns less from exposure to the normal socializing effects of his peers because he has less contact with them.

2. The gifted underachiever has identified less with his parents, who themselves seem to be less active than parents of overachievers and less supporting of him and of his increased needs.

3. Because the gifted underachiever is less sociable, and because most teachers are overachievers, he tends to find fewer surrogate parental models among his teachers. This added lack of identification with an adult model makes his behavior still more difficult to influence.

4. The gifted underachiever seems to have fewer salable skills, either to offer for part-time jobs, to bolster his economic situation, or to gain eligibility for college scholarship.

Employment is limited because he participates less and hence is less well adjusted; college is lost because of his poor scholastic showing. As a result, it is harder for him to become independent of an unsatisfactory family situation, harder for him to gain a sense of worth and participation through his job, and harder for him to keep going in college. The combination tends to push him out of school into an economic market where he has only marginal skills and into situations where he derives little if any job satisfaction.

Suggestions for Counselors

The following suggestions are offered for working with gifted underachievers.

1. Make a survey of the percentage of underachievers in your school. If it runs much higher than 15 per cent, there may be problems of morale, antisocial trends, or other factors in the school which should receive special attention.

2. Since gifted underachievers are usually boys by a ratio of two to one, make an effort to assign counselors who are most capable of reaching them; a male counselor may often be more effective than a woman with such boys.

3. Give attention to building up the gifted underachiever in the area where he has a real chance of outstanding success, whether this is athletics,

music, a hobby, or an academic course. The real and enduring interest of some strong adult model figure with whom the young person can easily relate should be secured.

4. Give attention to the anxieties which plague boys at this period. These stresses may include economic dependence on a hostile home figure, ignorance about sex, worry about the draft, concern with how a mediocre record can be brought up to college standards, anxiety over the rejecting attitudes of a fussy stick-to-the-rules type of teacher, and many others. If the manifold social roles which the adolescent male is called upon to play in our culture can be gradually and easily assumed, much anxiety and frustration can be prevented. Above all, the boy should sense that the counselor *has time to be for him*. He should be encouraged to go on with college plans.

5. Try to find membership roles for the gifted underachiever in clubs, activities, and student leadership. He should be engaged as much as possible in responsibilities commensurate with his social ability.

6. Because this type of young person feels insecure and is likely to lack a real peer group, attempt group therapy with a number of gifted underachievers if at all feasible. This may at least lead to confidences and possibly friendships among these people and ultimately to improved social adjustment. It may also help to establish stronger attitudes of personal worth.

16. *Dynamics of the Underachievement of Gifted Students* *

JOHN CURTIS GOWAN

IN RECENT YEARS, as manpower reserves of talent for scientific and professional occupations have become depleted, more and more attention is being directed to the salvaging of a significant portion of our ablest youths who qualify for the title of gifted underachievers. We are not concerned in this discussion with the economic and social factors which Stice has

* Reprinted by permission of the author and *Exceptional Children*, 24:98–100; November, 1957.

demonstrated as preventing over half of the high-ability high school seniors in our country from going on directly to college. We are rather concerned with the equally depressing fact, demonstrated by Wedemeyer, that of those who go, almost 30 per cent of the top decile of intelligence fail to attain significant achievement in scholarship because of emotional, educational, personal, financial, or other problems. Faced with the present economic and political rivalry with Russia, a nation turning out scientists at twice our rate, our country cannot afford this waste of its most vital resource—talent.

It is the purpose of this paper, therefore, to explore recent research on the causes and prevention of underachievement in gifted students. Moreover, a developmental hypothesis is proposed to account for agreements in research findings, and practical implications for education which seem warranted by these results are appended. By "gifted student" we shall refer to a student two or more standard deviations upward from the mean in general intelligence: loosely, an IQ of 130 or above. Recognizing that practically all gifted children are technically underachievers to some extent, we may define "underachievement" for our purposes as performance which places the student more than a full standard deviation below his ability standing in the same group. Roughly, this works out to about 30 percentiles' difference, so that we may call gifted children "underachievers" when they fall in the middle third in scholastic achievement in grades and "severe underachievers" when they fall in the lowest third. It should be noted that these definitions are made merely for clarity and convenience and are by no means uniformly used by all those whose research is later to be reported.

It may be of value first to note data concerning the number and percentage of underachievers in secondary schools represented by the previous definitions. Figures have been presented elsewhere to show that in one California high school where 7 per cent of the students were gifted, 42 per cent of these were underachievers. In another high school where 2 per cent of the students were gifted, 16 per cent of these were underachievers. In an outstanding independent secondary school, 12 per cent of the students were gifted, and 9 per cent of these were underachievers. In the same paper, it was suggested that where the per cent of underachievers "runs much higher than 15 per cent, there may be problems of morale, antisocial trends, or other factors in the school which should receive special attention."

There is considerable research evidence to indicate that achievement both in high school and later stems from habits, interests, attitudes, and motivation established in elementary school. With gifted children, these latter factors seem to be facilitated by special curriculum adjustments.

Terman, for example, reported that gifted youth who were accelerated in school outstripped those who had not been accelerated, both in college and in success in later life. He concluded that "the exceptionally bright student kept with his age group finds little to challenge his intelligence, and all too often develops habits of laziness that later wreck his college career." The Los Angeles School District in 1931 reported a high school comparison between 284 opportunity A students and 381 equally gifted controls; the opportunity A group, which had been segregated in the fifth to seventh grades, had higher high school grade averages, earned more honor grades, and had fewer failures. Cohler found in a similar study that the effect of acceleration was improved performance and stressed the need for vital school experiences to motivate the child. Sanford, after a discussion of the bright child who fails, considered boredom, lack of motivation, and home problems as major causes of underachievement. Engle, in another study of accelerants, found acceleration generally conducive to more favorable educational and vocational results than nonacceleration. The same results in even more specific terms were reported recently for the Ford scholarship holders. It seems evident from the weight of the foregoing reports either that special curriculum methods for the gifted have some value in themselves in reducing underachievement or that the increased attention, interest, recognition, and personal contact which accompany them result in increased motivation and consequent increased achievement.

A number of investigators have reported on college level achievement and underachievement of gifted students. Nason found achievement at this level more related to clearness and definiteness of academic and vocational plans and to parental influences than to personal adjustment. Burgess, in a study of engineering underachievers, described them in these terms: "less intellectually adaptive . . . less emotional control . . . more dependent in attitudes toward others . . . motivation weak . . . tend not to enjoy the school situation . . . unable to see the value of an education." Dowd, in a college study of underachievers in the top decile, found no personality difference, but more incidence of males, and concluded that the factors are operative before college entrance. Morgan in a similar study concluded generally that college achievement of high-ability students is "related to (1) maturity and seriousness of interests,

(2) awareness and concern for others, (3) a sense of responsibility, (4) dominance, persuasiveness, and self-confidence, and (5) motivation to achieve." Similar results were secured by Pearlman.

Studies on younger gifted underachievers have tended to emphasize home backgrounds, parental problems, and emotional immaturity. A study by Bonsall and Stellfre emphasized the importance of not overlooking the socioeconomic factor. Basic causes for the behavior of thirty-eight gifted children referred to a metropolitan clinic as maladjusted and reported elsewhere included disagreements between parents over methods of raising the child, transference of problems of parents to the child, over-anxiety or overprotectiveness on the part of the parent, fears of the parents regarding the children's health and safety, divorces and separations, and sibling rivalry. The school problems of these gifted children were seen in such symptoms as "not interested in school, didn't like teacher, work was too easy, didn't have any friends, liked to stay home with mother." Another inquiry into the family backgrounds of high school underachievers of IQ 130 or better found that they differed significantly from gifted achievers in that the underachievers were predominantly boys, had parents who took little part in community activities, had fewer books in their homes, had less often received private lessons, and expressed a desire in choosing a vocation to get away from the family. The pattern which emerged was one of indifference and rejection on the part of the parent, or behavior so interpreted by the underachiever. In addition, he had less time for outside activities, had more problems with time and money, and seemed lacking in ability to conduct himself easily in social situations and to make easy adjustments.

A recent study meriting attention was made by Barrett in the Toronto, Ontario, high schools. He concluded: the pattern of underachievement is apparent by the fifth grade with weakness in arithmetic characteristic; and parents of underachievers tend to exhibit a neutral or uninterested attitude toward education, to be overanxious, oversolicitous, or inconsistent in their attitude toward the child. In general, such homes show evidence of conflict, authoritarianism by the parent, or domination by the child. In the school situation, the underachievers exhibit a predominantly negative attitude toward school, win less acceptance from their classmates, tend to show less interest in reading. While both show feelings of inadequacy, the achievers are aware of their difficulties and constructive in their efforts, while the underachievers withdraw and refuse to compete.

Another study deserving special attention is that of Gough. In an effort to construct and validate an achievement scale on the California Psychological Inventory, he investigated personality items among a large number of underachievers. From this group he selected paired groups of gifted achievers and underachievers, dichotomized for both high school and college as well by sex. While there were a number of personality differences, the major ones were that underachievers were significantly higher on the scale for delinquency and achievers were higher on the scales for social responsibility and academic motivation. The scale for academic motivation correlated over .50 with scales for good impression, lack of dissimulation, social responsibility, tolerance, social participation, antidelinquency, intellectual efficiency, lack of impulsivity. Gough concludes that "academic achievement among intellectually gifted persons is a form of social behavior, and academic underachievement is a form of asocial behavior." He summarized that underachievement among the gifted is akin to delinquent behavior. A consonant finding had been previously reported by Terman in comparing 150 of his most successful gifted men with 150 least successful. The A group seemed to have greater enthusiasm for living and activity. They read more books, made more collections, engaged in more hobbies, were more successful in school and popular with classmates and teachers.

The common elements from these research reports indicate that achievement in gifted students versus underachievement seems related to the following factors.

1. Clearness and definiteness of academic and occupational choices versus the opposite.

2. Strong ego controls and strength versus weak ones.

3. Socialization and social interaction versus withdrawal and self-sufficiency.

4. Good use of time and money versus lack of such habits.

5. Reading and arithmetic ability versus lack of such competency.

6. Positive character integration versus psychotic or neurotic tendency.

7. Permissiveness, intraception, and creativity versus authoritarianism in the parental home environment or the gifted individual himself.

8. Parents who motivated and took pains or interest, versus dominant, autocratic, or laissez-faire parents.

9. Some tension in task demands in childhood (the imposition by parents of goals which are clear and possible to attain) versus either no goal or impossible ones.

10. Maturity, responsibility, and seriousness of interests versus opposites.

11. Awareness of and concern for others versus lack of interest.

12. Dominance, persuasiveness, and self-confidence versus their opposites.

13. Enthusiastic, socialized, activity-oriented view of life versus apathetic withdrawal.

As such a summarization is inspected critically, it appears to be a description of healthy personal attitudes and behaviors which are associated with the accomplishment of growth patterns on schedule. These skills and attributes are connected with cognitive ego development and singularly related to various developmental stages of childhood. As each new adaption is resolved successfully, a new strength and vitality is incorporated into the ego. An excellent description of this developmental process is given by Erikson, especially in his "industry" stage which coincides with the early latency period when the child turns outward from the family to peer group recognition in which, in Erikson's words,

He can become an eager and absorbed unit in a productive situation. . . . He develops industry, that is he adjusts himself to the inorganic laws of the tool world. . . . The danger in this stage lies in a sense of inadequacy and inferiority. If he despairs of his tools and skills or of his status among his tool partners, his ego boundaries suffer, and he abandons hope for the ability to identify early with others who apply themselves.

Parents who are either too autocratic, too dominant, too protective, or too laissez-faire arrest the child's development into and through this industry stage where he learns the joy of real work and accomplishment as an aid to status getting among his peers and with outside authority figures. As a result, he is thrown back for libido rewards to the earlier and more primitive satisfactions of the oral, anal, narcissistic, and oedipal periods. Because boys are slightly less mature than girls, and because parents sometimes expect more of them, their introduction to cultural tasks demands may be more difficult, and hence more problems may accrue.

To be sure, public schooling in the primary grades does much for those children whose parents may not have been successful in aiding the child through these critical adjustments; but while doing well by the generality, it frequently misses meeting the needs of two important groups. First is the minority group member who does not identify with the alien culture of the school; and second is the gifted child whom it does not challenge during this crucial period. Such a hypothesis explains most of the observed differences between gifted achievers and underachievers and also points up the vital necessity of adequate stimulation of gifted children during the primary grades, instead of forcing them to remain bored and inactive.

In contrast to gifted underachievers, the childhood of the gifted achiever appears to involve a constant, but not severe, pressure toward tasks and responsibilities which are perceived by the child as security- or affection-producing and which are neither capriciously administered nor impossible to attain under the aegis of interest-stimulating parental guidance. Thus, early experience in realistic goal setting and achieving leads to a personality with strong superego demands and strong ego strength to complete these demands. Such a personality tends in adulthood to have a high sense of social responsibility and large performance needs. He is not without anxieties, but these are oriented toward reality and tend to be ameliorated by his or others' modification of the environment rather than by changes in his attitudes toward it.

The gifted underachiever, on the other hand, appears to be a kind of intellectual delinquent who withdraws from goals, activities, and active social participation generally. As a child, his initial attempts at creative accomplishment may not have been seen by others as "worth while" but only as "queer" or "different." The blocking of this avenue of rewarding behavior by others, tending as it does to reinforce his often overcritical appraisal of the disparity between his goals and achievements, may blunt his work libido, stifle his creativity, and consign him to a routine of withdrawal and escape as the most tolerable method of insulating his ego from hurt in an alien and uninterested world.

Thus, achievement and underachievement in the gifted may be viewed as social and asocial responses of the individual to proper stimulation regarding developmental tasks either tendered or denied by the parental and educational environments.

17. Factors of Achievement in School and College *

JOHN CURTIS GOWAN

THE CENTRAL POSITION of achievement in the education of the academically talented student has engaged increased attention recently. The related problem of the reduction of underachievement in students of high-

* Reprinted by permission of the author and *Journal of Counseling Psychology*, 7:91–95; Summer, 1960.

level ability has come in for equal interest (Barrett, 1957; Gough, 1955; Gowan, 1955; Haggard, 1958; McClelland, 1953; Suttcliffe, 1958; Westfall, 1958). The problem appears more complex than was first indicated, and contradictory and unexpected findings have muddied the waters. In an effort to formulate a comprehensive picture of the various factors contributing to underachievement or fostering achievement, it has seemed desirable to attempt to organize the findings of a half-dozen research studies into a meaningful whole. Space does not permit either a discussion of these studies or a general clarification of the semantics of the terms *achievement* and *underachievement,* though both would be desirable in an introduction to such a formulation.

The following studies are notable in stating factors of achievement or underachievement in able students: Bishton (1958), Bowman (1959), Broedel and others (1958), Gowan (1957), Heath (1959), Morgan (1952), Nason (1954), Middleton (1959), Strodtbeck (1958), Terman and Oden (1947). Some of these were actual factor analyses; others were the results of surveys of literature; some were doctoral dissertations; and a few, perhaps, armchair speculations.

If the factors isolated in the previous research studies, plus occasional others, are collected and sorted into a logical format and grouped by categories, a rather interesting psychological panorama is unfolded in which the factors are called "measures," since all appear susceptible of measurement. Three large categories are evident: measures of *input,* measures of *process,* and measures of *results.* Each measure is supported by the specific findings of some research study in the same way in which the test items of a factor analysis load on the isolated factors and so serve to define them operationally. Wherever a statement refers to the underachiever rather than to the achiever, it has been prefixed with the symbol "negative."

Measures of Input

1. *Environment and Parents*
   (*a*) Socioeconomic level of parents (Terman, 1947; Frankel, 1958).
   (*b*) Educational level of parents (Terman, 1947; Frankel, 1958).
   (*c*) Lack of family disruption through death, divorce (Goldberg, 1958).
   (*d*) Parents more active in church, community (Gowan, 1955).
2. *Consonance of Parental and Individual Values*
   (*a*) Father's value system identification (Bishton, 1958).
   (*b*) (Negative) Conflict in values (Broedel, 1958).

 (*c*) No parental disagreements on vocational plans (Nason, 1954).
 (*d*) Values and convictions out of own experiences (Heath, 1959).
 (*e*) Achiever's values like those of supportive teacher (Battle, 1957).
 (*f*) Parents who motivated or took interest (Gowan, 1957).
 (*g*) Improvers had supportive teacher (Goldberg, 1958; Bowman, 1959).

3. *Parental Involvement in Task Demands*
 (*a*) Some tension in task demands in childhood (Gowan, 1957).
 (*b*) Early independency training (McClelland, 1953).
 (*c*) Emphasis on educational and verbal expression (Bowman, 1959).

Measures of Process

4. *Cathexis of Satisfactions from Libido to Superego Areas*
 (*a*) (Negative) Need for pleasure (Middleton, 1959).
 (*b*) Postponing immediate pleasures for future gain (Strodtbeck, 1958).
 (*c*) Orientation to life as a game, not a struggle (Heath, 1959).
 (*d*) (Negative) Frustrated emotional needs (Broedel, 1958).
 (*e*) A sense of responsibility (Morgan, 1952).
 (*f*) Ego controls and strength (Gowan, 1957).
 (*g*) Achievers project selves further into future (Drews, 1957).

5. *Purpose, Motivation, Inspiration, Morale*
 (*a*) Individual inspiration to succeed (Nason, 1954).
 (*b*) Motivation to achieve generally (Morgan, 1952).
 (*c*) Perseverance, desire to excel (Terman, 1947).

6. *Self-confidence, Self-acceptance, Positive Self-concept*
 (*a*) Belief in oneself (Bishton, 1958).
 (*b*) Dominance, persuasiveness, and self-confidence (Morgan, 1952).
 (*c*) Self-objectification in interview behavior (Heath, 1959).
 (*d*) Dominance, persuasiveness, self-confidence (Gowan, 1957).
 (*e*) Optimistic self-confidence (Gough, 1949).
 (*f*) Self-confidence (Terman, 1947).
 (*g*) Reasonable risk taking—the "reasonable adventurer" (Heath, 1959).

7. *Antiauthoritarian Behavior*
 (*a*) Permissiveness, intraception, and creativity (Gowan, 1957).
 (*b*) Tolerance of ambiguity (Heath, 1959).
 (*c*) A lively and benign sense of humor (Heath, 1959).
 (*d*) Fascinated by a wide range of interests (Heath, 1959).

(*e*) Belief in the efficacy of human planning versus superstitious fatalism (Strodtbeck, 1958).

8. *Interest-Maturity*
    (*a*) Maturity and seriousness of purpose (Morgan, 1952).
    (*b*) Maturity, responsibility, and seriousness of interests (Gowan, 1957).
    (*c*) High seriousness of purpose (Gough, 1949).

9. *Early Strong Set on Industry Tasks*
    (*a*) Strong reading and arithmetic skills (Gowan, 1957).
    (*b*) Good use of time and money (Gowan, 1955).
    (*c*) Improvers mastered basic skills with help (Bowman, 1959).
    (*d*) (Negative) Have study habit problems (Westfall, 1958).
    (*e*) Academic effectiveness, accomplishment, and good study habits (Gough, 1949).
    (*f*) (Negative) Difficulties in arithmetic (Barrett, 1957).

10. *Positive Personality Integration*
    (*a*) Positive character integration (Gowan, 1957).
    (*b*) Personality adjustment (Nason, 1954).
    (*c*) (Negative) Intense personal problems (Broedel, 1958).
    (*d*) Personal efficiency, vitality, and integration (Gough, 1949).
    (*e*) Strength and force of character (Terman, 1947).

Measures of Results in Developmental Tasks

11. *Breakaway from Home*
    (*a*) Freedom from family clannishness and consequent social mobility (Strodtbeck, 1958).

12. *Peer Socialization*
    (*a*) Affinity for peer relationships (Bishton, 1958).
    (*b*) Formation and maintenance of close peer friendships (Heath, 1959).
    (*c*) Socialization and social interaction (Gowan, 1957).
    (*d*) Acceptance of others, denial of animosity, lack of interpersonal friction (Gough, 1949).
    (*e*) Leadership, popularity, sensitivity to others (Terman, 1947).

13. *Economic or Vocational Adjustment*
    (*a*) (Negative) Remoteness of goals (Broedel, 1958).
    (*b*) Parent-pupil agreement on specific occupational plan (Nason, 1954).
    (*c*) Clearness and definiteness of occupational goals (Gowan, 1957).
    (*d*) (Negative) Goals set by others or not in line with interests (Armstrong, 1955).

14. *Intellectual Adjustment: College Aspiration Level*

(*a*) Parent-pupil agreement on college level aspiration (Nason, 1954).
(*b*) Intrinsic interest in liberal arts studies (Heath, 1959).

Measures of Results in Cultural Artifacts

15. *Independence versus Hostility*
  (*a*) Behavior maturity and freedom from adult supervision (Bishton, 1958).
  (*b*) (Negative) Hostility and rebellious attitude (Broedel, 1958).
  (*c*) Need for independence and resentment (Middleton, 1959).
  (*d*) Desirability of working for oneself (Strodtbeck, 1958).
16. *Need for Status and Approval from Adults*
  (*a*) Achievement, satisfaction, need for approval and status from adults (Bishton, 1958).
  (*b*) Need for social status and influence (Middleton, 1959).
  (*c*) Need to secure approval of adults (Drews, 1957).
17. *Power and Approval*
  (*a*) Power and approval (Middleton, 1959).
  (*b*) Achievement, status, male superiority, self-preoccupation (Bishton, 1958).
18. *Cultural Aggression*
  (*a*) Hostile aggressive denial of tender socialized feelings (Middeton, 1959).
  (*b*) (Negative) Extroversion (Middleton, 1959).
  (*c*) Aggressive constrictive pattern (Heath, 1959).
19. *Cultural Conforming Social Adaptation*
  (*a*) Conforming socioeconomic adjustment (Bishton, 1958).
  (*b*) Social adjustment (Nason, 1954).
  (*c*) Strong dependence (Middleton, 1959).
  (*d*) (Negative) Disavowal of social shortcomings (Middleton, 1959).
  (*e*) Awareness and concern for others (Morgan, 1952).
  (*f*) Submissive constrictive pattern (Heath, 1959).
  (*g*) Acceptance of conventions (Gough, 1949).

While this listing of factors appears to have the form of a factor analysis, it is important to realize that it is *not* a factor analysis but a construct of several studies of which some were factor analyses. In a factor analysis the factors are usually placed in order of extraction, which is the order of decreasing variance; whereas in this listing, factors have been arranged to conform to an emerging structure.

Discussion

The three input factors all point to the importance of the parents as the premier agents of the culture. Much about these factors is obvious; much else cannot easily be changed by parents or the school. Perhaps the most important implications for the intelligent parent or educator are the importance of agreement on parental and children's value systems and the necessity for lack of conflict of values at home. Parental involvement in independency training is another important area where many improvements can be made. Last, the school's facilitation of special programs for the talented through acceleration, enrichment, and grouping can be facilitated.

The next seven factors (called Measures of Process) represent rates of development. Of these, the first, factor 4, is probably the most important. This factor appears to measure the degree to which basic libidinal satisfactions have been encumbered with the "higher" satisfactions of ego and super-ego aspects. Such areas will be concerned with future rather than present gratification; with planning, orientation to reality and objectivity; with a growing sense of duty, conscience, and responsibility; and with other ego-strength aspects, such as frustration tolerance, ability to cope with novel situations without panic, and the general inhibitory processes involved in holding emotions in check.

Adolescent developmental task factors comprise the next group of four, measuring results of process. All the tasks except sexual adjustment appear herewith, and it is not surprising that the latter would be missing.

It is the last set of five factors that really compels attention. These, called Measures of Results in Cultural Artifacts, are obviously not developmental tasks. They appear instead to be results of ways in which individual achievers may cope with the particular pressures of our culture. Not all of them need be found in the behavior pattern of any one individual achiever. They are obviously not all desirable, but for this we may be more inclined to blame the culture than the individual. If we consider the cases of some highly individualistic and "inner-oriented" personages of history, such as Socrates, Thoreau, or Gandhi, it is obvious that these great innovators did not pick up these cultural artifact factors nor value them to any extent, as a result of which they suffered considerably. More conventional and less eminent achievers seem to acquire the societal yokes as the price for the recognition and approval of contemporary society. Space does not permit a detailed analysis of these factors here, but it is clear that they give important clues to the cleavage planes in which societal stresses are felt by the individual.

Nineteen factors to account for achievement seems a lot, and the question will be asked: "Are they independent?" The author confesses surprise that there seem to be so many and can offer no reassurance that future research will not reduce the number. Factor analysis can also do the opposite. Factors 16 and 17, *Need for Status and Approval from Adults* and *Power and Approval,* seem much the same, but they were differentiated by each of two factor analyses, and the latter factor was the first one extracted in *both* analyses. It is also interesting to note that over two-thirds of the loadings of the two factor analytic studies (Bishton and Middleton) were in this area of cultural artifacts. This concentration suggests the dark possibility that future research may establish that the factors we have dubbed "cultural artifacts" are really the only genuine factors and that the rest are merely surface ways of looking at them. Should this contingency turn out to be true, it may signal the passing of an age which examined achievement and other aspects of personality from the basis of psychological differences in individual development to an age which will be mainly concerned with the societal and cultural values in which any development must take place. It suggests also that the need structure which produces achievement may not be the same as the need structure which produces creative innovation. It finally whispers that achievement, like leadership, may turn out to be far more a complex situational variable than a simple personality trait.

To summarize, achievement is an indication that the individual has successfully transferred a large enough portion of his basic libidinal drives to areas of cultural accomplishment so that he derives a significant portion of his gratifications from them. We need always to consider how an individual is to receive psychological pay for tasks accomplished. The art of education consists in making the new task palatable "until the id catches up." The success of education can be measured by the degree of this transformation as it occurs in the individual or by the percentage of the group brought to a reasonable level of achievement. The problem of underachievement, then, is a direct challenge to education in its central task of acculturation. Since cultural demands constantly force this level higher, the achievement of youth becomes a paramount issue.

18. Group Counseling for Slow Learners *

FRANCIS J. LODATO, *Bedford Public Schools,*
Mount Kisco, New York
MARTIN A. SOKOLOFF, *Bedford Public Schools,*
Mount Kisco, New York

IN RECENT YEARS the American secondary school has made special provisions for the academically talented, the seriously retarded, and the emotionally disturbed. Little has been done, however, for a relatively large group of students who do not fit into any of these categories. These are the youngsters who are limited in intelligence, though not retarded, and who are unable to adjust their behavior to the demands of a school, though they are not seriously ill.

In order to explore the suitability of group counseling as a method of helping students in this category, a pilot study was undertaken at The Fox Lane School during the 1961–1962 academic year. In general, the objectives of the group counseling project were to assist slow-learning students in adjusting to their teachers, to the curriculum, and to other students. This adjustment was to be assisted by helping these students to increase their self-understanding and by specific assistance in making realistic vocational choices. It was also considered desirable to develop an increased awareness of the realistic intellectual limitations of these students, both by their teachers and by themselves. It was thought that this latter objective might lead to the establishment of an in-service program which would assist the teachers to serve these pupils more effectively.

Method

Ten students were selected from among students in a special, nongraded class in the seventh and eighth grades of the junior high school. The students selected were characterized generally by an IQ range of 77 to 90. They also failed to meet achievement goals set for the particular classes they ordinarily would be attending. Their behavior was characterized by lack of impulse control, negativistic attitudes, hyperactivity, lethargy, stealing, and the malicious damaging of property. These characteristics manifested themselves in the classroom situation by short attendance spans, excessive dis-

* Reprinted by permission of the authors and *Journal of Counseling Psychology,*
10:95–96; September, 1963.

tractibility, daydreaming, and other escape mechanisms. Further, these students appeared to have an unrealistically low self-concept as well as extreme feelings of inadequacy. These feelings, coupled with inadequate sexual identification and feelings of hostility, made it impossible for them to adjust to their peers and to teachers.

The students were evaluated initially, during, and at the conclusion of the project both by their classroom teacher and by staff members participating in the project. Test materials included the House-Tree-Person test, Human Figure drawings, Bender-Gestalt test, and a rating scale measuring observed personality traits.

Counseling sessions were held three times a week for the first half of the school year and were increased to five times a week for the remainder of the year, after the completion of the scheduled remedial reading program. Group activities included directed and nondirected group discussions, role playing, pantomimes, athletics, field trips, parties, dancing, and record playing.

While the approach used was essentially persuasive, certain limitations were consistently imposed by the staff participants. Students were required to attend all group sessions unless excused from a particular session by the group leader. Students were prevented from exhibiting behavior which might be disruptive to other phases of the school program (excessive noise, destruction of school equipment). Physically aggressive behavior toward the group leader or any other member was prohibited.

Results

Three students, originally members of the group, left the group early in the year because of their families' moving from the community. Of the remaining group:

One student, a girl, was sufficiently adjusted to be transferred to regular class sections after half the year had elapsed. She was offered the opportunity to receive supportive counseling on an individual basis.

The six remaining students (five males and one female) were originally characterized by frequent acting-out behavior, hyperdistractibility, lack of impulse control, low self-esteem, and poor academic achievement. By the end of the school year, it was the consensus of the counseling staff, classroom teachers, and the administration that four of the six had shown marked improvement in behavior, in their attitudes toward schoolwork, and in their relationships with school personnel; one had shown no change; and one appeared to be regressing.

Discussion

That positive changes in the behavior patterns of these children had taken place was concluded by all who observed them—staff working directly with these children, teachers, and administrators. The most significant gains were in the areas of self-confidence, social confidence, and the appropriateness of expressions of nonverbal aggression. Less significant gains were made in areas such as responsiveness to educational approaches and attempts to be self-directing. It is interesting to note that the attendance of the members of the group, after the initiation of the program, was significantly better than the attendance record of the over-all school population.

The over-all language patterns of these students are limited, uncommunicative, and characterized by poor articulation. These qualities did not appear to show any improvement.

It appears to the staff that some of these children could function in an academic setting providing that there was sufficient self-respect developed to keep them functioning effectively.

19. Counseling Underachievers *

C. H. PATTERSON, *Professor of Education and Co-ordinator of Rehabilitation Counseling at the University of Illinois*

A CADEMIC FAILURE is one of the major problems confronting counselors in schools and colleges. Not all failures are a result of lack of academic ability or aptitude. Mental or intellectual ability is not the exclusive determinant of academic achievement. The discrepancy between potential and achievement identifies a group of students who are known as underachievers. Underachievement is a problem both to the individual, who may suffer

* Reprinted by permission of the author from a speech made at the 1961 APGA Convention in Denver. This paper has now been expanded into a chapter of Dr. Patterson's book, *Counseling and Guidance in Schools: A First Course* (New York: Harper and Row, 1962), copyrighted by Dr. Patterson.

from the sense of failure, and to society, which loses the full potential contributions of an unestimated number of its members. Underachievement is, therefore, a legitimate concern of counselors.

Underachievement may be the result of a number of different factors or conditions. First among these in terms of historical attention is the deficiency in tools or techniques basic to academic proficiency, such as reading or other specific deficiencies. These deficiencies may be of a so-called innate nature or origin or the result of inadequate training or experience. On the basis of this assumption as to the origin of underachievement, diagnostic studies of specific disabilities, such as reading, have been stressed. Emphasis has been placed on programs of remedial work or tutoring where the deficiency was deemed to be the result of inadequate preparation or training. Training in methods of study has also been used to remedy defects in study habits or skills.

This approach was not found to be effective in many cases. In others, no such specific deficiencies could be uncovered. The factor of *interest,* or *motivation,* was then recognized as important in achievement. Dragsgow (1957) states that in his experience underachievers are usually in the wrong curriculum, and he proposes changing them to a curriculum more appropriate to their interests and aptitudes. But what about the underachievers in high school, where there is little if any choice of curricula? And again, what about those cases where interests and aptitudes are consistent with the curriculum being followed?

The importance of emotional factors in underachievement is being increasingly recognized (Feyereisen, 1948). Students may fail or achieve below their potential because of the presence of personal and emotional problems. This suggests that therapeutic counseling or psychotherapy may be effective in helping underachievers.

Several studies have indicated that interviews by teachers or counselors, dealing with the personal interests or problems of students, are effective in improving achievement of students (Bradt and Duncan, 1951). Hoehn and Salts (1956), however, found that teacher interviews were not effective. Other studies (Calhoun, 1956) involving counselors have also yielded essentially negative results, although Calhoun found improvement in grades but none in standardized achievement tests. Group therapy has also been reported as effective in improving achievement (Gersten, 1951). It would appear that the results are somewhat commensurate with the competence and duration and/or intensity of the counseling.

Serene (1953) reports an interesting experiment in "motivational counseling," involving one or two interviews with students and one with parents, with positive results. It may be of interest to note that while Schoenhard (1950) found that interviews with parents in the home did not raise academic achievement, a result which he explained as resistance of the students to parental control, Drews and Teahan (1957) report that mothers of high achievers were found to be more authoritarian and restrictive than mothers of low achievers. Thus the effect of Serene's interviews with parents is problematical.

A study conducted by a student of the author is pertinent here (Baymur and Patterson, 1960). Thirty-two members of a class of 220 juniors in a midwest high school were identified as underachievers on the basis of discrepancy in standing on grades and aptitude tests. They were divided into four groups of eight each, matched for aptitude, achievement, degree of underachievement, socioeconomic status, age, and sex. Then one group was provided individual counseling, and a second group was given group counseling. The counselor met once with the third group and informed them they were underachievers and encouraged them to work harder, pointing out the importance of good grades for further education and employment. The fourth group received no help. All groups were given copies of the book *Study Your Way Through School* (Gerken, 1953). Counseling continued for a period of twelve weeks and was conducted in a client-centered manner. All students were given the Brown-Holtzman *Survey of Study Habits* and a Q-sort (a measure of personal adjustment) before and after counseling.

The results indicated that the two counseled groups did not significantly improve their scores on the *Survey of Study Habits*. The two counseled groups combined did show greater positive changes in self-concept. This change was the result of improvement in the students who received individual counseling, however, since the students receiving group counseling did not improve. The two counseled groups improved in grade-point average. In this case, the students receiving group counseling seemed to show greater improvement in grades than those receiving individual counseling.

Considering the many factors involved, the results of this study might be considered encouraging. The duration and extent of the counseling were limited; the group counseling consisted of only nine sessions. The group counseling sessions tended to be rather superficial, in the opinion of the counselor. None of the students had requested the counseling; many were not aware that they were underachievers. In spite of these factors, some of the students were benefited. It appears possible that group counseling which does not concentrate on problems of personal adjustment may result in improvement in grades. On the other hand, counseling which involves consideration of personal problems, as in the case of the students given individual counseling, may, at least in the short run, have little if any effect on grades. In fact, as in a study of gifted underachievers to be mentioned later, grades may even decline. The concentration on personal problems may affect application to schoolwork.

It is interesting that the selection of students who were underachievers resulted in the selection of students manifesing personal and social problems, supporting the hypothesis that underachievement is related to general problems of adjustment. Some underachievers, however, appear not to have such general problems. A student may accept, or choose, underachievement in order to gain social acceptance or in order to concentrate his time and efforts in other areas, such as extracurricular activities. The influence of social attitudes on achievement was expressed by a student in counseling as follows: "That's one problem today with the schools of America—the intelligent person is ridiculed, and the person who may be average or a little below average is the one who gets all the recognition. And that I imagine has frustrated many people of potential ability, just as I think happened to me."

The failure of the attempt to stimulate underachievers in one-session motivational "counseling" is of interest. This group declined in all three measures employed in the study, falling below the control group at the end of the study. The approach used with this group is one commonly employed by parents and teachers who attempt to raise the achievement of students. The results of the study suggest that it may be better to leave underachievers alone than to point out their failure to achieve adequately and exhort them to do something about it. Perhaps the failure of underachievers to respond to such exhortations is related to the hostility which appears to be present in able underachievers. Shaw and Grubb (1958) write, "It seems reasonable to infer . . . that a basically hostile person would not react favorably to demands for better performance or to higher standards of work, as has been suggested in some quarters." A particular concern at the present time is the utilization of high-level talent. This has directed attention to the gifted or talented underachiever.

Numerous writers have been pointing out the tremendous waste of talent in America. This waste occurs through the failure to utilize the talents of many able people who, for one reason or another, do not obtain the education and training which would make it possible for them to develop their talents. Large numbers of students who have the ability to do so do not go on to college. Estimates of the proportion of high-ability students who do not go on to college are as high as 50 per cent. It is generally agreed that students in the upper 30 per cent of the distribution in ability are qualified for college level training. However, only about 60 per cent of this group enter college, and of those entering only about two-thirds finish (Wolfle, 1960). Russell and Cronbach (1958) estimate that if every person with the ability to graduate from college did so, we should have nearly 660,000 college graduates per year instead of the actual 270,000. And if everyone who could reasonably expect to attain a Ph.D., on the basis of ability, did so, we should have 300,000 such degrees awarded each year, compared to the 8,000 which are actually awarded. They correctly point out that "our scientific manpower problem is not a shortage of talent but a failure to attract enough students into advanced and specialized training."

There are, of course, many reasons why able students do not continue their education. Socioeconomic factors are important in many cases. Wolfle refers to a study which found that 90 per cent of those children whose fathers were engaged in professional and semiprofessional occupations, and who were in the upper third of their graduating class, went to college; 80 per cent of those whose fathers were in managerial occupations entered college; 70 per cent of the children of salesmen, clerks, and service workers went on to college; 60 per cent of the children of farmers did so; and only 50 per cent of the children of factory workers and laborers, although in the upper third of their class, continued their education to college (Wolfle, 1958). Beilin (1956) points out that it is not only lack of financial resources which prevents youth from the lower socioeconomic group from attending college. An important factor is the attitude toward education.

The loss of the talent of many gifted students is no doubt directly related to the various factors which have been mentioned. These factors prevent achieving gifted students from continuing their education or training. But in many instances these factors are indirectly responsible for the loss of talent, because they lead to underachievement in many talented or gifted students who are often not recognized as possessing talent or the capacity for greater achievement. This is particularly the case in students from the lower socioeconomic classes. Wolfle (1958) refers to a survey of 7,000 students who had received the highest scores on tests of science and mathematics. Many of the children and their parents were not aware of the abilities possessed by the children.

In many instances, high-ability youths are not aware of their potentialities or become aware of them too late to be able to utilize them. Attitudes, goals, and expectations have become fixed, so that even if they were persuaded to continue their education, many would have difficulty, and many would quit or fail before completing college. Preparation for college begins long before high school and requires more than the appropriate sequence of college preparatory courses. The importance of early identification of the talented, before they become fixed in a pattern of underachievement, is obvious.

The problem of underachievement in gifted students is a real one, although the extent of the problem is not clearly known. Its extent depends on the definition of underachievement. But even under the same definition, the number of underachieving gifted students identified varies from study to study. Gowan, using as a criterion a difference of 30 percentile points or more between ability and achievement, reports percentages of underachievers from about 10 per cent to almost 50 per cent in different schools (Gowan, 1955).

Evidence of underachievement at the college level is clear. One study revealed that almost 30 per cent of students in the top decile in ability who go to college fail to achieve adequately (Wedemeyer, 1953). The reasons for underachievement in college are many, including financial difficulties requiring excessive time devoted to employment and worries about financial problems.

Achievement in high school and later is also related to habits, attitudes, interests, and motivations established at the elementary school level. Personal, emotional, and home problems also are important factors in underachievement in the gifted (Wedemeyer, 1953; Gowan, 1957; Shaw and Brown, 1957; Sanford, 1952).

The fact that the underachievement of gifted students is related to personal-emotional adjustment suggests that counseling would be indicated. Experience suggests that counseling is difficult, however, perhaps because of an element of hostility which may be present in such students (Shaw and Grubb, 1958). Gowan's summary of findings indicating that gifted underachievers tend to be unsociable, self-sufficient, and hard to reach would also suggest that counseling would be difficult (Gowan, 1955). Both Shaw and Grubb and Gowan suggest that group counseling might be an effective approach to gifted underachievers. There appear to be no reports in the literature of the effectiveness of either individual or group therapy with gifted underachievers.

Studies of group counseling of gifted underachieving adolescents have recently been completed at the University of Illinois (Broedel, 1958). Twenty-nine freshmen in a large midwestern high school were studied. These students ranked in the top 10 per cent of their class in intelligence in the eighth grade but below the ninth decile in grade-point average. The total group was randomly divided into four smaller groups, two of which took part in group counseling, while two did not. The counseling consisted of two 43-minute sessions a week for eight weeks. An eclectic, group-centered approach to counseling was used.

The results of the study indicated that the two counseled groups made greater gains in acceptance of self and others during the eight-week period. Ratings of interpersonal relationships by the investigators, by observers, and by the parents indicated improvement in behavior. On the other hand, counseling did not result in better academic performance as represented by grade-point averages. The counseled groups declined in grade-point average slightly. There was also no improvement in achievement test scores by the counseled groups. However, scores on an achievement test administered sixteen weeks after termination of counseling were significantly higher. These results suggest that improvement in personal adjustment did not affect classroom performance, at least immediately, but did result in greater achievement as measured objectively at a later date.

The investigators report that most of the students questioned whether they were gifted; they showed evidence of disturbed behavior prior to counseling and were not the kind of persons one would expect to seek counseling.

Following the completion of this experiment, the two groups which had not received counseling were then counseled. Some of the members of these two groups showed some improvement in acceptance of self and others, but the improvement was not significant for the groups as a whole. Grades of students in these groups did not improve during counseling, although their grades improved the following year. In this study, the findings were affected by the fact that one of the two groups appeared to benefit from counseling, while one did not. It was felt that because of the relatively serious disturbance of the students, it would be expecting too much to achieve great changes in an eight-week period. The results of these studies are promising enough to suggest that underachieving gifted students, even though not presumably desirous of counseling, may be helped to improve personal adjustment by group counseling. This improvement in personal adjustment may lay the foundation for future gains in achievement.

Underachievement is a problem with a variety of causes, ranging from inadequate preparation or instruction on through deliberate efforts not to achieve at a high level because of fear of being considered a grind or an "egghead," through preoccupation with family problems, to emotional disturbances and lack of recognition of potentiality. Poor or inadequate background or preparation may be remedied by special instruction or tutoring.

The other factors or causes are matters for counseling rather than instruction or exhortation. More and better counseling services in our schools would undoubtedly lead to the reduction of underachievement and the more efficient utilization of the talent of students. It would not, however, eliminate the problem of underachievement, since this may be the result of factors not amenable to counseling. These include socioeconomic factors, social pressures, and the free but considered choice of the student to accept lower achievement academically in order to achieve better in some other area.

20. The Nonachievement Syndrome *

ROBERT M. ROTH, *Department of Psychology, Illinois Institute of Technology*
H. ARNOLD MEYERSBURG, *Staff member, Hampton Institute, Hampton, Virginia*

IN THE Psychological Services counseling program at Hampton Institute, many of the students who apply for help do so because they have been unable to succeed in their academic work. Also, there is a large group of students who fail in their academic work but do not apply for help at the psychologist's office. We became interested in this problem because of the large number of students involved and because of the lack of any effective methods with which to help them. Our first line of approach has been help for those who apply voluntarily for counseling. In time, we hope to be able to extend this help to the larger group.

In the course of our clinical experience, it became necessary to develop a frame of reference for achievement problems. Numerous studies have reported the ineffectiveness of current treatment approaches (vocational, educational, or personal counseling, reading improvement programs, academic advisement, etc.). It appeared to us that if we were going to help students with these problems, we would have to have a fresh perspective.

* Reprinted by permission of the authors and *Personnel and Guidance Journal,* 42:535–540; February, 1963.

We chose to develop constructs directly from our experiences in counseling students with achievement difficulties.

It is not our intention in this paper to present a definitive theory of achievement. Nor is the description of this syndrome intended to refer to all nonachievement problems. So far, we feel warranted in presenting our experience and thinking in presenting:

1. The constructs which we have evolved.
2. A description of the counseling process.
3. A formulation of "nonachievement" as a syndrome of character organization.

Constructs

1. The student's poor achievement does not arise from an incapacity to achieve.

Our clinical work indicated that achievement was related to factors other than an inborn capacity, and any new perspective must take this into account.

2. Poor achievement is an expression of the student's choice.

This construct presents achievement problems in terms of motivation toward goals which have meaning in the phenomenal world of the individual. The poorly achieving student is perceived in terms which delineate his motives for choosing poor achievement.

3. The student's choice for poor achievement operates in the preparation he makes for achievement.

The scrutiny of a student's preparation, including the actual amount of preparation time, the intensity of studying, the subject areas emphasized or avoided in the preparation, etc., indicates the kind of choice for achievement which a student makes. The student who has chosen poor achievement tends to spend his "preparation time" with friends, relaxing, watching TV, etc.; he spends much time in fantasy; he prepares only partially for exams; and when he does prepare he is not sure of what he is reading or writing. Although individuals vary in the way their choice for poor achievement operates, the description above seems representative.

4. Poor achievement is a function of the preparation for achievement which a student makes.

It follows that successful achievement is improbable in light of the preparation for achievement described under 3.

5. Poor academic skills are related to poor achievement and are an outgrowth of previous choices for poor achievement.

The progress of academic experience moves from the learning of skills to the use of these skills to acquire systematic knowledge. When choices for poor achievement appear early in the academic life of the individual, skills which at that time are the content of achievement are not learned adequately. In later periods of academic life, the poor skills either support the individual's choice for poor achievement or limit the achievement of those who no longer choose poor achievement.

6. The choice for poor achievement may be expressed as over-all limited achievement or as achievement in deviant channels.

In "over-all limited achievement," the student's energies seem to be directed against experiencing and toward the maintenance of a *status quo*. In "achievement in deviant channels," the student does expand his world of experience, but he avoids those avenues specifically related to accredited study.

7. The patterns of choice for poor achievement are enduring and do not undergo spontaneous change.

8. Achievement patterns, like other enduring behavior patterns, can be considered to be related to "personality organization."

In modern personality theory, enduring behavior patterns are considered expressions of the psychodynamic equilibrium of personality organization. We view poor achievement as an enduring behavior pattern related to a specific psychodynamic organization, a "character trait."

9. The counseling relationship can serve as the impetus to change the achievement patterns.

Changes in the psychodynamic organization can result in changes in character pattern. To induce such changes would require the use of psychodynamic techniques; the counseling relationship can be used to serve this end.

The Counseling Experience

The student is asked to express his complaints as completely as he is able. He is encouraged to include complaints in as many different areas of his living as he is aware of. These complaints may indicate academic difficulties, financial problems, problems with parents, wife, friends, with peers, with deans, etc., as well as depression, anxiety, lack of self-confidence, bodily symptoms, etc.

Regarding academic problems, the students make statements of which the following are typical: "I can't concentrate," "I freeze up on exams," "I study very hard, but the teacher always asks questions about the material

I did not get to study," "I don't attend class regularly," "I can't get interested in anything I do." The counselor views these expressions as symptomatic of a personality difficulty and directs the attention of the student to the ways in which he prepares for achievement. When sufficient examples are secured, the counselor interprets deficits in preparation in terms of their value in predicting failure. The counselor describes each deficit as it is related to subsequent failure, and he presents his view that these errors in preparation seem to be intentional (though not necessarily conscious). The client is presented with the inference that if this is so, then it would seem that the student is seeking or choosing failure. The counselor then indicates that this self-defeating behavior is evident in other areas of the student's living. Examples of this are given. If the client decides that he wishes to change his choices, the counselor can indicate the areas and directions to change. The extent to which this is done is contingent on their relationship and the readiness of the student to see this type of choice problem in other areas of his living. For instance, he might see his problem only in terms of study, or he might be able to see his academic problems as part of a general self-disparagement process. Regardless, the counselor helps the client to stop self-disparagement as soon as it has been recognized. This is necessary so that deleterious impulses in the form of intense anxiety become limited and controlled. If this is not done, alternative choices cannot be made by the client and changes cannot be tested.

The control of his impulsive self-disparagement is the key at this point. He is directed to concentrate his efforts on this task between interviews and to return at the next appointment and discuss his progress along these lines. This continues until the student is adept at halting the disparagements, at which point a steady increase in the duration of effective study times and a decrease in time between effective study periods occurs. The effect of self-disparagement on studies is the focus of all early sessions. (This is consistent with the college setting and its demands on the student.) In time, the student is led to see other effects of self-disparagement (i.e., family relations, peer relations, depression, etc.), to reject the mechanistic, self-defeating patterns. Freed of the shackling effects of disparagement, he selects new behavior patterns as hypotheses and proceeds to test them.

At first, the counselor helps in this selection. The amount of help required ranges from near-total, for those who cannot derive their own hypotheses and must be supplied with them, to scant, for those students who are able to formulate their own hypotheses. (We think that the point on this continuum at which a student operates at any given time is a measure of the severity of his disability.) In time, all choices are made by the student. It is extremely important for the counselor to view these attempts at hypothesis testing as trial-and-error runs, the results of which will serve as a basis upon which to accept or reject new hypotheses to the solution of problems. The students in this group are apt to interpret the rejection of a hypothesis as evidence of their own failure and use it for further self-disparagement. If this is allowed by the counselor, the situation reverts to the beginning and all the previous work may be lost.

When successful patterns of study are found and adopted, the counselor allows or leads the counselee to use the same methods for establishing successful patterns of behavior in situations dealing with peers, family, and self. Attention is then focused on these changes in terms of their significance to the client's view of his own life, present and future, and to his pleasure with his new achievement.

As these changes start to occur, the student is usually able to understand his own actions in terms of his new perception of self and the altered self-image which imposes changes in the view of him by peers. New relationships evolve. During this process, the counselor helps the student to recognize the significance of these new events. Because he views himself differently, his peers view him differently. His personal goals have changed, and so has his scholastic performance.

His relationship with parents must change, too. These students seem to have been covertly battling with parents for acceptance over long periods of time. Some students report that their parents view schoolwork indifferently, while others report that their parents attend only to the failures. We get the impression that these students originally sought to do whatever they could to arouse the parent's attention to them—that the parents could relate only through hostility. In this way an identity with the family is sought through the only channel available (i.e., self-devaluation). Thus, through the counseling experience this last channel is eliminated. The student can then recognize that what he wanted his parents to give him is not available. The final move from being a helpless, manipulating infant to becoming a competent self-directing adult can be made. When behavior which implements this choice has been selected and successfully tested, the counseling relationship is usually terminated by the student.

The Nonachievement Syndrome

The recognition of the dynamic processes involved in poor academic achievement serves to bring our perspective of this disorder into line with other personality problems. A rather prevalent group of symptoms and related to it, taken together, can make a consistent syndrome:

1. Poor academic achievement.
2. General self-depreciation; lack of recognition of pleasure at "being."
3. No clear system of personal goals or values.
4. Vulnerability to disparagement by others.
5. Immature relations with parents.
6. Frequent depressions.
7. Lack of insight about self and others.
8. Free-floating anxiety.

Etiology

From the sociological viewpoint, the role of scholar in our society has had relatively low status except among a small middle-class group. This is quite manifest, for example, in a comparison of the regard accorded a professor in Japan and that accorded a professor here. The ideal of a "self-made man," until the launching of the Soviet's Sputnik I, was dominant over the "well-educated man" on the American scene, and a college education was a "nice" formality rather than an intellectual growth experience. The more recent elevation of the "educated man" as an ideal above the "self-made man" has not as yet become a firm social reality.

The psychogenesis involves a series of very subtle devaluations of the child, stemming from the parent-child relationship. In our experience, the most frequent pattern is that of the parent who pays no attention at all to the accomplishments or failures of the child. (These students frequently exclaim, "What's the use, nobody gives a damn," in reference to their current college failure.) The life space of the child and the life space of the parent are in different realms: a state of affairs which constitutes a parental rejection. The only way a child can bring the life spaces together, albeit momentarily, is through the production of a crisis, occasionally necessitating outsiders such as police, teacher, principal, or a counselor.

Next in frequency is the parent who attends only to the child's failures and rarely to his successes. The latter are taken for granted, but the failures are punished. Thus, the contact between parent and child is through failure. If the child succeeds, he is alone; but if he fails, he is part of the concern of his parents.

Both of these early experiences lead to three devastating, incipient pathological processes.

The first of these is a process of self-denigration. In order for the child to maintain some kind of identity with the parent, he must learn to see himself as a failure. He must hold back his productivity and blame himself for his lacks. Hostility, he is taught, is received by him and never expressed toward others. When he does experience resentments, he directs them against himself and thus supports his own constructs about himself as being worth little.

As a consequence of this devaluation of self, the opinions of others come to occupy a position of greater importance than his own, and the development of a set of values for himself is arrested. This interference in the development of autonomy leads to the retardation of other self-functions and establishes the disparaged picture of the self.

In the early years, the learning of scholastic skills becomes the object of this child's choice for failure. As a result, the acquisition of such skills is minimal. Later, when these skills are prerequisite to new learning, the choice for failure is unavoidably maintained by their lack. The growth of the child's phenomenal world is curtailed and his development as a student impeded.

The impact of the individual psychogenesis with its burden of unsatisfied longing for approval makes the child particularly susceptible to the cultural approval given the unscholarly, and he derives important gratification from the acceptance accorded by his peers. Should he have "survived" the elimination processes along the way and reached college, he has not had the kinds of developmental experiences the institution assumes he has had. The new experiences at college are difficult for him, and he comes to faculty attention because of his limitations.

Lesser degrees of involvement may be associated with later time of onset in the developmental cycle or with relieving features in the parent–child relationship. The observation that many poor achievers read well, write well, and have a good basic mathematical knowledge tends to support this notion.

Psychodynamics

The personality organization of these students seems to follow a definite discernible pattern. There is a lack of self-boundaries which is expressed in an apparent inability to accept or reject others' evaluations, opinions, attitudes, and beliefs. Whatever they hear becomes introjected without modification, as with a sponge. They seem to have no value system of their own; this is particularly so when others' expressions are directed toward them and are disparaging.

Onslaughts against self are derived also from the inability to contain affect. When feelings well up, they become uncontrollable and impulsive. The impulsive expression of hostility is directed inward and rarely permitted outward expression. Thus, whether the self is attacked from the outside or from within, the self-structure decompensates with each new blow. Anxiety and distress are experienced. Guilt and depression tend to bind the anxiety, and the self-structure re-establishes its dynamic equilibrium. These students report depressions which come at frequent intervals. Each episode of depression begins outside awareness until it snowballs; functioning is impaired during these periods and is restored only after the depression subsides.

Each experience of devaluation leads to increments in self-disparagement and the level of free anxiety. The capacities of these individuals to bind free anxiety are severely taxed, owing to the already excessive production of anxiety from previous disparagement. The inability to cope with the distress feeds back in terms of further self-depreciation, thus establishing a destructive circular process which tends to perpetuate the disorder.

These processes are inimical to personality growth. There is an incessant expectation of change in the parental attitude which is not forthcoming. This continual disappointment adds to the hopelessness and despair. Since the disappointment is too difficult to bear, the student attempts to become the fulfillment of the parental expectations as a compromise. Thus, the student's desire for parental changes in attitudes toward him on one hand and his attempt to fulfill the parents' expectations (as the student views it) on the other live side by side. He acts on the latter. He seeks to become the fulfillment of his view of his parents' expectations of him through his choice for poor achievement. Experience of poor achievement feeds back into self-disparagement.

All these processes are supported by such expressed attitudes toward the self as "I have no interests," "I am a poor student," "People like you when you act right," "It's wrong to be angry," "I have no special abilities," "I am not as good as other people," "You must love your mother and father," and so on.

The entire dynamic picture is similar to that encountered in depressive disorders. This syndrome might be a special case of depression.

Summary

The delineation of this syndrome of poor academic achievement enables us to recognize a psychopathological organization closely resembling depressive disorders. A psychotherapeutic approach specifically designed to interrupt the circular processes of disparagement, anxiety, functional disability, hopelessness, frustration, disparagement, etc. has been found useful, and the constructs to guide this approach are set forth. We are thus in a position to revise the currently held view that counseling methods are ineffectual in bringing about changes in such achievement patterns.

21. Challenging the Underachieving Gifted Student: A Study of Programs in Thirty-Seven Schools *

HELEN G. STERN, *School Counselor, Nyack, New York*

THE PURPOSE of this study was to obtain detailed information about the programs and services for underachieving gifted youth in a cross section of schools and systems across the country. A simple questionnaire sent to the guidance personnel was designed to elicit reports on such topics as identification, scheduling, counseling and guidance services, referral procedures, personnel assigned to work with underachievers, active programs for gifted, further problems encountered, resources schools would like to have.

.   .   .   .

Summarizing the findings briefly, it was noted:

Of the thirty-seven schools, thirty-three stated that they had active and systematic methods of identification.

Most of the systems identified gifted underachievers by checking the IQ against teacher grades.

Of the tests used, the CTMM and the DAT were most frequently mentioned.

The majority of schools placed underachievers in regular classes.

* Extracted from a longer paper of the same title and published by permission of the author.

Only nine schools met Conant's recommendations of one counselor to every 300 students.

Twenty-one schools provided gifted underachievers with individual counseling or held conferences with faculty, parents, or administrators.

Seventeen schools referred underachievers to school psychologists. Fifteen did not refer at all. Eleven referred to remedial reading.

Twenty-three systems used one referral. Seven referred twice. Twenty-one assigned guidance personnel. Eight used a special teacher.

The most frequent problem ecountered was lack of a special program. College placement, motivation, and parental acceptance were next highest in frequency.

A majority of the schools wanted more guidance resources. Eleven wanted better faculty.

22. Personality Traits and Discrepant Achievement: A Review *

RONALD G. TAYLOR, *Professor of Education, Ferris College*

A REVIEW of the literature relating personality to discrepant achievement indicates with few exceptions the lack of a theoretical orientation which would adequately account for those variables influencing achievement. A logical order then would be to (1) suggest several personality traits, (2) support these traits by reviewing the research which appears to pertain to each trait, and finally (3) attempt a synthesis in order to emphasize areas potentially significant for future research.

Personality Traits

A review of the literature revealed certain recurrent references to seven basic personality traits connected with overachievement and underachieve-

* Reprinted by permission of the author and *Journal of Counseling Psychology*, 11:76–82; Spring, 1964.

ment. A basic difficulty in reviewing this research literature occurred in trying to determine the interpretive direction which each researcher implied in his individual study. The hypothesized "summary" traits are presented in Table 1.

The traits listed in Table 1 can be conceived as continua with the over- (or high) achiever characteristics hypothesized as falling at one end of the scale and those of the under- (or low) achiever occupying the other. The assumption is made that such groups represent motivational extremes. Farquhar (1963) has noted the significant lack of comparability in selection techniques used for isolating discrepant criterion groups. This fact suggests caution in accepting many of the comparisons found in the following review.

Academic Anxiety

DIRECTED ANXIETY

Horrall (1957) indicated that the overachiever has less deep underlying anxiety but more inner tension with better outer control than the under-

TABLE I—SUMMARY OF HYPOTHESIZED PERSONALITY TRAITS

Direction Low Achiever	Trait	Direction High Achiever
Free-Floating Anxiety	Academic Anxiety	Directed Anxiety
Negative Self-Value	Self-Value	Positive Self-Value
Hostility toward Authority	Authority Relations	Acceptance of Authority
Negative Interpersonal Relations	Interpersonal Relations	Positive Interpersonal Relations
High Independence- Dependence Conflict	Independence- Dependence Conflict	Low Independence- Dependence Conflict
Socially Oriented	Activity Patterns	Academically Oriented
Unrealistic Goal Orientation	Goal Orientation	Realistic Goal Orientation

achiever. Similar results are reported by Holland (1959) and Gough (1953), who concluded that the overachiever, or high achiever, has more self-control. His anxiety does not manifest itself in a readily apparent form such as misconduct, conflict over sex, maladjustment, and neurotic tendencies. Gowan (1957) found that tensions in task demands during childhood prevailed among overachievers. The result was the development of strong self-control.

FREE-FLOATING ANXIETY

Two investigators conclude that the underachievers tend to have a high degree of anxiety which demoralizes personal academic activity (Bond, 1960; Mitchell, 1959). Horrall (1957) reveals that the underachiever has a high conflict over conduct and sex, has a high degree of emotionality, and exhibits instability and maladjustment. Roth and Meyersburg (1963) indicate a general self-depreciation and free-floating anxiety relating to non-achievement.

Other investigators (Middleton and Guthrie, 1959; Kimball, 1953) have obtained similar results regarding the underachiever's denial of normal shortcomings and his attempt to maintain a superior self-image. An earlier investigation by Gerberich (1941) suggests that the underachiever has difficulty paying attention in class and studying. In a study of elementary school males, Walsh (1956) concludes that the underachiever feels restricted, hemmed in, and helpless. The underachiever expresses exaggerated free-floating emotion or represses all emotion when some emotional response seems appropriate.

Self-Value

POSITIVE SELF-VALUE

Several investigations indicate that the overachiever is optimistic, self-confident, and adequate as a person and holds a relatively high opinion of himself (Gough, 1953; Gowan, 1957; Horrall, 1957; Kurtz and Swenson, 1951; Lum, 1960; Morgan, 1952). A number of other investigations conclude that the overachiever has positive character integration and a personal and intellectual efficiency which is persistent and enduring (Gough, 1953; Gowan, 1957; Krug, 1959; Merrill and Murphy, 1959; Pierce, 1959). An investigation by Morgan (1952) finds the overachieving male to have insight and realistic attitudes which make for satisfactory self-value. A somewhat similar study of elementary males by Walsh (1956) indicates that the overachiever's acceptance of self results in freedom and adequacy of emotional expression.

Two investigations present some findings that disagree with the investigations cited above (Holland, 1959; Mitchell, 1959). The investigators found that the overachiever has feelings of unworthiness about himself and worries more about the impression which he makes upon others.

NEGATIVE SELF-VALUE

A number of investigators have discovered that the underachiever is self-derogatory and depressed in attitudes toward self (Horrall, 1957; Kimball, 1953; Kirk, 1952; Roth and Meyersburg, 1963; Shaw, 1960). The underachiever has feelings of inadequacy, a concern about health, and a poor over-all adjustment. In these studies it is also concluded that the underachiever has strong inferiority feelings and passivity which result in deliberate failure. Borislow (1962) suggests that the underachiever has a poor conception of his scholastic performance. In other investigations, it is indicated that the underachievers lack confidence in themselves and tend to withdraw, attempting to be self-sufficient (Gowan, 1957; Kurtz and Swenson, 1951).

The literature discloses only one investigator (Holland, 1959) who disagrees with this theory of negative self-values. He indicates that the underachieving student has positive self-attitudes.

Authority Relations

ACCEPTANCE OF AUTHORITY

Several investigations indicate that the overachiever has a good relationship with parents (Gowan, 1957; Gough, 1953; Horrall, 1957; Kurtz and Swenson, 1951). The parents are interested and supportive in regard to their children's academic success, and the children in turn respect their parents and attempt to please them by doing well academically. The child conforms to the demands and conventions which are important to the parents. Additional investigations have obtained similar results regarding the overachieving student's relationship with authority outside the home (Erb, 1961; Gerberich, 1941; Holland, 1959; Merrill and Murphy, 1959). The overachiever seems to like most of his instructors and feels that he receives fair treatment. The overachiever attempts to create favorable impressions and is eager to please authority figures. This he does by getting his work in on time, turning in extra assignments, exhibiting great interest in the course, and creating no discipline problems in the classroom.

Several other investigators indicate that there may be a negative relation between overachievers and their parents (Drews and Teahan, 1957; Haggard, 1957; Hoffman, Rosen, and Lippitt, 1960; Horrall, 1957), the theoretical assumption being that a child unable to obtain love, warmth, and understanding at home will compensate for these needs by seeking, in their place, a teacher's approval of his academic achievements.

HOSTILITY TOWARD AUTHORITY

The underachiever's hostility and aggression toward authority have been recognized by many investigators to be directly influenced by his relationship with his parents (Hopkins, Molleson, and Sarnoff, 1958; Horrall,

1957; Kimball, 1953; Kurtz and Swenson, 1951; Shaw and Brown, 1957). The parents do not express their love for the child and are somewhat indifferent or uninterested in the child's academic success. In general, there seems to be a great deal of conflict between one or both of the parents and the child. The underachiever feels that his parents have not given him the material things in life that he would like to have. In an investigation involving males only, Kimball (1953) concludes that the underachiever does not have much chance of directly expressing his aggressive and hostile feelings as he grows older; in most cases the father is felt to be very distant, strict, and dominating. Hopkins, Molleson, and Sarnoff (1958) conclude that the underachiever chooses his school subjects because of parental pressures rather than genuine interest.

This conflict and hostility seem to be carried over to authority figures outside the home. This is indicated by several studies (Dowd, 1952; Kirk, 1952; Lum, 1960; Shaw and Brown, 1957; Shaw and Grubb, 1958; Walsh, 1956). They conclude that the underachieving student dislikes his instructors and is resistant to such externally imposed tasks as homework. The underachiever's dislike and hostility are a pronounced characteristic which tends to create a less favorable impression, and as a result he is less acceptable to the instructor.

An investigation of elementary school males by Walsh (1956) indicates that the underachiever acts defensively either through compliance, evasion, escape, blind rebellion, or negativism.

Interpersonal Relationships

POSITIVE INTERPERSONAL RELATIONSHIPS

Investigations have indicated that the overachieving student seems to be aware of and concerned with others (Gebhart and Hoyt, 1958; Gough, 1953; Gowan, 1957; Holland, 1959; Kurtz and Swenson, 1951; Morgan, 1952; Pierce, 1959). The overachiever is interested in and responsive to the feelings of others and accepts them. He denies feelings of ill will and animosity toward anyone and is free of interpersonal friction. Peer relationships are strong and supportive. Middleton and Guthrie (1959) conclude that the overachiever's achievement is motivated by social acceptance. An investigation of elementary school males by Walsh (1956) found that the overachiever has a present feeling of belonging.

A number of other investigators seem to be in conflict with the theory of positive interpersonal relationships (Holland, 1959; Horrall, 1957; Krug, 1959; Merrill and Murphy, 1959). These researchers found in their respective studies that the overachieving student tends to be unsociable in his attitude toward peers. Rabinowitz (1956) indicates that one of the reasons for the overachieving student's excellence in the academic area is his doubt and confusion in the areas of family and peer acceptance. It would appear, though, that it is not so much a factor of not getting along with peers as it is a result of spending more time in individual tasks and therefore socializing less.

NEGATIVE INTERPERSONAL RELATIONSHIPS

Three investigations conclude that the underachiever has conflict over his conduct and heterosexual adjustment (Horrall, 1957; Kurtz and Swenson, 1951; Snellgrove, 1960). Similar investigations support this statement and indicate that the underachievers are overly critical of others and exhibit asocial behavior (Gough, 1953; Gowan, 1957; Shaw and Brown, 1957). The underachiever also tends to be withdrawn, self-sufficient, uninterested in others, and apathetic in many of his relationships with peers and adults. An investigation by Armstrong (1955) reports that underachieving girls are not chosen for positions of responsibility in extracurricular activities, while the male underachievers prefer companions who are older than themselves. The underachiever obtains lower ratings on co-operation, dependability, and judgment. Walsh (1956) indicates that the underachiever tends to feel rejected and isolated from others. Holland (1959) seems both to agree and disagree with the theory of inadequate interpersonal relationships. He observes that the underachiever creates a less favorable impression upon peers and authority figures and yet seems to be poised, socially skillful, and flexible in his attitudes.

Independence-Dependence Conflict

LOW INDEPENDENCE-DEPENDENCE CONFLICT

Several investigations have indicated that the overachiever's interest and emotional maturity are high. He tends to be dominant in his group (Cohler, 1940; Horrall, 1957; Merrill and Murphy, 1959; Morgan, 1952). A number of investigations have concluded that the overachiever is dependable and responsible, having a basic seriousness of interests which enables him to perform in leadership capacities (Holland, 1959; Holland, 1961; Kurtz and Swenson, 1951; Morgan, 1952). An investigation of elementary school males by Walsh (1956) found that the overachiever feels free to make choices and initiate activities.

Other investigators (Holland, 1959; Middleton and Guthrie, 1959) disagree, to some extent, with the theory that the overachiever is more independent. They indicate that the overachiever's success is motivated by dependency and that he is more oriented toward achievement than toward independence. It is also indicated that the overachiever does well academically under direction but is not as adept in situations demanding independent judgment.

HIGH INDEPENDENCE-DEPENDENCE CONFLICT

A number of investigations have indicated that future goals, occupations, and subjects are influenced by parental pressures and aspirations (Armstrong, 1955; Brown, Abeles, and Iscoe, 1954; Hopkins, Molleson, and Sarnoff, 1958; Mitchell, 1959). The underachiever lacks a decisiveness to act, and future occupations are chosen because of the influence of others. One study of males only by Kimball (1953) found that the underachiever has prominent dependency needs.

Contrary findings are reported by Stagner (1933), who concluded that the underachiever has a high degree of self-sufficiency.

Activity Patterns

ACADEMICALLY ORIENTED

Several investigators have indicated that the overachiever derives self-satisfaction through work and has a high motivation to achieve (Gebhart and Hoyt, 1958; Krug, 1959; Lum, 1960; Mitchell, 1959; Morgan, 1952). Additional studies indicate that the overachieving student spends most of his time on studies, gets assignments in promptly, has good study habits, and generally has a feeling of academic effectiveness (Dowd, 1952; Gerberich, 1941; Gough, 1953; Horrall, 1957). Two investigators (Holland, 1959; Pierce, 1959) conclude that the overachiever is able to work effectively under direction but is not as adept in situations demanding independent judgment. It is indicated that the overachiever is achievement-oriented rather than individuality-oriented. Kurtz and Swenson (1951) conclude that the overachiever is academically inclined, is happy in a classroom situation, derives satisfaction from book learning, has high educational and vocational goals, relates schoolwork to future goals, and tends to regard education for more than its job value.

SOCIALLY ORIENTED

Various investigations indicate that the underachiever lacks motivation and interest in the academic area but obtains self-satisfaction in other areas

(Brown, Abeles, and Iscoe, 1954; Holland, 1959; Mitchell, 1959; Terman and Oden, 1947). One example is that he is considered more socially skillful than the overachiever. The underachiever is unwilling to conform to academic requirements and has strong "activity" interests, as opposed to intellectual interests. Several other investigators emphasize the underachiever's tendency toward pleasure seeking and extroversion and the tendency to go to college for social reasons, e.g., joining a fraternity or sorority (Gerberich, 1941; Hopkins, Molleson and Sarnoff, 1958; Horrall, 1957; Middleton and Guthrie, 1959). The underachiever is found to have strong affiliation needs, and he reaches out immaturely for contact experiences. Gowan (1957) indicates that the underachiever has unclear and indefinite academic and occupational choices.

Goal Orientation

REALISTIC GOAL ORIENTATION

Several investigations of overachieving males indicate that they have a drive to organize and plan their lives. They are dependable, consistent, and responsible in relationship to task demands and requests from others (Diener, 1960; Gebhart and Hoyt, 1958; Holland, 1959; Krug, 1959; Morgan, 1952). The overachiever also has a basic seriousness of purpose, is intellectually efficient, energetic, conscientious, and has an insight and realistic attitude toward himself and others. A number of other studies conclude that the overachiever is conservative in setting goals, has persistent and effective study habits, has a capacity for sustained and diligent application, rejects the frivolous and diversionary, is orderly and planful, and has a basic seriousness of purpose (Dowd, 1952; Gerberich, 1941; Gough, 1953; Gowan, 1957; Holland, 1961; Kurtz and Swenson, 1951; Merrill and Murphy, 1959). These investigations indicate that the overachiever tends to relate schoolwork to future goals and is intellectually efficient.

UNREALISTIC GOAL ORIENTATION

A number of investigators indicate that the underachiever is highly emotional, lacks decisiveness to act, is restless, changeable, and unhappy (Brown, Abeles, and Iscoe, 1954; Dowd, 1952; Kurtz and Swenson, 1951; Holland, 1959; Lum, 1960; Mitchell, 1959; Stagner, 1933). It is also concluded that the underachiever lacks motivation to complete tasks that are assigned either in school or at home. Several of the investigations emphasize the underachiever's inability to decide upon educational and vocational goals and the difference between measured interests and stated future vocational goals. It is indicated that many underachievers have no stated goals or else have stated goals impossible to achieve (Armstrong, 1955; Dowd, 1952; Gowan, 1957; Hopkins, Molleson, and Sarnoff, 1958; Kurtz and Swenson, 1951; Lum, 1960; Mitchell, 1959).

Conclusions

The weight of evidence in the literature would seem to support the following conclusions concerning the relationship of certain personality traits to academic achievement.

1. The degree to which a student is able to handle his anxiety is directly related to his level of achievement.

2. The value the student places upon his own worth affects his academic achievement.

3. The ability to conform to and/or accept authority demands will determine the amount of academic success.

4. Students who are accepted and have positive relationships with peers are better able to accept themselves. Students who do not have peer acceptance generally go outside the school environment for their satisfactions.

5. The less conflict over independence-dependence relationships a student copes with, the more effort he places on achievement.

6. Activities which are centered around academic interests are more likely to produce successful achievement.

7. The more realistic the goal, the more chance there is of successful completion of that goal.

Suggested Readings

Demos, G. D., and Spolyar, L. J. "Academic Achievement of College Freshmen in Relation to the Edwards Personal Preference Schedule," *Educational and Psychological Measurement,* 21:473–479; 1961. Compares EPPS results on 245 Long Beach State College freshmen with respect to SCAT scores and GPA. No significant EPPS differences were found between achievers (high SCAT, high GPA) and underachievers (high SCAT, low GPA) or between overachievers (low SCAT, high GPA) and nonachievers (low SCAT, low GPA).

Drake, L. E. "MMPI Patterns Predictive of Underachievement," *Journal of Counseling Psychology,* 9:164–167; 1962. Found 4–9 pattern (elevation on psychopathic deviate and manic) to be characteristic.

Froehlich, H. P., and Mayo, G. D. "A Note on Under- and Overachiever Measurement," *Personnel and Guidance Journal,* 41:621–623; March, 1963. A technical report on naval school cadets which points out that instead of isolating criterion groups on the basis of the relationship between ability and achievement, we may express this relationship as a single variable which is useful for prediction of course grades and hence guidance. The index is based on the ratio of the actual final GPA to that average predicted by a set of ability measures.

Gill, Lois J., and Spilka, B. "Some Nonintellectual Correlates of Academic Achievement Among Mexican-American Secondary School Students," *Journal of Educational Psychology*, 53:144–149; 1962. The purpose of this study was to determine personal and maternal correlates of academic achievement among Mexican-American secondary school students. Four groups (fifteen each) of achieving and low-achieving boys and girls were identified and equated in age, IQ, grade level, and courses taken. Employing standard objective measures, it was shown that achievers manifested reliably less hostility and more social maturity, intellectual efficiency, and conformity to rules. Achieving girls and underachieving boys appear to come from strong mother-dominated homes. Since these findings seem meaningful with respect to this subculture, it is suggested that such study of achievement in minority groups may better clarify the nature of relationships among hypothesized variables.

Golburgh, S. J., and Penney, J. F. "A Note on Counseling Underachieving College Students," *Journal of Counseling Psychology*, 9:133–138; 1962. Suggests attention to (1) reading disability, (2) study habits, (3) the degree to which the curriculum meets student interests, (4) techniques to keep the counseling on the subject of underachievement, (5) attention to that part of the student's ego which wants to succeed.

Heath, S. R. "The Reasonable Adventurer," *Journal of Counseling Psychology*, 6:3–12; 1959. After characterizing three types of failure-prone college students as the amiable noncommitter, the aggressive hustler, and the erratic plunger, the author discusses the status of the "reasonable adventurer," who has solved the problem of a balancing rhythm between impulse and control. The latter individual is able to apportion his risk-taking input to the expectation involved; consequently he has found the ideal program for optimum achievement.

Locke, E. A. "Some Correlates of Classroom and Out-of-Class Achievement in Gifted Science Students," *Journal of Educational Psychology*, 54:238–248; 1963. The forty-seven variables measuring intellectual abilities, personality traits, personal habits, and demographic characteristics were intercorrelated for a group of 112 gifted science students and developed into eleven factor index scores. These were correlated with classroom and out-of-class achievement factors developed in an earlier study. Vocabulary and self-control were found to be most highly related to classroom achievement, and school and city size and originality most highly related to out-of-class achievement. There were considerable differences between sexes in the obtained relationships.

Matthews, C. G. *Differential Performances of Non-Achieving Children on the*

Wechsler Intelligence Scale, Ph.D. thesis, Purdue University, 1958. Non-achieving children grouped under etiological headings, including emotional disturbances. IQ 94/99/96 was the highest of all groups for the emotionally disturbed. Most subtest scatter, least perseveration.

Peterson, "The Researcher and the Underachiever: Never the Twain Shall Meet," *Phi Delta Kappan,* 14:379–381; May, 1963. Critical review of studies, with numerous citations.

Phillips, B. N. "Sex, Social Class, and Anxiety as Sources of Variation in School Achievement," *Journal of Educational Psychology,* 53:316–322; 1962. The hypothesis that social class interacts with sex and anxiety to produce differences in school achievement was tested, utilizing a sample of 759 adolescents classified into eight subsamples involving two levels of anxiety and social class and both sexes. Eight measures of school achievement were employed, including standardized tests and teacher grades. The results supported two major findings of previous research: females had higher anxiety scores than males, and highly anxious Ss had lower achievement and intelligence scores. Both first- and second-order interactions between sex, social class, and anxiety were found. Difficulties were encountered in integrating these findings into anxiety theory, and certain proposals are offered to accomplish this.

Pippert, R., and Archer, S. "A Comparison of Two Methods for Classifying Underachievers with Respect to Selected Criteria," *Personnel and Guidance Journal,* 41:788–791; May, 1963. From a population of 126 ninth-grade students scoring 110 or over on the Otis, underachievers were identified (1) by low GPA or (2) by low achievement test score. Neither method identified the underachievers by the other method.

Powell, W. J., and Jourard, S. M. "Some Objective Evidence of Immaturity in Underachieving College Students," *Journal of Counseling Psychology,* 10:276–282; 1963. Twenty male and twenty female college underachievers were compared with similar numbers of adequately achieving students on measures of self-disclosure to parents and friends and security. There were no differences in mean scores between the underachieving and achieving students. However, significant correlations were found between measures of disclosure to parents and security among the underachievers only. In the achieving groups, significant correlations were found between disclosure to peers and security. The findings were construed as evidence for lack of emancipation from parents on the part of the underachievers.

EMOTIONALLY DISTURBED children constitute a category recognized only recently. Besides the social importance of rehabilitation, however, the technical importance of this problem arises from techniques developed for identification and therapy which have applications to other types of exceptional children. The identification problem has been cared for in this chapter by two papers illustrative of the general method, those of Bower and of Weisbrod. The therapy aspects are most clearly indicated by the paper of Hollister and Goldston, especially in the appendix, which represents a part of the original manuscript. Students of this subject should consult other works of Bower and Hollister (both of whom are at the National Institute of Mental Health) for additional contributions to diagnosis and therapy. The Golburgh paper is a useful contribution to the vocational aspects of adult guidance for disturbed patients. Llorens and Rubin contribute a discussion of activity programs for disturbed children. The developments in this area show graphically what can be done in a short time through the influence of an organization such as the National Institute of Mental Health in opening up the guidance possibilities for these children and in providing a guideline for similar guidance procedures in other areas.

23. How Emotionally Handicapped Children Can Be Identified and Diagnosed *

ELI BOWER and others, *Consultant, National Institute of Mental Health*

EARLY IDENTIFICATION is essential if the school is to provide for the emotionally handicapped child maximum help in making school progress commensurate with his ability. The later the identification, the greater the handicap and the less likely the school will be able to provide the required help through its regular educational, psychological, and administrative services.

California schools employ established procedures for making early identification of children with hearing and vision handicaps. As a first step, screening tests are used to identify the children who may be handicapped by either of the causes. The difficulties thus identified are reported to the children's parents, and their assistance is sought in securing a diagnosis of the child's condition. For example, the Snellen chart and the Plus Spheres test are used in determining which children are likely to have less than normal vision and are therefore handicapped in their schoolwork in some degree, perhaps to the point of failure. The condition of the children found to be visually handicapped is reported to their parents, and the parents' assistance is sought in securing diagnoses by specialists and the correction possible. Where full correction of the difficulty is impossible, the school takes such steps as it can to help the children. In some instances, special consideration may be given to the child in the regular classroom. In others, the necessary provisions are made in special classes. The important point is that the child with a visual handicap is identified early in his school life or soon after the onset of the handicap and given the help he needs before his difficulty has involved him in a multiplicity of problems.

Some plan similar in nature to those used for the identification of visually and aurally handicapped children should be developed for the early identification of emotionally handicapped children. The schools should then be

* Reprinted by permission of the author and the State of California Department of Education and excerpted from *The Education of Emotionally Handicapped Children* (Sacramento: The California State Department of Education, March, 1961).

in a position to take the required steps to provide each child the special help he needs at a time when it would do the greatest good.

The procedures for early identification of children who are emotionally handicapped to the extent that they are having difficulty in doing schoolwork entail two separate but interrelated steps. The first of these steps involves the use of a screening procedure to identify the children who are having difficulty in school probably because of emotional handicaps. The second of these steps involves identifying the children in this group whose emotional handicaps are sufficiently great to cause extreme difficulty in school or even failure. When these steps are followed, the amount of effort expended and the costs of making the necessary identification are held to a minimum. In screening, coarse but better than rule-of-thumb measures that can be rapidly administered to large numbers of individuals are used. In such a process, the attempt is to identify all children who are having or will have learning difficulties because of emotional handicaps, including those children whose problems or severity of difficulties may not be readily apparent to teachers or parents. Administration of valid and reliable screening instruments and cross-checking the results with other data, such as the school records of the children's difficulties in learning and in working with others, are the essential mechanics of effective screening.

Once a child is identified by screening as emotionally handicapped, his parents are advised of the nature of the finding, and a plan is developed for individual study of the child and his difficulty. This study can be made by the appropriate school staff or by community mental health or private agencies. The specific purpose of the study is to determine the nature and extent of the child's problem, steps most likely to remedy or reduce the problem, and the best procedures by which the school and the child's teacher can provide for him the educational opportunities that will give him the help he needs to progress at the rate and to the point that his potential permits.

Research studies made by Rogers, Ullmann, Smith, Bower, and others have demonstrated the effectiveness of school screening procedures in the identification of emotionally handicapped children. Some of these procedures were subjected to analysis by Bower, Tashnovian, and Larson in 1954 and reported in a bulletin published by the California State Department of Education. As part of this project, it was noted that although many instruments and ratings were available for screening purposes, few were used by teachers because of the time requirements and the difficulty of administering them and because most of the instruments were better suited for diagnostic purposes than for screening. It was also found that practices in which both the separate and combined teacher, peer, and self-perceptions were utilized were best for screening purposes. The problem for this study, however, was to develop instruments which the teacher could use successfully in the regular classroom situation. The following ten conditions were, therefore, set up for the development of screening instruments and procedures.

1. The information to be collected by the teacher would be usable with large samples of school children, and the instruments used for collecting the data would be designed for group administration.

2. If so desired, the teacher could administer and score the screening instruments with little or no help from administrative or psychological personnel.

3. The administration and scoring of rating scales and tests would require a minimum amount of time and work on the part of the teacher.

4. The data should be obtainable as part of regular classroom routine and not involve the teacher in extra classroom duties, extra home visits, or individual test administration.

5. The data collected should help the teacher to obtain a comprehensive perceptual picture of the child from as many sources as is economically possible.

6. The data collected would not involve the use of questions pertaining to information of a highly personal nature to parents or children.

7. The major purpose of collecting the data should be to identify children with emotional handicaps, not to diagnose them.

8. Screening would provide for earlier referrals of children in need of help to sources prepared to give the help required.

9. The information collected should be of such a nature that, in collecting and analyzing the data, the teacher would gain a better understanding of each child and be better able to provide for him the help he needs.

10. Collecting and analyzing the data should motivate the teacher to seek help for children with moderate or severe emotional handicaps.

All instruments employed in this study were designed, developed, and utilized specifically for the purpose of identifying children with moderate to severe emotional maladjustment. The instruments used at different grade levels are perceptually similar but are geared to the intellectual and maturity level of the children. With one exception, each of the instruments met the ten conditions set forth.

Three types of instruments are used for screening purposes. These instruments are designed to collect three different perceptions of each child in a classroom: the teacher's perception of the child's day-to-day behavior, classmates' perceptions of the child's classroom and school behavior, and the child's self-perception. On the basis of previous studies of the screening procedure on large school populations, a ranking method has been found to be most effective for combining scores for screening. Children who score above a certain rank on any two or three of the screening instruments are those who are likely to be handicapped emotionally and therefore need diagnosis. The population thus selected through the screening process will include between 10 and 15 per cent of the school population.

The instruments employed in this research study were developed specifically for the purposes of this study. They are as follows.

Teacher Rating: *Behavior Rating of Pupils*—all grade levels

Self-Ratings: *Picture Game*—primary grades
              Thinking About Yourself—elementary grades
              A Self Test—secondary grades

Peer Ratings: *Class Pictures*—primary grades
              Class Play—elementary grades
              Student Survey—secondary grades

A summary of the conclusions reached in this study of the use and effectiveness of the screening process follows.

1. It is possible and practical for the regular classroom teacher to use screening instruments to locate in the general school population those children who are most vulnerable to or handicapped by emotional problems. To administer all the screening instruments takes about 45 minutes of class time for the students and about three hours of work for the teacher. No special training is necessary for the teacher, and he is not required to make judgments that go beyond his responsibilities as a teacher.

2. The screening tests for primary, elementary, and secondary grades which were developed and tested during this research project on the education of emotionally handicapped children are as reliable as most standardized ability and achievement tests commonly used in school.

3. The validity of the screening procedure has been subjected to many different tests. Nine out of ten children who were identified through the screening process were found to have moderate to severe emotional problems on the basis of individual studies. By cross-checking school referrals of children with emotional problems, it was found that seven out of ten children who had moderate to serious emotional problems and who were identified by the screening instruments had not been identified or reported by the principals or school psychologists. It was evident that without some

screening procedure a great proportion of children who need guidance services or school assistance because of their emotional difficulties would be missed.

4. The screening procedure enables the teacher to identify children with a variety of emotional problems. Each instrument used will help the teacher to identify children with specific kinds of emotional problems. For example, teachers and peers are sensitive to all the types of emotional handicaps described [earlier], and children themselves are aware of some kinds of emotional difficulties of a more intrapersonal nature.

5. Blind analyses of children identified through the screening procedure corroborate the effectiveness of the procedure. A total of thirty pairs of pupils were tested by two clinical psychologists without the psychologists having prior knowledge of the school histories or case histories of the children. In each pair, one pupil had been selected through the screening procedure and the other picked at random from the class. The psychologists were able to identify correctly twenty-seven out of thirty children who were selected through the screening procedure at the primary and elementary grade levels. When the psychologists' ratings for each pupil were totaled, the scores for the group of children who were identified through the screening process and those of the children picked at random were significantly different. Research evidence of this kind indicates that through the screening procedure children are identified who have real emotional difficulties of a variety of types and of sufficient magnitude to warrant diagnostic study.

6. A screening procedure is an essential phase of the total program for emotionally handicapped pupils. Research evidence indicates that without an effective screening procedure, a significant number of pupils with moderate or severe emotional handicaps are not identified. When a screening procedure to identify children in need of clinical study is employed, the amount of school staff time necessary to identify emotionally handicapped children is minimized, and the results are obtained with the expenditure of considerably less time for the school and the staff than otherwise possible. The process also eliminates unnecessary work by the specialists whose responsibility is to make a diagnosis of the children indicated by the screening procedure as likely to be emotionally handicapped.

7. The use of screening processes is helpful in getting teachers involved in the educational needs of children with emotional handicaps before the problem has become sufficiently severe or ingrained to be relatively unreachable. The involvement of the teacher is at this point positive, less motivated by frustration and anxiety, and conducive to the seeking of positive ways of educating the child.

24. Vocational Counseling with Psychiatric Students *

STEPHEN J. GOLBURGH, *Assistant Professor of Psychology, Boston University*

WHILE PSYCHIATRY has enabled large numbers of patients to leave mental hospitals, much remains to be done if they are to take their places as independent and productive members of society. Vocational counseling is a logical step to aid these individuals in becoming self-sufficient. This, however, is not easy to accomplish, since it requires a great deal of time and effort.

It is not enough for a counselor to see a patient, ask some questions, suggest an occupation, make phone calls, and get the patient a job. This can hardly be called vocational counseling. Such a perfunctory service is likely to be totally unsuccessful vocationally, therapeutically, and educationally.

Relationship and Scope

The counselor–patient relationship is more important and delicate in working with psychiatric patients than with normal people. Working with the patient for counselor satisfaction instead of working for patient satisfaction introduces negative factors into the relationship. These factors interfere with the counselor's potential usefulness in the undertaking.

It is important for the counselor to focus on the vocational problem. If he is acting as therapist, that is another matter; but when he is doing vocational counseling, he will be most successful if he focuses chiefly on that sector of the patient's life. This is not stated dogmatically, since human problems cannot be disconnected from each other, and vocational problems seem to represent and often symbolically duplicate more basic disturbances. This does not mean that they cannot be treated with a resulting beneficial effect on the more basic problems. The counselor can and at times needs to deal with other material, but he must focus on the vocational problem and its many ramifications.

When vocational counseling is indicated, it should be begun as early as

* Reprinted by permission of the author and *Vocational Guidance Quarterly*, 11:216–218; Spring, 1963.

possible. Psychiatrists sometimes refer patients for counseling two or three weeks before they are to be discharged from the hospital. It is usually impossible to accomplish anything in so short a period. It is the counselor's responsibility to aid the therapeutic team in understanding the need for early referral.

The Process

The counselor provides a permissive and human relationship where the patient is helped to talk freely and thoroughly about his vocational difficulties. The counselor's attitude should be one of sincere interest and vital concern. He should have a personal need to be of value to the patient. These attitudes cannot be successfully feigned, and probably no counselor can experience them toward all patients. When he cannot, it is best for him to refer the patient to another counselor.

The counselor helps the patient in a somewhat organized process of exploration and stocktaking. He talks with the patient about what the patient has thought of doing, what he has done in the past, and what he feels he would like to do. They talk about his hobbies, leisure-time activities, previous educational background, present skills, possibilities of future training, persistent and pertinent fantasies, and available opportunities. Above all, the counselor attempts to understand the patient's feelings and the degree of meaningfulness and significance they have for him.

This stocktaking is much more than a data-gathering procedure. While different theorists explain it in different ways, something does seem to happen in such an atmosphere that is helpful to patients in understanding their feelings about work, with the result that they are better able to handle their lives in the vocational sphere.

The counselor helps the patient to integrate what has been discussed. This is very difficult to accomplish. What it implies is putting this information together in a meaningful way while taking into consideration the patient's emotional reactions, his assets and liabilities, and reality factors. In the final analysis, vocational counseling may be regarded as a kind of sector psychotherapy in the area of vocational adjustment.

Psychological Testing

Psychological testing can be helpful in this process. Interpretation of results of test batteries must be done quite tentatively with psychiatric patients. Patients should be helped to draw conclusions primarily on the basis of their own experience and feelings rather than on the basis of psychological tests. Test results are useful in verifying what has been decided upon, in opening new areas for discussion, and in reconsidering plans that have been decided against.

Care must be taken to avoid overrating tests, especially when they are applied to psychiatric patients on whom they have not been sufficiently studied in terms of reliability and validity. To illustrate: if a patient shows, by means of psychometric tests, a high interest in the mechanical area supported by a high score on a mechanical aptitude test, the counselor is justified in suggesting to the patient that this area is one he might consider and talk about. The counselor is not justified in telling him he should enter mechanical work.

Implementation of Team Approach

The information that the vocational counselor and patient can obtain from the occupational therapist, psychotherapist, social worker, and nurse seems to be useful in the same way as are psychological tests. From these specialists the counselor can learn something about what interests the patient acts upon, what his physical and emotional tolerances are, what the environmental situation is like, and how other psychodynamic factors are related to his vocational conflicts.

The industrial therapist plays a significant role as he is able to provide patients with actual job experiences and thus add important information. Clear communication between disciplines lessens conflicts between personnel and facilitates the patient's progress.

Supplying Information

The counselor must at times supply the patient with certain types of information. It is surprising how little psychiatric patients often know about the kinds of work that are available and what people who have specific job labels actually do.

When information has been integrated and when plans are formulated in such a way that they seem appropriate to both counselor and patient, the problem arises of the patient's actually getting a job. It is usually better if the counselor does not arrange jobs for his patients, although there are, of course, exceptional cases. The counselor should rather continue talking with the patient about jobs, about feelings and attitudes toward work, fellow workers, making applications, having interviews, and perhaps about being accepted or rejected.

There are also mundane but nonetheless important factors which the counselor needs to discuss with the patient. For example, where to get job leads, how to apply, how to fill out application blanks, and how to dress for an interview. Role-playing employment interviews can be quite helpful to some patients, especially adolescents.

Follow-up

The counselor's work has not ended when the patient finds an appropriate job. The number of psychiatric patients who have unsuccessful vocational experiences could be reduced if counselors would continue to see them regularly after they begin working. This is the time when their feelings in relation to the vocational situation are actually brought to the fore. The problem is no longer "What will happen to me when I am working?" but rather "Look what is happening to me right now." Patients often need help in dealing with such feelings. It is useful for some discharged patients to see the vocational counselor at intervals, perhaps bimonthly, for an extended period after hospital discharge and successful placement.

Vocational counseling should not be considered unsuccessful because a patient loses one or even several jobs after his discharge from the hospital. This experience, though difficult, can provide important material for discussion and can be worked out so that unsuccessful patterns of behavior become more controllable for the patient.

As stated earlier, vocational counseling with psychiatric patients is a complicated and extended process. If we expect to help patients with this significant aspect of their lives, we must be prepared to expend the amount of time this process requires.

25. Psychoeducational Processes in Classes for Emotionally Handicapped Children*

WILLIAM G. HOLLISTER, *Chief, Research Utilization Branch, National Institute of Mental Health, Bethesda, Maryland*

STEPHEN E. GOLDSTON, *Training Specialist, Pilot and Special Grants Section, Training Branch, National Institute of Mental Health, Bethesda, Maryland*

Is THERE a unique educational methodology for emotionally handicapped children? Are there some specific procedures for working with emotionally handicapped children which differ significantly from those usually employed in the regular classroom? Is there merit to the use of the term *special education* in our approach to this group?

In search for answers to these questions, we reviewed and analyzed a sample of program descriptions from schools, located in various sections of the country, that are currently providing classes for emotionally handicapped children. Twelve of the programs reviewed are in public school systems, while six are in private day or residential settings (see List I). In addition, we studied more abbreviated reports from fifty other classroom programs for emotionally handicapped children. A number of the listed programs were visited to supplement our information. We also discussed these three questions personally with a number of the mental health and educational leaders in this field: Birch, Bower, Cruickshank, Deno, Dunn, Jones, Lambert, Mackie, Morse, Newman, Phillips, Rabinovitch, Rashkis, Redl, Reynolds, Rhodes, Trippe, and others.

By gently pursuing the deceptively simple questions: "What are you trying to do with these children? How are you going about the doing? What do you think is happening?" we became aware that (1) a considerable range of different procedures is being tried and (2) communication between various investigators and practitioners is extremely limited. It is also evident that a considerable number of schools throughout the nation have initiated classes for emotionally handicapped children, but most have not described their activities in sufficient detail to permit a thorough analysis of these

* Reprinted with permission of the authors and *Exceptional Children,* 28:251–256; March, 1962.

programs. Nonetheless, the brief descriptions available provided some clues to the wide variety of approaches and practices now being used.

Pamphlet Available

By focusing our attention on trends or on areas of common concern and practice, we were able to identify certain commonalities and gaps in these various classroom programs. We became aware that some system of description of the various psychoeducational processes being used was sorely needed in order to implement planning, communication, and preparation of teachers for such classes and for evaluative research. Therefore, we undertook the task of organizing the data from existing reports into a "beginning taxonomy" of the procedures and considerations involved in conducting classes for emotionally handicapped children.

The result of our efforts is a lengthy outline of the processes, factors, and procedures being employed or advocated for use in various classes for emotionally handicapped children. Through the insight and courtesy of The Council for Exceptional Children, this material has been gathered into a pamphlet entitled *Some Basic Considerations in Planning and Studying Classes for Emotionally Handicapped Children,* which is available from their headquarters office. We should like to emphasize that this document is only a preliminary taxonomy which has been collected, organized, and published principally to stimulate the various professions involved to do more definitive work.

It is our hope that this classification of procedures will enable school administrators and teachers to effect more comprehensive planning of their programs and that this outline will help teacher-educators to broaden their programs of preparing teachers to work with emotionally handicapped children. Beyond this, we hope such a taxonomy will set in motion more efforts at program description, inspire some comparative studies, and stimulate research to evaluate these various proposals and procedures.

The Psychoeducational Processes

In our attempt to order the data we had collected, it was necessary to erect a classification of the essential psychoeducational processes we found to be operating in these various programs. Eventually, we settled on the twelve principal processes described below, which we grouped into Administration, Pupil Selection and Study, Classroom Operations, and Supportive Operations. We were not able to order our information into mutually exlusive categories, nor was it possible to integrate procedures based on uch widely diverse premises into a unified approach. The sections that ollow represent an attempt to summarize and combine the best features nd procedures of the programs studied into a meaningful continuum. The rincipal headings in the pamphlet have been abstracted and are presented elow to provide a quick overview of the material available.

LIST I—DESCRIPTIVE PROGRAM REPORTS REVIEWED

Public School Classes
    California—Fontana Unified School District
    New York—New York City "600" Schools—East Meadow Public Schools
    Michigan—Lansing Public Schools—Detroit Public Schools
    Minnesota—Minneapolis Public Schools
    Missouri—Kansas City Public Schools
    Illinois—Chicago Public Schools—Quincy Public Schools
    Virginia—Arlington County Public Schools
    Wisconsin—Milwaukee Public Schools
    New Jersey—Wayne Township Public Schools
    Massachusetts—Newton Public Schools

Private School Classes
    New Jersey—The Forum School, Paterson
    Tennessee—Nashville Mental Health Center
    Rhode Island—Bradley Home, Providence (residential)
    Massachusetts—Gaebler School, Metropolitan Hospital, Waltham
    Florida—Montanari Clinical School, Hialeah (residential)
    New York—The League School, New York City

DMINISTRATION

1. Administrative Processes. The initiation, organization, planning, co-rdination, and operation of classes for emotionally handicapped children equires intensive and extensive administrative implementation. Since the levelopment of policy and program in this area involves not only the school dministrators and the school board but also considerable interdisciplinary nvolvement and community backing, the mechanisms of decision making nd plan implementation need to be clearly formulated. Consideration eeds to be given to the following important administrative areas: legal esponsibility; need assessment; definition of program goals and objectives; taff and consultant involvement in program development; policy develop-nent; designation of administrative and technical authority and responsibili-ies; administrative placement of the program; responsibilities for liaison nd co-ordination; relationships with pupil personnel, school health, and nstructional staffs; staffing patterns; teacher selection; staff role relation-

ships; staff development programs; personnel practices to fit a more difficu
teacher role; communication mechanisms; budget; administrative reviev
program evaluation by staff; as well as provision of such auxiliary service
as transportation and food service.

PUPIL SELECTION AND STUDY

2. Screening and Diagnosis. Need assessment and program develor
ment involve provisions for screening the school or community populatic
to detect already emotionally handicapped children and to identify childre
who are "susceptible or vulnerable" to emotional disorder so that early c
preventive help can be given. A screening program entails defining th
group to be screened, choosing the screening methods, training the pe
sonnel to be used, interpreting to parents and children, and establishin
criteria of which children shall be given individual study. Full develor
ment of the diagnostic aspect of the program encompasses not only separat
educational, medical, psychological, and psychiatric appraisals but a cor
certed attempt to define educational and psychological assets and deficier
cies. Emphasis is on usable descriptions instead of classifications and score
Such a diagnostic program involves use of referral resources and interprete
tions and clearances with parents as well as the difficult task of mobilizin
and co-ordinating the efforts of an interdisciplinary group to evolve
comprehensive diagnosis.

3. Planning, Placement, and Continuous Assessment Processe
The formulation of recommendations and plans for care and educatior
based on the individual needs of each child, is contingent upon integratin
diverse diagnostic findings into a meaningful picture of the pupil and th
selection of feasible goals for extending help that are appropriately matche
to the resources available. Procedures are required to integrate a multi
disciplinary working diagnosis and plan, to define the range of resource
and the indications for their use, to determine placements and to involv
the staff who receive the pupil in the rationale for placement, to translat
recommendations into action plans, to interpret to parents, and to evaluat
periodically both the diagnosis and the placement.

CLASSROOM OPERATIONS

This broad category encompasses a variety of closely related processe
often not mutually exclusive, which foster the education and adjustment c
the emotionally handicapped child.

4. The Relationship-Building Process. Much of the success of th
educational program rests upon the skill and ability of the teacher to estab

lish with the pupil a mutually perceived climate of trust, understanding, and empathy. The various procedures involved in this relationship building include: steps to prepare the child for relationships before entering the class, patterns of introducing new children into the class, methods to increase psychological safety, ways of setting up expected behaviors, factors associated with the grouping process, provision of direct emotional support by the teacher, diagnosing and reinforcing areas of personality strength, utilization of rewards and reinforcement, and group cohesion-building patterns.

5. The Motivation-Development Process. Emotionally handicapped children frequently require special efforts to free and nurture their motivation to learn and to achieve meaningful relationships with others. Such special efforts include procedures to utilize interest assessment techniques and to employ clinical knowledge of the child's psychodynamics as cues to defenses needing strengthening or impulses requiring reinforcement that can be used as motivations for learning. A group of procedures, varying from those designed to utilize stimulus deprivation to ways of focusing or heightening responses, have been developed under the category of "motivational lure methods."

6. The Perceptual Retraining Process. Distortions in perceptual abilities may be either the cause or the result of a child's emotional handicap. Procedures for diagnosing perceptual deficits are available, and educational methods have been evolved to train or retrain the pupil to overcome some of the perceptual distortions that interfere with his learning.

7. The Classroom Behavior Management Process. Most emotionally handicapped children show impaired behavior control and capacity for relationships with others. In order to release energy and time for learning, the teacher must frequently provide structure and firm guidance for the pupil's behavior. She needs to use her understanding of individual and group functioning to lessen and prevent maladaptive behavior that interferes with relationships, group productivity, and individual learning. The procedures include structuring expected behaviors, use of peer controls, group-wide guidance methods, control of group misbehavior, and methods for coping with poor individual behavior. Many of the procedures under the following section also contribute to behavior management in a preventive way.

8. The Behavior Re-education Process. Some antisocial or asocial behavior can be regarded as a defect due to incomplete or improper learning. The amelioration of these disturbances often requires corrective learning experiences provided through a gradual, planned process of behavior re-education. Emotionally handicapped children frequently must unlearn inappropriate behaviors and learn new behavior patterns which maximize their potential to effect those attitudes and behaviors which will enhance their personal well-being, usefulness, and acceptance. Procedures placed within this process have been grouped as anticipatory guidance education, planned corrective learning experiences, and general education on personal and social behavior.

9. The Academic Education Process. The special class shares with the regular educational activities the objective of transmitting our cultural heritage and knowledges. Often an emotionally handicapped child will have significant capacities and energies still available for intellectual growth. To meet the needs of an emotionally handicapped child, a detailed educational diagnosis is needed in order to develop an individualized curriculum for him. The procedures in this process are tutoring methods, remedial education methods, and the use of special methods and materials. Efforts which increase the child's cognitive, memory, evaluative, and other thinking abilities become ego strengths which can be used by him in coping with and solving some of his life adjustment problems.

10. The Process of Rehabilitation to the Regular Classroom. The task of social, emotional, and educational rehabilitation to the regular classroom and school life is a gradual process which demands careful planning, involving both the special and regular education staffs, the clinical personnel, and the family. The procedures of rehabilitation include the establishment of criteria for transfer, planning for and methods of returning to the regular class, procedures for returning the pupil to the special class as needed, preparation of the regular teacher, and provisions for follow-up guidance and evaluation.

SUPPORTIVE OPERATIONS

Although Administration and Pupil Selection and Study are supportive in nature, the following two procedures are important operations which are supportive to the teacher working in the classroom.

11. The Clinician-Educator Liaison Process. A special class program for emotionally handicapped children requires a close working relationship between a clinical team and the education staff. Planning for each child is a continuous process, a joint multidisciplinary responsibility, that must deal progressively with the changes in personality and other psychosocial factors affecting the course of the child as he progresses through various stages of his problem and into the rehabilitation process. The following operations implement this process: use of conferences and consultations, use of group and individual supervision methods, therapeutic opportunities and supports for teachers, periodic case reviews, in-service training methods, and joint data-collecting and research efforts.

12. The School-Home Liaison Process. The development of communication with the home and the supplementary extension of special service to the parents complement and extend the impact of the school program and help to mitigate factors in the home which may work against the psychoeducational processes being used at school. Various procedures such as periodic interview programs, use of parents' group activities, provision of parent counseling, therapy, case work, or nursing services, as well as the use of parent-aides and home-school reporting systems are used to effect this liaison.

Summary

Our attempts to explore the current status of educational programs for emotionally handicapped children revealed to us the need for some orderly classification of the various psychoeducational processes we found being used in such programs. We have developed this beginning effort at a taxonomy of the methods used in these classes in the hope that this preliminary outline will be of value to those currently planning and operating programs and to those attempting to describe and evaluate the procedures being used in these classes. In addition, this categorization may be helpful to those exploring the issues related to the training and qualifications needed for teachers of the emotionally handicapped.

Returning to the three questions posed at the beginning of this paper, we believe there are emerging out of the rich variety of current practices some unique or special procedures for use in these classes and that the term *special education* is justifiably applied to this work. Since a look at educational history reveals that yesterday's special education procedure frequently became today's standard class method, it would be wise to reserve judgment about the eventual use of these procedures in general classes. It is quite possible that some of the motivational lure and perceptual retraining methods, along with the process of diagnosing and reinforcing ego strengths and using group development methods, might well be the precursors to methods that will someday be used in classes for all children.

We are certain this outline deserves further refinement and elaboration. Improving its semantics and resolving its theoretical heterogeneity will require considerable future effort. In essence, we believe we have outlined an important book needed in special education—a book whose chapter and verse will be written by creative educators and behavioral scientists within the next decade.

Appendix

The following section, lifted from the original monograph, is appended because of its excellent detailing of the various procedures which can be used by counselors with emotionally disturbed children.

CLASSROOM OPERATIONS

IV. THE RELATIONSHIP-BUILDING PROCESSES
   A. Initial Stage Prior to Classroom Exposure
      1. Home visiting—by teacher, diagnostic personnel
      2. Preopening school visits—parents and child visit school and empty classroom
      3. Individual hours with teacher before entering class—promoting a sense of familiarization and acceptance
      4. Play-group organization of class preceding classroom activity
      5. Pairing pupils for mutual support
   B. Patterns of Introducing Members to Classes
      1. Gradual—shortened school day
      2. By pairing children—"buddy" system
      3. Individual time with teacher first—precedes entering class situation
      4. Planned orientation experiences—acquainting newcomer with environs, structure, and other children in the class
   C. Methods to Increase Psychological Safety
      1. Strong emotional support
      2. Gradual weaning from home support
      3. Slow introduction of demands and expectations
      4. Low frustration, high reward, easy success tasks
      5. Small groups—minimize number of interpersonal relationships
      6. Opportunity to be alone, by oneself, not under pressure; "doing nothingness"
      7. Slow pace
      8. Setting limits
   D. Setting Up Expected Behaviors
      1. Through instruction—example, repetition, doing
      2. Role playing
      3. Through group discussion and adoption

E. Grouping Process
   1. Criteria for grouping—including an awareness of the history of the children's significant relationships
   2. Situations demanding grouping
   3. Use of sociometrics
   4. Experimentation in grouping
F. Use of Emotional Support from Teacher
   1. Warm sympathetic approach vs. avoiding an anxiety-provoking relationship
   2. Recognition and verbalization of child's feelings
   3. Quiet nonthreatening, nonverbal use of self and communication by the teacher
   4. "Protective mothering"—proximity
   5. Reassuring touch
   6. Verbal reassurance
G. Preparing Group for New Members
   1. Creation of attitude of tolerance to new members—rewards associated with entrance of new member, e.g., group rituals, parties, etc.
H. Diagnosing and Reinforcing Areas of Ego Strength
   1. Determination of areas of strength
   2. Development and implementation of an individualized curriculum based on pupil's past successes, interests, and strengths
I. Using Sociometrics
   1. In regrouping to deal with isolates, cliques, and power groups
   2. In building compatible groups and relationships
J. Use of Rewards and Reinforcement to Build Relationships
   1. Privileges—games, trips, etc.
   2. Increased responsibility commensurate with level of adjustment
K. Use of Common Tasks and Activities to Build Group Cohesion
   1. Singing, "show and tell," projects, bulletin board, decorations, and scrapbooks, etc.
   2. Discussion and study of the emotional and social problems pupils face (*Quincy, Wayne*)—seeking out and verbalizing commonalities—"leveling" function
V. THE MOTIVATION-DEVELOPMENT PROCESS
   A. Interest Assessment
      1. By observation—teachers and clinical personnel
      2. Instruments—interest inventories, etc.
      3. Interviews
      4. Trials and experiences—exposing children to a wide variety of educational experiences. (Through share-and-tell sessions, interviews, and observations, teachers attempt to find some area of behavior that is particularly satisfying to the student—(*Arlington*)

B. Use of Clinical Data As Cues to Motivation

   1. Recognition and utilization by the teacher of the defenses which a pupil is motivated to use

   2. Recognition of the feelings, drives, and conflicts that guide a pupil's behavior choice and that can be employed by the teacher to motivate learning

C. Motivational Lure Methods

   1. Use of high-stimulus-value cues

   2. Use of high-reward stimuli

   3. Graded tasks—early quick success progressing to difficult, delayed success

   4. Use of transference on the staff to redirect pupils' activities (use of students' crushes on teachers). (Yet care not to interfere with transference between the child and the therapist—*Milwaukee*.)

   5. Transfer of interest from one goal to another by association (pairing of tasks)

   6. Use of familiar tasks and materials as an approach to new tasks

   7. Task closure—demand completion approach (*Newton PS*)

   8. Meeting new experiences while paired with a closely related adult

   9. Imitation lure—encouraging identification

   10. Curiosity focusing and production lure

   11. Attention focus by limiting stimulation—add Cruickshank's cubicles—Rhodes's low-stimulus rooms and direct suggestion

VI. THE PERCEPTUAL RETRAINING PROCESS

A. Perceptual Deficit Diagnosis

   1. Instruments used:

      (*a*) Pediatric history and examination

      (*b*) Neurological and EEG examination

      (*c*) Psychiatric evaluation

      (*d*) Speech and hearing examination

      (*e*) Psychological examination including:

         Marble Board Tests (Strauss and Werner)

         Tactual Motor Test (Strauss and Werner)

         Tachistoscopic Test

         Bender-Gestalt Test

         WAIS Block Design and Digit Symbol Tests

         Draw-A-Person Test

         Benton Visual Retention Test

      (*f*) Intelligence evaluation

         Stanford Binet

         Ammons Full-Range Picture Vocabulary Test

        (*g*) Personality evaluation
           Rorschach Test
           Vineland Social Maturity Scale
        (*h*) Educational achievement
           Stanford Achievement Test
           Metropolitan Readiness Test

   2. Analysis of findings and translation into classroom program

B. Specific Programs to Deal with Deficit

   1. Measures to counteract distractibility and attention loss. (Individual cubicles equipped with built-in student desks fitted to the cubicle walls—*Cruickshank.*)

   2. Attention-span lengthening through drills

   3. Perceptual retraining programs

     (*a*) Use of form board programs

     (*b*) Tachistoscopic discrimination training
         (figure background, form discrimination, etc.)

     (*c*) Use of high-stimulus materials

     (*d*) Drill sequences and reinforcement methods; workbook, teaching machines

VII. THE CLASSROOM BEHAVIOR MANAGEMENT PROCESS

A. Teacher Structuring of Expected Behaviors

   1. Freedoms defined and provided

   2. Limits set—methods established for maintaining limits

   3. Placing day's educational program on blackboard each morning—build a sense of structure (*Milwaukee*)

   4. Assignment of well-defined tasks and homework (*Arlington*)

   5. "Regulation of behavioral and social traffic"—acting as a cop to provide children the basic rules (*Redl*)

   6. "Umpire services—mediation function" (*Redl*)

B. Use of Peer Controls, Group Behavior, and Guidance Methods

   1. Setting of a group behavior code

   2. Group "government" methods

C. Control of Behavior Contagion

   1. Through the use of sociometric and other data to guide regrouping, seating, etc.

   2. Change of seating and activity pace

   3. Restructuring tasks to meet individual needs

   4. Spatial control of class group

   5. Regrouping—on three levels (*Redl*):

     (*a*) Total regrouping—the exclusion of a youngster from an institution (or class) not necessarily because of the intolerability of his own behavior or his inaccessibility to treatment but because of the untenable complications which the clash between group psychological needs and his own pathology produces

(b) A shift in group composition within the institutional limits

(c) Distributional changes within a given group—subgroup factors are manipulated

D. Methods for Coping with Poor Behavior

  1. Social management methods

    (a) Rechanneling energies into acceptable activities—structuring and giving permission for new line of work, play, or relating

    (b) Reducing stimulation, limiting space and tools, reducing contacts

    (c) Deprivation of some privilege or task pupil likes to do (*Arlington*)

    (d) Isolation of the child to an isolated office adjacent to the general room with an assignment of work to do

    (e) "Antiseptic bouncing"—the removal of a child from a scene of conflict

      Criteria for removing a child:

      (1) Physical danger

      (2) Irritation through the group psychological scene

      (3) Uncheckable contagion effect

      (4) Need for a face-saving device

      (5) Limit rub-in

  2. Interpersonal methods

    (a) Direct appeal:

      (1) Appeal to a personal relationship

      (2) Physical reality limitations—"that's dangerous"

      (3) Outside role sensitivities—"people won't stand for that"

      (4) Superego demand and value sensitivity

      (5) Group code value

      (6) Narcissistic pride

      (7) Appraisal of community consequences

      (8) Awareness of peer group reaction

      (9) Hierarchical limitation awareness

      (10) Personal considerations

      (11) Pride in personal improvement

    (b) Physical control:

      (1) Restraining

      (2) Comforting

      (3) Isolation

    (c) Proximity and touch control: increasing the physical proximity between child and adult. Touch control: putting the arm around the child's shoulder or patting him on the shoulder in a friendly way while making a limiting demand

(*d*) Going with the child to quiet room to maintain relationship during behavior crises

(*e*) Authoritarian demand

(*f*) Personal conference

(*g*) Signal interference—the adult indicates a clear signal of unacceptability of certain behavior in a friendly way; this blocks the rising disorganization

(*h*) Tension decontamination through humor—"kidding the youngster out of it"

(*i*) Punishment and threats

(*j*) Promises and rewards

(*k*) "Hypodermic affection"—sometimes all that is needed for an ego or superego to retain control in the face of anxiety or impulse onrush is a sudden additional quantity of affection

(*l*) "Planned ignoring"—the skill of an adult in sizing up surface behavior and in limiting interference only to those behavioral trends which carry too heavy an intensity charge within themselves or which would not stop from their own exhaustion unless directly interfered with

3. Group methods

(*a*) Mobilization of peer pressure

4. Extraclassroom methods

(*a*) Direct psychotherapeutic intervention

(*b*) Psychopharmacological controls

VIII. The Behavior Re-education Process

A. Anticipatory Guidance Education

1. Educational experiences to prepare pupils for situations requiring certain expected behaviors

2. Use of stories, discussions, outlines, and role playing which depict desired behavior

B. Planned Corrective Learning Experiences

1. Detraumatizing

(*a*) Emotional desensitization and new learning

(*b*) Redoing well a previously hurtful and/or failure experience

(*c*) Planned limited re-exposure to traumatic situation or learning experience

(*d*) Desensitize to error making; ignore errors, omit grading devalue error made

(*e*) Denigration by humor—kidding the child out of tense response

2. Emotional need meeting re-education

(*a*) Diagnosing emotional need behind poor behavior—offering new legitimate channels and successes in meeting this need (*Louis Raths*)

3. Positive self-concept education
    (*a*) Promoting activities in which the child gets feedback regarding his potentials
    (*b*) Promoting activities helping the child to set up an ideal self-image (what he wants to be)
    (*c*) Manipulation of the boundaries of the self—includes "encouragement," inculcating a feeling of worthfulness and pride (*Redl*)

4. Coping mechanism or ego-strength-building education
    (*a*) "Reality rub-in"—the realities of a situation pointed out to the pupil in order to counteract the pupil's near-to-delusional misinterpretation of life (*Redl*)
    (*b*) "New-tool salesmanship"—helping a child see that there are other defenses than the ones he is using and that doing this may at least partially widen the youngster's adaptational skills (*Redl*)
    (*c*) "Symptom estrangement"—helping to alienate the child's ego from his symptoms—enlisting part of the child's insight into helping his ego want to liberate itself from the load of his pathology. Using many of his life situations to pile up evidence that his pathology really doesn't pay, or that he pays too heavily for what meager secondary gain he draws from it, or that the glee he is after can be much more regularly and reliably drawn from other forms or problem solving or pursuit of life and happiness (*Redl*)
    (*d*) Teaching child a way to use his thinking and doing to solve a problem—to substitute for a disorganized emotional response to a problem
    (*e*) Widening of the cognitive field (*Redl*)
    (*f*) "Massaging numb value areas"—pulling out of issues of fairness or similar values from the debris of the child's daily life events (*Redl*)
    (*g*) Interpretation as interference—helping the child understand the meaning of a situation which he has misinterpreted, or helping him grasp his own motivation in an issue
    (*h*) Hurdle help—help the child take care of frustrations coming from an actual problem-solving block

5. Social impact education (social sensitivity training)
    (*a*) Peer group feedback to child regarding impact of his behavior (Bethel "T" group, etc.)
    (*b*) Social adjustment classes and sessions

6. Social role training
   Restructuring and assisting child in new role in group (*Lippitt, Redl,* role-playing devices)
7. Frustration tolerance building
   (*a*) Graduated frustrations and gratification delay with emotional support and successes with new coping mechanisms (*Newton*)
   (*b*) Graduated introduction into group, into school, into regular classes
   (*c*) Introduction of competitive activities
8. Desensitization to avoidance responses (and the use of other defenses)
   (*a*) Step-by-step moving from the familiar and the similar toward the unfamiliar and the different (*Rhodes*)
9. Stimulus deprivation plus suggestion
   (*a*) Use of low-stimulus room or setting followed by corrective suggestion and trial with new behavior; including use of subliminal stimulation and reciprocal inhibition (*Rhodes; Milwaukee Public Schools; Cruickshank*)
10. Desensitization to adult figures (parents and teachers)
    (*a*) Pair with adults in activities requiring co-operation for reward
    (*b*) Verbal or writing experiences to safely describe counter-rejection followed by stereotype-breaking discussions: "What do parents think of me?" "How do they see themselves?" exercises
    (*c*) Breaking up undue spill-over (displacement) of hostility to new settings or person by use of sociometrics and group discussion
11. Reality-irreality differentiation lessons
12. Repetition-compulsion breaking experiences
    (*a*) Specifically structured classroom living experience by psychiatrist and teacher to make visible or set limits on a repetition currently being discussed in therapy
    (*b*) Devaluing conformity compulsion, offering alternatives
13. Group behavior code building—peer enforcement
14. Behavior consequence lesson units
15. Self-directed experiences—graded movement toward self-direction
    (*a*) Reinforcing satisfactions by giving the pupil time to indulge in this activity (*Arlington*)
16. Planned learnings to diminish the socialization and cultural deficit in the pupil's home life (*Quincy*)

        (*a*) Trips to store
        (*b*) Opportunities to use money and buy
    C. General Behavior Education
        1. Education for self-understanding and normal problems of living
           (includes personal hygiene, good health habits, good speech,
           responsibility for own actions)

26. A Directed Activity Program for Disturbed Children *

LELA A. LLORENS, *Head of Occupational Therapy, Lafayette Clinic, Detroit, Michigan*
ELI Z. RUBIN, *Chief of Division of Rehabilitation, Lafayette Clinic, Detroit, Michigan*

Introduction

SIMPLE MANIPULATION of objects in infancy is the basic exercise toward mastery of the skills of later life. Some emotionally disturbed children develop slowly in many areas and need a longer period of simple investigatory manipulation than would an average child in which to perfect coordination and manual skills.

It was in the interest of assessing the functional capabilities of the emotionally disturbed child in the area of manual skills and to what extent practice and mastery could improve the level of skill that a research study was undertaken with a group of eighteen children at the Lafayette Clinic.

The results of this study pointed toward the establishment of a graded activity program in occupational therapy, using a directive, group teaching approach which would encourage and contribute to the emotional growth of the child through the use of activities beginning at a level commensurate with the child's ability, allowing for successful accomplishment and mastery and presenting opportunities to raise his level of skill.

* Reprinted by permission of the authors and *American Journal of Occupational Therapy,* 16:287–290; November–December, 1962.

The program is designed to offer a step-by-step upgrading of skills which will allow the patient to move toward more age-appropriate functioning, independence, and increased feelings of adequacy.

Setting

The Lafayette Clinic is a research and training center providing intensive treatment for psychiatric patients, with a 25-bed unit for emotionally disturbed children. The children range in age from six to twelve years old and represent a variety of diagnostic categories, including chronic brain syndrome, childhood schizophrenia, early infantile autism, psychoneurotic reaction, and adjustment reaction of childhood.

The children receive intensive psychotherapy, also chemotherapy when indicated; and they participate actively in the activity therapy program which includes school, recreational therapy, and occupational therapy. These programs and others are co-ordinated by the division of rehabilitation.

Occupational Therapy Program

The occupational therapy activity program is designed to meet the specific needs of emotionally disturbed children. It has been stated that children may be frightened by too much freedom and lack of patterning in daily living. In an orderly environment, the child's anxieties may be lessened and his potentialities for growth and adjustment may be encouraged.

The over-all structure of the occupational therapy program is designed to provide patterning experiences through planned activities presented in a directive manner, with guidance and opportunity for practice and mastery. The over-all goal is aimed at improving the child's feelings of adequacy through improved skills and level of performance.

The children are grouped for occupational therapy primarily according to their particular needs pertaining to level of skill, motivation, and behavior, without regard to age or sex except in rare instances.

There are three basic groups within the activity program: (1) the basic skills group, (2) the intermediate skills group, and (3) the average skills group. The children in the first two groups are drawn from the entire population, regardless of age. The third group is reserved for the older children, of ten to twelve years. The size of the groups varies; however, eight is felt to be the maximum number that can be effectively worked with at one time. The children usually work seated around a table that easily accommodates eight.

The basic skills group, then, is composed of children six to twelve years old. These children have basically poor skills in manipulation, co-ordination, and motor control compared to that expected for their respective ages. They also demonstrate a high degree of distractibility, short attention span, and low frustration tolerance. They may be either hyperactive or inhibited in behavior and have low interest in participating in activities. All diagnostic categories are represented.

Their primary needs in the skill area are to develop the basic skills used in painting, drawing, cutting, and pasting; to increase awareness of sizes, shapes, form, and color; to practice and improve performance on previously learned skills. Simultaneously they show a need to increase attention span and frustration tolerance, to decrease distractibility, and to stimulate interest outside of self.

Activities

The activities used with this group are highly structured, repetitive, and nonstimulating. They consist of coloring pictures; tracing around objects; cutting out forms and pasting them into designs; drawing, stimulated by topics which are discussed and ideas from their own experiences; and modeling with plastic clay. These activities involve such visual motor skills as form recognition and discrimination. Other visual motor and visual perceptive activities are being considered and will be added to the program where most beneficial.

In coloring, the children are encouraged to stay within the lines, but color selection is usually left up to the child. In cutting out forms, the child is encouraged to cut on the lines. Suggestions are given to encourage experimentation with placement of shapes when pasting. Sample projects have proved quite helpful with this group and have not appeared to destroy the children's individuality, as they seldom copy the sample but rather use it as a model. Object lessons are used in clay modeling. For instance, when making animals, animals will be discussed, rubber animals are used to look at and handle, and then the children are encouraged to construct their own. The children often need help in placement of parts. The activities are planned and upgraded with thought toward helping the child learn and master skill techniques which will be reinforced by practice with each higher-level activity presented.

The intermediate skills group is also composed of children from six to twelve years old. These children have fair to good manual skills and coordination for their age levels, have a fair to good attention span, demonstrate some distractibility, and display some immaturity. The children placed in this group generally have some interest in participating in activities but may be poorly motivated.

The specific needs of this group are to further practice and master skills needed in painting, drawing, cutting, and pasting; to increase attention span; to decrease distractibility; and to increase relatedness to others.

The activities for this group are both structured and expressive. Drawing, painting, and paper crafts are utilized extensively. Drawing from their own experiences and in response to topic discussion is encouraged and stimulated verbally. Painting centers a great deal around the use of varied techniques such as yarn painting, rubber cement resist, and water color painting. Experimentation is encouraged, and opportunity for mastery is provided.

The children are encouraged to find expression using the varied craft media, to share tools and materials, occasionally to work together on a project, and frequently to help each other with activities. Adjustment in this group is essential to success in the average skills group.

The average skills group is composed of ten- to twelve-year-olds. These children have good skills relative to those expected for their ages; high interest; good motivation, attention span, and frustration tolerance; but they have a need to learn and practice self-organization and constructive independence. The specific aims for this group are to help maintain their positive functioning, increase independence and self-reliance, encourage group identification, increase interaction with peers, and encourage responsibility for their own behavior.

The activities for the average skills group are craft-oriented. The program is highly structured and is taught in units; however, within each unit there is much opportunity for creativity, self-organization, and independent functioning. The units taught are leathercrafts, metalcrafts, decorative printing techniques, creative art techniques, and ceramics and sculpture.

In decorative printing techniques, for instance, we begin with potato prints, then use linoleum block prints, then stenciling and silk screen process. These techniques are demonstrated to the group; the children then draw up their own designs, execute them, and experiment with them. The children are encouraged to build on each previously learned skill through association, repetition, and practice.

Evaluation

In order to determine which of these groups will most closely fit the needs of the newly admitted child, the occupational therapist observes the child's behavior and performance on two assigned tasks in a one- to two-hour evaluation session. The evaluation may be given with one to three children in one session. The first task is a drawing. The child is taken to the occupational therapy workroom, where paper, pencils, and crayons have been laid out for him. He is shown around the area, first, on a brief tour; then, when settled at the table, he is told in a general way about the occupational therapy activity program and about the various groups. He is introduced to the drawing activity and told that his picture may be about anything that he wishes. When the picture is completed, the child is asked to put his name on his picture and is given the second task.

The second task is a cut paper activity. The child is given a 12 by 18 inch sheet of construction paper and a pack of 4 by 5 inch sheets of paper in assorted colors. He is also given three sizes of circle patterns to trace. He is asked to trace as many circles as he can, cut them out, and paste them down, arranging them into a picture or design. The child is given pencils, scissors, and paste with this activity.

While the child is working, the therapist observes the child's reactions to the activity, his approach, his apparent interest, motivation, attention span, frustration tolerance, and degree of distractibility. The degrees of communication, relatedness, and reaction to limits are also observed and evaluated.

The child's performance on both tasks, along with behavioral observations generally, comprises the evaluation. From this information the decision is made as to which group the child will enter. This method has proved most helpful in placing children in the appropriate activity group early in hospitalization.

Special Considerations

Occasionally there are children in the hospital who are not ready to begin work in an activity group owing to their extremely short attention span, low frustration tolerance, hyperactivity, and high degree of distractibility. When this occurs, individual help has been most beneficial, and the child is seen for his activities alone with the occupational therapist. The goal is to prepare the child for entrance into one of the established groups by increasing attention span and decreasing distractibility through the use of patterning experiences.

There are also children who have specific dynamic conflicts which can be appropriately worked through in the occupational therapy area. These children may also most profitably be seen on an individual basis for therapy. The problem of suppressed anger and hostility may be worked through using specific activities, or the child who is extremely inhibited or obsessive-compulsive in performance may be helped through a series of activities from controlled to less controlled to accept less inhibition and obsessive-compulsive performance without guilt. Because the techniques used with these children are aimed at dynamic emotional conflict, they are most effectively carried out with the full and complete supervision and co-operative guidance of the psychotherapist. This aspect of the program should complement rather than supplement the regular occupational therapy activity program.

The Role of the Occupational Therapist

In an activity program of this kind, the occupational therapist is in the role of an enabler. The enabler helps the group to learn new ideas and to develop new skills. The occupational therapist is active in the initial direction of an activity, acquainting the children with the techniques involved in acquiring a particular skill. He then becomes less and less active as the child practices the skill and moves toward mastery.

Using the group teaching approach allows for more independence on the part of the children in carrying out their activities. They have an opportunity, after the initial instructions, to plan and organize their projects on their own. Help is given in all cases when needed, but the children are encouraged to seek help from each other.

Discussion

The activity program just described is graded to provide incentive for growth within its structure. The activities for each group are specific to that group, and overlapping is avoided as much as possible. The children can then strive to "graduate" to the next group and know what to expect when they achieve this. The attitude of the occupational therapist is supportive but at all times attempting to contribute to the child's feeling of self-worth by encouraging decision making and independence of functioning.

Social interaction is greatly enhanced by the use of the directive teaching approach, as the children have an activity in common about which they can converse with peers. The activity presents similar problems to all; however, those who successfully solve their own can extend help to others. The seating arrangement enhances the child's relatedness to others and offers greater opportunity for verbal interaction with peers.

Summary

In this paper we have described a graded activity program in occupational therapy for emotionally disturbed children based on the findings of a previous research study relative to the needs of this disability group. The findings of that study pointed toward a structured activity program using a directive teaching approach which could bring about significant changes in skills leading to improved performance in a group of emotionally disturbed children in a relatively short period of time. The program herein described follows the recommendations of the study and has been developed to make a definite therapeutic contribution to the treatment of emotionally disturbed children.

27. The Identification of Potentially Maladjusted Children in the Middle Elementary Grades *

KENNETH C. WEISBROD, *Co-ordinator, Pupil Personnel Services, Riverside County Schools, Riverside, California*

Purpose

THIS PROJECT is to determine to what extent certain information available to teachers in their day-to-day contact with pupils could be used by them to identify potentially emotionally maladjusted children in the

* Reprinted by permission of the author; abstract of unpublished Ed.D. thesis, University of Maryland, 1958.

fourth, fifth, and sixth grades. A further purpose is to develop an actuary method of identification suitable for teacher use with the entire class without the aid of psychological or psychiatric assistance.

Procedure

Clinicians were asked to identify children enrolled in regular fourth-, fifth-, and sixth-grade classes who, in their estimation, were emotionally disturbed. Two hundred classes, in which clinically designated children were enrolled, were identified, and their teachers were asked to gather data on each child in the class with reference to multiple criteria related to the school setting. Information was gathered by the teachers during the school year 1954–1955 and included the following.

1. Scores on group-administered intelligence tests.
2. Scores on arithmetic and reading achievement tests.
3. Scores on *Thinking About Yourself,* a personality inventory distributed by the California State Department of Education.
4. Scores on *The Class Play,* a projective sociogram distributed by the California State Department of Education.
5. The number of days of absence reported for each child.
6. Age-grade relationship.
7. Socioeconomic status of the family as indicated by father's occupation.
8. Rating by teacher of the physical status of each child.
9. Rating by teacher of the adjustment status of each child.

All instruments were administered and scored as prescribed by the authors. Each of the factors above was analyzed, and weights were assigned to those having the capacity to discriminate between the clinically designated children and their classmates. Factors showing the highest discriminatory quality were used to develop an actuary method by which teachers might identify disturbed children in the classroom. Those children in the class who deviated markedly on the total product factor or in a pattern making up the total product factor were believed to be potentially emotionally maladjusted.

Findings

1. Intelligence. Maladjusted children deviated significantly from their classmates on results of group-administered intelligence tests.

2. *Achievement.* Maladjusted children scored significantly below their classmates in both reading and arithmetic. Greater differences existed between the two groups in arithmetic than in reading. Differences between the two groups tended to increase from the fourth through the sixth grade.

3. *Self-perception.* A significant difference was found between the maladjusted and other boys in the extent of discrepancy between the perceived self and the wished-for self. Greater discrepancies were found among maladjusted boys. Owing to a limitation in the instrument, no significant difference was found for maladjusted girls and other girls in their class.

4. *Peer Ratings.* Maladjusted children were perceived negatively by their peers, while other children in the classes were generally seen positively. Differences in the ratings of the two groups were found to be significant.

5. *Absence from School.* Differences in rate of absence between maladjusted children and their classmates were not found to be significant.

6. *Age-Grade Relationship.* There was no significant age-grade difference found between the maladjusted and other children.

7. *Socioeconomic Status of the Family.* No significant socioeconomic differences were found between the maladjusted and other children.

8. *Rating by Teacher of Physical Status of Each Child.* This factor failed to discriminate between maladjusted children and their classmates.

9. *Ratings by Teachers of Adjustment Status of Each Child.* Teachers and clinicians tended to identify the same children as maladjusted. Teachers identified 4.4 per cent of all children and 26 per cent of the maladjusted as aggressive or defiant. Teachers rated 61 per cent of the emotionally maladjusted group ($N = 207$) overly aggressive or defiant either "quite often" or "most of the time." Teachers indicated twice as many boys as girls in the total group to be overly aggressive "most of the time." Seven boys to one girl in the group of maladjusted children were so rated by teachers. In the maladjusted group, 25 per cent were rated overly withdrawn "quite often" or "most of the time."

Finding the factors of intelligence, achievement, peer rating, and teacher rating to differentiate significantly between the maladjusted and other children in the fourth, fifth, and sixth grades, these factors were used for the purpose of this study.

How Teachers Can Use Results

It should be emphasized that this study was conducted primarily for the purpose of developing a method by which teachers might identify potentially emotionally maladjusted children in the classroom. In the present form, it does not define the nature or causes of any given condition, as there are many factors to be considered in addition to those found to be valid by the present study. This method is, therefore, recommended to interested, inquiring teachers as a means for identifying children whose problems may have formerly gone unnoticed and for exploring suspicions about the adjustment of children regarding whom there may be some question.

This study found the following factors to be sufficiently significant to be used for discriminating between children who were emotionally maladjusted and other children: (1) intelligence, (2) achievement, (3) peer ratings (*The Class Play*), and (4) teacher ratings. This study did not make any determination of the order of importance of the items or the relationship between them, since it was designed to discover those factors which were discriminatory. As indicated herein, other studies are in order which will determine this matter. Even though such studies are needed, a good and fairly practical method can be recommended for teachers from the results of the present study.

The following procedure is suggested for use by teachers, administrators, or guidance personnel for identifying maladjusted children in the school population of the fourth, fifth, and sixth grades:

1. Administer and score appropriate forms of the California Test of Mental Maturity and the California Achievement Test, or use results of these tests obtained within the past six months.

2. Administer and score *The Class Play*. This may be obtained from Educational Testing Service, Princeton, N. J.

3. Complete Item H on the "Adjustment Index Summary," which is as follows.

Rating by teacher (please place the number of the appropriate word or phrase on the line to the right).

(*a*) Is this child overly agressive or defiant?
1. seldom or never   2. not very often
3. quite often   4. most of the time   _____

(*b*) Is this child overly withdrawn or timid?
1. seldom or never   2. not very often
3. quite often   4. most of the time   _____

(*c*) Is this child a control problem in his present group?
1. seldom or never   2. not very often
3. quite often   4. most of the time   _____

Rating by teacher (please place the number of the appropriate word or phrase on the line to the right). (*Continued*)

(*d*) Is this child an instructional problem in his present group?
 1. seldom or never   2. not very often
 3. quite often   4. most of the time   _____

(*e*) Where would you rate this child's adjustment with respect to your present group?
 1. among the best adjusted
 2. among the average
 3. among the poorest   _____

(*f*) Would you rate this child among the two most maladjusted children in your class?
 1. yes   2. no   _____

(*g*) Would you rate this child among the two best-adjusted children in your class?
 1. yes   2. no   _____

4. Determine those children in the class who fall into the following categories for each of the four factors found significant.

(*a*) Intelligence—below 90 IQ.

(*b*) Achievement in either reading or arithmetic—one grade level below their present grade placement or two years below their age-grade placement.

(*c*) Peer rating—the two children in each class who show the most disturbance on the score: (1) those who are chosen for predominantly even-numbered roles, (2) those not chosen at all by most of the children, or (3) those who select even-numbered roles for themselves.

5. The rating of pupils in each of these factors is to be weighted as follows.

(*a*)	Intelligence	1
(*b*)	Achievement	1
(*c*)	Peer rating	2
(*d*)	Teacher rating	2

The determination of potentially maladjusted should be made on the basis of the total weighted minimum score of three.

The reason for weighting intelligence and achievement less than peer rating and teacher rating is that these factors are considered indirect indicators, whereas the other two, peer rating and teacher rating, are more direct descriptions of maladjustment. Also, it is judged by the values that the latter two are probably more valid indicators and from this standpoint alone warrant higher weighting of their respective ratings.

Implications for Education

Although mental health is acknowledged to be a complex, transactional, and highly individualized reality, it is believed that the present study shows a sufficient number of factors to be valid in the classroom situation to make judgments regarding the emotional involvement of groups of pupils through a group screening process.

This makes possible three types of implications. The first concerns the direct assessment of individuals. The second and third types of implications arise out of the possibilities for the first. The first type of implication relates to:

1. The identification of individual children who may be in need of preventive care, environmental adjustment, or clinical therapy.

2. The proportion of children in the grades needing such consideration.

The second type of implication relates to:

1. The stimulation of teacher self-appraisal of attitudes regarding certain pupils and pupil behavior in general.

2. The improvement of teacher-initiated referral of pupils for special consideration.

3. The manner in which teachers regard and resolve routine discipline and learning problems in the classroom.

4. The use by teachers of clinical findings regarding certain pupils under study.

The third type of implication relates to:

1. The adjustment of curriculum, teaching methods, and school policy concerning grouping, grade placement, reporting pupil progress, and annual promotion.

2. The adequacy of pupil personnel and other kinds of specialized services in the school.

3. The appraisal of mental health programs in the classroom.

4. The relationship between school personnel and parents of maladjusted children.

5. The need for, or the evaluation of, child study and other in-service education programs for teachers.

6. The estimation of need for school and community facilities to rehabilitate seriously maladjusted children.

Suggested Readings

Bower, E., and Rothstein, J. H. *Diagnostic Problems in Mental Retardation Bulletin of the California State Department of Education,* 27:7; August, 1958. Contains papers from mental retardation conference as follows: "Differentia diagnosis of mental retardation" by Wortis, "The private pediatrician's approach to the problem of mental retardation" by Korngold, "The contribution of the psychologist to the diagnostic team" by Bell, "The school psychologist's role in diagnosis" by Smith, "Factors in the appraisal of intelligence" by Skeels, "Research on pseudo-mental retardation" by Burks, "Cultural values and psychological diagnosis of mental retardation" by Kohs, "The mental health of families with retarded children" by Hormuth, and "Interdisciplinary teamwork" by Tarjan.

Lessing, Elise E., and Lessing, J. C. "WISC Subtest Variability and Validity of WISC IQ," *Journal of Clinical Psychology,* 19:92–95; 1963. Child guidance cases, IQ 100 (N = 188). WISC compared with a group test of intelligence to determine the effect of wide WISC scatter. Mental ability appeared to be underestimated when the pattern was markedly uneven.

McHugh, Ann F. "WISC Performance in Neurotic and Conduct Disturbances," *Journal of Clinical Psychology,* 19:423–424; 1963. Children diagnosed as adjustment reaction of childhood with neurotic traits or with conduct disturbances were compared (N = 28). "Neurotic" IQ's were 116/100/106; "conduct" IQ's were 108/104/107. Both groups had similar profiles and IQ's.

Oettinger, L., Jr., M.D. (University of Southern California College of Medicine) *The Medical Management of Behavior Disorders* (privately printed). (Cf. *idem.,* "The Use of Deanol in the Treatment of Disorders of Behavior in Children," *Journal of Pediatrics,* 53:671; 1958.) Believes that severe behavior disorders arise from organic abnormalities in the brain. When such are present, the patient is very sensitive to environmental stress, which may serve as precipitating agent. Drugs, while not curative, are valuable control and access agents. Psychotherapy has a function in altering environmental stress or helping patients adjust to it.

Patterson, C. H. *Counseling the Emotionally Disturbed.* New York: Harper and Brothers, 1958. A directive approach to counseling of the emotionally disturbed through the background of general clinical counseling. The book, however, is somewhat antagonistic to diagnosis. There is considerable discussion of vocational rehabilitation, although the vocational theories of choice are not explicated in much detail. The author presents a vocational-assessment approach rather than a clinical approach, however, in working with the problems presented by clients.

Spivack, G. "Childrearing Attitudes of Emotionally Disturbed Adolescents," *Journal of Consulting Psychology*, 21:2; April, 1957. (Also The Devereux Schools, Devon, Pennsylvania.) Using sixty-six disturbed adolescents versus seventy-nine normal controls on an attitude survey, it was found that disturbed adolescents express significantly more restrictive and overcontrolling attitudes than do normals.

Tobias, M. "Some Physiological Correlates of Emotionality," Conference Report, November, 1960, California Educational Research and Guidance Association. (Mimeo.) Points out that a large number of disturbed children have skeletal immaturity as revealed by X-rays, mixed dominance, or other physiological abnormality.

Trippe, M. F. "Conceptual Problems in Research on Educational Provisions for Disturbed Children," *Exceptional Children*, 29:400–406; 1963. Temptation to apply assumptions from other groups of exceptional children to the emotionally disturbed is a frequent miscalculation. The goal with this group is to eliminate the "disability" (not compensate for it as with many other exceptional children) and to effect changes in the child and his behavior. Each professional system (medical, legal-correctional, social welfare) handles these children with different services, conceptions, and operational patterns, and often they have similar problems. Education is assuming more responsibility, but as constructive, not reconstructive. There is a growing tendency to define all of these as emotional disturbances: (1) learning disabilities, (2) underachievement, (3) all other unexplained difficulties. Much of this "disturbance" is a conflict between the needs of the school and the needs of the children. They attempt to correlate the morale of industry with that of the child. Because we cannot "fire" a student, perhaps, like industry, we could "transfer" or "rotate" him. This makes the school the responsible factor, not the child. (If he cannot conform, change the atmosphere if you cannot change the child.) In adult society many roles are possible, but more than one is usually prohibited the child. Because of special services, many teachers are told to "refer" rather than to "handle" special problems and become custodians of the lunchroom, washroom, and playground.

Ullmann, C. A. *Identification of Maladjusted School Children*. Public Health Monograph No. 7, U.S. Department of Health, Education, and Welfare, 1957. Compares three methods of screening maladjusted children centering around teachers' ratings and forced-choice responses.

THE AREA of mental retardation is a very old area of interest but one which has been conspicuously lacking in guidance emphasis and development. When the area was being opened up, guidance was not recognized as a partner in the educational team, and the major emphasis even today of guidance practices for mentally retarded children comes through the school psychologist who tests them and makes the diagnosis. Since the major objective for these youngsters is some degree of social and vocational performance rather than academic development, there is an extensive literature of vocational counseling and training. Such efforts are represented in this chapter in their prevocational aspects in the papers of Menchel, Smith, and Syden. (They also appear in the next chapter in the rehabilitation aspect.)

Personal counseling aspects are found only in a few papers, most of which are represented here. The Davis paper, "Counseling the Mentally Retarded," is such a representative example. Another is Thorne's directive counseling view of the benefits of this type of guidance for the subnormal. It would be interesting to hear a nondirective rebuttal, but the compilers were unable to find one. Finally, the chapter concludes with Yates and Lederer's discussion of the effects of parental counseling in the case of mongolism.

28. Counseling the Mentally Retarded *

DONALD A. DAVIS, *Director, Counseling Bureau,*
Western Michigan University

A MORE ADEQUATE adjustment of the "forgotten child" is coming to be recognized as not only a desirable goal of society but an increasingly necessary one.

We no longer feel that institutionalization of the mentally handicapped relieves us of all responsibilities to him but that each life is a precious one and that each has something unique and valuable to contribute to our way of life.

This is the feeling upon which is predicted the philosophy of education in America, and underlying it are two important premises fundamental to this philosophy: one, that each member of society has the privilege and the right to be developed to his optimum growth through fulfillment of individual physical and psychological needs; two, that all pupils, unless severely handicapped either physically or mentally, should attend school for a minimum number of years in order to approximate this optimal growth and development. These two premises apparently pertain to all—the gifted, the normal, and the handicapped.

It has been in response to these demands that the schools have become more and more complex, and guidance and counseling have come to share in a significant way.

The counselor has the serious responsibility of aiding each student in his school toward better adjustment to his environment. Obviously this includes the mentally retarded. A mental retardate is a person whose measured intelligence quotient is roughly between the limits of 50 and 70 and who, with adequate training, can be expected to function as an essentially normal person. He must be identified as early as possible, must be trained in emotional control, must be helped to formulate a more realistic self-concept, and must be aided in choosing appropriate educational and vocational goals. As a precautionary measure, let it be understood that these areas of adjustment are not actually separable into distinct and unrelated subjects but are closely interrelated and interdependent. However, for the purposes of clarity and discussion, it seems best to approach them as entities.

* Reprinted by permission of the author and *Vocational Guidance Quarterly,* 7:184–190; Spring, 1959.

Problems of the Retarded

There seems to be general agreement in the field that the mentally retarded child has particular difficulty in making satisfactory resolutions of his problems. Mental retardates, unlike other deviates whose disabilities may be seen, receive from the public mind emotional dislike and repulsion. This, of course, leads frequently to withdrawal or antisocial aggressive behavior.

Parental attitudes toward children who are mentally retarded have definite effects on the mental health of the child. These attitudes may spring from guilt feelings based on mistaken concepts of heredity or on a feeling of being punished for past misdeeds. This sets up a barrier between child and parent, lessening the opportunity for a sound emotional development of the child, which in turn may bring about partial or even complete rejection of the child.

Self-respect seems to be based on good family relations, acceptance by others, achievements in both thought and action, and fostering of independence. The mentally retarded must not be pushed beyond his intellectual capacities. This will inevitably result in frustration, irritability, impatience, and hatred and rejection of self or society.

Dewan undertook to ascertain the frequency of emotional instability in 30,000 retarded and nonretarded subjects as measured by the Canadian Army "M" test. He found that there was a definitely higher incidence of emotional instability in the mentally retarded than in the nonretarded. He also notes that as the intelligence increases, the emotional instability decreases.

One of the most important factors influencing the emotional adjustment of the mentally retarded is the attitudes of the parents to the child. To most parents, the child is an extension of the self. He can be used to fulfill the hopes and desires which they were unable to attain in their own lives. If the child is mentally retarded, he presents a source of worry, frustration, and guilt. The "sins of the father" have been visited upon the child, and thus he constitutes a continual threat to the ego of the parents, constantly reflecting their own inadequacies. If the parents have these attitudes and thoughts of the child, they will find it difficult to understand and accept him. This, in turn, will seriously hinder the healthful development of the child's personality.

Counselors of the mentally retarded have probably failed much more often than they have succeeded in educational matters. The retardate, usually coming from an environment of rejection or overprotection and lacking socializing experiences with normal children, is prevented from adjustment through fears, anxieties, and frustrations. He is not able to gain status through academic achievement and will react with anger, aggression, or withdrawal.

The retarded person is subject to the same range and variety of emotional reactions as are those of normal intelligence. Rejection by parents, the community, relatives, peers, and in many cases by the school will have definite deleterious effects on the emotional adjustment and development of a realistic concept of self of the retardate.

He should be regarded as a normal child emotionally but with intellectual deviation. If the child is happy and contented, the result will be good mental health. Such people can be definite assets to the community and country.

The counselor should encourage parents and teachers to give lessons and training which are within the abilities of the intellectually subnormal so that he may achieve up to capacity. Social training and character development are more significant than academic attainment for these children. They will be accepted by society if they are cheerful, willing, and obedient. However, if they lack these qualities of adjustment, they will be shunned and disliked.

Good standards, values, and attitudes should be inculcated as early as possible, since retardates have difficulty distinguishing right from wrong and are easily influenced by peers and adults. With social problems under control, they will function passably well in areas of concrete thinking, but they find abstract reasoning and interpretation of symbolic material incomprehensible. The educational training must be tailored to the student. It is a waste of time and money to attempt to mold the student to a rigid concept of formal academic schedules.

Bobroff's follow-up study illustrates this point. He checked on 121 adults who had been given special training in the public schools twelve years before. Very few of these retarded people had failed to meet social standards of self-sufficiency and responsibility. He felt that as a result of this study more confident predictions can be made for people having had similar training.

Group counseling in a warm, friendly, and democratic atmosphere does much to ameliorate social attitudes, beliefs, and modes of conduct. Special attention and training will do much to mediate happier and more productive lives for the retarded.

An illustration of the problem is the case of a young man in Camp Brighton, a parole unit operated by the Michigan Department of Corrections. He is a mentally retarded youth twenty-two years of age. He has been judged a thief and has been isolated from society because of his behavior. However, a greater crime than this one has been perpetrated by society against the lad. He comes from an unfortunate family background, was expelled from school at an early age, and has been on his own for many years. He has numerous unresolved emotional problems and does not understand how and why he gets into so many difficulties. He has formed poor social skills, work habits, and moral standards. Most would agree that these are learned and not inherited. Had he had training and special education beginning at an early age, he would probably be a productive member of society at the present time instead of a ward of the state. The financial burden is ours; the emotional bewilderment and guilt feelings are his.

Functions of the Counselor

There seems to be considerable agreement that "self" is gradually becoming recognized as one of the most useful, integrative concepts yet developed for explaining behavior. An understanding of the self-concept and the ability to alter it through some sort of re-education would be a valuable tool for the counselor of the mentally retarded.

Counseling techniques available to the counselor which will aid in understanding the self-concept of a student are the autobiography in written or verbal form, test results, anecdotal records, and conferences with teachers, parents, or others who know the retardate well and are able to relate his behavior objectively. If there seems to be a discrepancy between what the student thinks of himself and the opinions of others in terms of interests, abilities, capacities, goals, values, and attitudes, then the counselor may utilize the counseling interview, talks by other people who have rapport with the counselee, or group interaction to bring about a more realistic view of himself by the student. Cotzin concludes, after a study of the effectiveness of group psychotherapy on mentally defective problem boys, that the results are entirely encouraging and indicate that group psychotherapy is useful with the mentally retarded.

Emotional self-control is necessary for the mentally retarded. Kaldeck feels that "most patients in state schools as far as they are able-bodied and have I.Q.'s above 45 or 50 are placed in institutions, not because of their intellectual deficiency but on account of their emotional difficulties." In another study, Nehan basing her statements on evidence presented in her investigation, proposes that high-grade mental defectives of the moron or borderline type improve with psychotherapeutic treatment in about the same proportion as do normals. This would mean that lack of intelligence within limits is not necessarily an inhibiting agent in learning emotional control.

In a study of the effectiveness of a comprehensive guidance program at the Brandon State School in Vermont, Thorne reports that counseling and psychotherapy are both possible and profitable. The therapy of sixty-eight retardates resulted in happier, better-adjusted children, total abolition of corporal punishment, increase of group morale, and lowering of uncontrolled emotional reactions. He indicates that 66 per cent improved, 23 per cent remained unchanged, and 10 per cent became worse.

The need for educational counseling will vary considerably, depending upon the size and philosophy of the school. If it is a large one and there is emphasis upon increasing individual differences, there will probably be special classes for the exceptional child. Early identification and proper placement will be the responsibility of the counselor. But if the school is a small one, in rural areas especially, the counselor will have greater difficulties. He must do what he can to ease tensions at home, to be sure the teacher understands the limitations of the child, and to provide learning experiences which are meaningful for the retardate. The retarded indivdiual's self-concept is being shaped by these experiences; and if he is made to fail, to feel guilty and worthless at an early age, it will be exceedingly difficult to change these attitudes later in his life.

There is probably no aspect of education of mentally retarded children which is more important than that which concerns itself with the social and occupational adjustment in adult life. Since these people will be filling unskilled and semiskilled occupations primarily, it is desirable that they be taught such things as cleanliness, courteousness, punctuality, co-operation, reading of simple notices, and filling out of simple blanks, rather than specific job skills. The counselor must see that the retardate understands the necessity for these attributes and that he does as well as he can within his limitations.

Personal and social skills and attitudes are most important for vocational success. Retardates can usually be placed if they have a desire to work, good personal habits, a sense of responsibility, and ability to get along with others. Placement is most difficult when emotional disturbances are added to mental deficiency.

These people can become good workers and citizens if they get good training. With acceptance at home and in school, adequate personalities can emerge; without acceptance, society's resources for the delinquent, psychotic, and criminal will become exhausted, and the real problems will remain.

29. Prevocational Evaluation of the Mentally Retarded *

JEROME MENCHEL, *Baltimore County Board of Education. Formerly Director, Sheltered Workshop, Maryland Society for Mentally Retarded Children*

THERE ARE three phases to be considered on a purely scientific basis among the activities of the prevocational evaluator for the mentally retarded young adult.

First, he must establish minimum requirements for performance that are to be expected. Second, he must determine by the same procedure the specific attitudes, skills, and information to be incorporated in the optimum existing performance of these functions. Third, he must develop, with due regard to maturation and abilities of retarded young adults, a prevocational evaluation designed to produce the indicated knowledge and skills.

The individual in charge of organizing an industry-geared prevocational evaluation center must not only adopt the criteria of content selection but also investigate for the type of components implied by them. This requires methods for the selection of work samples.

In some instances, the methods are based upon practical reasons and judgment. Some of these methods approach the rigor of scientific investigation, as in the case of experimental procedures and those planned to discover the skills that are most useful in the performance of a particular job.

A job is always complex. It calls for a variety of abilities or aptitudes. Since it is impossible to make out a complete list of wholly independent abilities which can be separately measured and related to the requirements

* Reprinted by permisison of the author and *Vocational Guidance Quarterly,* 8:209–211; Summer, 1960.

of the different jobs, the practical procedure is to analyze the job and to apply to its requirements the various means of discovering skills and aptitudes for it.

The analytical procedure is one of the most widely known of the methods of job analysis. It has been closely identified with the criterion of productiveness, although it has been used in the selection of content in accordance with other criteria. Generally speaking, it consists of an analysis of the things people do to discover the skills functioning in these various activities.

There are three forms of the analytical procedure, all more or less following the same pattern. The first form is the "activity" analysis, the object of which is to discover the general kinds of activities engaged in by people of a given group or area and then to reduce these to specific activities. The second is "job" analysis, which is the technique of activity applied to vocational operations. If anyone wishes to know what should be taught in operating a sewing machine, for example, an analysis would be made of what sewing machine operators actually do. This paper is concerned with this particular form of the analytical procedure. The third form of this procedure is simply the use of the process of investigation to determine the elements of knowledge or the skills having general utility.

Job analysis consists of fact-finding techniques applied to the work tasks under investigation. Therefore, the first step in the procedure is establishing the area of human concern, the specific function or specialized occupation to be investigated. The second step is breaking it down into more specific elements and selecting an appropriate technique for collecting data about these various elements. Although drill press operation may be divisible into a number of jobs, depending upon the complexity and nature of work being performed, the jobs may be defined under the heading of an occupation.

The analysis of the occupation or the activity by the worker is made step by step by someone considered to be an expert with the specific job or activity. He lists his duties or operations that he performs. A job that requires the fitting of a part into its place may, for example, start out with (1) searching for, (2) finding, (3) grasping, (4) putting the part into its place.

After the first analysis has been made, the operation must be studied as a whole. In this study any existing waste motions can be eliminated upon discovery. The evaluator must decide whether the work can be so placed that there is less searching, easier finding, quicker grasping, or moving over less distance. Such improvements will speed the operation and increase efficiency. The physical placement of the work is extremely important. If a part must be turned around before it can be put in place, naturally it takes longer to handle and becomes more tiring than when it is picked up in the position which is right for placing it accurately.

Fatigue is an important factor to be considered. Are all the motions being made that will produce the least fatigue? A well-arranged workplace and good tools will help simplify body motion and thus make the work easier.

It has sometimes been asserted that the analytical method is "atomistic" —that is to say that it breaks operations, skills, and knowledge into such small elements that the real identity of the original process is lost.

Job analysis is always essential. The pertinent questions should always be these: What is the analysis for? Is it sufficient for the purpose? Job analysis yields results in the discovery of what is actually done on the job: knowledge and skills that workers actually use in performing their various operations.

30. Vocational Planning for the Mentally Limited *

DAVID WAYNE SMITH, *Professor of Education, University of Arizona*

IN A COMPLEX social order such as ours there are many simple, routine tasks to perform. Because these jobs involve excessive repetition, they are too monotonous for people of average intelligence to perform creditably over any long period of time.

Certain mentally limited persons constitute an excellent source of man power to fill positions entailing these duties. Employment in a useful occupation is extremely important to an individual's success in community life. Providing the retardate with social and vocational skills may enable him to become a contributing member of society rather than a burden.

* Reprinted by permission of the author and *Vocational Guidance Quarterly,* 6:142–145; Spring, 1958.

Meeting Youth's Needs

Educators have long professed the belief that all children, regardless of mental or physical condition, have certain needs that must be satisfied, and the World Health Organization has stated that the education of all youth, both normal and subnormal, should be the responsibility of educational authorities.

To accept these propositions involves setting up the machinery to implement them. In the formulation of objectives of a vocational program for the retardate, these predications must be carefully considered.

Recent trends, evidenced in the practices found in many school systems, uphold the belief that the needs of the child must determine the learning process. This is particularly significant in determining learning goals for the mentally limited. The vocational training program, then, for the mentally retarded person must involve placement in a job that will prove satisfying and also contribute to the general welfare of the individual in relation to the community. If society desires to meet the needs of this group, it must provide the necessary facilities and the programs.

Planning the Program

An example of well-planned vocational training for the mentally limited functions as a part of the Special Education program in the public schools of Tucson (Arizona). The learning goals for this group are vocationally oriented, and adolescents assigned to this department follow a training schedule designed to give them practice in social and vocational skills necessary for living and being productive in the community.

Experience has shown that occupational success without social proficiency is rare, so that the training curriculum of the Tucson system includes experiences designed to help these youths develop adequate responses for competent living. Providing activities that show a direct correlation between the principle and the goal is extremely important to the success of this kind of undertaking.

In setting up learning goals for this group of the mentally deficient, the following objectives should be considered.

1. The maximal development of mental capacities (fundamental processes).
2. The realization of optimum physical health for more effective living.
3. The development of an adequate personality.
4. The acquisition of vocational skills for economic independence.

5. The development of social competence for personal adjustment in the community.

6. The development of ethical and moral standards and habits.

7. The development of recreational and leisure-time activities for personal enrichment.

Selection of Trainees

Selection of mentally limited individuals for a vocational program should be based on the results of (1) psychological and neurological examinations, (2) observations by teachers and other school and community personnel, and (3) complete analysis of the individual's cumulative record. From the results of this study, it should be possible to determine the extent to which the particular person could become proficient vocationally and socially.

In general, boys and girls of chronological ages sixteen to eighteen years, whose mental development ranges from eight to twelve years, are best suited for this kind of training. In addition, these youngsters should possess physical development and motor co-ordination commensurate with those needed for proficiency on the task assigned. The training program must also emphasize the development of self-control, since success depends many times on the way the trainee reacts to the feelings of others. Activities included in the training program, then, must be based on the individual's need to be socially skillful as well as vocationally competent.

Areas of Employment

The classroom activities made available to this group of the retarded must give actual experiences in performing the tasks expected on the job. A working relationship must be established between the school system and the employers, and the school-employer association must be one of mutual education. A partial list of some of the employment areas for the mentally limited is included here.

MALES	FEMALES

1. Simple horticulture
  Gardening
  Nursery helper
  Floral shop helper
	1. Homemaking
	  Domestic (maid)
	  Child care
	  Laundry
	  Ironing

2. Simple maintenance and janitorial duties	2. Nurse's aide

3. Construction work
  Laborer
	3. Restaurant employee
	  Waitress

MALES	FEMALES
Painter's helper	Kitchen helper
Hod carrier	Dishwasher
Carpenter's helper	4. Industrial kitchen
Plumber's helper	5. Sales clerk (not involving salesman-
4. Ranch hand	ship)
5. Farm labor	6. Garment industry
6. Helpers with small animals	Routine cutting
7. Stock control	Routine stitching
Inventory	7. Clerical (routine)
Sorting	8. Commercial laundry
Stacking	9. Janitorial
8. Carry-out boy	10. Stock wrapping
9. Commercial laundry and cleaning	

Urban communities that have diversified industry are in a good position to develop training and placement plans for the retardate. This does not mean, however, that communities lacking these qualities should not undertake to develop similar programs. In those school systems where periodic placements are large and where the follow-up and conference load is excessive, the employment of a full-time person is essential. Individuals responsible for these services must be well trained and have an understanding of the problems of the mentally limited group. The Tucson system, previously discussed, has made this provision.

Placement of Trainees

Actual placement of a boy or girl must be based on extensive planning. The school must provide a service for co-operating prospective employers that is of superior quality. These employers must be given adequate, frank information concerning the capabilities of the trainee. Periodic conferences of placement officer and employer are essential and contribute much to the mentally limited person's success on the job.

In addition to discussions with the trainee, frequent parent interviews are recommended, since these serve to keep the parent informed.

Vocational Program Guideposts

The following criteria might serve to guide a school system's efforts in establishing a vocational planning program.

1. The duties of the particular job must be simple and routine, involving only minor decisions.

2. The employer must be willing to assist in the training program and recognize both the capabilities and the limitations of the trainee.

3. The fellow employees must be willing to accept the retardate. They should be the type who will exert a positive influence on his development.

4. The parents must be willing to accept what the school is trying to accomplish.

5. The trainee must realize his obligations toward his employer and fellow employees and must want the job opportunity.

6. Teachers involved in the training program must be cognizant of the goals of the retardate.

7. Distances from the youngster's home and the school must be considered.

8. The legal limitations relative to the employment of youth must be recognized.

Facets of Evaluation

Determination of the success of a vocational program for the mentally limited involves an examination of employer reports, length of service records, success on the job, and the individual's all-round contentment. Failure often involves such unforeseen complications as home environment, transportation difficulties, and unsuitable or premature placement.

It is essential, therefore, that in the assignment of an individual due cognizance be taken of his capabilities, preferences, and temperament—plus the very practical problems of relative geographic location of the employer's place of business, desires of the youngster's parents, and requirements of the job itself.

31. Preparation for Work: An Aspect of the Secondary School's Curriculum for Mentally Retarded Youth *

MARTIN SYDEN, *Chairman, Department of Social Science and Pre-Teaching, Nassau Community College, Mineola, New York*

D URING THE PAST decade leaders in education for the mentally handicapped, such as De Prospo (1954), Fouracre (1955), Kirk (1951), and others, have advocated a socio-occupational-oriented curriculum for the educable mentally retarded, especially for those of secondary school age. The school has begun to realize that it is responsible not only for the academic phase of the course of study but also for the individual's personal, social, and occupational growth, development, and adjustment.

This philosophy, when properly applied, has extended the education of the retarded adolescent from its terminal position at the conclusion of elementary or junior high school at the age of sixteen and has placed him in high school programs which parallel in time and schedule those of his age peers with normal intelligence. As school systems are attempting to fulfill their obligations toward the older retarded, curricula and programs directed toward education for occupational competency are emerging and are being publicized in the professional literature. An overview of such programs is indicative of current practices. It should acquaint school authorities without such curricula with recent trends in the education for retarded adolescents and should serve as resource material for schools having provisions for the retarded of secondary school age and seeking to improve their programs.

Consequently, a review of the literature for the past ten years pertaining to secondary school programs for the mentally retarded adolescent serves as a basis for this paper. Any general statements concerning current practices made herein are based upon the programs examined and are not to be interpreted as referring to all programs in operation for retarded teenagers.

These programs are discussed, therefore, in the light of how some communities are meeting the challenge and providing education of a practical

* Reprinted by permission of the author and *Exceptional Children*, 28:325–333; February, 1962.

nature for the retarded adolescent. Six areas are explored, namely, the student and the program organization, teacher's functions, formal curriculum provisions, work-study or work experience education, parent and student counseling, and curriculum evaluation and revision.

The Student and the Program Organization

Not all retardates are admitted to a high school program. Some school systems set up criteria and a process for this procedure. The entrant completes the junior high school phase of the over-all curriculum when he is about fifteen or sixteen years of age. His IQ, as prescribed by New York State law, ranges between 50 and 75, with a possible five-point tolerance at either extremity. The prospective student has a reading ability and mathematical achievement that place him between the second and sixth grades. Furthermore, he has a favorable prognosis, as determined by an entrance committee, for independent living as a contributing member of society.

In Des Moines, Iowa, for instance, the decision as to the student's placement is made by the high school psychologist along with the teacher and the Director of the Department of Pupil Adjustment (Des Moines Public Schools, 1959). The student is also expected to have a potential to adjust socially and personally to the high school environment, to perform in industrial art shops for the normal students, and to complete successfully other nonacademic subjects. He should also possess a potential to adjust to departmentalized scheduling.

The high school program usually requires three years to complete in a 6–3–3 school system or four years in an 8–4 school system. This time interval in special education corresponds with high school programs for normal pupils. In New York City, however, plans are being made to develop a program for youths between the ages of seventeen and twenty-one, the feeling being that the retarded need a longer time and increased services to adjust to the world of work (Allen & Harnett, 1960).

The organization and daily scheduling of secondary school programs for mentally handicapped youths have emerged in two major forms. One pattern requires a departmentalized schedule of 40- to 45-minute daily periods and the completion of prescribed subjects prior to granting a qualified diploma. The second pattern is the core curriculum containing graduated problems in life education.

The system prevailing in California is representative of the first type mentioned above. This consists of three phases: academics, electives, and work experience. However, these aspects of the curriculum are not unrelated to each other but interwoven to develop the individual socially, occupationally, and personally. Although the academic areas taught by special class teachers bear the classical titles of English, mathematics, science, and social studies, the content matter of these courses is not similar to that in a high school curriculum for normal students but is geared to occupational education. Elective subjects in classes for normal students such as industrial shops, home economics, music, typing, and art are available to the special education student provided that the elective is within the individual's scope of learning. During the initial year or two years in high school, academic subjects and electives listed above constitute the daily program. However, the schedule for the remaining two years is divided: a half-day in school is devoted to academics, and the rest of the day is given over to work experience (Daly & Cain, 1953).

The second schedule outline is illustrated by the core curriculum. The duration of the core curriculum pattern is three or four years. Its daily schedule is subdivided into block time unit studies. These consist of the study of persistent life problems and possible solutions of everyday life situations as they may arise in the experiences of the retarded adolescent. Electives and work experience are also integral parts of the curriculum and are placed in the scheduling and organization as indicated above.

In some school systems, special education students are assigned to regular home rooms in order to provide a social experience with their age peers as well as an additional experience in complying with rules and regulations both necessary in vocational adjustment.

Realizing that all educable retarded adolescents are not of equal ability, some schools have or contemplate having a differentiated curriculum for this group. In Baltimore, those more capable of self-sufficiency are directed to occupational classes, whereas those less capable are directed to shop center classes (Baltimore Public Schools, 1953). Minneapolis has reported that its future program for adolescent retardates will be on four levels. Students functioning higher intellectually will participate in a minimum diploma pattern in a regular high school. However, students who have low potential for independent living and are in need of more specialized training will be accommodated in the transitional pattern (Deno, 1960).

Teacher's Functions

The duties of the teacher of educable retarded youth are being identified as programs evolve. In Hayward, California, he is designated as Counselor-

Teacher of Mentally Retarded Students (Carson, 1956). In Lansing, Michigan, his title is Teacher-Coordinator (Lansing Public Schools, 1957). However, his duties are virtually alike in both instances. In essence, the teacher is accountable not only for the academic instruction in the school but also for other tasks outside the school environs.

In some smaller communities, where no single person supervises the work experience program, the teacher of the mentally retarded conducts this program and co-ordinates it with the academic phase in school. It is he who co-operates with community agencies such as Rotary, Kiwanis, and chambers of commerce in a common endeavor to place his students in training positions. He follows up these placements with visits to the employer-trainer to discuss the progress of his students, assists the employer-trainer with any problems, and counsels with the trainee when necessary. In school, he guides the student in the selection of electives, consults with teachers who have special education students in their classes, and counsels students with problems relating not only to work experience but also to adjustment in school and at home. The special educator also counsels with the retardate's parents in order to guide their thinking in accepting realistic occupational goals for their children. Thus, he attempts to create a wholesome atmosphere within the home surroundings necessary for the student's occupational success. He also co-operates with governmental agencies such as the Division of Vocational Rehabilitation in the operation of a work-study program for the retarded.

Some Curriculum Provisions

In general, the academic phase of the curriculum is oriented to provide the retardate with information and experiences which should assist him in learning to meet his everyday problems, find his place in our economic world, and give him an understanding of his responsibilities as a citizen of his community. The academic aspects, functional and practical, constantly relate to the individual's life experiences.

Although the format of daily scheduling may differ as indicated above, nevertheless content material appears to bear a great similarity. Pasadena, California, for example, which has subject scheduling, requires vocational English, taught by the special education teacher, each year that the student is in the program. However, its guide warns that this subject "must be vocational in nature in order to relate to the need of it within given job areas. Abstract ideas and concepts, except for the most elementary ones, have no place in the curriculum of the mentally retarded. Only those things which are immediately practical and useful should be employed" (Pasadena City Schools, 1957).

However, Altoona, Pennsylvania, subscribing to the unit study curriculum organization, also emphasizes practicality in its Communications Techniques Unit (Altoona Public Schools, 1961). Curriculum content in this field, in both of these communities, includes such topics as various forms of letter writing, completing many types of application forms, reading signs, a knowledge of some business forms found in business, industry, and the community, the use of the dictionary and telephone directories, and vocabulary pertinent to job areas. Good oral expression is developed by requiring students to report and relate their experiences on the job. Another form of improving speech is attained by practicing telephone conversations.

Similar comparisons may be made in mathematics or arithmetic, which contains not only such topics or units as banking, budgeting, insurance, taxes, traveling, money, and credit buying but also wages, deductions, and related mathematics as needed by the student on the job.

Common trends in social studies or social living such as in Sacramento, California, include units on the structure of the local economic community and occupational information as well as a survey of the types and requirements of jobs (Sacramento Public Schools, 1957). The State of Texas suggests that the major emphasis for the retarded adolescent should be occupational education and training. A combination of these should assist the prospective employee in becoming a better worker (Texas Education Agency, 1960).

High school science for the retarded aids him in job preparation by teaching him safety on the job, good health through proper living habits, and the effect of narcotics and tobacco on health. Personal guidance in terms of developing a sense of achievement, pride in one's work, understanding one's limitations, and developing a feeling of security assist in the creation of good mental health.

Besides the academics, students are permitted to benefit from choosing electives which may assist in evaluating interests and possible abilities in some areas of employment. Special education students may choose from several industrial shops such as woodworking, metal and printing, sewing, cooking, and typing. Driver education has also been made available to selected students either in a normal class or through the facilities of the special education teacher. In either event, more time is devoted to behind-the-wheel driving and sign reading than to the study of the theoretical aspects of the four-cycle gasoline engine.

Furthermore, teacher-developed materials have been marketed to aid the student in preparation for assuming his place in the economic community. Carson's *Teen-agers Prepare for Work* (1957), Tripp's *I Want a Driver's License,* Lawson's *Everyday Business* (1958), Tudyman and Groelle's *A Functional Basic Word List for Special Pupils* (1958), and Baltimore, Maryland's, *A Handbook for You the Worker* (1960) are examples of such materials.

Work Experience

Although work training is inaugurated in the elementary grades for educable mentally handicapped youth, it is not brought to fruition until the student attains the senior high school years. Work experience is not merely the employment of an individual but, according to Tyler, a systematic plan whereby young people, while still in school, gain realistic employment experience through paid part-time work performed under the following conditions: that certain things be clearly defined, such as (1) the roles of the student, the school, and the employer and (2) co-ordination by qualified school personnel; that legal aspects of the job be observed; and that announcement be made of how much accreditation will be given for the work training as a regular high school course (Tyler, 1956).

There are various types of work experience on the high school level. However, the pattern that is developing consists of two stages, in-school and out-of-school. During the tenth year in school a student may be assigned to cafeteria, shop, homemaking room, or office for one period a day as helper in order that his abilities, as well as his desires and adjustment to several work situations, may be explored and evaluated. Periodic reports are made by co-operative teachers and other employers relative to the student's adjustment and performance. The special class teacher, who supervises in-school work experience, also contributes his evaluation as a result of periodic visits and observation of the trainee.

In Texas, for example, provisions are made for prevocational training in several shops. Students are given an opportunity in several job areas in order to provide them with varied experiences. It is generally felt that work experiences should not train for one specific job but rather for general skills, proper attitudes toward work, and the development of positive habits. Usually this work is compensated not monetarily but in terms of school credit. The in-school work experience program for retardates at Hayward, California, is known to be integrated with that of normal high school students in a work experience program for all students (Carson, 1956).

The ultimate step in the transition of the mentally retarded from school to work is the student's placement in industry on a part-time basis during his last two years in school. The usual pattern for work-study programs is for the student to attend school in the morning and participate in work training in the afternoon for three or four hours. However, Baltimore has a variation of this pattern. It permits the trainee to be on the job full time for two weeks and return to school for the following two weeks, alternating on the job with another student. The procedure provides the employer-trainer with a full-time trainee (Baltimore Public Schools, 1953). Another variation of work experience is the Lansing, Michigan, program which permits the student to work full time during his last year in school provided that he attends school one night a week. His experience is credited toward his high school diploma (Lansing Public Schools, 1957).

The student is usually paid the minimum wage rate for his services during the training period. This permits him to learn first hand the meaning of wages, deductions, savings, and budgeting. However, this practice is not universal, for Altoona, Pennsylvania, does not require its employer-trainers to pay the student-trainee except in the form of gifts at the conclusion of the ten-week training period (Altoona Public Schools, 1961).

Since the philosophy in special education is not to train for one specific type of work but rather toward the development of general skills, attitudes, and habits, the experiences of the student are not limited to one job in out-of-school experience. Furthermore, some firms and employers have voiced their desire to train their own employees in the use of equipment and the performance of tasks which may vary as technological progress affects industry and business. Variations in the timing and number of experiences exist. Examples of local needs are Albany, New York, and Altoona, Pennsylvania, which have arranged for at least three experiences of ten weeks each during the final school year. Santa Barbara County, California, permits its students to remain on the job until the student desires a change of position or the employer requests the school to withdraw the trainee in favor of another student (Santa Barbara County Public Schools, 1956).

Usually students are placed in positions which are classified as unskilled, semiskilled, and service types of jobs. Very few are placed or succeed at skilled tasks, although these may not be beyond the reach of some. Hospitals utilize the services of the retarded as ground and building maintenance men, ward aides, tray girls, and laundry helpers. Factories employ the limited student in such routine tasks as porter, drill press operator, assembler, and maintenance man. Garages hire the retarded as car washers, gas pump attendants, and car parkers.

This phase of the retardate's education could not materialize without the co-operation of businessmen, community organizations, and governmental agencies in the locality. In Lansing, Michigan, for example, the Excalibur Club has a committee of its members assisting in the placement of the handicapped student (Lansing Public Schools). In some communities, the Division of Vocational Rehabilitation is co-operating with local school authorities by evaluating student-clients for possible training and giving financial support to them upon qualifying for on-the-job training. In other cities, such as Albany, Altoona, Baltimore, and Cincinnati, the willingness of employers to work with the school directly in training retardates is evident from descriptions of community-supported work experience programs.

Parent and Student Counseling

The school has realized that the student is in need of knowing how to adjust socially and is not devoid of influence from pressures at home and in the community. It has created formal and informal counseling situations with parents under the guidance of the special education teacher or the co-ordinator of special education for the following purposes:

1. To orient parents to the limitations and assets of their children.

2. To present them with information which should assist them to regard their children's future realistically.

3. To solicit their co-operation in the high school program by having them sign agreements to abide by the school's plan for work experience and school attendance.

These functions appear to fall within the realm of a social service agency. However, such an agency may not be available to assist the school. Consequently, the educational institution has assumed these obligations. Simultaneously, the school has included counseling sessions and mental health objectives in the retardate's curriculum in order to have him better understand himself, his family, and the environment and learn within his limitations to accept himself, as well as learn to cope with many problems confronting him in the immediate future in school, on the job, at home, and in the community. All these efforts are directed toward assisting the retardate in becoming a worth-while citizen and a contributing worker in our society.

Curriculum Evaluation and Revision

Although educators have created work training programs for educable retarded youth in the hope that these youth, upon completion of the program, will become well-adjusted citizens in the community, provisions have not been incorporated within the curriculum framework to determine the effectiveness and the need for modification of work experience. However, some educators, such as McGinnity (1957) in Paterson, New Jersey, Dinger (1959) in Altoona, Pennsylvania, Cassidy (1955) in Columbus, Ohio, and Beekman (1957) in Lansing, Michigan, have within recent years conducted follow-up studies of postschool adjustment of retardates in order to evaluate the school's curriculum. The consensus of the aforementioned follow-up studies is such that the special education curriculum for educable mentally retarded youth in these communities is accomplishing its goal favorably. Surveys and studies such as these tend to keep current curriculum provisions up to date in our dynamic society. Whether formal or otherwise, this practice should become an integral facet of the curriculum.

Summary

During the past decade, many school systems have inaugurated programs for the educable mentally retarded of secondary school age. Special classes for these students have been introduced into the communities' secondary schools. In this manner the teen-age retarded student has been given an opportunity to associate with his age peers and become an integral part of the secondary school organization. Thus, he is assisted in developing himself personally and socially—factors which are necessary in his preparation for employment.

Curriculum content, whether organized under traditional subject titles or under core units of study, is socio-occupationally oriented. The goals of the program are to develop the individual's capabilities and assist him in discovering his place in the economic society upon completion of his formal schooling. In addition to academics taught by special education teachers and electives in classes for normal students, the special education curriculum provides for work experience as a bridge between school and the world of work, co-ordinated and correlated by special education personnel. Some schools provide counseling for both students and parents as a function of the mental health provisions in the over-all curriculum. Finally, follow-up studies have been introduced for the purpose of evaluating these emerging curricula as well as a means for implementing the special education curriculum in light of our dynamic society.

32. Tutorial Counseling with Mental Defectives *

FREDERICK C. THORNE, *Brandon, Vermont*

Rationale

THERAPEUTIC and rehabilitational procedures with mental defectives may have different objectives from the goals sought with normal or superior persons. Whereas an important educational objective with the normal or superior child is to teach him *to think for himself* independently and creatively, with the mental defective a more tenable goal may be to teach him *to think what a normal person would do* in specific situations. *The functional intelligence of the mentally deficient may be greatly improved if they can be taught to act in any given situation as a more intelligent person would do.* The deficiencies in logical reasoning so typically displayed by the mentally deficient can be compensated for to great degree by a system of tutorial education and counseling designed to provide standard solutions of problem situations *learned by rote memory.*

Clinical experience indicates that many children with moron or borderline intelligence become completely frustrated by modern educational methods which attempt to stimulate original thinking by training in inductive and deductive reasoning. Unable to "think it out for himself," the mental defective becomes thwarted, frustrated, hostile, or demoralized and soon ceases to make any effort to learn. As a result, he soon becomes socially isolated and rejected by both teachers and other students. Unable to change her method for one pupil or to give the time necessary for intensive drilling, the teacher also becomes frustrated and threatened to the point

* Reprinted by permission of the author and *Journal of Clinical Psychology,* 16:73–79; 1960.

where her main objective is to get the child out of her class. The only solution of this educational impasse may be to provide special tutorial education and counseling designed to provide a subject matter which the mental defective *can* learn.

Technique

In lecturing to students on methods of counseling and training with mental defectives, we have often used the analogy that educating the defective is much like photography on a dull day—the subject must be exposed longer to the material to be learned. The same principles of learning apply to mental defectives as to normals with the exceptions that much more attention must be given to creating conditions conducive to learning and much longer practice periods than usual must be provided.

1. Suitable Conditions for Learning. In our experience, mental defectives may require a much more *friendly, accepting, tolerant,* and *supportive* learning situation than do normal children. Mentally defective children have usually experienced much larger amounts of failure and defeat than more competent children and therefore are typically more demoralized and inhibited by fear or anger at the start of learning. For these reasons, the mentally deficient typically react adversely to competitiveness, frequently giving up immediately because they are unwilling to risk another failure. Therefore, the teacher or counselor should provide strong support in the form of personal attention, affection, and appreciation for effort even though the level of learning may be poor.

2. Use of Rewards. In intelligence testing, the testee is constantly praised and encouraged to continue, even though making errors, in order to achieve the highest levels of accomplishment. This lesson is often forgotten in education where subtle punishments in the form of marking systems, grades, failure to promote, and other discriminatory practices are common. Similar deterrents may occur in therapy, as, when clinics refuse to accept the defective for therapy, they are referred to institutions where there is less hope or assigned to less competent professional personnel or students. In work with mental defectives, rewards and praise should be dispensed profusely, *whether earned or not in terms of normal standards,* on the assumption that anything gained is that much to the good.

3. Practice Periods. Depending on the level of retardation, practice periods must be lengthened to whatever point necessary to permit rote learning. It may require two or three times as long in training periods, but if the moron acquires the equivalent of an eighth-grade education by, say, age twenty-five, he becomes reasonably adequate to work in many occupations and get along in the community.

4. Individual Prescriptions. Each mental defective may require a specially planned course of education and counseling, standardized as to general objectives but individualized in the rate and method of training. Thus, it is important for the defective to learn to tell time, to count money, to handle commonly used appliances, and what to do in basic social situations. This is best accomplished by meeting situations as they are encountered and with special emphasis on what the particular child is having difficulty with.

5. Tutorial Methods. Tutoring implies individualized training, specifically tailored to each child's needs. It usually requires that each child be dealt with singly, noncompetitively, gently, acceptingly, and patiently, with sufficient time assigned to achieve limited objectives.

6. The Principle of Overlearning. Because mental defectives forget quickly, large amounts of overlearning may be required to ensure retention. Here, again, the greatest patience is necessary if the child is not to be discouraged and demoralized. It may be necessary to repeat the same teaching or counseling six thousand times, i.e., one or more times daily for twenty years.

7. Directive Methods. While nondirective methods may be used to secure limited objectives, and as long as they are effective, the teacher-counselor should not hesitate to be directive and authoritative in outlining programs and securing objectives. Many mental defectives are confused by nondirective techniques, which may place too much dependence on their inadequate resources, but are reassured by positive directiveness and being told what to do.

8. Communication. Effective tutorial counseling will depend upon the ability to talk in basic English on the mental level of the defective. The counselor will benefit from spending several years in an institution for defectives, learning to communicate on their level. The problem is largely solved when communication is established.

9. Organismic Learning. Many mental defectives are able to learn organismically, utilizing all their faculties *by doing* a task, i.e., by directly acting it out in imitation of another person, whereas they may not be able to comprehend the task if it is presented purely on verbal levels. We need to discover more ways to let them "see" how to do it.

.   .   .   .

Discussion

Mental defectives are capable of learning high social skills, including psychological techniques which were formerly considered beyond their limited comprehension. For example, in case 1,* a low-grade moron was counseled concerning the nature of ambivalence and how to deal with it. Over a period of months he learned to expect ambivalence from the environment, to tolerate it, and even how to cope with it actively. When untrained, most mental defectives have low frustration tolerance, but with suitable counseling they can be taught how to cope with frustration, hostility, and aggression. In case 2, a moron with a low retention span and her employer were counseled concerning methods of compensating for poor retention span by simplifying overcomplicated instructions and by preparing lists of reminders. The failure of case 3 to adjust in the placement home could have been predicted in view of the lack of provision and planning for suitable friendships and recreational outlets for her leisure hours. In subsequent placements, she received much more detailed counseling about romance and how to occupy her leisure. Case 4 illustrates how a person with a low actual IQ may develop functionally normal intelligence through long-term tutorial counseling.

The mental defective should be regarded as a marginal person, incapable usually of adapting on his own resources alone but capable of almost normal adjustment if his resources can be supplemented by the higher intelligence of relatives, friends, teachers, and counselors. The tutorial relationship is one of directiveness, recognition of self-inadequacies, acceptance of authority, and willingness to seek co-operative help from those who know more. There is nothing undemocratic, subservient, or unduly dependent in the relationship of a person of higher intelligence systematically supplementing the inadequacies of a person of lower intelligence where the goals and end results of such a relationship are constructive and healthy. Under such conditions, an otherwise defective and inadequate person may function almost normally and with healthy dignity.

Summary

The rationale and technique of methods of tutorial education and counseling are outlined in this paper. The functional intelligence of mental defectives may be greatly improved if they can be taught to act in a given situation as would a more intelligent person. Special educational and re-

* Details of these cases have been omitted in the ellipsis above. *Ed.*

habilitative techniques are necessary to accomplish these objectives. Illustrative cases are presented to demonstrate the relatively complicated behaviors which may be acquired by defectives with suitable tutorial counseling.

33. Small, Short-Term Group Meetings with Parents of Children with Mongolism *

MARY L. YATES, *Clinical Psychologist, Bureau of Maternal and Child Health, Washington, D.C.*
RUTH LEDERER, *Clinical Psychologist, Bureau of Maternal and Child Health, Washington, D.C.*

Introduction

VARIOUS MEANS have been used to help parents cope with the knowledge that they are the mother and father of a retarded child. These may include the group approach or individual counseling, both of which have been successful. An attempt was made to find out whether in a clinic setting short-term, undirected group meetings would help both parents of retarded children. Since parents of children with mongolism (Schipper, 1959) raised similar questions with regard to the developmental prognosis of their child, regardless of their degree of acceptance of the diagnosis, it was decided to include such parents in a first attempt to try out these groups. It was felt that four couples should be the maximum number included in any one group because the emphasis in the meetings was to be on the sharing of experiences and that more than this number would perhaps be a deterrent to this goal.

A series of three evening sessions was planned with each of three groups, meeting at monthly intervals, so that both parents could attend. In the course of a year ten meetings were held. A total of sixteen parents participated, all of whom had had their children evaluated in the clinic and had

Reprinted by permission of the authors and the *American Journal of Mental Deficiency,* 65:467–472; 1961.

received interpretation. The children represented ranged in age from one year to four years, with the exception of one child who was seven. There were five boys and four girls included.

Services for the Retarded Child is a special program of the Bureau of Maternal and Child Health of the Government of the District of Columbia Department of Public Health. The clinic offers diagnostic as well as treatment and follow-up services. The diagnostic study is an unhurried process, often involving several contacts with the various staff members, because it is felt that these appointments can be of therapeutic value as a step in preparation for interpretation. Interpretation is given by the pediatrician-director, and efforts are made by the staff members immediately concerned to help parents carry out the recommendations. In many instances parents need help in accepting and understanding the diagnosis, and this is offered through continued case-work service. Or, if the child is in need of stimulation in developing self-care skills, help in this direction is provided.

Following interpretation, parents' reactions may vary from seeming acceptance to hostile rejection and inability to use help. The question was raised as to whether it is possible, regardless of the degree of acceptance, understanding, and awareness of the situation parents may have, to provide something in addition to facilitate their ability to restructure their way of living to include this experience.

Although in the last few years the public has become more enlightened about mental retardation, much misconception still persists. Mongolism, for example, is still equated with idiocy, even among professionals. Historically, the term *mongolism* embodies characteristics which have been associated with the concept of the fool or idiot. Because of this, the parents of these children have to cope with their own feelings about their child as well as with the ambivalance shown toward him in their contacts outside the home.

In other situations, group meetings have been utilized successfully in helping parents. It was felt that the group process might be of use here to assist parents to find their equilibrium more easily and handle more appropriately their feelings about what has happened to their child.

Purpose, Goals, and Form of the Meetings

The purpose of these meetings was to encourage parents to share their experiences and concerns with each other by permitting them to assume responsibility, not only in conducting the meetings, but also in bringing up subject matter for discussion. It was hoped parents would feel free to bring up common concerns, what they did about them, and their feelings about having such a child and that the very sharing with each other would help them make a more satisfying adjustment. All the families who participated in these meetings were told individually about them and their structure. It was emphasized that these were their meetings, a time during which they could bring up and discuss any concern they might have about their child, and that all parents invited had a child with mongolism. Thus, the groups were to be composed of parents who met the following criteria: (1) children with the same diagnosis; (2) both parents able to attend when possible and who were not so severely disturbed about the diagnosis as to need special individual help.

As members of the group, the staff participants did not function in their usual professional roles of psychologist and social worker but rather as sponsors of the group, taking leadership only to get discussion going and to keep it along lines within limited goals. The social worker assumed the responsibility for the meetings, and the psychologist participated as cosponsor. They acted as sympathetic listeners, redirected questions back to the group, took initiative at the beginning of the sessions and at the end, answered questions, and gave information only if it was obvious that the group had misinformation or lacked knowledge about the subject.

The meetings were held in the conference room of the clinic, and as the parents arrived they were invited to sit around the conference table. In order to stress the informality of these meetings, light refreshments were available, and informal conversation was encouraged because it was felt best to wait until the majority had gathered so that all parents could have equal benefit of the exchange of ideas. This went on until such time as the sponsors indicated that the meeting would begin. Although the sponsors had in mind some time limit as to when the meetings would draw to a close, they were not rigid about this. Sessions were permitted to go on until they reached a logical and natural termination point, and it usually turned out that they lasted for approximately one hour and a half. At the close of the meetings there was always a pulling together of what had gone on. This was done by either a parent or the social worker. However, if the social worker took responsibility for doing this, every effort was made to include the parents in the summing up.

Pattern of the Initial Meetings

The initial meetings of all three groups seemed to follow a similar pattern. The sponsors usually had to take more initiative in the first session of each group than during the remaining meetings of the series. They opened with a review of the purpose for which the group had been called together and with clarification of the role the sponsors would take. It was then suggested that the parents describe their child, in order that he might be identified for the group. This was eagerly responded to by the parents. Some took this quite literally and described him in physical appearance, size, and weight, while others immediately brought up problem areas.

One of the concerns presented first in all three groups centered on growth and development. The earlier questions in this area usually involved the onset of the basic achievements in motor development skills, that is, at what age a child sat up, walked, talked, and the like. This immediately set up a contact point between the parents. It was more than just an exchange of information: a sort of emotional interchange. Most of them had not known the parents of any other child with mongolism, and this was their first opportunity to really discuss mutual concerns. This led to a very rapid feeling of relatedness among them and enabled them to move quickly into other areas.

Almost immediately following this physical description of the child, the question was raised as to when the others had learned of the diagnosis. Another question that came up early was whether they had told anyone else, and, if so, how they had handled it. These questions were emotionally charged and were brought up by the parents who had experienced difficulty in dealing with them. There was usually a parent in the group who had been able to handle his own anxieties in this area and could help clarify the underlying feelings the parents had about this. Those involved seemed able to listen to what was said.

Having shared this kind of information with each other seemed to release a certain tension that had existed, and they began to participate very actively in discussion. In a first meeting, they seemed to cover the whole gamut of concerns: diagnosis and timing of being told the diagnosis; their feelings about having such a child, not only now but at the time they were given the diagnosis; rate of development; resources; and schools. They also raised questions about what can be expected of their child in the near future as well as in terms of long-range plans, reaching into adolescent and adult years. One group broached the possibility of some type of insurance plan.

These subjects were really just skimmed over and gave the impression that these questions had been on their minds and they had to get them out. It was usually very difficult for the first session to break up because there seemed so much more still to be said.

The Pattern During a Series of Three Meetings

In all three groups, the trend seemed to be that most areas that were discussed in later sessions had already been touched upon in the first meeting. The emotional tone of the first meeting was one of a positive feeling for the sponsors and for each other. They seemed glad to have an opportunity to meet with other parents with similar problems. It was more or less a sharing with people who feel very close, but not in an intimate way. The deeper feelings they might have about their particular situation did not usually come up. Although many factors enter into this, one might be that they were grateful for the opportunity to share information with others who can be sympathetic out of experience.

At the second meeting, the same subjects were raised that had been brought up during the first session, but, in addition, some of the more serious details as well as their deeper concerns came out. They tended to look to the sponsors for answers, and when redirected to the group they displayed hostile feelings toward them. Since the sponsors did not grasp the responsibility for answering questions or taking over, usually a member of the group assumed leadership, and they were able to work out some of their feelings and answers to the questions. Those persons who took the role of leader seemed to rise to the position and to gloss over some of their deeper feelings about their own situation in order to help others with theirs. The way they handled this was to display extreme acceptance of having a retarded child, pointing out some of the assets and actually distorting some of the situation.

The subject came up of whether they had found it necessary to conceal the fact that they had a retarded child. How had they handled this, and what were their feelings about sharing the information with others? They wanted the details of whether you tell other members of the family and members of the community and, if so, how one goes about it and how much one tells. It was the parent leaders who were able to help the other members of the group look at this more realistically and work out how this could be handled. Although this was not resolved to the point where some of the more reluctant parents would agree that they would tell others, there was a feeling of relief from having expressed their feelings about why they had not told others about the child. This was a rather uneasy session, one during which they had to face up to reality. No matter how they attempted to couch many of their problems and feelings, someone in the group always saw through it. The parents seemed to look forward to the third session. They appeared to need each other, and they even planned what they would cover.

The last meeting of the series was usually a more intellectual type of session, during which there was some attempt to solve their problems and an evaluation of what had come out of the meetings. The solutions they offered were usually beyond their immediate problems, reaching into adolescence and adulthood. There was some criticism of the sessions, what they had expected of them and still needed, and also some criticism of the role the sponsors took. They seemed to have expected more informative and instructional-type sessions but were able to see what the sponsors meant by setting up limited goals within which they themselves would attempt to face their situation. Once having "hashed out" what had gone on in these sessions, they seemed to feel that they had gained some benefit from this kind of meeting. Often they felt that some of the needs that had not been met in these brief sessions could be found within existing community resources, such as the Association for Retarded Children, or could be fostered through such facilities.

Evaluation

The impressions gained are based upon a limited number of cases and are therefore tentative.

Small, short-term, undirected group sessions, spread over a three-month period, with both parents attending, appeared to the sponsors to be quite helpful and useful. This approach would seem to work best with persons who have some ability to put their feelings into words. The number of meetings was restricted because goals were limited and the sponsors wanted to help these parents during their period of adjustment to the diagnosis and its implications. Three meetings seemed to be ideal because the first meeting served to throw open the problems; the second, to delve more deeply into certain aspects of the problem; and the third, to help them pull together and integrate what had been accomplished during the sessions and begin to think more realistically about the future.

With the first group, a fourth meeting was held in compliance with the demands of the parents. During this session the parents planned for expansion of the group. They were interested in increasing the members, bringing in speakers on various topics, and also changing the role of the sponsors to include discussion of the more emotionally charged issues. As this did not fall within the purpose and goals of this project, the sponsors discussed with the parents the resources in the community where this could be met. It would appear that this type of group might not be able to maintain its nondirective character beyond three sessions but would tend to become more therapy-oriented or educational and informative in nature.

The focus in these group meetings was to encourage parents to discuss their feelings about their child and help them come to grips with the situation. The small group sessions were effective because the size made it a face-to-face relationship, yet different enough from a one-to-one relationship to present a nonthreatening situation conducive to sharing and enabling parents to bring up areas of concerns one might anticipate they must have.

The meetings did not change the parents' basic attitude but did enable them to see, for example, that although it was "terrible" to have such a child, it was all right to feel this way, and this seemed to relieve some of their shame and guilt. Although their problems and feelings were not resolved, in some it had been so bottled up that they had been unable to express any feelings except hostility, withdrawal, and denial. As the meetings progressed, there seemed to be less need for denial toward other people and a more realistic appraisal of their situation and their feelings about it. As a result, the parents seemed better prepared to consider the next steps in planning. For example, they seemed more aware of their own needs in relation to such planning and in a position to recognize the need for direct help, whether in relation to their feelings about the diagnosis or in the area of management. They also seemed able to look at the broader implications of mental retardation and to wonder what they could contribute as parents in areas outside their immediate situation.

In the group setting, with both parents present, the sponsors became more aware of how difficult it is for fathers to accept the diagnosis of mental retardation, since they tend to cover up their real feelings. Their early comments were more general, with a tendency to intellectualize the problem. Mothers, on the other hand, responded in a more personal way. Their comments were closely related to specific incidents from their experience with their child. Fathers and mothers looked upon the sponsors differently, too. The mothers used the sponsors in their role more appropriately, and the fathers tended to place the sponsors on a more social level. One factor of significance which emerged from these meetings is that fathers do want to be included in planning for their children. It was pointed out that fathers were not always able to participate as much as they would like, but they felt strongly that they wanted to be the ones to decide to what extent they could be involved rather than have it assumed that they could not participate.

At a first meeting, either the father or the mother seemed to take over, and the couple functioned as "one," with the less verbal parent reinforcing the other. In later meetings, the husband and wife spoke up as individuals, free to express their own ideas regardless of whether their comments were in agreement with the spouse. In one case they even sat on opposite sides of the table. The emphasis was on clarifying their own thoughts. This was made possible because they gained support from the other couples. What occurred was different, for example, from mothers supporting mothers and fathers, fathers. At the end of the sessions, they again seemed to be united, voicing more or less similar feelings.

It is important for parents to be able to attend meetings together. Although the couples seemed to speak to the point of the reality factors in the situation, when only one person of a couple was present, the members of the group seemed to jump to supporting that person more quickly. Also, when there are couples present, the core of the issue is forced because they do not have to accentuate their sex-linked role.

These meetings appeared to help parents in their adjustment during the period following interpretation. The spacing of the meetings at monthly intervals seemed to give them time to absorb some of what they had brought up during the meetings. The role the sponsors took was different from their professional one in the clinic. It took time for the parents to accept this, and occasionally their hostility was aroused. But they went along with it, selecting their own leaders who were able to assume the role they wanted the sponsors to take. Because in the third session they were able to evaluate what had gone on quite objectively, being able to discuss both the negative and positive aspects of the meetings, it was felt that steps toward adjustment had been initiated.

At first the parents felt a very strong link with each other because of the factor of mongolism.. Discussion was unproductive when they attempted to analyze and understand the physical attributes of mongolism per se. Only when they realized the futility of this were they able to examine the basic issue of retardation and discuss their children who had varying degrees of retardation rather than "having to deal with a mongolian idiot."

It should be remembered that the children represented by the parents in these groups were still young. The children themselves had not yet had to face the community. The parents will, perhaps, have to analyze their feelings again in terms of mongolism when they meet situations as their children grow older.

This type of group can be effective as a regular part of such a clinic program and is thought of only as an intermediary step in the process of adjustment.

Suggested Readings

Bolduc, T. M. "Social Value Need Patterns in Mental Retardates," *Journal of Consulting Psychology*, 24:472–479; 1960. Factor analysis of fifty mental defectives' performance on a research instrument of 120 items indicated the following: (1) preference for submission to adult authority, (2) preference for loyalty and protection of others, (3) compliance with adults but domination with peers. Three additional factors each had less than 10 per cent variance.

Erdman, R. L. *Vocational Choices of Adolescent Mentally Retarded Boys*, Ed.D. thesis, University of Illinois, 1957.

Mahan, W., Jr. "Unique Aspects of the Low-Ability Student: A Challenge to Counseling," *Journal of Counseling Psychology*, 10:78–82; 1963. Characteristics of forty low-ability (IQ 90 or below) eighth-grade pupils on three non-intellective measures are contrasted with those of average (N = 90), above average (N = 49), and superior ability (N = 33). Low-ability pupils were found to differ significantly from others in (1) inadequacy of school performance as reported by teachers; (2) correlation between self-as-pupil and self-as-ideal-pupil based on a fifty-item Q-sort; (3) correlations between self-as-pupil and the school's modal-ideal-pupil concept. No significant differences were found among the other three groups. It is suggested that low-ability pupils may comprise a different population, and the implications of this for counseling are discussed.

Throne, Frances M.; Schulman, J. L.; and Kaspar, J. C. "Reliability and Stability of the Wechsler Intelligence Scale for Children for a Group of Mentally Retarded Boys," *American Journal of Mental Deficiency*, 67:455–457; 1962. Three to four months after the original test the same examiner retested on the WISC thirty-nine mentally retarded boys, ages eleven years to fourteen years eleven months, with original WISC IQ's in the retarded range. The correlation coefficients indicate that the Verbal, Performance, and Full Scale IQ scores are reliable. The reliability of the Comprehension, Arithmetic, Picture Completion, Block Design, and Coding subtests was adequate; but the reliability of the remaining subtests was somewhat less than adequate. The means of the Verbal, Performance, and Full Scale IQ scores showed no significant gains (or losses) between the first and second administrations—a further indication of the stability of the WISC for this population.

THE VERY CONSIDERABLE guidance literature which has recently grown up about the vocational rehabilitation of mentally retarded youth appeared to deserve a special chapter in this book of readings. The sheltered workshop appears to be a socioeconomic invention of such importance, both to the patient and to society, that descriptions of it need the space here accorded. In this respect the Mayo article, authored by the chairman of the President's panel, gives the guidelines for this development. Papers by Appell, Williams, and Fishell; Dubrow; Goldman and Soloff; and Hunt explore the objectives, procedures, atmospheres, and effects of the sheltered workshop. The chapter is concluded by two more theoretical papers: the first by Nadler and Shontz on a factor study of the various patterns in a sheltered workshop and the last by Rusalem on the counselor's perception of the therapeutic aspects found therein.

34. Significant Factors in Placing Mental Retardates from a Workshop Situation*

MELVILLE J. APPELL, *Director, Mental Retardation Demonstration Project, Rochester, New York*
CLARENCE M. WILLIAMS, *University of Rochester*
KENNETH N. FISHELL, *University of Rochester*

THE DEVELOPMENT in recent years of sheltered workshop facilities for special disability groups has been an event of unusual significance in the field of rehabilitation. In a directory (1961) now being completed by the National Association for Retarded Children, there are listed 203 workshops for the mentally retarded, operated either directly by member units or in affiliation with other community organizations. However, as in most areas of rapid growth where service becomes the focus, research needs appear to be of secondary importance. Goldstein and Heber refer specifically to "the severe limitations in our knowledge of the factors critically related to vocational and social adjustment" and "the need for research data bearing on vocational and social adjustment."

Even though there is little research related to successful vocational adjustment of retardates, there is even less in reference to successful workshop experience (successful in the sense that workshop training leads to competitive employment). Most studies are concerned with factors that distinguish employed from unemployed retardates. These factors generally fall into three categories: (1) level of intelligence, (2) personality characteristics, and (3) specific vocational skills.

In relating intelligence and vocational success, it is generally conceded that the IQ or mental age does not differentiate the successful from the unsuccessful groups with competitive employment as the criterion. However, this is probably too broad a generalization, according to studies reported by Davies.

The prevailing attitude in this field regarding intelligence and employment is probably best summed up by Goldstein and Heber. "The IQ has been too frequently regarded as a highly efficient predictor of an individual's level of vocational and social adjustment and of his ability to profit from

* Reproduced by permission of the authors and *Personnel and Guidance Journal*, 41:261–265; November, 1962.

an education and rehabilitation program. . . . The problem is not so much the test as the interpretation which has been given it."

Most researchers are agreed that certain personality and social factors are much more important in distinguishing the placeable from nonplaceable groups (placeable referring to those able to secure employment). Warren found self-confidence, cheerfulness, co-operation with supervisors and peers, sociability, initiative, as well as other factors, important in distinguishing the employed from an unemployed group. Coakley indicates that "personal traits and characteristics determine success or failure on a job." She notes the employer's interest in the individual's "dependability, his ability to get along with other workers and to accept criticism, his interest in the job and his desire to do his best." Employers gave as reasons for an unsuccessful exposure to the world of work the following: talked too much; not punctual; couldn't follow instructions. In no instance was intelligence or inability to do the work mentioned.

Discussion concerning specific vocational skills and placement in competitive employment must often involve a comparison of specific versus general training. It is obvious from the foregoing discussion that success in a workshop is related to general training such as one might get in personal adjustment training programs in workshops. Many surveys report that pupils are not able to find work in the specific skills in which they have been trained. Furthermore, the mentally retarded generally work at semi-skilled laboring jobs or service jobs which modern industry has so simplified that few if any skills are necessary.

A review of the literature, then, would seem to indicate that there is relatively little research which significantly distinguishes the retardate who is competitively employable from the retardate who is not. Yet burgeoning programs supported by federal and local governments and voluntary agencies make it necessary to know what distinguishes these groups so that adequate training can be provided. Therefore, this study is an attempt to supply partial answers to the question, "What are the differences between retardates who are considered to be terminal (long-term) trainees in a workshop and retardates who have achieved competitive employment after a period of exposure in a workshop?"

Method

Population. The comparison groups (Table 1) for this study were trainees in the Work Training Center of New York State's Mental Retardation Demonstration Project in Rochester. The trainees were divided into two groups, twelve in an Employed Group who had been in training in the workshop and who had been placed, and twenty-five in a Terminal (Long Term) Group still in training at the time of this study.

In accordance with the original project plan, enrollment was limited to the "mentally retarded of both sexes, age 17 or older, whose vocational adjustment needs were not otherwise capable of being met." A maximum IQ of 75 was noted as the "rough threshold for entrance screening purposes," but no minimum IQ was stipulated.

Situation. The Work Training Center, a subcontract shop, is staffed with a director, assistant director, director of counseling (staff psychologist), a social worker, a group social worker, a case worker, two evaluation and training supervisors, a part-time recreation director, and a placement director. There are also a number of consultants associated with this Work Training Center, such as a psychiatrist, a mental retardation specialist, and an engineer. The Evaluation Panel for admitting and discharging trainees consists of members of the workshop staff, augmented by certain interested professionals.

Materials. A medical check list, an individual psychological test battery, and interview data were obtained from candidate and parent to establish criteria for admission.

TABLE 1—CHARACTERISTICS OF EMPLOYED AND TERMINAL (LONG TERM) GROUPS

		Terminal	Employed
IQ	Range	36–74	48–80
	Mean	61.2	69.3
	S.D.	9.57	9.34
Age in months	Range	215–335	218–358
	Mean	255.4	259.5
	S.D.	29.34	38.65
Reading grade	Range	1.1–7.8	1.6–10.1
	Mean	4.0	4.8
	S.D.	2.15	3.34
Arithmetic grade	Range	2.0–5.1	2.3–8.3
	Mean	3.4	4.2
	S.D.	0.92	2.13
Time (days) in work-shop (as of 3/10/61)	Range	137–420	20–239
	Mean	290.0	107.5
	S.D.	84.87	63.81

A Work Evaluation Report (WER) modeled after the Jacobs and Weingold Behavioral Check List (1958) was completed on each trainee by a supervisor during the last half of the first seven-week orientation period.

The WER was thereafter administered at six-month intervals. It was divided into six areas: (1) general abilities, (2) work approach, (3) social attitudes and adjustments, (4) work tolerance, (5) observed interests and aspirations, (6) summary and recommendations. Each item in any one area was rated in accordance with the following scale: A—Industrially Acceptable, B—Workshop Standard, Problem in Workshop.

Procedures. The candidates for this Work Training Center came from many voluntary and public agencies and a state institution. Prior to admission by the Evaluation Panel, all candidates were examined by a medical doctor, a psychologist, and a social worker. These examinations were conducted within the twelve months before consideration by the Evaluation Panel. The thirty-seven trainees under discussion met the admission criteria.

The initial period of orientation and evaluation was determined by the panel in accordance with what was determined necessary for any one particular trainee. Shortly before the end of this period, the trainee was re-evaluated by the panel as to his progress. When a trainee had shown an ability to profit from his workshop experience, the Evaluation Panel recommended a further training period on re-examination of his progress. This process of re-examination was continuous.

As soon as appropriate evidence was obtained, a tentative division into the Pre-Employment and the Terminal (Long Term) Group was made. Placements to competitive (outside) employment were made from the Pre-Employment Group by the placement director of the workshop or through the trainee's own initiative. Until placement was obtained, however, this group continued in training. The Terminal (Long Term) Group was composed of those for whom placement was doubtful or for whom long-term training was indicated. Appropriate evidence consisted of data collected from the previously mentioned instruments, the weekly staff conferences, and the weekly panel meetings.

Results

The pooled ratings by separate judges on the WER for the two groups were compared for significant differences using Chi-Square. Table 2 shows the items which were significant in favor of the Employed Group. Also shown are the items from the WER on which there were no significant differences.

A comparison of time spent in the workshop for the two groups showed the Employed Group to have spent an amount of time which was less than the Terminal (Long Term) Group. This difference, proved significant beyond the 1 per cent level using the Mann-Whitney U test.

The groups were also compared on the basis of IQ scores. Full-scale scores and verbal scores for the two groups showed no significant difference, but nonverbal scores as measured by the Wechsler (both the WAIS and the WBI were used interchangeably) did show a significant difference (Mann-Whitney U test). This difference, as shown in Table 3, is in favor of the Employed Group, revealing that they were significantly higher in nonverbal scores.

Discussion

Some of the characteristics found significant in regard to the items of the WER, which distinguish between the two groups, substantiate the findings of previous studies. However, other characteristics which show significant differences between these groups have not been stressed in previous reports. These are in the area of general abilities (WER), such as learning speed, attention span, manual dexterity—gross, and following instructions —oral. (Following instructions—written was found to be of no significance.)

In the area of work approach (WER) a number of characteristics which significantly separate the two groups were found, as shown in Table 2.

The significant items in the section on social attitudes and adjustment (WER) have generally been reported where comparison of these groups was under discussion.

Much previous work has been accomplished in which the IQ was not a significant distinguishing factor contributing to employment from the workshop. In none of the previous reports investigated was there found a discussion of the various scales of the intelligence tests used. In analyzing the verbal and nonverbal scales of the Wechsler tests, it was found that, while the verbal scale did not distinguish these groups, the nonverbal scale did. This is an interesting finding, since it might be used by workshop personnel in conjunction with the WER for purposes of differentiating those long-term trainees from those who might achieve competitive employment.

As indicated in Table 1, age for the range represented in the sample for this study was not found to be a significant distinguishing factor.

By far the most important of the factors found to be significant appears to be time in the workshop (Table 1). It is recognized that these trainees come to the workshop at various stages of preparation for employment and that this complicates the issue concerning time in the workshop. Furthermore, a considerable turnover of professional and nonprofessional staff

TABLE 2—TABULATION OF ITEMS: WORK EVALUATION REPORT

Items	Significant	Not Significant
I. General abilities	Following instructions—oral Learning speed Retention Attention to job Attention span Job comprehension Manual dexterity—gross	Following instructions — written Manual dexterity fine—finger fine—small tools co-ordination— both hands
II. Work approach	Interest level motivation Bizarre behavior amt. of attention seeking speed accuracy complexity of work responsibility initiative perseverance degree of supervision Adjustment to variety of work Adjustment to repetitive work	Attendance Punctuality Bizarre behavior judgment Care of tools, office equip- ment, maintenance
III. Social attitudes and adjustment	Grooming Self-confidence Co-operativeness Acceptance of supervision Group response acceptance of group acceptance by group communication	

TABLE 3—COMPARISON OF THE TWO GROUPS ON SCALES OF THE WECHSLER
BY MANN-WHITNEY U TEST

	Full Scale, IQ	Verbal Scale, IQ	Nonverbal Scale, IQ
Employed group Terminal (long- term) group	> not significant	> not significant	> significantly higher for employed

during the course of this study probably contributed to a longer stay for some trainees in the workshop than might have occurred otherwise.

Nevertheless, of the original thirty-seven, only twelve obtained employment outside the workshop up to March, 1961. All of those placed found employment within eight months of entrance into the workshop. The average time spent in the workshop for those trainees was slightly over three and a half months, while the terminal trainees averaged slightly over nine and a half months in training. The results raised serious questions as to training in a workshop of this specific type. It is unlikely that the trainees who were placed in competitive employment were actually workshop-trained in the sense of "making proficient by instruction and practice."

However, it is possible that a workshop of this kind, in which training is general rather than specific, does provide an orientation and reinforcement of good work habits and thereby increases a trainee's prospects for employment. This might suggest, then, that more intensive placement efforts by competent placement specialists ought to be provided for those who, after sufficient evaluation and orientation, are considered good prospects for employment.

This is not to imply that those who remained in the workshop as terminal workers did not benefit from their experience. The workshop allowed for work activity that in many ways was similar to that engaged in by those gainfully employed workers. This in itself is a worth-while objective for a workshop. However, the worth of this workshop or any other workshop to any community or any individual must be determined in the light of appropriate goals and purposes. Since almost 70 per cent of all trainees remained in the workshop, the question is raised as to whether a greater effort should be made to provide for acceptability on the part of the community of the workshop as a terminal facility. In this connection, the development of contract work and other trainee remunerative activities ought to be emphasized to ensure continuous work flow and resultant workshop stability.

It would appear, then, that the rate of placements to outside employment decreased as a function of time, while the long-term trainee became numerically a greater factor in the workshop. Further investigation of this aspect of workshops for the retarded is recommended.

Summary and Conclusion

In order to answer the question, "What are the differences between retardates who are considered to be terminal (long-term) trainees in a workshop and retardates who have achieved competitive employment after a period of exposure in a workshop?" an attempt was made to identify certain factors which would distinguish the two groups. For this purpose a Work Evaluation Report (WER) was developed. A Termination Report filled out by the workshop staff and an intelligence test administered before entrance into the workshop contributed other factors which were found to be useful in distinguishing between the comparison groups. These groups were compared, using ratings derived from the WER and the other factors previously mentioned. The Terminal (Long Term) Group was composed of twenty-five trainees in the Work Training Center, while the twelve in the Employed Group had been in the workshop but at the time of the study were in competitive outside employment.

On the WER, sixteen items were found to be significantly higher for the Employed Group. Time in the workshop and the nonverbal scales of the Wechsler test distinguished the Employed from the Terminal (Long Term) Group.

Certain questions were raised by this study. One involved the training of that group for whom outside employment could be predicted. It was felt that further study should be undertaken to determine the kind of training which would most benefit these trainees for whom outside employment seemed a realistic conclusion to their workshop efforts. Because of the tendency of the majority of workshop trainees to remain in the workshop, the question was raised as to whether workshops handling this type of trainee ought to concentrate their resources on providing a workplace as a terminal facility. Further investigation seemed warranted in this area. From the point of view of this workshop and workshops devoted specifically to the retarded, a study of goals and purposes was considered necessary.

35. Sheltered Workshops for the Mentally Retarded As an Educational and Vocational Experience *

MAX DUBROW, *Director of the AHRC Training Center and Workshop, New York City*

THIS ARTICLE is based on the experience of one workshop—the AHRC (Association for the Help of Retarded Children) Training Center and Workshop in New York City. This workshop dates back to 1953 when the

* Reprinted by permission of the author and *Personnel and Guidance Journal,* 38:392–395; January, 1960.

AHRC, a parents group organized in 1949, opened its first unit, which outgrew a number of locations through the years. When special project funds became available through the 1954 Amendments to the Vocational Rehabilitation Act, we were able to establish our present facility in June, 1955. We received a five-year grant from the Office of Vocational Rehabilitation for research and demonstration. The grant made it possible to investigate such large problems as the factors inhibiting the vocational rehabilitation of mentally retarded young adults; the type of organization, program, and staffing pattern of an appropriate rehabilitation workshop; the development of diagnostic, evaluation, and training methods; etc. Just as important, from a human and practical point of view, was the extension of our service to meet the pressing needs of the many retardates in the community and the utilization by the State Division of Vocational Rehabilitation of our vocational rehabilitation facility for the many retardates who were not eligible for or accepted by the then existing community resources.

At about this time, the middle of 1955, we were designated by OVR as the prototype project in this field, so that the many workshops for the retarded that received OVR grants subsequently have been patterned to some extent after ours. We are now completing our fourth year of operation under the OVR grant.

Workshop Clientele

The AHRC Workshop serves young men and women over seventeen years of age whose primary disability is mental retardation. Our capacity, because of space and budget restrictions, is limited to about sixty-five persons. During any one year we serve from ninety to one hundred individuals. There is no upper age limit; yet our group of trainees is a predominantly younger one, averaging about twenty-two years of age.

In accordance with the legal and educational definitions of retardation in New York State, our IQ ceiling is 75. We have fixed no lower limit on IQ, but the lowest IQ score we have worked with is 27, for a young man currently in the workshop, who, we would all agree, has made a satisfactory if minimal adjustment. The average IQ for the entire population during the past year was 57.4, a figure which has remained fairly constant from year to year.

Referrals come from two main sources. The State Division of Vocation Rehabilitation refers up to twenty trainees at a time, who usually stay for a limited period only, and AHRC has referred most of the forty-five long-term trainees, who will remain with the workshop for indefinite periods of time.

Obviously, if we are to talk of an educational and vocational experience, it is not sufficient to describe our clients according to sex, age, and IQ alone. How can we classify them more meaningfully?

The terms *educable* and *trainable,* so dear to many educators and legislators, are not particularly helpful. For one thing, our clients are young adults who have had all the formal schooling that was available to them. Also, we have found that some of the so-called educables do not profit from training, while many of the so-called trainables can, in fact, be educated if we think of appropriate behaviors, habits, attitudes, motivations, interests, etc. rather than formal academic skills.

In a sheltered workshop, the major dimensions for a classification system, consistent with the objectives of vocational rehabilitation, are employment and work adjustment. Clients may be differentiated meaningfully according to such variables as presenting problems, diagnoses, rehabilitation goals, treatment and training programs, and outcomes. About a year ago, we set up four categories which included all the mentally retarded young adults likely to be served in a sheltered workshop.

1. Readily Placeable. This group is mildly retarded with IQ scores ranging usually from 60 to 75+. Individuals in this category demonstrate relatively positive and active orientation to work, superior performance on our evaluation tests, fairly mature self-concepts in their acceptance of adult roles, and relative ease in relations with peers and adult authority figures. Some had work experience prior to their admission to the workshop or had engaged in some job-hunting activity. Awareness of retardation or "slowness" is usually present. General behavior in the workshop usually confirms our initial impressions of essentially healthy and well-integrated personalities. Rather early in their stay in the workshop, they show accessibility and responsiveness to treatment.

We are sometimes successful in placing these trainees in competitive employment within six or eight months. In some cases, the jobs found are totally unrelated to the trainee's initial and often unrealistic job preferences.

2. Placeable with Special Help. IQ scores for this group range from about 50 to 65. Persons in this category seem less mature; they are less sure of themselves and demonstrate less initiative and self-direction. While expressing positive orientation to work, they are more passive and show fearfulness and anxiety concerning work and their acceptance of the role of adult wage earner.

These trainees are relatively high producers and earners in the workshop and give an impression of operating efficiently. They are somewhat more dependent and less at ease in adult and peer relationships than the first group. Intensive individual and group counseling with the trainee and often with the parents is necessary. A highly concentrated and focused workshop program, integrating the efforts of all the staff, enables members of this group to move into competitive employment after a period of one to two years.

3. Sheltered Workers (A). The most striking characteristic here is the disparity between potential and level of functioning. With respect to IQ and academic achievement, these trainees are most like the members of Group 1, the readily placeables. Emotional instability, rather low physical energy level, and poor socialization are commonly observed. Workshop productivity and earnings tend to be low, although spurts occur from time to time.

They show little awareness of problem and little capacity for change. Counseling tends to be ineffective except in moving toward restricted, limited objectives. These trainees have made what appears to be, for them, a reasonable adjustment to the workshop, although they tend to shun group activities and situations and to prefer social isolation.

4. Sheltered Workers (B). This group is most clearly a long-term or permanent group and includes all trainees whose stigmata alone, such as mongolism, hydrocephaly, gargoylism, etc., might limit their acceptance in other work settings. IQ's range from under 30 to about 48. Trainees in this category are characterized by fairly low potential and a level of functioning which approaches their ceiling. They tend to operate at close to maximum or optimum levels. They are consistent if slow shop producers, but on some contract jobs which provide lengthy training and practice periods some can earn relatively high wages.

Trainees socialize rather freely with each other but rarely with higher-level trainees. Shop staff are usually perceived as parent or teacher figures. Trainees tend to be childlike in their relations with adults, seeking approval through attention-getting devices or parroting parental and other adult standards of good behavior. For these individuals, paid work has more meaning as a constructive, satisfying experience than as a symbol of adult status and self-sufficiency.

For this last group particularly and for many of the third group, the workshop provides considerably more than a vocational and educational experience. It becomes, in effect, a way of life and is probably a significant factor in keeping these retardates in the community and out of institutions.

These descriptive categories have been confirmed by our subsequent experience. A generalized resistance to employment, however, was found to be much more characteristic for the first two groups than we found earlier.

Investigation Findings

We have recently completed two major studies: (1) an analysis of 85 records of cases referred to us by OVR over a two-year period and (2) a follow-up study of 106 cases that had been in any of the AHRC workshops since 1953. (There were a total of 138 cases in the study, but data were available for only 106.)

Because relatively small numbers are involved and because we plan to analyze the data much more intensively, the findings presented must be considered tentative. Generalizations at this point would be unwarranted and premature. Some distillation of our experience of the four years of operation under the OVR grant will also be presented.

1. Using competitive employment as a criterion, the most favorable trainee characteristics appear to include (*a*) being a male; (*b*) twenty-two years of age or older; (*c*) without psychosis or serious emotional disturbance; (*d*) acceptance of mental subnormality; (*e*) some previous work experience; (*f*) fairly realistic job preference; (*g*) some reluctance to enter the workshop.

2. Characteristics of competitive employment include stability with very little turnover or job hopping and jobs in service industries and within institutions generally. The majority of men are successfully employed as messengers; earnings range from $35 to $60 per week, averaging $43 for the group successfully employed.

3. For those capable of entering competitive employment, "workshopitis" or the tendency to prefer the sheltered workshop to other more demanding types of employment did not constitute a problem.

4. The most common problems, varying in intensity from individual to individual, was a generalized resistance to employment.

5. Factors which did not differentiate success from failure groups, using competitive employment as a criterion, include IQ, reading level, friendlessness, and adequate knowledge of job culture.

6. There are indications, not too reliably established at this time, that those trainees who returned home following the workshop experience were more useful family members, were more self-directing, and displayed more initiative and self-reliance.

7. The efficacy of group counseling in particular, and individual counseling as well, in inducing change and in consolidating the trainee's gains

has been demonstrated as a significant piece of the total workshop program.

8. Paid work (in our case, contract work) in a simulated industrial setting, consisting of bench-type tasks including assembly, packaging, and other comparable operations, has proved to be an indispensable medium for training.

9. Evaluation tests of the work sample variety, carefully standardized on a population of mental retardates, have been found to be useful in prediction when considered together with careful observations during the evaluation process and a standardized psychological evaluation.

10. The total workshop atmosphere provides a therapeutic milieu and a program individualized as far as possible to include (*a*) appropriate stimulation and outlets for increased self-assertive and self-directed behavior; (*b*) opportunity for retardates to assume and act out adult roles; (*c*) staff which is perceived by retardates as sympathetic, accepting, understanding, and nonpunitive, at the same time that the staff makes reasonable demands and enforces general rules.

11. Counseling with parents tends to be most effective when goals are fairly concrete and limited.

12. Our program, which we feel has been successful to date in assisting trainees to achieve their highest level of functioning, has included such programs as a weekly workshop meeting of all trainees, newspaper committees and a biweekly workshop newspaper, an employable group, a job preparation group, section meetings, improvement groups, housekeeping committee, grooming groups for men and women, trainee council (an elected, quasi-grievance committee), instruction in travel, word recognition, and reading.

Research in this field is painfully slow. We are dealing with severely handicapped human beings whose growth toward improved functioning moves in barely perceptible steps. We need to investigate larger numbers over long periods of time before we can identify and study many of the variables that have implications for the vocational rehabilitation of the mentally retarded. Particularly intriguing research suggestions that have already emerged include (*a*) study of the self-concept of the retardate and his perception of social roles; (*b*) study of the dynamics, process, and techniques of individual and group counseling with mental retardates; (*c*) determination of the behavioral components which constitute maximum or optimum functioning for the retardate within a sheltered workshop setting; (*d*) development of differential teaching and training methods for

various diagnostic and etiological categories of mental retardation; and
(e) study of effect of controlled environment manipulations on attitudes
and behavior of retardates.

The ongoing and pressing needs of a service program require continuing
research as well in such areas as refinement of diagnostic and prognostic
measures, development of scales for tracing movement and change, and
methods of helping pseudo retardates whose emotional disturbances present special problems. As a vocational rehabilitation facility which has
attempted to integrate or at least reconcile the often conflicting service
and research elements of our program, we are grateful for the support of
the Office of Vocational Rehabilitation, which has made this beginning
possible.

36. Issues in Rehabilitation Workshops *

EDWIN GOLDMAN, *Supervisor, Work Therapy
Center, Chicago Jewish Vocational Service*
ASHER SOLOFF, *Research Supervisor, Chicago Jew-
ish Vocational Service*

IT IS PERHAPS time for those of us in the workshop movement to take
stock and ask ourselves some important questions. While we have been
able to report some success with workshops as a form of help, we have
not always been clear in our thinking as to exactly what is happening to
clients in our programs. Perhaps we could be even more successful if we
could stop and take a look at what we are doing. In this paper, we hope
to contribute to the process of self-evaluation by raising some of the important issues that need clarification. While we do this by presenting some
of our own ideas, it is done in order to provoke discussion and controversy
which could lead to heightened understanding for all of us.

* Reprinted by permission of the authors and *Personnel and Guidance Journal,*
40:169–173; October, 1961.

Four Workshop Purposes

To begin with, what are the purposes of workshops? What do we hope to accomplish with them, and in what terms can we justify their existence? It is not enough to say that their purpose is to help people who have been seen as vocationally disabled to get to work. Other techniques might fill that role. Intensive counseling and testing, for example, might be sufficient help for many people who are now considered for workshop entry. Active support by a counselor prior to job seeking and during the initial period on a job might be help enough for others. We must distinguish our goals from those of counseling, testing, and training before we can be clear as to our objectives.

We would like to suggest four purposes that set off rehabilitation workshops from other forms of help and, in combination, define what we are trying to accomplish.

First, workshops provide a *concrete* work experience. A situation simulating actual job conditions provides opportunities for clients to participate in a realistic work setting. In such a setting, a client can see for himself how he functions on various jobs, what it feels like to work, or how he feels about taking orders. He can begin to see and feel what it means to say that a work situation is different from a school situation or other social situations. Actually being in the setting provides its own kinds of learning.

The work atmosphere as a social situation is as important in this respect as the specific learning of manual or social skills. This is the milieu therapy aspect of the workshop. The atmosphere helps provide learning, goals, and emotional support for clients and helps them to adjust to work and to job relationships. It could be argued that this is a genuine acculturation process in which an individual confronts a novel situation much as does an immigrant arriving in a country. The manner in which this happens in workshops is still largely unexplored, and we would do well to investigate it further.

The counselor is also aided by the concreteness of the experience, for the workshop provides specific answers to some of his questions about clients. He is likely to discover what kinds of work his client relates to best, what levels of productivity his client reaches, whether productivity problems are related to relationship problems, and how his client relates to co-workers. By having available the observations of the workshop staff, the counselor can compare what is actually happening in the work setting to the client's statements about his abilities, goals, and problems.

Second, the workshop provides a sheltered setting. While attemping to simulate work conditions as closely as possible, we are usually gradual in our imposition of controls and standards on individual clients. Thus, a young man without work experience may test various ways of dealing with his superiors without fear of being fired before he settles on what is most appropriate for himself. Again, a client learns that he can test himself without fear of suffering from the consequences of his actions. He may experiment with different methods of doing a job, with the amount of talking he can do while working, or with the necessity of keeping regular hours. He can test these activities and relationships in a setting in which he learns that he is respected and given time to learn what is most appropriate.

Third, the workshop provides a therapeutic setting for some. This area must be approached cautiously. We suggest, however, that the reality functioning of the ego is often strengthened in a positive workshop experience and that the defenses which are preventing adequate adaptations to work demands can be modified. This has often been true, we think, for some of the most fearful and most withdrawn. On the other hand, we question whether there are any radical changes in personality organization of clients or any major changes in the defense systems. There are likely to be therapeutic results for some clients, but the extent of therapy is limited.

Fourth, the workshop provides a group setting. Clients are working together under supervision. Each person is able to compare his own work with that of others. He is able to see that his problems are not unique and need not provide so much of a reason for shame. He can develop friendships and compare notes on work experiences. He is not trying to overcome problems on his own.

These, we suggest, are the four interdependent purposes served by rehabilitation workshops. Are there others which are just as important? We feel that this question of purposes is one of the most important needing discussion within the workshop movement.

Who Is Helped

We would like to consider next whether experience has yet taught us whether there are certain kinds of clients with whom we tend to succeed, as against others with whom we do less well. It should be understood that we are not referring to the traditional diagnostic categories but rather to the dynamics observed, no matter what the initial diagnosis.

It is our contention, based on our own experience, that certain broad generalizations can be made. Certainly, as with any generalization, exceptions will be found. However, we think that some guideposts have become evident over a period of years. It is possible that other workshops have had different results. If so, it would be instructive to learn how and why.

Let us discuss first the types of clients with whom we have tended to be most successful and postulate why this might be so.

For many coming to the workshop program, the main defect in the work personality is an inability to understand the demands of work or the role of a worker. However, in these clients, emotional problems of severity have not developed, and they have been fairly well trained socially. These clients are mainly in need of an educational experience specifically relating to the demands of work. Often, too, they are in need of support regarding self-concept. The workshop functions primarily with these people as an educational experience focused on building appropriate work habits and as a security-giving agent in terms of both productive achievement and an emerging awareness of adequacy in the co-worker setting. The workshop has tended to be most successful with this type of individual.

Another type of client with whom we have done well is the so-called non-achiever. Often, from an early age, this person has not achieved to capacity.

The workshop, to this kind of client, is a liberating experience. It gives the individual a chance to achieve in competition with co-workers very much like himself and to feel adequate for, perhaps, one of the few times in his life. The workshop has not been as successful with nonachieving individuals whose years of low functioning have caused deep emotional insecurity and disturbance.

The client characterized by anxiety and/or withdrawal is often a good candidate for the rehabilitation workshop, though not as promising as the aforementioned two categories. The security-giving ability of the workshop program comes forcefully into play with the anxious client. Through the skillful offering of support around achievement and the manipulation of the work and co-worker environment so that success is possible, a better self-image can slowly be built. With the withdrawn person the reality of a work setting often forces him into some greater degree of awareness of environment. The job, then, is to make this environment seem more desirable. The danger, of course, with the withdrawn client is that awareness might be too quickly pushed upon him and cause further withdrawal. Success of workshops with these people often depends on the degree and deep-seatedness of the disturbance.

Where the defect seems to be one of motivation or a lack of desire to play a productive role, the workshop has more difficulty. Here the program is often attempting to deal with a concept or philosophy entirely alien to or rejected by the ego. Here we struggle against great odds because we are attempting to cope with a problem area which is well established in the basic pattern of the personality. Where the shop has been successful, it has impinged a new or different reality and set of values upon the person. This has been accomplished best when the values of society, as related to work, were never really perceived in the first place. Success is much more difficult when values are perceived by the client but are in variance to those of society.

Perhaps the single most difficult category for workshops is that of the acting-out client. This person will constantly break rules and provoke rejection. He views society and all authority figures with great distrust. The workshop has been effective in instances where the acting-out client has been given some latitude in which to express impulses, where he has been assigned to tasks which he views as carrying status, and where the workshop and foremen have avoided mirroring other authorities and their typical rejection of the impulse-ridden person. This, however, is a very difficult client with whom to deal effectively, since he must, sooner or later, come to understand and partially accept the routine demands of a work situation.

These, then, are the guideposts. We should consider them and begin to think whether some type of screening and prediction is now possible, given our years of experience. We have, for some time, been the passive recipients of referrals from other sources. We have been "the court of last resort." The theory has been that we should not screen out clients since we did not yet know enough about our workshops and their effectiveness to set up any real intake criteria. Is this caution as warranted today as it was at the inception of workshop programs? Has our experience taught us something about people and their work potential? Can we now begin to make some more definitive statements about our assets and our liabilities? Perhaps it is time to come to grips with these very important questions.

Finally, and perhaps most important, are there people whom we actually harm by placing them in the workshop programs? If failure in a program such as ours is destructive, then it becomes even more important that some type of criteria be set up, if this is at all possible.

In conjunction with the last point, it seems well to discuss our experience with a category of individual for whom not only the workshop program seems to be unsuccessful, but, further, harm is a very definite possibility. This is the person with deep feelings of inadequacy, whose main defense is an unrealistic and blown-up self-concept. We should be very careful in judging the efficacy of our programs with clients of this nature. Though the defense of inappropriate self-concept is not the healthiest one, it is, indeed, the only one that these people seem to have.

Placement in a workshop program which deals so obviously with marginal people robs the person of this defense and tends to reinforce feelings of inadequacy, no matter how skillful the manipulation of the professional staff. Often the person responds to workshop placement by defending himself even more vehemently and by verbalizing an even more unrealistic self-concept. However, this seems to be accompanied by even greater feelings of inadequacy. When this set of dynamics is picked up during the intake process, it is useful to seek psychiatric advice and to be as certain as possible that the risk of greater damage is not too severe.

It would be interesting to discover whether our results fit those of programs in other agencies. Whether or not they seem to, it may be time for us to concentrate some of our future efforts on research that might tell us what criteria of success to use and what kinds of people—diagnosed vocationally—seem to profit most.

How We Help

Let us turn now from the question of whom we help to the question of how we help people. Techniques in workshops include, of course, such things as physical arrangement, job assignments, methods of pay, etc. We will take just one example and discuss the staffing pattern and staff behavior as a technique of help in a rehabilitation workshop setting.

Techniques in workshops should be related to purposes. How we work depends on what we are trying to accomplish. This can be seen in how we choose staff, how we assign staff to clients, and how the staff is instructed to behave toward the clients.

The staff serving as foremen in the kind of workshop we are discussing is likely to consist of professional personnel. The rationale for this has to do with the emphasis on individualizing programs. Professionally trained personnel would more quickly observe subtleties of client behavior and would be more skilled in understanding the meanings of such behavior than would industrially trained foremen. They would be more skilled also in structuring situations for clients that would be more likely to provide the kinds of experiences that clients need. On the other hand, most professional personnel are quite limited in the amount and thoroughness of industrial experience.

In this respect, they are limited in their efforts to provide a genuine work atmosphere for clients. They may also be slow in seeing the possibilities of improving work methods and of conveying, by example, the importance of this to the clients.

The number of staff members is also an important consideration. Within limits, it is likely that the greater the number of foremen, the better the chances of individual attention. One might think that the greater the chances for individual attention, the more likely it is that the client will be helped. Yet there are questions to be raised here also. There are some clients who prefer to be left alone for long periods of time and whose work suffers from too much attention. Is this a serious issue? What role do the foremen actually play in helping the client? Are they most useful in helping to provide a work atmosphere or in helping individual clients with individual problems, and is the answer to that the same for all kinds of clients? Finally, is there a difference in the degree of foreman usefulness for evaluation purposes and for adjustment purposes?

STAFF BEHAVIOR

The staff members who serve as foremen participate with the clients in a joint endeavor to help the latter move toward competitive employment. In doing so, the members of the staff, self-consciously or not, assume certain roles with the clients which influence the way they are seen by clients and the manner of client participation. These roles, if consciously adopted, can vary with the client and with different stages in any one client's progress. The same foreman may adopt different roles with different clients or with the same client at different times.

The behavior of the foreman has various purposes. His presence and activity serve to contribute to the creation of a work atmosphere. In addition, he may try, through his approaches to people, to provide a permissive atmosphere in which clients can become aware that there is less to dread in work relationships than they had feared. On the other hand, being more stern and demanding with some clients may provide the kind of support and security they need in order to learn how to function on a job.

One typical pattern of foreman behavior toward a client may serve as an example of the kinds of questions that can be raised. The client is introduced to the program in a benign, accepting, encouraging manner. He is given a good deal of support, and his errors or difficulties are only gently pointed out, if at all. As he becomes more comfortable, greater demands are made on him and support is lessened. Eventually, the relationship becomes distant, matter-of-fact, almost impersonal. In part, the evaluation of the client focuses on his ability to adjust to and tolerate the changes in supervisory practice, while continuing to improve his work. The role changes will, of course, have been interpreted to the client in one manner or another.

Role playing, as a technique, appears to be very useful, but again certain questions can be raised. To what extent does the playing of different roles at different times by the same person involve confusion for the clients or for the foreman himself? Do clients peg individual foremen as particular kinds of persons anyhow, no matter what the variations in behavior? Is the opportunity to see the foreman as a helping person the only real issue as far as the clients are concerned? How we behave toward clients depends partly on how we answer such questions.

Summary

In summary, we have attempted to raise issues which we feel confront the entire workshop field. The issues we have tried to discuss are (1) the definition of workshop purposes as distinct from the purposes of other forms of help; (2) the possible classification of the kinds of clients who may best or least be able to benefit from workshop help (this necessarily includes a consideration of what constitutes benefit and what are the criteria for improvement and for success); (3) the best methods of staff training to help provide clients with corrective experiences; and (4) the use of role playing as a staff technique.

We have suggested some answers to the questions we have raised. We have argued, for instance, that there are four purposes—a concrete experience, a sheltered setting, a therapeutic situation, and a group setting—which define the distinctive contributions of the workshop as a form of help. We have argued further that it is likely that there are some kinds of individuals who benefit most from our programs and some who might even be harmed. In addition, we have suggested that staff training in industrial methods is important, that the size of the staff influences the results of the program, and that role playing by foremen is a useful technique.

We do not feel that there are any hard and fast answers. Our suggestions are, at best, tentative. Further, there are other issues needing discussion which we did not cover in this short paper.

We are aware that there are practical limitations in all workshops which limit the things that can be done. We certainly do not insist that any program do more than is practicable. We do suggest that each of us think about what we are doing, what purposes we are trying to serve, whom we are trying to help, and what our techniques help us to accomplish.

37. Factors in Determining the Employability of Mentally Retarded Youth: Some Findings of the Detroit Special Education-Vocational Rehabilitation Project *

PAUL R. HUNT, *Project Director, Detroit Special Education–Vocational Rehabilitation Project*

W HEN WE ADDRESS ourselves to the topic of factors limiting the employ-ability of mentally retarded youth, we tend to think immediately of those factors involving their limited resources. For example, we are con-cerned with their reduced mental ability to work through the problems encountered in daily living. We are concerned, too, with their safe conduct in this fast-moving world, particularly in areas where they are disadvantaged the most. One such area is the world of work.

Youths living in complicated metropolitan surroundings, such as Detroit and other great cities, are having a particularly difficult time in gaining employment. Even high school graduates in these cities are experiencing considerable delay in entering their first employment. Dropouts, too, are finding their employment status being aggravated by the lack of prepara-tion to enter a complicated and competitive job market.

Most severely disadvantaged, however, are those youths who border on the fringe areas of normal intelligence: our educable retarded. These youths, particularly those living in the culturally deprived areas of the large cities, are truly the least employable of all the employables in our society today. The Detroit–Vocational Rehabilitation Project addresses itself to the prob-lems of this latter group.

Although the demonstration portion of the project is fully operational, the research program is still in a formulative stage. There are, however, factors we have observed through our research which seem to influence and control the employability of these youths. It is the purpose of this paper to comment briefly on these factors.

Essentially we are talking about three main conditions (factors) in the

* Reprinted by permission of the author. A report prepared for the Council for Exceptional Children, 42nd Annual Convention, 1964, Chicago.

life space of these mentally retarded, culturally deprived youths. These three conditions are (1) the youth's community and social mobility, (2) the opportunities for growth through work, (3) the adult guarantors in the youth's life.

Each factor is treated separately as follows.

Community and Social Mobility

Mentally retarded slum-area youths tend to have limited contacts outside the immediate range of their homes and schools. For example, we are finding teen-age youths who have lived all their lives within the glow of Detroit's downtown skyscrapers and have not had such experiences as riding on elevators or escalators and otherwise negotiating the city. In addition, they lack daily contact with vital social situations which, together with knowledge of the community, combine to produce a sophistication necessary to function in today's urban world of work.

Through field trips, social experiences, and resource persons, we are finding that these youths' concepts of the world of work are being broadened. In addition, they are provided with actual practice in social behavior found more appropriate than the behavior they generally display. To some extent, then, we feel that the disadvantaging factors associated with their immobility and social stagnation can be offset through a "higher horizons" approach to their alienation.

Growth through Work Experience

Preparation for the world of work starts at an early age. Attitudes about work are learned from parents and neighbors and particularly through those early experiences youths encounter in paid employment such as yard work, paper routes, and running errands for the corner grocer.

It is not unusual, however, to find teen-age youths enrolling in the project who have never worked at even these most menial tasks. In addition, absent in the lives of these youths are those early work experiences gained by doing household chores. Youths living in public housing projects, for example, have no lawns to rake, windows to wash, or garages to clean. They are, interestingly enough, victims of an imposed system of leisure—leisure that can become a way of life. Is it any wonder, then, that youths coming to the project have little, if any, concept about work and how it is performed? They lack the basics, such as a fundamental appreciation for quality and quantity in work so essential in succeeding on a job. In addition, they are found to be extremely awkward and uninformed concerning their relationships with employers. Their responsibility to the employer is not part of their understanding, nor are they at all informed about the employer's responsibility to them.

To provide for the kinds of growth that come through work experiences, the project invites youths to participate in three experiences producing occupational growth. First, they are given an opportunity to earn money within the project school from the very first week they enter. The jobs they are doing—packaging, manufacturing, and custodial—are necessary and meaningful. Once they have developed a physical and emotional tolerance for work (it is found that such tolerance for work usually does not exist in these youths), they are given their first opportunity to work with two or three private employers in an actual work setting. These short-term experiences are called "job tryouts" and generally last about four weeks.

After observing the client on the job tryouts, it becomes possible to talk with him in terms of a longer-range work experience program. Such a program is referred to as on-the-job training. Generally this training (also paid for by project funds in the form of a small stipend) usually matriculates into a job and stable employment with the employer who provided the on-the-job training.

Adult Guarantorship

It is not new to those of us who work with youths living in lower socioeconomic surroundings to find these young people leaving their adult guarantors voluntarily, or involuntarily, much before the time they are thought old enough to cope with the sordid environment to which they are exposed. We recognize, too, that even youths in more advantaged circumstances, when extricating themselves from family and school ties as we expect youths to do, become disadvantaged if they do not find as replacements sound adult guarantors. An adult guarantor, for the purposes of definition, is one who may take the position of employer, counselor, parent, or friend. His main purpose, however, is to provide a point of stability in the adult world through which his image and counsel can give support to the youth. Certainly youths are finding such adults in employers and friends, where these models are available. However, it is generally conceded that these models are not available or congenial to most slum-area retarded youths.

And so it is in the Detroit Special Education–Vocational Rehabilitation Project that we provide available adults as images and the kinds of models these youths are willing to accept. The counselors, group workers, teachers, and employers all serve to provide the adult guarantorship these youths so desperately need.

In summary, then, we are finding that positive changes in behavior are occurring. The kinds of experiences centered around improving the client's social and community mobility, affording opportunities to grow and develop occupationally through combined school and work experience and providing the stabilizing support which can come only through adults who can be counted upon, can do much, it is being found, to improve the employability and assure the vocational success of these least employable youths.

38. Philosophy and Recommendations of the President's Panel on Mental Retardation Relating to Education, Vocational Rehabilitation, and Training *

LEONARD W. MAYO, *Executive Director, Association for the Aid of Crippled Children, New York City; former Chairman, the President's Panel on Mental Retardation*

To APPRECIATE its full value and flavor, Section V on "Education, Vocational Rehabilitation, and Training" in the Report of the President's Panel on Mental Retardation must be read and studied as an integral part of the entire report. The report consists of nine sections, including introductory material on the nature and volume of mental retardation and recommendations.

* Reprinted by permission of the author and *Exceptional Children*, 29:425–430; May, 1963.

The section on education opens with a paragraph which sets the stage for the subsequent recommendations. Unlike many reports, however, the more or less orthodox introduction setting forth the widely accepted advantages of rehabilitating a child "from a role of idleness and dependency to the status of a full-fledged wage earner and citizen" is not followed by platitudes. Just three pages later the tempo quickens with a straight-from-the-shoulder declaration: "Although the Nation has long been committed to the objective of providing all children with opportunities for developing their potential to the fullest, this goal has not yet been realized for those who are handicapped."

Education and Rehabilitation Needs

From this point, and on this thesis, the panel proceeds to examine the extent, nature, and volume of the problem insofar as the educational and vocational rehabilitation needs of the mentally retarded are concerned. Only about 250,000 of the nation's one and one-fourth million school-age retarded children are enrolled in special education programs in public schools. Although "tremendous advances" have been made in both public and private programs of special education and the number of pupils enrolled in such programs has doubled since 1948, a large majority of retarded children simply do not have educational opportunities open to them.

There is a serious dearth of opportunity for early acquisition of intellectual and social skills by children who come from deeply deprived homes where stimulation and adequate care are severely limited or completely lacking.

Diagnostic and evaluative services and facilities for the early detection of learning disabilities are scarce. There is a deficit—a serious deficit (55,000) —of teachers trained to instruct the mentally retarded; and by the same token, standards of teacher qualification are needed as well as reciprocal certification agreement among the states.

State vocational rehabilitation programs must be stepped up to increase the rehabilitation of the retarded.

Counseling programs in the schools must be extended and strengthened; far too frequently young people who are retarded complete the special education program of the public schools only to be lost to vocational training opportunities.

Only a few communities have adequate workshop training facilities for the trainable or activity centers for the severely retarded, and employers are largely unaware and to some extent uninterested in the potential of the retarded as reliable workers.

Thus, the panel found that the situation surrounding the education, vocational rehabilitation, and training of the retarded is still one of serious deficit. The panel noted and applauded the obvious signs of movement and leadership in many states but strongly urged a national effort locality by locality, state by state, and at the national level to give the educational and vocational training needs of the retarded the visibility, the attention, and the emphasis they require.

Blocks to Progress

The panel recognized certain substantial blocks to immediate progress, such as the hard fact that the cost of maintaining special classes is twice that of regular classes. The limited financial resources of many states and communities act as a major deterrent in this connection.

The lack of qualified teachers is a universal problem, and that of recruiting and training instructors for special classes is even more acute. At present there are probably no more than twenty thousand teachers for the mentally retarded in the country, and it is estimated that at least one-fourth of them fail to meet minimum certification requirements. In 1963 only five hundred new teachers, or possibly a few more, will graduate from colleges and universities having teacher-training programs in mental retardation. This number is pitifully small, even when it comes to replacing those who will leave the field during the year.

There are more than five million handicapped children of school age in the United States, including the mentally retarded, and the expansion of special education opportunities for them will require citizen and governmental leadership and both public and voluntary financial assistance from local, state, and national sources.

State and local school systems are now spending over $200 million dollars annually for education of the retarded. States usually reimburse local school systems for a portion of the excess cost of special education. Therefore, unless communities are given some assurance that an increased subsidy will follow expansion on their part, they are reluctant to move ahead.

In training and employment, a practical problem lies in the fact that we are just beginning to absorb the physically handicapped in business and industry and have been slow to recognize the potential of the retarded.

Hence, there has been little steam and enthusiasm to date behind measures and policies designed to provide the retarded with vocational counseling and specialized training for productive employment.

Vocational counselors in rehabilitation centers and in the local offices of the Vocational Rehabilitation Administration in most parts of the country have recently been dealing with an increasing number of the physically handicapped. Many counselors, consequently, have not had the time or, in some instances, the special knowledge to give concentrated attention to the special needs of the retarded. By the same token, employers in business and industry, including organizations where service personnel are employed, have not been aware of the wide variety of functions that many retarded persons can perform.

Administrative Recommendations

In a series of some twenty major recommendations designed to help meet the critical educational and vocational rehabilitation needs of the retarded, the panel called upon the U.S. Office of Education for increased administrative leadership in the development of state and local programs for all exceptional children. The leadership and staff of this program in the U.S. Office of Education should, the panel stated, be brought to a level commensurate with the importance of exceptional children in the nation. With full recognition of the contributions made by the office to date, the panel called upon it to expand its efforts in the following specific ways.

1. The extension of present programs for exceptional children. This would entail a review of proposed and current legislation and an analysis of present services of the Office of Education in the area of exceptional children as these relate to other Government agencies such as the National Institutes of Health, the Office of Vocational Rehabilitation, and the Children's Bureau.

2. The development of new programs which would stimulate and assist state and local school systems in the extension of services for exceptional children.

3. The administration of programs which provide funds to assist colleges and universities conducting programs for the preparation of special educational personnel.

4. The administration of programs of intramural and extramural research on exceptional children.

Research Recommendations

With reference to the fourth point above, the entire report is undergirded and laced with recommendations on the need for research—research in causes of mental retardation, in methodology in special education, in the intellective process, and in the development of teaching materials. Also stressed is the need for adequate fellowships and other provisions for the professional education of qualified men and women to conduct such research.

Section II of the Panel Report, entitled "Research and Manpower," presents the findings of the Task Forces on Biological Research and Behavioral and Social Research, chaired respectively by Seymour S. Kety and Lloyd M. Dunn. This section, quite naturally, includes findings and recommendations germane to special education.

The need for additional research in the Office of Education is stressed, and a major recommendation deals with the establishment of an "Institute of Learning." This is of such importance that the following quotation from the report is included.

The major functions of an Institute of Learning would be to encourage and support studies of the structure, development, and function of intellective processes; characteristics of simple and complex learning; the extension of theories of learning and elaboration of these theories to include individual differences in human learning; and the neurological basis and biobehavioral correlates of learning. The development of methods of measurement and of training are essential as are further studies on creativity and programmed instruction. The Institute would also be a center for the co-ordination and stimulation of research, for the initiation of programs to determine the conditions under which, and context within which laboratory findings can be applied to facilitate classroom learning.

The Institute should have a broad base involving several agencies within the Department of Health, Education, and Welfare. The National Science Foundation would have great interest in such an Institute and should be consulted in its planning and development. . . . The Institute should include an intramural as well as an extramural research program. There are a number of universities in the country where there is an active interest in research and education . . . and it would be the purpose of an Institute of Learning to encourage and support such programs of competence and promise.

The panel stipulated that "the conservation of human resources so essential for humanitarian, defense, and scientific reasons must now specifically include a new emphasis on the education and rehabilitation of the less capable as well as the typical and the talented."

Recommendations for Special Education Programs

Moving from research to the need for improving present programs of special education, the panel was specific in outlining ways and means by which specialized educational services in local school systems might be enhanced. Stating that "any substantial extension of the specialized educational services for retarded children will require assistance and stimulation from sources beyond local and State school systems," the panel pointed out that such assistance could readily and logically be provided through the federal extension and improvement procedure (augmentation of P.L. 531) administered in such a way as to assure the use of available funds for expansion of present services, development of new ones, or both.

The panel urged the appointment by the Office of Education of a group of experts to help the states develop standards for special class teachers and for the organization and operation of special classes. In addition, a professional advisory committee was suggested to assist the Office of Education in the administration of the extension and improvement program.

The panel outlined five areas of need for extended or new services, which it strongly urged should be given emphasis and priority in the awarding of grants under the extension and improvement program and the education aid programs proposed by the President:

1. Projects to enrich the learning opportunities of preschool children who live in homes where such opportunities are inadequate.
2. Instructional materials centers in the special education units of State departments of public instruction or in university departments of education.
3. State and local community leadership in the development, administration, and supervision of school services for retarded children.
4. Specialized classroom services to provide for all mentally retarded children.
5. Services of educational diagnosis and evaluation to provide for early detection of school learning disabilities and to enable appropriate school placement.

With respect to man-power needs, the panel pointed out that six thousand new teachers must be added to the national roster each year for the next decade in order to meet the increasing need. The panel recognized that this is nearly twelve times the number of new teachers who graduated in 1962 with adequate training for teaching the retarded. In order to reach the goal of six thousand a year, it was recommended that (*a*) the federal government as well as foundations and other private groups provide increased funds for scholarships and for the support of training programs; (*b*) each state provide funds in its annual budget to be used specifically for teachers who wish to prepare for work with mentally retarded children; (*c*) local school systems (through the granting of leaves of absence with pay), community agencies, and civic and service organizations contribute to the cost of preparing teachers for the retarded: the panel stated that in its view the concerted efforts of such groups should produce a total of three million dollars a year, or an average contribution of $1,000 from each of the three thousand local school systems now operating programs for the mentally retarded; (*d*) federal funds awarded under the administration's proposal should be allocated to universities for scholarships and support of teaching programs. The task force also recommended that high priority be given to training more instructors for the college level and that federal funds under Public Law 85-926 be increased and authorized for this purpose.

In another thrust at the man-power problem, the panel urged that the U.S. Office of Education initiate a national recruitment program to interest students in careers in the education of exceptional children and that attention be given to discovering new ways by which the limited number of professional personnel working with the handicapped might be more effectively utilized.

Recognizing the increased mobility of the population, the panel pointed out the importance of making teacher certification requirements uniform or at least comparable in all states and called on responsible certification agencies such as the National Council on Accreditation of Teacher Education and regional groups such as the Southern Regional Education Board, the Western Interstate Commission on Higher Education, and the New England Board of Higher Education to assist in facilitating interstate reciprocity agreements.

Recommendations for Vocational Programs

The panel stated that more than 75,000 of the retarded youths who leave school each year have a potential for self-support. Hence, in addition to its general recommendations concerning increased vocational rehabilitation appropriations by the states and the extension of counseling programs in the schools, the panel cited the following work education services as essential to all communities if they are to preserve the productive capacities of the nation's mentally retarded:

1. Vocational evaluation, counseling, and job placement.

2. Training courses in appropriate vocational areas.

3. Joint school–work-experience programs operated co-operatively by schools and vocational rehabilitation agencies.

4. Clearly defined and adequately supervised programs for on-the-job training of retarded workers.

5. Employment training facilities for those who require further vocational preparation after completion of the public school program.

6. Sheltered workshops for retarded workers capable of productive work in a supervised, sheltered setting.

7. Vocational rehabilitation services in conjunction with residential institutions.

8. Counseling services for parents to provide them with an adequate understanding of the employment potentials of their children and to provide guidance which will enable them to participate more fully in the rehabilitation process.

9. Co-ordination of vocational counseling with the entire school program.

The panel then set forth in some detail how vocational rehabilitation services for retarded youths could be expanded through special federal expansion grants under the federal-state vocational rehabilitation program.

The need for new facilities, including sheltered workshops for those capable of preparing for productive employment and activity centers for those who could profit by that type of facility, were carefully spelled out. "Every effort must be made and all available services used, to equip and train the retarded and assist them in finding suitable employment." To implement this broad mandate the panel made the following specific suggestions.

1. Relate the education and training of the mentally retarded to employment requirements, especially through expert evaluation and counseling.

2. Advise the mentally retarded and their employers about the kinds of jobs they can perform and how jobs can be redesigned so that the mentally retarded can perform them.

3. Refer the mentally retarded to jobs they can perform or to training opportunities.

4. Advise the mentally retarded and their fellow workers and employers about the best ways for working together.

5. Expose the mentally retarded to work in competitive work situations.

6. Provide the mentally retarded with employment in noncompetitive situations if competitive employment is not possible.

Acknowledgments

The task force which produced the portion (Section V) of the report of the President's Panel which has been briefly reviewed in this article was most ably chaired by Ernest Willenberg, Ph.D., Director of Special Education, City of Los Angeles; the panel staff member who worked with Dr. Willenberg on a comparable professional level was Rick Heber, Ph.D., Director of Special Education, University of Wisconsin.

Members of the task force were Ernest Willenberg, Ph.D.; Monsignor Elmer H. Behrmann; Darrel J. Mase, Ph.D.; Mr. F. Ray Power; Mr. Henry Viscardi, Jr.; and Mrs. Irene Asbury Wright. In addition, more than a score of able advisers from various parts of the country who were invaluable to the task force aided in the pursuit of its work. Numerous groups in this and other countries also gave unstintingly of their advice and assistance, including the Section on Special Education of the U.S. Office of Education, the Association of State Directors of Special Education, the National Association for Retarded Children, and the Council for Exceptional Children.

Responsibility for the recommendations made and the entire text rests, of course, with the task force and the panel as a whole.

Underlying Philosophy

It is important to include some elements of the basic philosophy on which the task force based its recommendations.

1. The concept of assistance to the states via the extension and improvement formula rather than outright aid to education.

2. The emphasis on the needs of all handicapped children and youth, except when attention to the specific needs of the retarded is clearly indicated as essential in order to give them the visibility they have lacked and the attention they sorely need. (The panel's philosophy concerning the dangers of setting the mentally retarded aside as an isolated categorical group is clearly expressed in several sections of the report.)

3. The importance of advancing the entire program for the exceptional child as a means of benefiting every classification and category.

4. The need for wider public awareness and understanding not only of the exceptional child but of the essential and key role of special education and vocational rehabilitation.

5. The basic importance of primary and secondary prevention: primary prevention through research and the application of present knowledge; secondary prevention through every known means of minimizing the hazard of retardation and enriching and otherwise improving the lives of all retarded children and adults in our society.

6. The urgent need as a nation to face the full implication of the fact that "deprivation in childhood of opportunities for learning intellectual skills, and childhood emotional disorders which interfere with learning . . . appear somehow to stunt young people intellectually during their developmental periods."

As the introduction to the panel report succinctly states, "The majority of the retarded are the children of the more disadvantaged classes in our society." That fact alone should be quite enough to shake us out of any complacency of which we may be guilty and to compel educators, social workers, research scientists, physicians, city planners, and all related professional groups to find common cause in a crusade of research and action aimed at raising the whole level of community life in our society.

That will come tomorrow; but today there is something tangible, practical, immediate, and constructive in this report for every school official—local and state—for every legislator, and for every employer, teacher, vocational counselor, and parent.

39. A Factor Analytic Study of Motivational Patterns in a Sheltered Shop *

E U G E N E   B .   N A D L E R ,   *Case Institute of Technology, Cleveland*

F R A N K L I N   C .   S H O N T Z ,   *Psychologist, Highland View Hospital, Cleveland*

TWO PATIENTS with severe physical disabilities receive services in a rehabilitation center. Although their illnesses are identical and they are alike in other important ways, one of them utilizes the physical therapy, occupational therapy, and vocational guidance services in an effective manner, while the other does not. Why?

It has become popular in rehabilitation work to ascribe such differences to "motivation." In usage, the concept has referred variously to the patient's underlying needs, his acquiescence to rehabilitation demands, his adjustment to severe illnesses, and at times to his moral character. Regardless of usage, the unitary character of motivation is the common assumption, i.e., a single dimension along which persons may be ordered.

The little research that has been done on this question has tended to be guided by this unitary concept. By and large, this research has made use of the "extreme groups" design, in which differences have been sought between individuals rated high and low, respectively, on "motivation" or "adjustment to illness" (e.g.). While some valuable insights have been gained in this way, whatever differential response tendencies have been discovered have tended to lose their meaning when lifted out of the context of interrelated behavior patterns.

Shontz has summarized some of the theoretical arguments against a unitary concept of motivation. On the basis of clinical experience, he has described certain behavioral configurations and environmental demands which must be considered in the prognosis of rehabilitation success. Concerning motivation, these configurations define *patterns of behavior,* some of which operate to facilitate the rehabilitation process, while others impede it.

The present study proceeded from the view that an individual's reaction

* Reprinted by permission of the authors and *Personnel and Guidance Journal,* 37:444–449; February, 1959.

to severe disability and the manner of his utilization of rehabilitation services represent instances of more general and relatively enduring modes of response, factors of life style. From the standpoint of rehabilitation requirements, these may perhaps be ordered along a single dimension of "success in rehabilitation," but such an ordering would represent an externally imposed value judgment rather than multidimensional behavioral reality. Specifically, the study undertook (1) the empirical demonstration of multiple patterns of one kind of rehabilitation behavior—work in a sheltered shop—and (2) the preliminary description of some of these patterns. The taxonomic approach offered by the method of inverse factor analysis suggested itself as the method of choice in achieving these purposes and promised to shed some light on the nature of the life styles exhibited in sheltered-shop behavior.

Method

SUBJECTS

The subjects were twenty-eight patients hospitalized with chronic physical illnesses. All had sufficient physical recovery to be employed in a sheltered workshop attached to the hospital, but none were yet well enough to compete in normal jobs in the community; indeed, some never would again. There were fifteen males and thirteen females ranging in age from twenty-four to eighty-four, with a median of fifty-seven and a half years. Their primary diagnoses included complex fractures, paralyzing spinal cord injuries, rheumatoid arthritis, multiple sclerosis, diabetes, and pulmonary emphysema. Educational achievement was probably somewhat lower and the number of social service problems was probably somewhat higher than in the general chronic hospital population; in other respects the sample appeared representative of that population.

THE Q-SORT

A 63-item Q-sort was constructed which called for sorting descriptive phrases into a forced quasi-normal distribution, as follows: 3, 5, 7, 10, 13, 10, 7, 5, and 3. Coverage of the content universe was attempted by constructing items around the Spranger categories of theoretical, political, social, economic, aesthetic, and religious values; a global adjustment category was also included. Examples of the items in each category are shown in Table 1. All items were worded positively to offset tendencies on the part of the judges toward making "good" and "bad" value judgments.

As many items as possible presented gross behavioral descriptions, i.e., called for a minimum of inference on the part of the judges.

TABLE 1—EXAMPLES OF Q-SORT ITEMS

Category	Item
Religious	3. has religious faith
	7. quotes Bible
Political	11. a leader among his fellows
	14. seeks the limelight
Economic	21. remembers instructions
	24. economizes on materials
Theoretical	29. a clear thinker
	32. figures things out in advance
Aesthetic	38. wants to do beautiful work
	42. more interested in quality than quantity
Social	48. equally at ease with men and women
	52. understands another person's point of view
Adjustment	57. confident
	60. relaxed

PROCEDURE

Prior to the beginning of the study each patient had been working in the shop for at least two months and in a few cases as much as one year. Pairs of shop supervisors most familiar with the patients independently used the Q-sort to describe their behavior. All interjudge reliability coefficients were significant beyond the .01 level; the mean of these coefficients, averaged by Fisher's z' method, was .48. A composite Q-sort for each patient was obtained by summing the item placements of the two supervisors and resorting the items into the original distribution on the basis of these scores; in cases of ties, items were randomly assigned to adjoining categories.

Pearson product moment correlations among the composites yielded a 28 by 28 correlation matrix.* The matrix was factor-analyzed by means of Thurstone's centroid method, with the highest correlation in each column or row entered as an estimate of the communality of each patient. Six factors were extracted and rotated to approximate orthogonal simple

* The following tables have been deposited with the American Documentation Institute: (1) The Q-sort items, (2) the matrix of original and residual intercorrelations, (3) the unrotated factor loadings, and (4) a table showing the rank, for each factor, of each of the 63 Q-sort items. Order Document No. 5801, remitting $1.25 for 35-mm. microfilm or $1.25 for 6 by 8 inch photocopies. Make checks or money orders payable to: Chief, Photoduplication Service, Library of Congress.

structure. The median absolute residual correlation after extraction of the sixth factor was .00, with 92 per cent of the residuals between ±.15.

IDENTIFICATION OF FACTORS

Items were arranged in factor-arrays by means of a procedure described by Cresser in which each item in a person-array is multiplied by the weight of the person's contribution to the factor-array, the value of each item being the sum across person-arrays of the weighted scores. The final factor-arrays were the arrangements of the items in ascending order of their total scores. Items with the highest and lowest scores were then used to identify the factors.

RELATIONS OF FACTORS TO EXTERNAL CRITERIA

The possibility that certain factors might be artifacts of age and sex differences was examined by determining the relation of these variables to the factor loadings, using the Mann-Whitney U test for sex and the rank-difference correlation for age.

Additional quantitative data that could be drawn upon in interpreting the factors consisted of WAIS Performance IQ's prorated from the Picture Completion and Picture Arrangement subtests and scores on a criterion-rating scale of job performance which was made up of six equally weighted elements: the number of jobs the patient could perform, his productivity, steadiness of work habits, attendance and punctuality, independence from supervision, and quality of work. Comparison of Performance IQ and job performance with each factor was done with rank-difference correlations.

Finally, factor loadings were compared qualitatively with interviews with the psychologist and with the available social history material.

Results

The rotated factor matrix is presented in Table 2. Descriptions of these factors in terms of the salient items in the Q-sort factor-arrays are presented below, along with the names used to identify them. The relationships of the factors to the variables of sex, age, Performance IQ, and job performance rating are presented in Table 3.

Factor I included remembering instructions, following directions, and ready comprehension. Individuals characterized by this factor were described as getting along well with their supervisors; however, they were not leaders among their fellows, did not understand or think of others, and had

TABLE 2—ROTATED FACTOR MATRIX

| Subjects | Factors | | | | | | h^2 |
	I	II	III	IV	V	VI	
1	49	−37	50	−03	35	−22	799
2	04	66	−21	10	−07	−07	501
3	66	−17	−15	04	13	21	550
4	−06	74	−07	19	10	−15	625
5	−24	18	65	31	−05	21	655
6	01	01	30	17	−45	−07	328
7	23	47	53	−08	−14	18	613
8	−08	67	38	−01	15	11	634
9	48	−05	16	10	−24	−18	359
10	23	59	32	−05	10	−11	528
11	58	−05	47	−11	43	−15	779
12	26	13	15	68	09	28	656
13	55	−13	36	−04	−25	23	566
14	03	37	−28	53	33	14	626
15	−08	05	85	06	−08	11	754
16	58	−13	01	43	−21	07	587
17	15	−05	88	−22	−13	14	884
18	10	70	36	11	07	−18	679
19	69	−18	−14	40	−10	−12	713
20	65	−13	−19	08	−16	28	586
21	11	−16	23	50	−14	−39	512
22	33	36	10	28	35	−18	482
23	−13	55	60	08	23	11	751
24	01	−12	71	07	−28	−22	650
25	67	−24	45	18	24	−04	801
26	12	−09	74	−23	−08	07	634
27	38	−28	49	37	18	21	676
28	66	−16	04	16	−36	−22	666

TABLE 3—RELATIONSHIP OF FACTORS TO EXTERNAL CRITERIA

Variable	Statistic	I	II	III	IV	V	VI
Sex	U	88	118	76	91.5	86.5	146.5*
Age	rho	−.21	.04	.18	−.18	−.05	−.08
Work Rating	rho	.64†	−.79†	.17	−.43*	−.02	.25
Performance IQ	rho	.55†	−.75†	.20	−.05	.08	.18

* Significant beyond .05 level.
† Significant beyond .01 level.

little influence with others. They asked questions about work, paid careful attention to detail, and were neat and tidy in their work. Among their least characteristic qualities were being calm, relaxed, and well adjusted. Factor

I was not significantly correlated with age or sex; however, it was correlated .64 with job performance ratings and .55 with Performance IQ, both correlations significant beyond the .01 level. Factor I was named *drivenness toward work*.

Factor II was defined primarily by items placed at the *least true* end of the Q distribution. A typical person loaded on this factor was not a clear thinker, did not comprehend readily, and did not come up with good ideas. His work did not show advance planning, organization, or attention to detail. Socially, however, he got along with others in the shop and with his supervisor; he was equally at ease with men and women and appeared generally well adjusted and realistic. Despite this seeming social ease, this person was not sought by others and was described as a "moral" person having religious faith. Factor II was not related to age or sex. It was correlated −.79 with job performance and −.75 with Performance IQ, both correlations significant beyond the .01 level. For reasons discussed later, it may have been an artifact that this factor was not more clearly bipolar. Factor II was designated *intellectual deficit*.

Individuals typified by Factor III were described as getting along with their supervisors and with others in the shop. They remembered instructions, followed directions, wanted to learn, and were said to be good people to have on the job. More generally, they were well adjusted and realistic. Their least characteristic traits were: seeking the limelight, acting important, attracting attention, and taking charge of other people. They did not quote the Bible or preach; they did not appear to believe in miracles or require spiritual help. None of the variables of sex, age, job performance, or Performance IQ was significantly related to this factor. Factor III was named *laissez-faire realism*.

The individuals who were characterized by Factor IV were described as having religious faith, being "moral," liking to preach, and believing in miracles. They knew the right thing to say when they met someone, asked questions about work, and got along with others in the shop. On the negative side, they were self-critical and were not realistic, well adjusted, relaxed, or calm. They were not leaders among their fellows. Factor IV was not correlated with sex, age, or Performance IQ. It did, however, show a moderate negative correlation with job performance, −.43, significant at the .05 level. Factor IV was named *hysteria*.

Factor V was bipolar and showed only a few loadings of moderate size. The positive pole of this factor included being humble, self-critical, considerate of the feelings of others, and thinking of others before oneself. These individuals were also said to be artistic, to have religious faith, and to quote the Bible. Persons at the negative pole were said to seek the limelight, act important, and influence others. In addition, they were realistic, confident, well adjusted, had drive, and said what they thought. None of the variables of sex, age, job performance, or Performance IQ was correlated with this factor. The most appropriate name for Factor V seemed to be *submission-dominance.*

Factor VI was a bipolar factor with such low loadings that its precise identification must remain in doubt. The positive pole was described by individuals who dressed neatly, were neat and tidy about work, and paid careful attention to detail. They had drive and liked to preach. They also knew the right thing to say when they met someone, influenced others, and enjoyed the feel of different materials. Factor VI was not significantly correlated with age, job performance rating, or Performance IQ. Women, however, tended to achieve positive loadings; men, negative ones, significant beyond the .05 level. Factor VI was tentatively identified as *constrictiveness-expansiveness.*

Discussion and Conclusions

1. The most important general conclusion that can be drawn is that the evidence does not support a unitary concept of motivation in rehabilitation. Rather than finding clusters of traits characterizing each end of a single dimension, this study showed the presence of several dimensions. If the study had employed an "extreme groups" design, based on the criterion job performance rating scale, several of the factors would have been indiscriminately lumped together at the ends of the job performance continuum, whereas others would have been left out since they were neutral with respect to job performance. In accordance with the conception advanced in the introduction, the factors isolated in this study may be viewed as neutral, contributing to, or impeding one kind of rehabilitation effort, but their psychological distinctiveness cannot be ignored.

2. While factor analytic studies have often been criticized for yielding factors that are clinically meaningless, to greater or lesser degrees the present factors have some standing as previously explored clinical entities. This makes it possible to formulate some hypotheses regarding the nature of the life styles exhibited in the sheltered shop, such hypotheses having more general implications for other aspects of the psychology of physical disability and the rehabilitation process.

Generalizing from studies of the blind, Cutsforth has focused on two reaction patterns to physical disability: the compensatory reactions of compulsive personalities and the retreat reactions of hysterical personalities. These reactions agree rather well with the patterns here labeled *drivenness toward work* and *hysteria,* respectively. In turn, *drivenness toward work* bears some resemblance to the factor postulated by Shontz, energy level. The merely moderate correlation of Factor I with Performance IQ, compared to Factor II, and the strong presence of least characteristic qualities of calm, relaxed, and well adjusted argued against an interpretation of Factor I as an intellectual factor. Rather, it appeared that these individuals had intellectual avenues available to them for developing compensatory reactions. The case history material showed that individuals with high loadings on either factor had poor life achievement records, certainly for different reasons in view of the present evidence. The stimulus characteristics of the hospital and sheltered shop—permissiveness, routine, protectiveness, and relaxed authority—probably heightened the difference between groups. For Factor I people, there was less conflict over the competitiveness of compensatory reactions and a greater chance of these reactions meeting with social approval. For Factor IV people, there was tolerance of labile, narcissistic, and dependent behavior.

It is no surprise that intelligence emerged as a separate personality factor, albeit in the form of *intellectual deficit,* in view of the previous findings of investigations like those of Cattell. A previous study which included the same subjects used here also showed rated job performance to be partly a function of tested intelligence. Although Factor II showed only a slight tendency toward bipolarity, this was probably due to the perceptions of the supervisor judges who may have been prone to focus on intellectual deficit as a source of inconvenience in their work, paying little attention to intellectual distinction above a certain level. The presence of religiosity and moralism in Factor II may indicate the importance of external rules and values in the adjustments of these persons, including their adjustments to severe disability and rehabilitation.

Factor III, labeled *laissez-faire realism,* is of interest primarily because it was not correlated with job performance in the shop. Clinicians would probably rate this factor as the "mentally healthiest" of those that emerged, excluding the intellectual factor; the social histories of Factor III people support this hypothesis. On the other hand, the social histories of Factor I people were easily more pathological than those of the other groups; yet they were the best workers. Thus, it appears that the requirements of mental health may be unrelated to the requirements of working in sheltered shops in institutional settings as these are presently constituted. One implication of Shontz's discussion of a postulated factor of *reality orientation* is relevant here; the *reality-oriented* patient may perform quite differently in different rehabilitation settings, depending on the specific requirements of the latter. The same thing, of course, may be said regarding the other factors.

In terms of the magnitudes of factor loadings, Factors V and VI, labeled *submission-dominance* and *constrictiveness-expansiveness,* lack the clarity of the other factors. In terms of relevant Q items, however, Factor V appears to be identical with the pattern isolated in other studies, concerning which special scales have been constructed. The identification of Factor VI is more doubtful, particularly because of its relationship with sex. Several interpretations are possible, all of which involve cultural sex differences, e.g., conventionalism-individuality. The tentative naming and description of these factors represent hypotheses for future research which would make use of relevant items in the Q-sort both for more precise identification of these factors and for clearer comparison with various criteria.

3. The present study points toward a specific methodology for studying the psychology of physical disability and rehabilitation. It also has certain implications for psychological diagnosis, prognosis, and treatment.

Research must begin with inquiry into the differential impact of various physical disabilities upon individuals differing in already existing personality patterns. A similar consideration holds for the interaction between personality factors and specific aspects of the rehabilitation process. As the nature of these interactions becomes known, diagnosis and prognosis will more closely approach the recommendations of Holt for combining both clinical and statistical methods of assessment. At the same time, treatment recommendations would be placed on a more realistic footing; in the words of Cronbach, the pay-off function would be maximized.

Summary

The present study undertook the empirical demonstration of multiple patterns of behavior in a sheltered shop and the preliminary description of some of these patterns. The view was taken that reactions to physical disability and the patient's utilization of rehabilitation services are largely understandable from the standpoint of previously existing personality factors. Factorial analysis of the interperson correlations of twenty-eight severely disabled patients working in a sheltered shop led to the extraction of six factors and their preliminary description. The relationships of the factors to certain external criteria were presented. The implications of the study for research, diagnosis, prognosis, and treatment of the physically disabled were briefly discussed.

40. Counselor Perception of the Therapeutic Aspects of the Sheltered Workshop *

HERBERT RUSALEM, *Assistant Professor of Education, Hunter College of The City University of New York*

WHEN THE ELEMENTS of a sheltered workshop structure are selected and combined to create a workshop culture, decisions have to be made regarding the quality and degree of each component to be incorporated into the environment. For example, each workshop has to arrive at decisions regarding physical setting, type of supervision, production pressures, interpersonal climate, remuneration policies, supportive services, shop atmosphere, relationship to other rehabilitation facilities and the community, use of client time, degree of individualization, and roles of workshop staff members. It is desirable for each component to make a substantial contribution to the rehabilitation process and to bear a rational relationship to the other components, thus making up a therapeutic workshop culture.

Currently, there is relatively little evidence offering guides for making such decisions. Most often, the administration and staff of a workshop arrive at a priori decisions and adopt them on a tentative basis. If they seem to work, they are retained; if not, they are modified. Gradually, through an evolutionary process, a relatively stable workshop environment takes shape, serving more or less effectively and helping clients achieve their therapeutic goals.

* Reprinted by permission of the author and *Personnel and Guidance Journal*, 41:705–708; April, 1963.

A body of experience is being developed regarding desirable combinations of workshop elements. Hopefully, the day will come when study and experience will have combined to produce general agreement about the nature of the therapeutic workshop environment and the components which constitute it. Although we may be moving toward this goal, there is a need from time to time to ascertain our current distance from it. Thus, the scope of this research is limited to ascertaining the level of current agreement within a population of state rehabilitation counselors about the desirable components in a therapeutic workshop environment. Two hypotheses will be tested:

1. Among state rehabilitation counselors making use of workshop facilities to obtain therapeutic benefits for their clients, a consensus does not exist on the desirable characteristics of a therapeutic workshop setting.

2. The preference among state rehabilitation counselors is for a workshop structure possessing a high degree of flexibility rather than a high degree of conformance to consistent industrial working conditions.

Procedures

A questionnaire on "The Characteristics of a Therapeutic Workshop Environment" was devised, consisting of twenty multiple-choice items. The items dealt with various phases of the workshop atmosphere, including remuneration to the client, hours of work, types of work available, types of clients, general setting, location, punctuality demands, production demands (after the learning period), absenteeism, sponsorship, counseling, supervision, maximum stay, mental health services, general health services, socialization, group counseling, termination procedures, readmission, evaluation, and ways of handling work problems. These areas were selected by listing the characteristics of therapeutic workshops found in the literature on this subject. The areas having the greatest frequency of mention were retained.

The instructions given to respondents were as follows.

Workshops have many functions. For the purposes of this questionnaire, limit your thinking to the "Therapeutic" function, that of helping to prepare disabled persons for industry by increasing their employability. Theoretically, when the client enters such a workshop, he is not ready for placement in industry owing to his lack of one or more essential characteristics. It is assumed that his stay in the workshop will increase his readiness for placement by strengthening him in the areas in which he has these lacks. Among the areas in which help may be given are personal adjustment, work tolerance, work habits and attitudes, self-concept as a worker, self-confidence, general work skills, and adaptation to the physical and social conditions of work.

Within this limitation, what kind of a workshop setting would be most helpful to him? In other words, what workshop characteristics will help the client who is not ready for placement in industry become more ready for placement in the shortest possible time? In each case below, select the alternative that seems most applicable and write in the space provided.

A tentative form of the questionnaire was administered to five state rehabilitation counselors during a "dry run." On the basis of this experience, five items were replaced and twelve were modified. With the co-operation of the New York City Office of the New York State Division of Vocational Rehabilitation, the questionnaire was distributed to sixty-five state rehabilitation counselors in the New York City office. Returns were received from fifty-eight counselors (89 per cent).

Findings

With one exception, only those responses selected by 30 per cent or more of the counselors will be reported.

Remuneration to the Client. Thirty-one counselors (53 per cent) suggested a piecework rate as the preferred means of remuneration in a therapeutic workshop.

Hours of Work. Forty-one (70 per cent) suggested flexible hours of work.

Types of Work Available. Fifty-six (95 per cent) recommended that the workshop should offer a range of jobs extending from low- to high-skilled.

Types of Clients. Twenty-nine (49 per cent) favored the inclusion of clients representing all types and classes of disability in the therapeutic workshop. Twenty-three (39 per cent) preferred limiting admission to clients with the same types of problems, such as need for improved work habits or need for improved job skills, regardless of disability.

General Setting. Twenty-two (37 per cent) suggested that the therapeutic workshop should have a variety of physical work environments under the same roof, some resembling a rehabilitation center, others similar to an ideal industrial plant, and still others resembling typical places of work in the community. Another eighteen (31 per cent) counselors favored a work environment that is physically just like plants in the community doing the same type of work.

Location. Nineteen counselors (32 per cent) felt that the therapeutic workshop should be located off the grounds of a comprehensive rehabilitation agency, but nearby. Another nineteen (32 per cent) would locate the therapeutic workshop wherever firms in the community doing the same types of work are located.

Punctuality Demands. Thirty counselors (51 per cent) suggested that clients should be required to come precisely on time. Twenty-one (36 per cent) recommended that there should be a variety of punctuality standards, with different standards maintained for different clients.

Production Demands (After the Learning Period). Twenty-seven (46 per cent) believed that there should be a whole range of production standards, with individual standards set for different clients. Twenty (34 per cent) felt that clients should meet the same production standards as those required by industry on the same jobs.

Absenteeism. Thirty-two (54 per cent) felt that clients should be excused for visits to clinics or rehabilitation services. Twenty-one (36 per cent) felt that clients should come to the workshop every day on the same basis as workers in industry.

Sponsorship. Thirty (51 per cent) felt that the therapeutic workshop should be part of a rehabilitation center or a comprehensive rehabilitation program. Twenty (34 per cent) believed that it should be part of a vocational counseling or vocational rehabilitation agency.

Counseling. Thirty-three (56 per cent) believed that counseling should be available to the worker any time he requests it.

Supervision. Thirty-seven (63 per cent) believed that the supervisor should be a foreman who is interested in production but who puts the welfare and mental health of the client first. Twenty-two (37 per cent) suggested that the supervisor should be a vocational counselor whose main concern is the personal adjustment training of the client. None of the respondents favored a foreman-psychologist whose main concern is the treatment of the client or a foreman whose main concern is production.

Maximum Stay. Thirty-four (58 per cent) felt that the client should remain in the therapeutic workshop indefinitely if he needs the experience.

Mental Health Services. Twenty-five (42 per cent) thought that a psychiatrist, psychologist, and/or social worker should be physically present in the workshop, coming in on a regular basis. Seventeen (29 per cent) suggested that these personnel should be available for referral at other agencies but should not be part of the direct workshop setup.

Socialization. Twenty-six (44 per cent) felt that the therapeutic workshop should set up special provisions and personnel to encourage client socialization, such as a planned recreation program. Twenty (34 per cent) suggested that clients should be left to form their own social relationships, as in industry.

Group Counseling. Thirty-three (57 per cent) felt that group guidance should be offered through trained rehabilitation counselors.

Termination. Forty-three (73 per cent) felt that clients should be terminated in the therapeutic workshop only when they have gotten as much as they can from the workshop environment, regardless of placement possibilities or training schedules.

Readmission. Twenty-seven (46 per cent) felt that workshop clients leaving for employment should know that they can return only if this is made part of a rehabilitation program. Twenty-four (41 per cent) thought that clients leaving for employment should know that they can return if the reason for failure in industry is related to their original workshop program.

Evaluation. Thirty-four (58 per cent) felt that clients should be evaluated on the basis of norms developed in industry for nondisabled workers. Nineteen (32 per cent) suggested that clients should be evaluated on norms that are individual to them as clients, revealing their own individual degree of progress from the time that they entered the workshop.

Work Problems. Thirty-three (56 per cent) felt that work problems in the shop setting should be handled by the client's rehabilitation counselor.

Discussion

These data have limitations which should be taken into account in evaluating the results. The fifty-eight rehabilitation counselors were drawn from a single office of one state rehabilitation agency and may not represent rehabilitation counselors in general or even in that state. Furthermore, since all these counselors worked in metropolitan New York, their perceptions of the therapeutic workshop were influenced by their experiences with this type of facility in that community. The nature of the instrument contributed other problems. In certain instances, respondents were not clear about the intent and meaning of some of the choices. In others, the forced-choice technique led to the selection of multiple responses or, in a few cases, no response at all. Finally, as some counselors noted, their responses would have varied if they had had different clients in mind. They felt it difficult to generalize their responses to cover all clients.

Agreement among these counselors exceeded 75 per cent on only one item—Types of Work Available. Agreement exceeded 60 per cent on four items—Types of Work Available, Hours of Work, Supervision, and Termination Procedures. Thus, the degree of agreement reached was something less than a consensus. The lowest degree of agreement appeared in items having a broad administrative significance, such as types of clients, general setting, location, and mental health services. The greatest agreement occurred in items which had relevance for the rehabilitation counselor's day-to-day relationship with the workshop, e.g., types of work available, hours of work, supervision, and termination procedures.

Whenever items contained choices reflecting both rigid and flexible limits, the counselors tended to give preference to the latter. Thus, they recommended flexible hours of work, a piecework rate, a range of workshop jobs at different skill levels, a varied client load, constant availability of counseling, indefinite maximum stays, terminations based upon client needs, and flexible readmission procedures. The counselors were least flexible in regard to such workshop components as punctuality demands, the use of industrial norms, and the provision of on-the-job counseling by rehabilitation counselors rather than other personnel. Most of the data reflect counselor attitudes suggesting the perception of the therapeutic workshop as a facility capable of great flexibility in adjusting to individual client needs. However, some of the respondents had conflicts in trying to reconcile simultaneous beliefs that the therapeutic workshop should have flexibility and at the same time should reflect competitive industrial conditions. Many workshops are experiencing the same type of ambivalence and are attempting to work out policies and procedures which will reduce the degree of inconsistency and discrepancy resulting therefrom.

Conclusions

Within the limits of this study, the data tend to support the two hypotheses offered earlier in this paper.

1. Among rehabilitation counselors, there is a tendency for majority agreement on most components of a therapeutic workshop environment. But this falls short of a consensus.

2. Rehabilitation counselors tend to favor flexibility in the therapeutic workshop environment, perceiving the workshop more often as a facility which adapts to individual client needs than as one which reflects consistent industrial working conditions. This perception of the workshop is not always stable. At times, counselors seem to be reaching simultaneously for both the flexibility of a therapeutic environment and the reality structure of competitive industry.

Suggested Reading

Burdett, A. D. "The Role of the Counselor in Rehabilitation," *Rehabilitation Literature*, 21:6; June, 1960.

Ferguson, R. G. *A Manual of Operations for a Sheltered Workshop to Serve Mentally Retarded Young Adults*, Ed.D. Thesis, University of Pennsylvania, 1959.

Jarrell, A. P. "A Project to Assist Public Schools to Meet Some of the Major Rehabilitation Needs of the Mentally Retarded." (Paper reported at 41st Annual Council for Exceptional Children Convention, Philadelphia, Pennsylvania, 1963.) This project of the Georgia Rehabilitation Agency is based on the premise that counselors can provide rehabilitation services to the mentally retarded when they have assistance at critical points in the rehabilitation process. Evaluation and prevocational training are two of these points, where effort is concentrated. The project started in 1961 with seven school systems; it includes a supervisor, vocational counselor, resource committee, teachers, and exceptional child consultant, who render vocational appraisement and prevocational training. The pupil is in the school work-in program from fourteen to sixteen; he is then considered for work-out prevocational training in six to a dozen vocational experiences in the community. The vocational rehabilitation counselor makes the ultimate placement. As of March, 1963, 608 pupils had been referred to the project, of which 465 had received vocational appraisal, 136 were in training stations within school, and 36 in work-out situations in the community, while 48 had been transferred to local counselors.

Katz, G. H. "Re-educational Therapy," *The Nervous Child*, Vol. 2, No. 1. (Also The Devereux Schools, Devon, Pennsylvania. n.d.) Rehabilitation efforts for the feeble-minded child should start from the earliest ages and be a part of all his education.

Scura, G. *Similarities and Differences in Social and Vocational Adjustment of Young Adult Sheltered Workshop Trainees in an Institutional Setting and in an Outside Facility*, Ed.D. Thesis, Yeshiva University, 1959.

Speiser, A. *Adjustment in a Sheltered Workshop*. Ed.D. Thesis, New York University, 1960.

FOR VARIOUS REASONS, which the reader might find interesting to itemize, the blind appear to have fewer special guidance problems than any other group of exceptional children. As a result, it is very hard to find any guidance articles written specifically about them, and the five reproduced here are virtually all to be found in the literature. The Jordan and Hunter article is particularly helpful in discussing the subject directly and thoroughly. The vocational aspects are handled by the Hoffman and Thume papers, while the Kenyon presentation discusses the aspects of counseling with the disturbed blind child. Cantoni and Cantoni begin the chapter by helping us to understand the way the blind person wishes us to relate to him.

41. Helping a Physically Disabled Friend *

LOUIS J. CANTONI, *Associate Professor of Education and Coordinator, Rehabilitation Counselor Training Program, Wayne State University, Detroit*

LUCILE CANTONI, *Formerly Supervisor of Social Casework, Detroit and Flint*

PHYSICAL DISABILITY may persist through months, years, or a lifetime. Many of the crippled, the blind, the deaf, and the chronically ill can hardly hope to be relieved of their disablements.

Initially, in your relationship with such an individual, there may be no way of helping him to resolve a personal problem. Thus your disabled friend may have a personal problem which, to you, is so glaring that only with great effort can you turn your attention away from it. Yet there is apparently nothing you can say or do about it because, although the physical disability itself is not an acute problem, the fact of the disablement pervades your entire relationship and creates barriers to easy communication.

To develop a healthy relationship with such an individual, you must cultivate a healthy attitude toward human disablement. For if you are to be the friend of a disabled person, you must, as he must, learn to live with his disability.

A realistic, matter-of-fact attitude toward disability is a healthy attitude. It neither exaggerates nor denies the disability. It focuses attention on the healthy aspects of the total person, never forgetting, however, the limitations imposed by the disabling condition. It encourages the disabled individual to become as independent as possible, applauding him for the gains he makes along his difficult path.

Thus, the youngster with cerebral palsy is encouraged to carry his own tray in the school cafeteria. When he spills his milk, it is wiped up and his plastic cup refilled without fuss. His family, his teachers, and his friends rejoice when he can carry his tray and eat his meal without incident. What for a normal youngster is a simple feat becomes for this disabled child an act of heroism.

On the other hand, it is foolhardy to commend a disabled individual who refuses to accept limitations imposed by his disability. It is false bravery

* Reprinted by permission of the authors and *Vocational Guidance Quarterly,* 9:111–113; Winter, 1960.

for a youngster with a severe heart condition to play in competitive sports. A physically disabled person must learn to live as effectively as possible within his limitations.

But is that not the fate of all of us? Each man must learn to live as effectively as possible within his own special set of limitations. For example, you may have what, in effect, constitutes an artistic disability. Let us say that you are enraptured by a sunset—your whole being aches to record your impression of that sunset on canvas. But you know from past efforts that your brush can never catch what you see with your eyes and with your imagination. You would be a fool to spend your life trying to become a painter, because you are too limited in artistic talents. So you accept your limitations and capitalize upon abilities which you do have.

Since most of the people in the world share your disability for painting, you do not consider yourself an object of pity. You do not expect your friends to think of you as an artistically disabled individual. Rather, you expect their esteem for the skills and talents which you do possess.

Let's explore the implications of this kind of thinking. Let's say that you know a physically disabled individual—a blind man. You may have much in common with this man, sharing his occupation or profession, attending the same church, or living on the same block. You have many things you can talk about with him, just as you would with a sighted friend. He may have a special quality which you respect, perhaps an unusual musical talent. Your respect has nothing to do with his blindness. He may also have remarkable personal qualities, such as a keen sense of humor, tolerance for the foibles of others, a tempered optimism. Again your high regard has nothing to do with his blindness. On the other hand, he may have one or two annoying traits; he may be illogical at times, argumentative. And again your response to him as an individual has nothing to do with the fact of his blindness. You see him as a person; you respond to him as a person; you accept him as a person.

If you are not comfortable with his blindness, that one fact of his life may keep you from developing a satisfying friendship with him. Let us say that his lack of vision disturbs you. You may find yourself weighing your every word to avoid making any reference to his blindness. This becomes a formidable task because, in the English language, the word "see" is used in scores of ways to yield a great variety of meanings. Thus, good conversation is precluded; you have permitted undue concern for his visual disability to raise a linguistic barrier.

Such concern may also occasion many unnecessary and uncomfortable acts in his behalf. If you are anxious about his ability to go up stairs or get into a car, you may half carry him, causing him to lose his balance. Or you may push him ahead of you as you walk, trying to steer him from behind but actually leaving him to encounter every obstacle in his path. When he wants to sit, you may find yourself trying to push him into a chair. Or you may shout at him; or use another individual as interpreter when you address him because you think his blindness affects all his means of communication. A blind person is subjected to these and many other unpleasant attentions by well-meaning individuals who are uneasy with the fact of blindness.

If you will sit back and observe a blind friend carefully, you will find many effective ways to assist him. As you are about to walk down the street, offer him your arm. He will hold your arm at the elbow or wrist. Then walk a little ahead of him so that he can sense hazards before reaching them. If there are stairs to climb, just put his hand on the rail. To offer him a seat, place his hand on the back of a chair. Since he cannot see you, it is courteous to greet him when you come into his presence and to say good-by when you leave him. When you are dining together, it is in order to tell him what is being served and to cut his meat for him. These and other courtesies will put you and your blind friend at ease, minimizing his disability.

You will discover many ways to help a physically disabled friend—if you are comfortable with his disability and if you take time to observe him carefully. But keeping a list of things to do will hardly improve your relationship. More than this, you need to develop a healthy attitude toward his disablement; then you will be free to react toward him as a whole person. Accepting his limitations realistically, you will find many avenues to reduce the impact of his disabling condition and to offer him constructive help with personal problems.

42. Some Predictors of the Manual Work Success of Blind Persons *

SIMON HOFFMAN, *Supervisor of Vocational Services, New York Guild for the Jewish Blind*

A N INDIVIDUAL'S CONCEPT of his manual ability is one aspect of his self-concept. This concept of manual ability develops from experiences of success and failure with manual tasks in daily living and work. By the time even the blind person reaches maturity, he has had some experience in manual activities such as chores, hobbies, school courses, work, etc. and thus an opportunity to develop some concept of his manual ability. This concept may be more valid than his estimate of his performance in an unfamiliar task, such as an aptitude test, and may be more valid than his actual performance in that unfamiliar task.

Three of the manual dexterity tests most widely used in the evaluation of each blind person who requests vocational rehabilitation are the Pennsylvania Bi-Manual Worksample, the Minnesota Rate of Manipulation Test, and the Purdue Pegboard.

Other Studies

In *Psychological Abstracts,* section on the Physically Handicapped, for the entire decade 1946 through 1956, only two reports of studies of the manual dexterity of the blind were found. Bauman's 1946 reported results, based on her adaptations of the Pennsylvania and the Minnesota, were considered of such value that they were incorporated into a manual which serves as a standard reference in the field of the rehabilitation of the blind. The same study noted that the Purdue had been "tried but discarded" on the ground that this test requires too accurate orientation in space for the totally blind client.

In 1950, Curtis reported favorably on his use of the Purdue Pegboard, with minor modifications of the standard instructions, for vocational guidance and placement of the blind. He did not differentiate between the totally blind and those with some useful vision.

In 1954, in another study, Bauman reported significant differences

* Reprinted by permission of the author and *Personnel and Guidance Journal,* 36:542-548; April, 1958.

etween "employed and generally well adjusted" and "not successful in mployment and generally poorly adjusted" blind persons in the speed of ssembly and disassembly of the Pennsylvania.

During the same decade, many authorities pointed to the great need for 1ore research to establish adequate norms for the blind.

It was thus decided to study the relative value of self-rating of manual bility, biographical information about manual life experience, i.e., chores, 10bbies, school courses and work, and aptitude test results in predicting he manual work success of blind persons.

Procedure

The subjects were all the blind adults with $5/200$ or less vision who were eferred for vocational services at the New York Guild for the Jewish Blind luring a seventeen-month period ending November, 1956. The guild is a >rivate, nonsectarian, rehabilitation agency which has a professionally rained social service and vocational counseling staff.

The vocational service program is one of the several services available o help the visually handicapped client and his family. The vocational ervice staff conducts a program of counseling, evaluation, training, business >lanning, and job hunting.

The number of subjects was 36. Twenty-one subjects were males, and 5 were females. Twenty-six subjects had less than $1/200$ vision, and 10 1ad visual acuity of $1/200$ to $5/200$. The mean age was 46.5, with a standard leviation of 13.4. The age range was 21 to 71 years. The mean number of years blind was 16.9, with a standard deviation of 13.7. The mean number f years of schooling was 9.4, with a standard deviation of 2.5.

Early in the vocational intake interview, the counselor asked each subect four questions designed to evoke self-ratings of manual ability on a ive-point scale. These questions were arrived at in a brief pilot study.

Later in the same interview, biographical information about previous nanual life experience, i.e., chores, hobbies, school courses and work, was licited from the subject and filled in on an individual biographical inventory card.

Within two weeks after this interview, a psychometric battery which ncluded the Purdue Pegboard (Right, Left, and Assembly), the Pennylvania Bi-Manual Worksample (Assembly and Disassembly) and the Minnesota Rate of Manipulation (Placing, Turning, and Displacing) tests vas administered to each subject. The Pennsylvania and the Minnesota ests were administered in accordance with the Roberts and Bauman adaptation for the blind. For the Purdue Pegboard, this investigator expanded on the Curtis adaptation of the standard administration.

About one week later, the counselor interpreted the test results to the subject in relation to the "sighted norms" in the manual. Following this the subject was again asked to rate himself on the four manual ability scales referred to above.

Within the next month, the subject was referred to the guild's subcontrac assembly shop for a four-week paid-work trial. Each subject was instructed in and assigned a number of manual operations, such as assembling o. packing of simple toys, novelties, hardware, electrical supplies, automotive parts, etc. The variety sampled the subject's aptitude and development o skill in fine, intermediate, and gross manual dexterity and one-hand ma nipulation and bimanual co-ordination tasks. Daily production and earning records were kept. Each subject was paid for work produced at the curren community rate for the same or similar job, extrapolated on a piece-rate basis. Jobs are time-studied, and piece rates vary with each task in relatior to the time required to complete the operation.

The piece rate is a real incentive. When an individual approximate average hourly earnings of 90 cents or more, he is capable of meeting the quantity production demands of competitive employment. The work weel varied from 32 to 35 hours. Average hourly earnings for the four-weel trial in this industrially simulated assembly shop of the New York Guild was considered the criterion of manual work success.

The work trial was followed by another interview in which the subjec was asked to rate himself on the scales of manual ability.

Findings

For the 36 subjects of this study, the statistical treatment of the data revealed the following results.

1. The variables *not* correlated significantly with earnings were: age sex, vision, years of school, years blind, the prebiographical inventory self-rating, the posttest self-rating, the Pennsylvania Bi-Manual Worksample Assembly and Disassembly tests, and the Minnesota Rate of Manipulatior Turning and Displacing tests.

2. Selected aptitude tests correlated significantly with earnings. The Purdue Pegboard (Right, Left, and Assembly) and the Minnesota Rate o Manipulation (Placing) tests proved to be the most valuable predictors o manual work success, contradicting the findings of an earlier investigator using a less appropriate criterion. That first study had compared the

performance of blind subjects with the manual's norms for sighted persons, showing that the blind are handicapped in these tests. A second study by the same author compared employed and unemployed blind persons. This present study, however, used an external criterion—earnings—for correlation with test results, demonstrating that performance on the tests is related to performance on the job. The output criterion seems more appropriate.

3. A simple tally of each subject's biographical inventory of manual life experience, i.e., chores, hobbies, school courses and work, correlated significantly with earnings, proving to be as good a predictor of success in manual work as selected dexterity tests.

4. Of the three self-ratings of manual ability—the first made before completing the biographical inventory of manual life experience, the second made after testing, and the third made after the paid-work trial—only the self-rating made after the work trial correlated significantly with earnings.

5. The group with enriched manual experiences was significantly differentiated from the impoverished-experience group. The former were significantly better earners.

6. The enriched-experience group made the greater change in self-rating of manual ability as a result of the experimental experience. However, the change in self-rating favoring the "enriched" group was not significant.

43. Counseling the Blind *

JOHN E. JORDAN, *Associate Professor, College of Education, Michigan State University*
WILLIAM F. HUNTER, *Clinical Psychologist, The Range Mental Health Center, Virginia, Minnesota*

WESTERN SOCIETY has for the past several centuries accepted the right of blind children or adults to a full and progressive education. However, society's stated acceptance of the blind has not often been put into operational use. The blind have been accepted and then located in schools where

* Reprinted by permission of the authors and *Personnel and Guidance Journal,* 9:210–214; 1960.

they were entirely segregated from society. They have been regarded as being acceptable only in certain locations or as having certain personality deficiencies which were inherent in the problem of blindness.

The blind, from an educational standpoint, have also been viewed as "people without vision." There has not been the recognition or the realization that the blind are not just sighted people who have lost their vision but that they possess some distinctively and qualitatively different problems. This is particularly true of the congenitally blind.

The emotional problems of blind children and adults have been of growing concern to the psychological profession in recent years. Samuel Hayes was one of the first individuals to collect and interpret data relating to the intellectual capacity and academic achievement of blind children. However, educational and other types of programs devised by society for the blind have not taken into account the full range of opportunities available for rehabilitating this group. These programs have been mainly academic and vocational in nature. This has assumed that the primary needs of the blind were for academic preparation and vocational placement. There has been little operational awareness of the fact that the personal-social implications of blindness far outweigh the differentiating factors of academic and vocational needs.

The growth of guidance and counseling services within the public school and the growing consciousness of the total mental health picture in modern society have, at last, posed an awareness of the personal-social needs of all handicapping conditions, including loss of vision and blindness. Thus, within many school settings, counseling is now being viewed as preventive rather than only remedial.

The Counselor's Approach

Immediately following blindness, the individual enters a tightly knit program directed toward his rehabilitation or habilitation. The congenitally blind child is also a participant in a tightly knit educational program from nursery school through college. It is the purpose of this article to discuss some of the theoretical assumptions, practical problems, procedures, and methodology involved in counseling the blind and to outline an operational approach to guide the counselor in helping such individuals to adjust to the world at large. Too frequently the adjustment of the blind individual is accomplished by providing a special set of circumstances removed from the frustrations which would ordinarily confront him in the everyday world. This level of adjustment represents no more than a compromise and does not lead to the development of realistic attitudes which help these individuals to function in the normal situations of a sighted environment.

Literature on counseling the blind has emphasized the commonalities of all children and the fact that blind children do not differ significantly from regular children. These articles have further emphasized the integration of blind with sighted in all areas such as education, community living, and reality of blindness on an integrated basis within his self-concept. In other words, the blind person must be able to see himself as blind but not conceptualize this condition as a limiting factor on his possibilities to be a whole person.

The counselor needs to know the basic medical information about blindness itself. This includes such things as etiology, course of the disease or condition, treatment, prognosis, concomitant effects, and psychological characteristics such as intelligence and academic achievement. The counselor should also understand the societal provisions for the blind, including the educational, medical, economic, and vocational rehabilitation. This obviously includes knowledge of the community agencies which can be of service to the blind individual.

The attitudes of the counselor toward blindness are very important, and he should come to know and understand them before he can be regarded as having an adequate education or preparation as a counselor of the blind. These attitudes and feelings about blindness, as a disabling condition, will affect the quality of his voice, including intonation, inflection, and rhythm. The counselor must be aware of the effect of extraneous noise and nonverbal communication in counseling the blind. Extraneous noises, such as shuffling papers, can denote to the blind that he is being ignored or that the counselor's attention is being directed elsewhere during the interview.

The sighted person receives many cues in counseling from nonverbal communication. Behavior like glances, turning the head, raising the eyebrows, etc. connote many things in the counseling interview. Since these cues are not available to the blind person, nonverbal communication with him relies primarily on auditory cues.

The Problem of Acceptance

In blindness there is a need for the individual to develop psychological acceptance of his handicap. The person who becomes blind must adapt, in various ways, his former self. The inner person may be altered. His aspirations, his interpersonal relationships, his body image, his concepts of self, and his relationship to the physical world may be strongly affected, if not completely changed. Barker and associates refer to this as the somato-psychology of blindness.

A blind person may refuse to accept his blindness for a number of rea-sons. Perhaps he cannot accept this handicap because it means he is being punished for his own or his parents' sins. Another person may give blind-ness sexual meanings. Another may feel it means an end to his acceptance by society as a valid person. Another is traumatized by the economic prob-lems of blindness. Still another cannot accept his blindness because he resents the feelings of pity he believes the sighted feel for him. However, it is basic to any rehabilitation that he accept this change in self. It must take place before he can effectively accomplish all the new learning that is essential for his future development. The counseling process is one means which may be used to assist the blind person in reorienting his self-concept.

Counselors are cognizant of the emotional difficulties arising with the onset of puberty and adolescence, and individuals working with blind students should be on the lookout for such problems during this period. In our society, adolescence is possibly the most painful period of life, owing to its physiological and psychological upheavals. It is a time of emotional turmoil which accompanies development of sexual maturity. The dependent role of the child is being discarded for that of an adult; defiance of authority during this period is not unusual and is accompanied by a strong need for group acceptance and identity.

Some of the following preoccupations of the adolescent make acceptance of blindness especially difficult: (1) The importance of bodily-attractive-ness in the female and masculine strength and independence in the male. These preoccupations are related to sexual fears which are accentuated in the blind adolescent. (2) The problems of developing independence in an adolescent who must accept certain dependencies which are characteristic for blindness. (3) The exhibitionism accompanied with the desire for anonymity of the adolescent.

Formidable resistance is sometimes put up by the blind person to any change in his self-concept. This may be due to a lack of ability on his part. A complete diagnostic evaluation, including a medical examination, social history, psychological examination, and an educational evaluation, should be accomplished prior to the initiation of any counseling with a blind individual.

For counseling to be effective, a minimum level of intellectual ability and verbalization is necessary. During the testing situation the examiner can gain a great deal of clinical information in order to make a prognosis as to the outcome of any counseling which may be done. Many times blind children, due to a lack of early environmental stimulation and training, seem to lack the ability and insight to make a satisfactory change in their self-concept. This is especially true of the deaf-blind.

In assisting the blind individual in changing his self-concept, the counselor should offer himself as a relatively fixed, warm, nonthreatening figure. He must not take responsibility, since the blind individual tends to be hostile toward authority figures during this period of self-reorganization. A facilitating atmosphere is one in which the client sees the counselor as an available resource for the resolution of his many internal stresses which holds the minimal threat.

It will be wise to remember that the client is first an individual and then a blind person. When he can deal with his personal situations adequately, he will deal more effectively with problems of blindness. Sometimes problems that are usually found in adolescence occur earlier, and the counselor should be aware of this possibility.

Intercommunication Difficulties

Many blind individuals have exceptional difficulty in expressing their emotions. Even in cases in which they are in constant contact with teachers and peer groups, superficial relationships are the rule rather than the exception. Especially impressive is the difficulty many students show in discussing their reactions to emotion-filled situations.

This reticence toward the expression of emotion is not limited to the blind. Our culture views emotional experiences as a most intimate aspect of the individual and the expression of emotion as something of an exposure of the inner self. Consequently, such communication of feeling is a measure of trust and closeness reserved for close relationships.

This difficulty in discussing feelings, moods, and emotions has many derivatives in the inner life of blind individuals. For example, many clients feel that their fears, anxieties, and emotional problems are peculiar to themselves. It is amazing to a blind client to learn that another blind person feels uncomfortable in silence or is very fearful when lost.

While such feelings of uniqueness of emotions are not unusual in the sighted, they are probably much more common with the blind, because of their limited ability to observe the emotional reactions of others. In some cases, blind clients feel that their emotions are mental anomalies which serve to make them different from others. A more stable self-concept is attained when they learn that their strong feelings need not be signs of pathology and that sighted individuals possess them also.

The Counseling Process

The psychological make-up and age of the blind client are prime factors in the counseling interview. The young client or child can be dealt with in a more matter-of-fact manner than the older individual, who may expect a more solicitous attitude. Whether the client is a child in school or comes as a counseling client to a vocational counseling center will make a difference in the kind of arrangement necessary.

Children in a school setting, and especially those in an institutional setting or residential school for the blind, are accustomed to a more informal type of appointment. The nature of the problem or situation which initiates the counseling interview is also important. A vocational problem, a personal-social situation, or a school discipline case may necessitate a different approach to the counseling interview.

The counseling process with the blind is qualitatively different from that of the sighted in certain aspects. It is necessary to be more specific in making appointments and arranging other conditions, since the blind may have to depend upon others for transportation and direction to the counselor's office. The counselor's readiness for the appointment is more important for the blind than for the sighted client.

The counselor should be ready for the interview and not be required to shuffle through papers or the case file looking for various items of information. If this becomes necessary, he should make some comment, such as "It will take me a few seconds to find that information." Such apparently innocuous activities as tapping the pencil may connote to the individual client irritation of the counselor or the desire to hurry the interview.

Mobility is a problem of the blind which the counselor should be aware of and handle properly. While the blind individual may require direction or assistance to the counselor's office or to a chair in the counseling room, he must not be maneuvered in a manner which appears to be a manipulation of his rights as an individual.

It is necessary to orient the blind individual to the room if it is unknown to him. Such statements as, "This room is eight by ten feet and your chair is located here, facing the light," will give the individual the necessary environmental orientation. A more or less detailed explanation may be required, according to the client.

It is usually necessary to structure the surface of the interview for the blind individual. He comes expecting a certain kind of structured activity, owing to the fact that he has been dealt with in this manner much of his life. If the interview is a situation which is aimed at dealing with personal-social conflicts, the counselor may desire to allow the client to structure the interview. If the interview is to be a specific one, such as vocational counseling or a disciplinary problem in school, the purpose of the interview should be structured for the blind individual so that he knows its purpose. While this is also true for the sighted individual, it is more so for the blind, since he must depend on auditory cues more than the sighted individual.

The perceptual difficulties of the blind are a differentiating factor in the counseling interview. A blind person's perception of a certain kind of job or a certain idea may differ markedly from that of the sighted person. The perception may be in spatial relations, abstract ideas, or concrete life experiences. The blind individual has often experienced less of the everyday acculturation, such as visiting stores and acquiring the life experiences of the sighted individual.

It is apparent that the intellectual level of the client will also be a significant variable. This must be considered, as the same condition which caused the blindness may bring about some damage or restriction to the brain that will exert a limiting effect on intellectual development. The emotional stability of the blind individual will also be a significant variable in the counseling process. If the individual has been subjected to repeated and severe emotional stress because of his blindness, he may be in need of more intensive psychotherapy or psychiatric care.

Counseling Relationships

In order for an individual to express feeling with any degree of comfort, he must be aware of the manner in which his communication is received. As the sighted person offers some indication of his emotions, he receives permission to proceed from the smiles, sympathetic face and nods of the counselor. In short, the client must receive, in some way, constant stimuli from the counselor in order to sustain the necessary verbalization to proceed with the counseling.

The visual cues which are used by the sighted are not available as stimuli to the blind individual. The blind consequently substitute other cues not usually necessary for those who have sight. For example, a blind client may observe the counselor's rate of breathing, the shuffling of his feet, or the number of times he clears his throat. These and other audible cues are substituted for visual cues relating to the attentiveness, interest, sympathy, and general response of the blind person's listener. Often these audible cues are not sufficient to permit free expression of emotion. This inability to assess clearly the listener's reaction may explain the relative ineffectiveness noted in some of the communications of the blind.

There are some techniques available which may help to facilitate the counseling process with blind personnel. It is helpful to interpolate frequent grunts, *un-hum's, yeses,* and various audible cues to substitute for the visual cues which indicate to the client that his communication is being received and understood. The verbal note of expression lets the blind client know the counselor's position in regard to his communication.

Another point to be considered in dealing with the blind is the difficulty in assessing emotional reaction by studying facial expression. The face is generally a poor indicator of emotion in blind individuals, and especially so in the congenitally blind, who must learn about facial expression through secondary sources. For this reason it is helpful to watch the fingers and hands for movements and evidence of tension in attempting to assess the emotional state of clients. In the blind, the fingers are substitutes for the eyes and are the most expressive of emotional states.

Summary

The article has intended to indicate some of the needs in the counseling of blind individuals, particularly of children and adolescents. It has attempted to point out some of the theory on which to build a qualitatively different approach in counseling the blind. An operational approach to counseling the blind was tentatively outlined, including such things as the significant factors in the counselor's education as well as the counseling interview itself. The research on perceptual difficulties points to a need for establishing whether there is a qualitative difference in the counseling methodology for blind individuals.

44. Counseling with the Atypically Blind Child *

EUNICE KENYON, *Executive Director of the Center for Blind Children, Boston*

MY ASSIGNED TOPIC is "Counseling with the Atypically Blind Child." If by "atypical" we mean simply "not typical" rather than a more or less specific diagnostic category, then it is probably correct to assume that this is the child about whom I intend to talk with you today. However, to discuss the problems of this altogether too large group of children, I think it will help us to clarify our thinking if we divide all blind children into six rough categories: (1) the strictly educable, (2) the educable retarded, (3) the moderately disturbed but educable, (4) the disturbed child whose prognosis for educability is in doubt, (5) the trainable retarded, (6) the grossly retarded child in need of custodial care. Children with physical handicaps in addition to blindness are purposely not mentioned, since some of these children fall into each of the six listed groups.

Now, as we look at these six categories in terms of available services, I believe we can have considerable confidence that thoroughly adequate programs exist for the first group: the strictly educable. In an increasing number of settings, the second group, too, the educable retarded, are being offered programs suitable to their needs. The fifth group, the trainable retarded, are probably third on the list in terms of available resources to assist them in their growth. The sixth group, the grossly retarded child in need of custodial care, usually has a setting available to him, although there is considerable variability in the quality of such programs. The third group, the moderately disturbed but clearly educable child, can usually be offered a helping program. Although few schools have enough man power in their guidance departments to offer this youngster the therapeutic help necessary if he is to function at his optimal level, there are usually community therapeutic resources which can be applied to his need in conjunction with the school facilities.

But what of the fourth group: the disturbed child whose prognosis for educability is in doubt? Any of you who have tried to find suitable resources for one of these children know how few and far between such

* Reprinted by permission of the author. Speech given at the Council for Exceptional Children Convention, Philadelphia, 1963.

facilities are. It is certainly understandable that this is the group of children to whom we offer the least, for any number of reasons. They do not fit well into a program for "normal" blind children whose educational needs must be met; indeed, in addition to the handicapping influence on other children, the seriously disturbed blind child cannot be adequately served in a program geared exclusively to educational needs. He requires much more. His needs are also different from those of the retarded child, so he is usually not well served in a program intended for the training and/or care of the retarded. It is clear that the seriously disturbed youngster needs a program which is highly specialized to meet his requirements.

What sort of program does he need? To answer this question, one must first acknowledge that the seriously disturbed child is correctly considered multiply handicapped in that he is blind, emotionally disturbed, often somewhat retarded in his functioning level, quite often also afflicted by some degree of demonstrable or suspected neurological involvement; he is usually experiencing disturbed family and/or social relationships; he has almost invariably suffered in his concept formation and fund of information through lack of suitable learning opportunities; and, altogether too often, he has some additional physical handicap. Obviously, a program which is going to serve him well strives to understand and help him cope with his specific difficulties in each of these handicapping areas. Since the problems with which the individual child is struggling in each of these categories are quite different from those with which another equally disturbed child is struggling, the difficulty of serving him well is further compounded.

The problem of helping such multiply handicapped youngsters presents a tremendous challenge and undoubtedly appears too discouraging for the majority of settings to have succeeded in setting up suitable programs. However, I speak to you about the problem today because something can be done. It is being done in our own Center and a few other scattered settings; but this is not enough. More such programs are needed to serve this increasingly large group of children. I do not mean to suggest that all these seriously disturbed children can be "cured," so to speak, but experience has already shown us that even with our present knowledge, skills, and understanding, a great many can be helped to a point where they are considerably happier people, able to contribute to our society on a higher level than would have been the case had they not had such help. A great deal more needs to be learned, but the learning will accompany our continuing efforts with these youngsters.

So, how, at our present stage of knowledge, can we help this group? In view of the tremendous complexity of the problems of a given child, the first step is a complete, accurate, and thorough diagnostic study. By this, we mean not the application of diagnostic labels but a study which results in as thorough an understanding as possible of this child, his specific limitations and strengths, his anxieties and frustrations, his fears, his feelings about himself and his world, his unmet needs. We need to know what medical problems he has. We must learn what his mental capacities are, how he uses them, and what, if anything, prohibits his use of his optimal abilities. We need to understand his educational needs: what has he learned, how he learns, and what is holding him back from further learning. We need to know his background: how do his family feel about themselves, about him; what have been his relationships, his opportunities, as well as limitations of opportunity. It has been our experience that from such a combined pediatric, psychiatric, psychological, educational, and social service diagnostic study, a fairly well-rounded picture of the child in his environment emerges which allows us to make wise recommendations for helping him to further growth. So far, we have not found the real problems which are preventing more adequate service to these children, for such diagnostic studies are available.

However, when we have arrived at an understanding of the child and his present needs, workers in most areas are faced with a most discouraging lack of suitable resources to meet these needs. At the Center for Blind Children, we have developed a treatment setting for disturbed children and therefore are able to admit a child in need of such service from our own diagnostic program into our own treatment facility. Since more such programs are badly needed, it seems worth while to take a few minutes now to state the broad outlines of this treatment program in which the divergent problems of disturbed blind children can be met. Since the needs of these children as understood following diagnostic study are very individual, the program must also be individualized if these needs are to be met. Yet, while there must be flexibility to meet these varying needs, there must also be structure, for many of these youngsters rely heavily on structure and routine for support to their usually very weak or fragmentary ego structures.

Obviously, an educational program must be available which is prepared to offer class room and/or tutorial help not only at any grade level where a given child is functioning but also where the child's emotional needs can be adequately met. This in itself is often difficult, for, in many cases, superimposed on the youngster's basic emotional disturbance is a reaction to prior failure in school settings and a gross lack of information and concepts resulting from his lack of educational opportunity.

The child's teacher needs to work very closely with other members of the professional staff, chiefly with the child's psychotherapist, who seeks to help the child come to a better understanding of himself and the world around him. It is often with his therapist that the youngster first dares to experiment with new and, hopefully, more effective ways of relating. When this has occurred in psychotherapy, it is imperative for others working closely with the child to know about it in order to offer him other opportunities to practice his new learnings about himself. For example, a little girl recently came to us who was markedly withdrawn. Her relationships with other people had been so unsatisfactory to her that she seemed to prefer her own company, her own thoughts. She did nothing in class or in the program. Then, in psychotherapy, she became well enough acquainted with her therapist and felt safe enough to share her fantasies, showing the therapist how very angry she was. Shortly, this anger began to "spill over" into the classroom and program in general. Had the child's teacher and child care worker not been in close touch with the therapist, had they not understood these new angry outbursts as necessary steps to better personality integration, the child could very well have been squelched again as had happened in the past and might never have proceeded to abandon her withdrawn state.

Speaking of the child care worker (often referred to as counselor or house parent), I believe this is a key person in residential treatment. This is the person with whom the child spends large blocks of time, in the morning, at mealtimes, after classes, in the evening; and these must not be periods of empty waiting for the next class or therapeutic session. The whole point of residential treatment is to offer the child a consistent, 24-hour-per-day program geared to his particular treatment needs. Therefore, his child care worker must be an intelligent, warm, sensitive, creative person who understands the child's particular problems and his treatment needs; who, in conjunction with the teacher and therapist, decides on goals appropriate for the youngster and seeks to appreciate these goals through careful treatment planning. These children have almost invariably learned ineffective ways of relating to adults, and the child care worker is often the person who has opportunities to help him come to the realization that he is a loved and respected person, thus freeing him to relate more productively. The social worker who co-ordinates the treatment program with home and who helps parents come to a better understanding of their child and his needs is obviously another key person; for as the child makes gains in residential treatment, the parents need to understand these as thoroughly as possible if they are to be in a position to relate constructively.

Perhaps the key to residential treatment is "working together," for all these people are important to the child's growth; but it is imperative that his total program be consistent.

Our time is too limited to allow anything resembling thorough discussion of this almost forgotten group of children. However, since we have such a marked need for additional treatment resources, I hope that in the discussion period following these presentations we may be able to bring out in greater detail the methods through which our resources can be improved and expanded to meet the tremendously pressing needs of this increasingly large group of children.

In summary, the major needs appear to be:

1. Sufficiently thorough and accurate diagnostic studies to ensure wise placement and treatment planning. A simple intelligence test is surely not enough of a basis for differential diagnosis and deciding a child's placement.

2. Treatment resources which are available to these children and adequate to meet their multiple needs—these treatment resources in conjunction with ongoing diagnosis.

3. Careful research aimed at greater understanding and hence improved ability to serve these youngsters.

4. Careful consideration of and planning for the large group of young adults which these children are rapidly becoming, including decisions as to whether the majority of them must live out their lives in institutions or whether we can prepare at least some of them for constructive, happy, contributing careers. The successes we have already experienced are ample evidence that the latter is possible.

45. Vocational Counseling and Placement of Blind Youth *

LYLE THUME, *Psychologist-Counselor, Arkansas Enterprises for the Blind, Little Rock*

I T IS NATURAL to be final in the succession on a panel when one's subject deals with vocational guidance and placement of youth. In spite of this, I will dwell only briefly on the historical aspects of guidance as it has been in the past. At present we are undergoing extreme change, and much that has been said about the past may not be relevant to the future. Most references to guidance, as it involves blind persons, tends to emphasize some of the more unusual or atypical occupations that blind persons have entered into. The examples often given are such as is contained in the title of a book, *From Homer to Helen Keller*. Such a reference is always connected with the blind person who became an author, a poet, or some of the other more unusual things that these persons may have done and been. My thinking more often goes back to Robert Louis Stevenson and Blind Pew. I am not certain what the occupational reference handbook would say about the job description of a buccaneer, and it also may not be significant that he was eventually trampled to death by horses, as this is the type of violent end that those who enter this occupation often expect to encounter. The significance of this association is that there are no doubt many jobs, occupations, and professions that various blind people have or can enter into. Too specific a description of any one of these is in great danger of limiting both the flexibility and the horizons of any blind youth who may be seeking vocational guidance or counseling.

Not too recently, in 1955, research work sponsored by the American Foundation for the Blind under the authorship of Raskins surveyed some of the needs as they were being met for guidance of blind students in residential schools for the blind. One might expect that within the purview of the residential school the greatest emphasis would be given to the guidance needs of these blind students. His survey would contend, as well as does the limited support given the guidance workshop in the American Association of Instructors for the Blind, that there are still very many

* Reprinted by permission of the author. Paper read at the Council for Exceptional Children Convention, Philadelphia, 1963.

288

young blind persons who are not receiving the counseling and guidance that would be appropriate for the meeting of their needs.

Important considerations that need to be given are the type of guidance that will be provided and, most importantly, the individual's readiness to receive the type of guidance that is presented at a given time. Concepts that may deal with various jobs or occupations are sometimes found in quite concrete form; at other times they may be very abstract. The environment and the endowment of the individual himself not only may indicate the readiness and timeliness of the guidance that should be given but also may determine the kind of guidance that the individual may ever be able to deal with and to handle. There is no over-all panacean solution to this problem except that at the present time it is incumbent on those in guidance work to recognize that there is a difference in this type of material and to exercise their responsibility concerning the type of material that is appropriate and the time at which a given type of material can be presented. It is also important for them to consider the manner in which material will be presented, in terms of the kinds of concepts that the individual will be able to handle.

In a prevocational training situation, we are often dealing with many blind persons who have lost their sight after the time that most of their formal education has been completed or accomplished. There are also, of course, many blind persons who have gone through instructional experiences within the public school situation as well as some of those who have gone through their educational experiences in residential schools for the blind. As a result of this, the need of these young blind people will many times not be the needs that we typically ascribe to those persons who have received their formal educational experiences as blind persons. Today the pressures for change that have already been mentioned are resulting from the fact that demand for unskilled labor in all fields is becoming less. The Department of Labor contends that there is likely to be a 5 to 8 per cent core of unemployment at any given time. This can make the competitive placement of blind persons more difficult as well as increase the demand for better job training and the types of job training that will need to take place over a longer duration. This places us under pressure to begin planning and vocational guidance much earlier. It has been said that at early ages fantasy largely determines the young person's choices of vocation. This is the time when a young person aspires to being an actor or actress, a nurse, doctor, policeman, fireman, or what have you. These are the choices that are common to most children, whether they be blind or sighted. Later on more realistic choices are considered. A parallel may be drawn here from dentistry, concerning the time at which the more realistic choices can be moved into. Dentists use a pulp test to determine whether the nerve in a tooth is dead or not. If the nerve is dead, the individual may be advised to have the tooth removed, as decay, infection, and perhaps abscess might occur later. On the other hand, he may wait, as there may be many, many years of good chewing left in that tooth before extraction becomes absolutely necessary. Some of this same form of indecision may pertain to some of the planning that should be entered into in a guidance situation.

Recently there have been some very specific progressive steps taken toward the meeting of the needs of blind persons. One of the most notable is the study by Bauman and Yoder, *Placing the Blind in Professional Occupations*. This publication, again, is not a specific enumeration of jobs that have been done by blind people but a very excellent beginning of the development of a source of information that can be obtained concerning some of the techniques, methods, and experiences that have been undergone by blind persons performing in some of the professional fields. Last year at the Southwest Rehabilitation Center, operated by Arkansas Enterprises for the Blind, we inaugurated a college preparation course, which will be significantly expanded this year. With this group we particularly attempt to meet certain needs of blind individuals who are all ready to matriculate on the college campus. Last summer this group's activity resulted in the operation of an evaluation factor, which was not initially anticipated. Five of the approximately thirteen full-term enrollees are not now, and probably will not be, in college in the near future. Original planning was not deliberately designed to include this evaluation factor but will probably receive continued important consideration in the future. The college prep course is a supplement to the ongoing prevocational training program of a center. The student in this course is considered as one of the trainees of the center, and the group in which he functions is mixed in terms of heterogeneous factors of age, sex, and background. There are only one or two periods a day that are particularly set aside for college preparation. In these groups such problems are dealt with separately. He is scheduled with the other trainees in needed areas such as mobility, communicative skills, daily activities of living, etc. The set-aside daily periods contain one period a week which is almost totally unstructured. During this time, with a leader, the students ventilate and exchange their ideas concerning problems that they feel may relate to college living. These included a variety of matters such as "drinking," "cheating on exams," "matters of one student's relationships to another"; and the problem of "student-owned cars" is about the only one that did not appear last summer.

The other sessions during the week contained more directively oriented instruction. Problems involving note taking, the taking of exams, the inter-relationship between student and professor, the responsibility of the student to make advance arrangements for taking his tests so that the problem will not be encountered as a fresh obstacle on the date that the examination is scheduled, as well as the amount of concession he will demand or refuse concerning such problems as taking lab courses, physical education, and such matters are prime considerations in these other sessions. College note-taking techniques developed as a particularly important problem, and guest speakers as well as center staff members were brought in to deliver sample lectures. Following these, rather difficult tests were given on the material. This was found necessary because many of the students had accepted the ancient stereotype that blind people have very "excellent memories." As many of them had been representative of a "bright group" in the schools from which they came, they had been able to do quite well academically and had not always been impressed with the necessity for note taking. Some of them were never impressed by this in the course either, and the rather severe lecture and exam pattern was necessary to convince those that were amenable of the value of note utilization as well as the practical experience of handling this process independently.

This college prep course and Bauman and Yoder's research are constructive steps forward in meeting the needs of blind youth. Primarily they represent blind people in college or entering into professional areas. An area of some neglect remains for the blind person who plans to enter business college or a trade or technical school or to engage in on-the-job training. In most cases these persons are not offered special prep courses. One major contribution in this area is the Visceli course in placement counselor training at the University of Southern Illinois. This deals directly with training counselors who will be working in the field of making industrial placements. It is not dealing directly with the blind individual who may have guidance needs, but it does represent a constructive step in the direction of offering more specialized services. An ideal overview of these developments resulted from the recent St. Louis Conference sponsored by VRA, AAIB, and the Hadley School. The minimum result of this conference will certainly be the selection of occupational text material and the adaption or authorship of counselor and teacher guides. Eventually these may be used by teachers and counselors or by blind youths in self-study.

Personnel of residential schools, those dealing with blind children, and classes in public schools, those in rehabilitation centers, and those in state rehabilitation agencies are probably to some extent unaware of each other's functions. There seems to be a need for exchange of information concerning each other's problems and resources. It is highly important for the school counselor to know something of the follow-up that a student will receive from a rehabilitation counselor after he leaves school. It is necessary to determine whether a transfer at this point is indicated, possible, or unwise. The rehabilitation counselor has a like need to know something of the experiences that the client received as a student prior to reaching him. These experiences are important, as they have contributed to both his educational experiences and his counseling needs. On June 24 we are having an institute of this type in Little Rock. The institute will be composed of personnel both from residential schools for the blind and from special resource people working with blind children in other school systems in the southwest region. In this instance the program content will be presented by the Rehabilitation Center staff and by persons connected with the State Rehabilitation Agencies who will come in. It would seem to me that other institutes or workshops would be important where school personnel would bring in rehabilitation center staffs and rehabilitation agency personnel to learn more of the contribution that each is making and of the potential opportunity for the use that each would have for the resources that the other can offer. This spring we have also had an exchange evening meeting between the Rehabilitation Center and the Arkansas State School for the Blind. These, as more or less informal occasions, are the kind of things that will make staffs and faculties on a one-to-one individual basis much more aware of the job that is already being done.

In work for the blind, as in other fields, there has always been a problem of the stereotyping of the occupation that many blind persons happen to be engaged in as that which perhaps should involve all blind persons. Historically, we may refer to the musician, to the piano tuner, to the broom maker, and probably now perhaps to the vending-stand operator. While vending-stand operations have tended to "mushroom" in recent years, it continues to be very important that development also needs to be encouraged in business, professional, industrial, and other areas. Many times after the administration of the psychological tests that are available—Wechsler, Occupational Preference Records, Personality Inventories, or Dexterity Measures—it is found that even after an individual may have gained insight into the competencies he most easily might develop and would enjoy most, he may be inclined to accept the secure offer of a "sure thing" in an occupation where he believes his earnings might be $50 or so a month more than he thinks they could otherwise have been. This tends to set aside the importance of counseling and evaluation that may have been done and, incidentally, contributes to the reinforcement of these already existing stereotypes. Oftentimes a blind person who functions successfully as a vending-stand operator probably possesses greater security and greater adequacy than many other blind persons who may not be dealing as directly with those elements of the public. On the other hand, it is not taking away from the respectability and dignity of these individuals to suggest that there are many blind persons who probably enter vending-stand or other programs because of the above-mentioned needs for apparent security and not because of the development of any particular insight. A discussion of the development of some of these problems that still contribute to job stereotyping probably relates back to our initial references in this paper to considering the vocational preferences of a number of blind persons. This, then, offers us an ideal suggestion to end our remarks at this point in the hope that further discussion will have an opportunity to occur.

Suggested Readings

Abel, Georgie Lee. "The Blind Adolescent and His Needs," *Exceptional Children,* 27:309–310, 325–334; February, 1961.

Clay, Frances. "Towards Competence in Serving the Blind," *Journal of Rehabilitation,* 26:14–16, 24; 1960.

Davis, C. J. (ed.). *Guidance Programs for the Blind: Report of a Conference.* Watertown, Mass.: Perkins School for the Blind, 1959.

Fields, Helen. "How New York City Educated Visually Handicapped Children," *New Outlook for the Blind,* 55:337–340; December, 1961. Discusses responsibilities of guidance counselor assigned to visually handicapped in New York City schools.

Hoffman, S. *Some Predictors of Manual Work Success with Blind Persons,* Ed.D. Thesis, Columbia University, 1957.

Lowenfeld, B. "The Blind Adolescent in a Seeing World," *New Outlook for the Blind,* 53:289–295; October, 1959.

Moor, Pauline M. "Blind Children with Developmental Problems," *Children,* 8:9–13; January–February, 1961.

New Outlook for the Blind. "Symposium—Self-Image: a Guide to Adjustment II," *New Outlook for the Blind,* 55:285–305; November, 1961.

New York Heart Association. *Vocational Counseling for Children with Heart Disease or a History of Rheumatic Fever: A Pilot Study.* New York: the Association, 1962. 236 pp.

Rusalem, H. "Attitudes toward Blind Counselors in State Rehabilitation Agencies," *Personnel and Guidance Journal,* 39:367–372; 1961. There are few opportunities for blind counselors in state rehabilitation agencies serving both blind and nonblind persons. Attitudes toward blind counselors may change with research.

Wallace, Helen M. "School Services for Partially Seeing and Blind Children in Urban Areas," *Sight-Saving Review,* 29:160–165; Fall, 1959.

Weiner, L. H. "Educating the Emotionally Disturbed Blind Child," *International Journal of Education of the Blind,* 11:77–79; 1962. Feels that the blind child may be consciously or unconsciously manipulating his disability to avoid facing reality. Hence his teacher should help him to face reality by making the child aware of expectations for life adjustment and putting pressure on him to meet them. Steps for achieving this goal are presented.

West, Doral M. *Attitudes of Rehabilitation Counselors for the Blind Towards Totally Blind Students,* Ed.D. Thesis, Missouri University, 1957.

I N CONTRAST to the dearth of guidance material on the blind, there is a spate of such material on the deaf and speech-handicapped. Perhaps the most informative of all the articles, however, is that of Myklebust, Neyhaus, and Mulholland on "Guidance and Counseling of the Deaf," *American Annals of the Deaf,* 107:370–415, 1962, which could not be reproduced here because of limitations of space. This monograph should be read by all who counsel or work otherwise with these students.

Our chapter commences with the paper by Jane Raph (then Beasley) on early speech problems related to parental pressures. Then comes a research report by Birch, Stuckless, and Birch of an eleven-year study in predicting achievement in deaf children. This is followed by Fuller's excellent advice to parents of deaf children. Levine, in a short extract from an excellent psychological paper which should be read in full, gives the counselor some guidelines for dealing with the deaf. Murphy continues with a top paper on counseling with deaf students. Rudloff discusses the problem of guidance which deaf children present in school, and Roy discusses the problems of vocational rehabilitation.

46. Relationships of Parental Attitudes to the Development of Speech Problems *

JANE BEASLEY–RAPH, *Formerly with Horace Mann Lincoln Institute at Columbia University; now Professor of Education at Rutgers University, New Brunswick, New Jersey*

PROFESSIONAL PEOPLE concerned with helping children are in agreement, as a rule, that parents are key figures in the child's situation, not only in the problems he may have but also in the progress he is able to make. This paper will call attention to certain cause-effect relationships thought to exist between parental attitudes and occurrence of language and speech problems. Some issues will then be considered which are related to the parent work carried on by a speech and hearing therapist. Suggestions for counseling will be discussed in the final section.

Effects of Parental Attitudes

Since a child develops communication in an interpersonal setting, speech or language difficulties inevitably mean that he has encountered emotional stress within his family deeper than or different from that of a child who has developed adequate speaking skill. Disorders such as mutism, faulty articulation, or stuttering may have occurred as a child's way of coping with unfavorable attitudes and treatment from family members. Disorders of other kinds, as those associated with cleft palate, hearing loss, or brain injury, may have been aggravated in the child as much by the expectations, disappointments, and anxieties of the family members as by the original organic involvement.

According to McCarthy, a number of investigators of language point to an emotional and functional explanation of most of the language disorder syndromes and indicate that the disturbances are for the most part environmentally determined. Exponents of this theoretical position, notably McCarthy, Sullivan, Wyatt, Goldfarb, and Ribble have emphasized particularly the possible effects of the mother-child relationship in the establishment of early vocalization and the ensuing enrichment and refinement

* Reprinted by permission of the author and *The Journal of Speech and Hearing Disorders,* 21:317–321; September, 1956.

of sounds. These writers and others, such as Lewis, Langer, and Mowrer, have explored the emotional coloring and nonlogical characteristics of beginning sounds. They hold that rudimentary stabilized word forms are not attached to particular events, objects, or persons. Rather these word forms represent the infant's attempt to call back the surprise, pleasure, or affection the mother has shown. If the infant should meet with indifference, particularly between the twelfth and eighteenth month, his sound combinations may remain variable and tenuous or tend to disappear altogether.

As the child develops, his growth in language continues to be in large measure a response to the kind of interpersonal climate around him. It is hypothesized that freedom and spontaneity in talk are more likely to exist if he meets with flexibility and encouragement in all his early experimenting and exploring and that unevenness and distortion are more likely to appear if he encounters rejection or exacting pressures from people significant to him. These causative factors affecting language are then reinforced by the child's verbal shortcomings. Interference with the normal development of language disturbs his equilibrium and that of his family in several ways: the child is deprived of much of the richness and warmth in relationships which come about through satisfying verbal interchange; he is isolated from the comfort of having what he says understood and approved by people important to him; furthermore, he is penalized by the rejecting effect of well-meaning admonitions to talk better and by the amused ridicule to which he is sometimes exposed.

The family, in turn, may become concerned and oversolicitous, thereby increasing demands on the child to talk differently. Such demands deepen the dependent patterns which the child finds somewhat necessary. As parents search for assistance for the child's condition, they may be motivated as much by their own guilt feelings and their need to direct blame elsewhere as they are by their desire to obtain help for the child. At best, the emotional climate is a charged one, intensified year after year by the cultural expectations placed on both the parents and the child by relatives, neighbors, and eventually school personnel.

Issues in Parent Counseling

From this assumption concerning the influence of the parent–child relationship on the development of language and speech problems, it would follow that parents who want clinical assistance for their child often need it themselves. Such assistance is often essential if the equilibrium of the household is to be brought into better balance for the child. In examining the work that might be done with parents in a speech program, two professional considerations merit some attention.

First, parent work is still a new venture for many speech and hearing therapists. Its scope has not been clearly formulated as yet. Many are still unsure of whose job parent counseling is, how one goes about it, how time for it can be found, and what is considered adequate professional background for the counselor. Procedures with parents vary from the fairly common ones of suggesting how they may help their child's speech at home or presenting information about speech disorders to the less common one of providing a therapeuticlike climate wherein parents discuss their own feelings and struggles. In some instances, contacts with parents are made only briefly on the occasion of the child's enrollment and dismissal from speech class. In other instances, lengthy interviews are provided or parents are actively involved in the child's education or therapy. The range of opinions regarding what constitutes satisfactory and appropriate help is very broad.

Secondly, the expectations for parents vary widely among those who counsel them. Some workers recognize the fact that the problems of parents are of long standing and cannot be eradicated easily, if at all. They see that significant changes in parental attitudes will be brought about slowly and painfully and that a few nostrums will have little effect on the long-range picture. Other equally realistic workers, understanding that human problems are amenable to change, believe that someone, be it a friend, teacher, counselor, or speech therapist who has faith in the possibility of change, can serve as a successful therapeutic agent.

These issues will require thought and planning for some time to come. Appropriate psychological and social agencies, increasing in number throughout the country, are extending their services in this direction. Colleges and universities will be broadening their course offerings to include work in counseling, guidance, and parent education for the therapist in training. In the meantime, many therapists who are concerned with the relationship of the child's speech to his total situation will be talking with parents and providing any assistance they can. Certain attitudes are considered basic to such assistance and are suggested in the ensuing section.

Attitudes in Counseling

The components of the relationship between the speech therapist and the parent are not essentially different from those comprising the relationship between the speech therapist and the child. These may be said to

nvolve *respect* for the parents' present functioning, *understanding* of their
need to preserve their defenses, whatever they may be, *acceptance* of the
parents as people of worth in their own right, *sensitivity* to parents' feelings
of hope and despair, and *compassion* for their situation.

While such qualities may be thought of as intrinsic to any parent coun-
eling, their real significance is frequently concealed in the worker's sincere
fforts to be objective and to function as an authority who can be of help
o parents. Assuming this authoritarian role is apt to place the therapist in
he position of an expert who knows answers, knows better, knows more.
He becomes one who should advise on the best theories and methods of
hildrearing, who can furnish intellectual information about speech dis-
rders, prescribe home treatment, and furnish reassurance for parents. This
s a big order, and yet many who have embarked on the task of helping
parents have set just such high standards for themselves. The therapist's
nvolvement in proving his competency to himself and others may serve
o blur his view of the parents' predicament. In the emphasis on *what* he is
o say, he easily loses sight of the *people* to whom he is talking. Parents
re likely to feel inadequate, anyway, when their child's speech is dis-
rdered. They may come away from a discussion with a speech therapist
eeling bewildered by the amount of advice they have been given, inferior
bout their handling of their child, and anxious or hostile about carrying
ut instructions incompatible with their own beliefs. Such efforts may serve
o make worse what was already an undesirable home atmosphere.

In contrast, if the worker can view himself less as an authority and more
s one who joins parents in seeking a better understanding of the child
nd how he can be helped, a somewhat different role emerges that is easier
n certain respects. The therapist reaches out to parents as people who are
perating in the best way they know at the moment, who probably have a
owered sense of self-worth because of the difficulties the child is having,
nd who have need to express their doubts and uncertainties. The therapist
hould understand that parents may wish to hold to their own regimes of
liscipline and standards and to experience acceptance of the job they are
loing.

The therapist should listen to what people are saying—really listen—
nd attempt to follow the emotional import of the topics parents choose to
aise, the problems they describe, the observations they make about their
hild, and the relationships among family members on which they comment.

The therapist should also attempt to clarify questions parents raise.
Parents ask many questions, although they are often threatened by the
nswers and may hear only what they want to hear or can tolerate hearing.

Certain questions merit simple, factual answers, of course. Certain other questions, often unanswerable, represent more a need for support and encouragement than a need for information. Parents may inquire about length of treatment and eventual outcomes but have considerable difficulty handling the reality situation of the here and now. When parents ask, "Will our child's speech ever be normal?" sometimes the best reply is another question, "What changes have you yourselves noticed in the past three months?" Their query, "What ought we be doing to help?," which so easily calls forth the therapist's preconceived ideas about ideal family instruction and shuts off the individual resourcefulness of parents, can be more profitably turned to "What ideas have you had that seem to be paying off?" When parents ask what speech they should work on at home with the child, it is often valuable to inquire what speech the child is using at home that could be profitably worked on in speech class. These functions can serve to increase the therapist's knowledge about the child and to decrease the threat to the parents of the expert's opinion.

In conclusion, even though parents are seen only briefly or occasionally by a speech therapist, the kind of relationship he establishes with them may serve as an example for parents in their relationship with their child. To the extent that parents themselves are granted acceptance and respect, they will be more free to give this to their child. If the therapist attempts to understand the parental situation instead of evaluating it or forcing change, they will be more free to seek understanding of their child's predicament, less likely to impose additional pressures on him. As the parents gain some small sense of their own worth because they are viewed in a positive way by the therapist, they will be more able to perceive their child favorably.

Since the problems of a child in language and speech originate and exist in an interpersonal setting, modifications of this environment may be highly important if change in speech is to take place. The viewpoint presented here has suggested that the speech therapist's knowledge and understanding of parents can do much to bring this about.

47. An Eleven-Year Study of Predicting School Achievement in Young Deaf Children *

JANE R. BIRCH, *Psychologist, Western Pennsylvania School for the Deaf*

E. ROSS STUCKLESS, *Instructor, Special Education and Rehabilitation, School of Education, University of Pittsburgh*

JACK W. BIRCH, *Professor, Special Education and Rehabilitation, School of Education, University of Pittsburgh*

THIS IS a report of an investigation of the use of ratings from the Leiter International Performance Scale to predict school success of deaf children and to examine the correlations with the Leiter Scale of certain educationally significant attributes of deaf children and their teachers' ratings. The following questions were posed.

1. Can the later school achievement of young deaf children be predicted with substantial accuracy by psychological measurements made when the children are four to eight years of age? How useful are such predictions?

2. Do supervising teachers of the deaf make accurate estimates of the intelligence of young deaf children after approximately six months of observation? Are their estimates of academic aptitude (intelligence) predictive of how the children perform later?

The study is based on and is an extension of earlier work done at the Western Pennsylvania School for the Deaf.

Previous Studies

More than a decade ago, Matthews and Birch and Birch and Birch reported on the potential usefulness of the Leiter International Performance Scale in the psychological assessment of young deaf children, the latter giving comparative data with other psychological instruments. In 1956, a follow-up was described on thirty-five children to determine whether the LIPS could furnish useful predictions of the school success of

* Reprinted by permission of the authors and *American Annals of the Deaf*, 108:236–240; 1963.

young deaf children and whether estimates of children's intelligence mad by supervising teachers would also yield an accurate prediction of schoc success.

The population of the 1955 study was thirty-five students: twenty-tw boys and thirteen girls. They ranged in age from three years and eleve months to eight years and six months. All were examined about six month after entering school. At the same time, each child's intelligence was rate by a supervising teacher. Twenty-two of the children had entered school i 1952, ten in 1953, and three in 1954.

In the spring of 1955, twenty-two of the children had been in schoc for more than three years, ten more than two years, and three more tha one year. At that time the supervisors rated the youngsters on curren educational achievements. The ratings on school achievement were on seven-point scale, with "seven" being the highest.

The Leiter intelligence quotients were transposed to a clinically derive seven-point scale as follows.

Leiter IQ Range	Prediction of Probable Success in School	Rating
111 and higher	Very Superior	7
100 to 110	Superior	6
95 to 99	High Average	5
85 to 94	Average	4
80 to 84	Low Average	3
60 to 79	Poor	2
59 and lower	Failing	1

The correlation reported in 1956 (2) between ratings from the Leite and student achievement approximately one to three years later was .7 yielding a prediction considerably better than chance and also accurat enough to be very useful in counseling parents and planning school pro grams. The r of .86 between Leiter ratings and supervising teacher's esti mates of intelligence indicated that the Leiter was measuring, to a significan extent, what experienced supervising teachers were looking for when the judged the intelligence of young deaf children. These results suggested th advisability of further study.

A longer-range investigation was planned. This, it was felt, would allo an opportunity to put this prediction from the Leiter ratings to mor severe tests. The criterion for school achievement in the 1955 study ha been the judgment of the supervising teacher, unsupported by achievemen tests other than the informal testing done in the normal course of teaching. The supervising teachers in the 1955 study had also been asked to rate the intelligence of the children, and there was some possibility that the estimate of achievement had been influenced thereby. It was also possible that the educational program in the early years was made up of activities much like, in principle, the items in the Leiter Scale.

By 1962 it was possible to use standardized tests of achievement with the subjects. Also it was possible to obtain and grade samples of written language. The character of the curriculum had become much more academic, and different supervising teachers as well as classroom teachers were assessing the children's educational development.

Twenty-five of the original thirty-five subjects were in school in 1962: fifteen boys and ten girls. Attrition had occurred from the usual causes. Inspection indicated that the boy–girl proportion was essentially the same, and the ten lost subjects were fairly evenly distributed over the range of intelligence as measured by the Leiter. The mean and standard deviation of the original population on intelligence ratings were 4.38 and 2.04, respectively. For the twenty-five remaining cases, the same measures were 4.40 and 1.67. The differences were not significant (t = .042).

The following data were subjected to correlational analysis.

1. Intelligence quotient from LIPS approximately six months after admission to school, median age five years.

2. Rank, from low of 1 to high of 7 on Leiter prediction chart.

3. Supervising teacher's rank estimate of each subject's intelligence, from low of 1 to high of 7, in 1952.

4. Supervising teacher's rank estimate in 1955 of each subject's achievement, from low of 1 to high of 7.

5. Supervising teacher's rank estimate in 1962 of each subject's achievement, from low of 1 to high of 7.

6. Mean rank estimate of achievement of each subject in 1962 by all the subject's present teachers.

7. Mean rating of three teachers for each subject on written language in 1962.

8. Paragraph-meaning raw score from Stanford Achievement Test administered in 1962.

9. Word-meaning raw score from Stanford Achievement Test administered in 1962.

10. Average reading raw score from Stanford Achievement Test administered in 1962.

11. Battery median raw score from Stanford Achievement Test administered in 1962.

Results

CORRELATION MATRIX FOR PREDICTORS AND ACHIEVEMENT CRITERIA *

N = 25

	Predictors			Achievement Criteria							
	1	2	3	4	5	6	7	8	9	10	11
1		.946	.603	.538	.490	.534	.431	.509	.442	.492	.632
2			.698	.685	.602	.617	.531	.555	.529	.560	.710
3				.796	.576	.458	.603	.411	.429	.433	.557
4					.784	.619	.744	.675	.705	.712	.748
5						.833	.846	.889	.943	.950	.950
6							.742	.811	.844	.858	.900
7								.773	.784	.807	.858
8									.854	.963	.905
9										.963	.912
10											.942
11											

* df = 23; r for significance at 5 per cent level of confidence = .396
r for significance at 1 per cent level of confidence = .505

1. The predictive validity of both Leiter ratings and supervising teachers' ratings obtained in 1952 remained relatively high for all the achievement criteria obtained in 1962.

2. Leiter ranks assigned in 1952 correlated .685 with supervising teachers' estimates of achievement in 1955 and .602 with the later estimate in 1962. The difference between the two correlations is not significant at the 5 per cent level of confidence (t = .812). The predictive validity of the Leiter rating for this criterion did not decline significantly over a seven-year period.

3. Supervising teachers' ratings of intelligence for the children in 1952 correlated .796 with their ratings of the children's achievement in 1955 and .576 with their ratings of the children's achievement in 1962. The decline in the predictive validity of the supervising teachers' original rating of intelligence is significant at the 1 per cent level of confidence over a seven-year period (t = 3.99).

4. Although the observed correlations of Leiter ratings in 1952 with six of the seven criterion variables of achievement in 1962 are higher than the correlations of supervising teachers' ratings in 1952 with these variables none of the differences are statistically significant. It is of interest to not

that the one criterion variable with a higher observed correlation with the supervising teachers' ratings is the rating of written language. Supervising teachers possibly weigh their estimates of intelligence more heavily than the Leiter with a language factor.

5. Strong positive relationships continued to hold between the estimates of the children's intelligence by supervising teachers and all other measures of intelligence and all measures of achievement.

6. Different supervising teachers were quite consistent in their estimates of the same children's achievement from 1955 to 1962. Their estimates proved to have strong positive correlations with objective measures of achievement made in 1962.

7. Supervising teachers and other teachers were in substantial agreement ($r = .833$) regarding their evaluation of the achievement of the subjects in 1962; the mean rank estimate of achievement by teachers at the same time was in very considerable accord with achievement on the Stanford Achievement Test Battery ($r = .950$); and its subtests included here are strongly related to teachers' ratings of the youngsters' achievement in written language ($r = .846$).

8. When a number of objective achievement measures of the language arts are applied to deaf children, there is considerable consistency among them. Relevant intercorrelations are those among items 7, 8, 9, 10, and 11. Inspection will indicate that they range between .773 and .963.

Conclusions

The findings of this study indicate that significant weight can be given to the LIPS in predicting school success among deaf children. There has been no significant decrement over an eight- to ten-year period in the correlation between ratings based on LIPS IQ's and school achievement in the language-arts area.

Cross validation is needed, and further longitudinal studies should be made to determine the generality of the conclusions drawn from the Western Pennsylvania School population and to learn about the extent to which the forecasts will hold up through and beyond secondary school. In the meantime, if proper caution is observed, the educator of the deaf and the psychologist working with deaf children can make telling use of information from the LIPS in planning special educational programs and in counseling parents and deaf children.

Teachers of deaf children are evidently in considerable accord as to how they evaluate success in school. The language-arts content, as measured by standardized tests and by teachers' ratings of written compositions, is closely correlated with teacher and supervising teacher appraisals of overall school achievement. It would be instructive to (1) analyze the content of standardized tests of paragraph meaning, word meaning, and reading, (2) determine the specific classroom responsive behavior to which teachers and supervising teachers give particular attention in evaluating the educational progress of their pupils, and (3) attempt, through factor analysis and other means, to identify the relationships of components of the LIPS and (1) and (2) above.

Language-arts content and processes are of acknowledged special importance in the education of deaf children. It is appropriate that teachers give particular and continuing attention to that curricular area. However, additional useful information might be found if the criterion for school success were broadened.

Working from the data analyzed to date, predictions from the LIPS regarding school achievement are global, with particular reference to what teachers of the deaf consider success in school and with reference to objective scores on tests mainly in the language arts. Also, the teachers' views and the achievement test results are much alike.

Through cross validation it should be possible to confirm predictions. Equally important, however, is the fact that work on factor analysis might reveal factors which, in turn, might give clues to educational methods and to curricular content especially appropriate to deaf children with certain psychological characteristics. If so, the education of the deaf might be increasingly particularized, to the end that each child receives the education most likely to allow him to realize his unique potentialities.

48. Your Child, Maturity, and You: A Talk with Parents *

CARL W. FULLER, *Assistant Director, Audiology and Speech Clinic, Indiana University Medical Center, Indianapolis*

ONE OF THE MOST conspicuous results of deafness in a child is inadequacy of verbal communication, and it is entirely natural for the child's parents to be anxious about his lack of speech and eager to help him learn to talk. So intense is this anxiety that some parents give the impression of believing that speech is the only thing the child has to learn and that, having speech, he will be free of other problems of living.

This, of course, is not true. Your children require more attention from their teachers than hearing children do for the development of language and speech, but they do not thereby require less attention for the development of other social skills. On the contrary, the deaf child faces the same pitfalls, obstructions, and frustrations on the road to adulthood that the hearing child does, and he needs as much help, if not more, from his parents in learning how to deal with them effectively.

Some of these pitfalls and frustrations involve the attitudes which deaf children and their parents have toward the problems which deafness creates. Nina Ridenour has pointed out:

Specialists who have worked with handicapped children agree in stressing two points above all others:

1. The type or degree of a child's handicap has little relation to the kind of emotional adjustment he will be able to achieve.

2. The single most important factor in determining the child's attitudes toward his handicap is the attitude of his parents.

In other words, the extent to which any handicap *handicaps* depends to an important degree on the way the child and his family feel about it.[1]

How should you feel if the handicap of deafness is to be minimized? What attitudes should you develop to foster favorable attitudes in your

* Reprinted by permission of the author and *American Annals of the Deaf,* 107:320–328; May, 1962.

[1] Nina Ridenour, *Building Self-confidence in Children* (Chicago: Science Research Associates, 1954), p. 37.

children? What attitudes can you teach your children to aid them in achieving a realistic emotional adjustment to deafness?

Attitudes Helpful to Parents

THE ATTITUDE OF ACCEPTANCE

Basic to all other constructive feelings about the handicap of deafness is acceptance—the recognition of the nature of deafness and the problems it creates without either deprecating or exaggerating its significance. Sometimes parents have feelings which inhibit their ability to accept the fact of hearing loss in their children and which, because of the distorted perspective they create, may lead the parents to make unwise decisions regarding their child's training and welfare. Some of these feelings appear to be widespread enough to justify their mention here. Avoidance of these feelings will help you accept your child's hearing loss in a realistic way.

First, do not blame yourself for your child's hearing problem. Few children, if any, are deaf because of something their parents did, or did not, do. Hearing loss and the circumstances which produce it are no more predictable for a given child than such other twists of fate as being struck by lightning or breaking an arm. Yet some parents reproach themselves for causing their child's deafness, and their self-blame keeps their relationship with the child from being a happy one.

I once saw a child whose father was a veteran of World War II. This man had been wounded in combat in such a way that both his legs were virtually useless. His daughter apparently had been born deaf, and the father was convinced that her deafness was somehow caused by his own handicap. Thus, the child's hearing loss daily reminded the father of what he regarded as his own inadequacies, and there were signs that the girl was aware of and sensitive to father's unhappiness with her and was reacting to it with her own undesirable behavior patterns.

You did not cause your child to be deaf. Take responsibility for your child's education but not for his deafness. You cannot accept deafness if you view it as a living reminder of your own negligence.

Second, do not view hearing impairment as a punishment. A child came to be examined, accompanied by her mother and her grandmother. In the course of interviewing the adults it became clear that the grandmother felt that a youthful indiscretion of the mother was responsible for the child's hearing loss, and she lost no opportunity to say so. The facts of the situation did not justify this accusation, but the mother had heard it so often that she had come to believe it herself. Furthermore, she came to believe that any effort she made to minimize the effect of the hearing loss was an attempt to evade deserved punishment for an admitted wrong, and this belief practically paralyzed her good judgment in managing her child. This is obviously a sketchy description of a very complex emotional situation; the essential point is that both the grandmother and the mother were so aware of their own guilt feelings and so in need of expressing them that they were relatively insensitive to the child's feelings, and the child, who should have been protected from emotional storms, received their full force.

Deafness is no more a punishment than is a common cold. You will find it difficult to accept your child's deafness if you regard it as retribution for your own mistakes.

A third attitude which interferes with the acceptance of the deaf child is the denial that deafness is a handicap. Clearly it is not the *same* handicap for all children. The degree, even the nature, of the handicap produced by hearing impairment varies with the severity of hearing loss, the age of the child when the loss occurs, the kind and variety of educational opportunities available to the child, the economic, social, and emotional stability of his environment, and many other factors. Yet—let us face it—no matter how the child's world is manipulated, no matter how favorable his circumstances may be, nothing will change his hearing loss from a liability to an asset.

Impaired hearing produces obstacles to effective communication and to other forms of social adjustment. It reduces to some extent the range of careers in business, industry, and the professions available to the deaf person. It imposes other burdens upon the deaf person which do not exist, or at least do not exist in the same way, for hearing persons. The effects of deafness are restrictive; accepting deafness requires accepting the restrictions it imposes.

This concept does not imply that we must be defeatist about deaf children. Perhaps deafness is, in a way, a cloud, but it does not fill the entire sky of the deaf person's life. We have every reason to feel optimistic about the future of the deaf child, though we know that as a deaf child he is a handicapped child.

Nevertheless, we see parents who apparently feel that the concept of deafness as a handicap is impossible to accept. I remember a child who seemed to be most unhappy and who was so unco-operative when she appeared for examination that it was nearly impossible to determine what her ability might be or even how much hearing she had. I learned eventually that when the girl's mother learned of the girl's hearing loss, she resolved that her daughter was not going to be handicapped by it. Her refusal to recognize the handicapping nature of deafness turned her from a loving, patient mother into a strict, nagging, driving tyrant, and it caused both her and her daughter much emotional turmoil and misery.

Denying that hearing loss is a handicap is one extreme reaction to deafness; the opposite extreme is the exaggeration of the degree of handicap which deafness involves. Some time ago I saw in clinic a three-year-old deaf boy who was bright, alert, friendly, and well behaved. When I asked his mother how he was making out in learning to dress and wash himself, she said, "Can deaf children learn to do that?" I assured her that they could. She had not begun to teach her son to perform these elementary tasks because she had assumed that deafness would interfere with his ability to learn them.

All people who work with deaf persons know that there are many things which deaf people can do as well as their hearing brethren. There is no reason to assume that because a child is deaf, he is also stupid, or mean, or disobedient, or devoid of feeling. Deaf children are deaf—that is regrettable. But they are also children, and they share with hearing children the play interests, the desire to please their parents, the pride of accomplishment, the curiosity about the natural world, the delight in new toys, the laughter and the tears of childhood. Do not be like the pessimist who looks at a doughnut and comments first about the size of the hole. It is important to know what your deaf child does not have. It is just as important to know what he *does* have. Almost invariably the deaf has more left than he has lost.

I have been discussing the attitude of acceptance as the most fundamental of the constructive attitudes you may develop. I have described four of the pitfalls on the road to acceptance. Obviously acceptance is only one of many constructive attitudes, all of which are important. Let us discuss one other attitude for parents to strive for: the attitude of objectivity oward your child's goals and accomplishments.

THE ATTITUDE OF OBJECTIVITY

The first step toward objectivity is to define your goals for your child in terms of his abilities and interests. A basic requirement in this respect is to recognize the limitations of educational achievement which are imposed by the language deficiencies resulting from deafness. It has been true for a long time—and it is still true—that deaf children are retarded in school achievement by two years or more (compared to hearing children) because of their late start and slow progress in acquiring the language skills necessary for academic learning. This retardation does not imply poor intelligence or lack of motivation or inadequate teaching. It is inherent in the nature of deafness. The acquisition of language, a process which we hearing people complete more or less automatically and take for granted, is a long and laborious procedure for the deaf child. It slows his rate of advancement through school, and in most cases it limits the ultimate level of his achievement. Because of this, the goals which some parents define for their deaf children are unrealistic, though they might be perfectly appropriate for children who hear.

Our culture seems to be on its way to setting a college or university degree as the minimum level of satisfactory educational achievement. Yet the usual bachelor's degree is probably beyond the reach of most deaf children. By the same token, certain vocations may be impossible for deaf children to enter. It is obviously most unlikely that a deaf person could be a successful piano tuner. It is less obvious but no less true that the so-called white collar professions may be out of reach for most deaf children. I do not mean that no deaf person can become say, a lawyer. I do mean that we cannot *take it for granted,* that a deaf child can become a lawyer, whereas we might take it for granted in the case of his hearing twin. The fact of deafness forces us to redefine our goals if we wish to maintain an objective attitude toward the deaf child's school achievement and eventual vocational choice.

A second step toward objectivity is to avoid overemphasizing the importance of speech. It may seem strange to you that speech could possibly be *over*emphasized in the education of a deaf child, and yet there seem to me to be many parents of deaf children whose determination to teach their children to talk is so strong that it distorts their sense of educational perspective.

There is no doubt in my mind that the deaf person who can talk intelligibly and who can read lips has some advantage in dealing with hearing people over the deaf person who does not have these skills. I remind myself, however—and I remind you—that learning to talk is not the equivalent of getting an education. In terms of his ultimate school achievement, it is probably more important that your deaf child learn to read than that he learn to speak; and this tends to be true, too, for the child with normal hearing. The minimum objectives of an educational program are to develop those skills which will enable each person to become economically independent as an adult and to acquaint him sufficiently well with our social customs and statutory laws so that he will not flout the one or violate the other. These are the bare essentials, and speech is not necessary for either. This level of educational achievement is far exceeded by most deaf adults who do not talk. Speech is desirable for all deaf people, and our schools should make every effort to teach it; but it should not bulk so large in our ambitions for the deaf child that we lose sight of his other educational needs.

There is another reason for not overemphasizing speech which is somewhat more specific to this discussion; that is that the quality and intelligibility of a deaf person's speech is largely irrelevant to his development of social competence and emotional stability. You know that among the hearing, talking people around you there is a wide range of social and emotional adjustment. The mere fact that hearing people can talk does not seem to save them from social inadequacy or from emotional confusions. There is no evidence to indicate that speech is any more effective in promoting social maturity or emotional stability in deaf people than it is among the hearing. Indeed, there is every reason to believe that good speech is a result of emotional maturity rather than a cause of it.

Good speech is a worthy ideal for the deaf child. If he can learn it, he should. But you should not consider your child to be an educational success if he can talk and an educational failure if he cannot.

I have suggested that your planning for your child's future should be oriented in terms of his interests and abilities and that it should avoid a distorted emphasis on speech. A third aspect of this planning is so thoroughly imbued with common sense that it is practically a truism—yet it deserves restatement here. It is this: remember that each child is an individual unto himself, with his own unique set of skills and desires and motivations and limitations. He is the only one of his kind. Because that is so, it is impossible for him to do things exactly the way that other children do them. Sharing the handicap of deafness does not imply sharing all other characteristics of behavior.

Johnny, the deaf boy up the street, may be a skilled lip reader at the age of six, but that does not mean that your son, who is just as bright and who has had the same amount of training as Johnny, should be a skilled lip reader. It is obvious that expecting your child to do what another child is doing, just because both of them have hearing losses, is grossly unfair. Comparing your child's accomplishments with those of another deaf child is almost invariably unwise, because it is probable that the only thing they have in common is deafness.

Finally, in evaluating your child's progress, put your emphasis on what he has learned and can do rather than on his failures. The following story illustrates the point. A duck hunter purchased a dog and trained him as a retriever. On his first hunting trip the man shot a duck and sent the dog after the dead bird. The dog walked across the surface of the water to the duck and brought it back to his master, who stared in amazement at this incredible feat. On his next duck-hunting trip the man brought along a friend, assuring him that the dog would perform an amazing trick. Eventually another duck was shot, and again the dog walked over the water to retrieve it. The friend, however, made no comment. The dog's owner asked, "What's the matter? Didn't you see anything unusual about my dog?" "Yes," answered the friend, "He can't swim."

This friend was like the pessimist I spoke of who looks at the doughnut and sees only the hole. Unfortunately, some parents have this tendency to see only what their children cannot do, to be blind to what the children can do. There is an old popular song whose lyrics contain the advice, "Accentuate the positive." This is an excellent maxim for all parents. Find out what your child can do and likes to do. Help him to do it well. No songs are sweeter than those which celebrate success.

Attitudes Helpful to Children

I have tried to describe two general attitudes which are important to you in dealing with your deaf child: the acceptance of him as he is now, and objectivity in planning for his future. This discussion would be incomplete if we did not devote some time to the attitudes which are desirable for your child to have and the contributions you can make to their formation and development.

THE ATTITUDE OF INDEPENDENCE

The first of these is the attitude of independence. Obviously achieving this depends to a great extent upon the *desire* to be independent. But the desire to become independent is not an ambition which appears automatically in the growing child. It must be fostered and encouraged from the earliest years of the child's life, and ordinarily it is well developed by the time the child enters school. What can you do to help your child learn that independence is a worth-while, rewarding attitude?

First, you can give your child freedom to investigate his world. Children need to explore the world at first hand, and the exploration seems to be more meaningful if it is done as a result of the child's initiative. Because of his communication handicap, your deaf child is more dependent on physical exploration and manipulation than the hearing child. Consequently, he rummages through the dresser drawers and the cellar closet and father's tool chest and the neighbor's garage, leaving behind the disordered evidence of his passing. The hearing child can accomplish much of this exploration verbally by asking, "What's that? What's in there?" The deaf child cannot ask, so he opens the drawer or cupboard and looks.

While some of these actions may be discomfiting, the attitude which engenders them is generally to be encouraged, for this attitude signifies that the child is willing and eager to strike out for himself in seeking knowledge. Time, growth, and patient instruction will teach him how to translate this attitude into action without inconvenience to others. But too severe a restriction upon his actions as a searching, investigating child will have the effect of teaching him that the attitude of independence is undesirable. His healthy, stimulating curiosity is then replaced by shyness, fearfulness, and inability to deal effectively with new or unusual situations.

Secondly, you can promote the attitude of independence by giving your child responsibility. Each new task that the child assumes responsibility for means less dependence on others and hence is a step toward social maturity. We expect responsible adults to decide for themselves when to buy clothes and what clothes to buy, when and how to look for a job and what kind of job would be most desirable, what kinds of social affairs are desirable and how to behave when attending them. The foundations for this adult behavior are laid in the preschool years when parents teach their children how to dress and undress themselves, how to perform household chores, how to wash themselves, how to play with other children without being selfish or destructive.

Giving responsibility to children often involves, at least temporarily, some inconvenience to parents. It may be exasperating to wait for a child who is learning how to dress himself. The child who is learning to wash himself is usually hard on the soap supply. The child who is left to care for his toilet needs will have "accidents." But these trials are transient; and when they have passed, the parents will find new pride and satisfaction in the fact that their child is not just growing, but growing up. Insistence on doing for the child what he should be doing for himself—that is, failure to give the child responsibility—produces dependency, passivity, and clinging. This is behavior typical of infants, and when we see it in older children or in adults, we are quite justified in calling it immature.

THE ATTITUDE OF CONFIDENCE

A second attitude which parents should encourage in their children is confidence. The encouragement I speak of is not that which takes the form of a pep talk. Rather, I refer to the establishment of a secure, stable emotional environment in the home and particularly in the relationships between parents and child. Confidence, for the child, is pretty much a matter of emotional security, and the maintenance of this security is a primary responsibility of the parents.

Your child needs to feel that the world is a safe, orderly place which runs according to rules. This is so because your child is not capable of judging complex situations, and the existence of rules often helps him reduce his judgments to the simple level of "Is this permitted to me or not?" Rules represent security to the child for the additional reason that they are the fruit of adult wisdom and thus symbolize strength and protectiveness. The absence of rules deprives the child of a standard by which to anticipate the results of his own conduct and increases the probability that a given experience will be painful. Thus, the child who lives in a world which is capricious and inconsistent will tend to behave with confusion and uncertainty.

You have probably sensed by now that I am using the term "rules" not just in the narrow, specific sense of arbitrary commands and regulations but also in the larger general sense of consistency and predictability of experience. For the child, it is a rule that the sun will rise and set daily. It is also a rule that the sidewalk is a painful place to fall, that mother will produce food at mealtimes, and that all the routine of living will be pretty much the same from one day to the next. Some of the rules which govern the child's life stem from the law of nature. The rest are imposed by his parents, and wise control by the parents can make a significant contribution to the development of confidence in the child. I wish to emphasize three aspects of rule making which parents need to be particularly conscious of.

Consistency of Behavior. The first of these, consistency of behavior, I have already discussed to some extent. Nothing is more disconcerting to a child than to find that what he was praised for doing yesterday he is criticized for doing today. Though the reason for the change from praise to blame may be quite clear to an adult, a child, and especially a nontalking child, may find the two different reactions to be totally incomprehensible. He has difficulty in understanding why father lets him play in the mud, while mother spanks him, or why mother lets him play in the bath, but father takes the toys away. Children have a deep-seated need to please their parents, but this need is inevitably frustrated unless children have some basis for predicting how their parents will react to their behavior. It is important, therefore, that parents be consistent with each other and that each parent be consistent from one day to the next if they are to establish that emotional climate which gives rise to the attitude of confidence.

Clarity of Boundaries. The second aspect of rule making which needs emphasis is that of establishing the boundaries of permitted and forbidden behavior. This is a corollary of the first, for consistency of management is obviously based on consistency of standards. The point here is that the standards need to be adequately defined for the child. He should have a way of expecting whether you will greet his proposed behavior with "Yes" or "No." Sharply defined "Yes-No" boundaries are a source of security for the child, for the areas of behavior covered by "Yes" represent the kinds of behavior which will always be approved of and which, therefore, will always please the parents. We usually think of "No" as a restriction which fences us in; but we must remember that fences face in two directions, and though being fenced in may be an inconvenience sometimes, "No" often means to the child that strange forbidden threats and dangers are, by the same word, fenced *out*. As the child grows older, the "Yes" areas are enlarged and the "No" areas diminish until finally the child is left to define them for himself. Clear-cut "Yes" and "No" boundaries help the child distinguish between desirable and undesirable conduct and so give him confidence in doing that which will gain approval.

The Parent-Teacher Distinction. A third aspect of rule making concerns the difference between the rules which govern parents and those which govern teachers. As you know, much of the emphasis in the training of preschool deaf children has been laid on parent education programs, and parent education has included both the concept of educating parents and that of training parents to educate their children, especially in speech and lip reading. Classes for parents have been established at many clinics and schools where training programs for deaf children are conducted, and most, if not all, of you are familiar with the correspondence course for parents of deaf children published by the John Tracy Clinic in California. To these programs of parent education I give my full sympathy and support.

I frankly wonder, however, whether some of these programs have sufficiently considered the risks which parents run when they set out to become teachers (in the formal sense) of their own children. The roles of teacher and mother are, in some ways, incompatible. Mother ideally is a source of boundless love, unfailing sympathy, never-ending support and encouragement. Teacher, on the other hand, must disapprove, must press for improvement, must be more or less objective and impersonal in evaluating progress, and may even have to flunk her pupils. The shift from the role of mother to the role of teacher and back again is difficult for some mothers and occasionally impossible. Apparently many women find it impossible to combine the roles and remain effective mother and effective teacher at the same time. This is not to say that most mothers make poor teachers. On the contrary, most mothers do effectively teach speech and language and lip reading to their children. There are some mothers, however, who seem unable to teach and play the role of mother *at the same time*. As a result, some stop being mothers in the best sense of the word and become full-time teachers. I have cited an example of the unhappy child such a situation can produce. Others go on being mothers and are such inefficient teachers that the lessons are an almost total waste of time for both mother and child. The great majority of the mothers I have known alternate between mother and teacher with some degree of success. When the child becomes confused as to whether the woman with him is mother or teacher and consequently does not know whether to behave according to the rules for mother and child or according to the rules for teacher and pupil, his security and his confidence suffer.

I do not mean to suggest that none of you should try to teach your child basic communication skills. I do mean that you should be aware of the dual role you will be playing and that you should be observant to see that this dual role does not confuse your child. Your first duty is to be parent. If you cannot be that and be teacher at the same time, give up the teaching. You will always be able to find a school where your child can get good teaching, but if he cannot have you for his parents, he will have to go without.

I have talked about the attitude of independence and the attitude of confidence. I will conclude this discussion of the child's attitudes by reminding you of the importance of your behavior as a model for your child. Children trust their parents' judgment and wisdom and fairness. And because parents know more about the world than their children, the children assume that their parents behave in certain ways because they are the ways which are wisest or most efficient or most enjoyable. So children tend to copy their parents' form of behaving. The hearing, talking child, when puzzled, may ask his parents why they did thus and so, and in a relatively short time he learns to distinguish subtle nuances of motivation and response and modifies his own behavior accordingly. The deaf child, however, can judge only by what he sees; one of your jobs is to ensure that he sees only behavior which it is desirable for him to imitate. In short, the instruction you give your child in helping him develop constructive attitudes toward deafness, toward social intercourse, toward emotional behavior, cannot be confined to preaching. You must practice as well as preach. You must demonstrate to your child the social and emotional maturity you wish to see him attain for himself.

Parenthood has many responsibilities and many burdens. Ultimately, success as a parent probably depends less upon the use of a specific technical skill than upon the exercise of some indefinable kind of artistry. Parents cannot be likened, however, to just any kind of artist. Certainly children cannot be raised in the way that the sculptor produces a statue, by hacking away at the raw material until it has finally assumed a shape and size pleasing to the creator. Neither can the parent be compared to a portrait painter, since the growth of a living child is not like the creation of an *illusion* of life. Rather, the parent might best be compared to a landscape gardener, who, confident of the inner strength and ultimate beauty of his flowers, provides light and warmth and nutritious soil for their sustenance. You, too, can be confident that if you provide adequate nourishment and a congenial atmosphere, your child will come with unwavering purpose to a full, rich, productive maturity, and you will be able to say with the gardener's pride, "Isn't this a beautiful flower? I helped it grow."

49. Implications of Early Profound Deafness for the Counselor *

EDNA S. LEVINE, *Consultant, Office of Vocational Rehabilitation, New York*

IN BRIEF REVIEW, the problems of early profound deafness represent the results of a voiceless environment upon human development, individual differences among the deaf, the results of varying methods of management, and differing innate capacities and abilities. Needless to say, the best outcome is to be expected from the deaf child who is mentally eager and alert, who comes from a loving, understanding family that works in close co-operation with a pupil-centered school in which the curriculum is based upon a *maturational* plan for personal as well as academic development. To be realistic, it must be admitted that such a happy combination of circumstances is the exception rather than the rule. Nevertheless, a surprising number of pupils manage to become successful "outcomes" notwith-

* Reprinted by permission of the author and publisher and excerpted from "Early Profound Deafness: Psychological Aspects and Problems," *American Annals of the Deaf*, 103:328–348; 1958.

standing. But again, I know of very few who could not have achieved greater success if the circumstances governing maturation and education had been more favorable.

For a counselor unfamiliar with the deaf to receive the full impact of an unsuccessful "outcome" is an assignment second to none in complexity. The usual rehabilitative approach falls short of its purpose in such instances. As Whitehouse points out:

Congenital or early disabled young persons have often been neglected, at least in a rehabilitative sense, until they reached an age where the usual rehabilitation resources come into effect, and at that stage the typical services are geared for a certain minimum work sophistication. Since this early disabled group frequently lacks the maturer experiences, work skills, and work history of the adult disabled, this group is rather patently or subtly unprepared to profit by these facilities.

The need in such disabilities is for the *habilitative* rather than the re-habilitative approach; education rather than re-education; basic adjustment rather than readjustment. Whitehouse cautions the counselor that here "the primary preparation for work is not so much training in specific skills as indoctrination in the attitudes with which an adult must approach his contribution to society." Interestingly enough, the term "habilitation" has long been used among workers with the deaf. But in view of the fact that the same habilitation problems and principles obtain for other childhood disability groups, Whitehouse has adopted the term to designate all those requiring "a different approach, set of values, an altered program and a special matrix." In adopting the habilitation approach, the counselor's program will therefore include provision not only for the development of vocational skills but also for the continued development of other client resources essential for vocational adjustment and capable of further improvement.

The first that come to mind in connection with the deaf are to be found in the areas of language skills, numerical operations, and attitudes. So far as speech and hearing are concerned, as much has usually been done as can be done by the time the young deaf adult reaches the rehabilitation counselor. Significant gains in these abilities are not likely. But the deaf worker must possess a sufficient command of language to understand directions and exchange intelligible communication with employer and co-workers; he must be able to employ the terminologies of his trade; he must be able to apply the numerical operations required by his job, whether they be, to quote Williams, "linear, square, cubic, dry, liquid, of time, or weight, or temperature, monetary, or any of the specific forms of measurement peculiar to a trade. . . ." He must understand the basic facts of job holding, its attendant responsibilities and benefits; employer-employee relationships; getting along with fellow workers; the need for flexibility in the give and take of daily work crises. He must know what co-operation is. In a word, the habilitation counselor takes over where the educator leaves off; and since the areas that must still be cultivated are essential to vocational success, they become thereby an integral part of sound vocational planning.

Where the counselor himself carries out habilitation procedures, his basic preparation must include familiarity with the range of language usage he will find among deaf persons, with their communications methods, and with the problems of psychosocial maturity that prevail. The basic aim of the counselor is always to get to the thinking of his client. Communications is the bridge that will get him there. But in order to understand what he finds when he finally arrives, familiarity with the language usage of his client is essential. The counselor must understand his client's thinking, no matter how defective or eccentric the language.

The language usage of the client will also provide the counselor with the cue to the wording of his own thinking so that he can get his own ideas across without misunderstanding. Here, again, communications is the bridge; but the content of thinking is contained in the language. For example, one counselor used magnificent signs and finger spelling to tell his client that he must "stand on his own two feet and break away from his mother." The young deaf person understood the methods of communication all too well, for he carried out the counselor's advice to the letter and ran away from home that very day to "break away from mother." It was not until ten days later that he was found wandering about. As far as he was concerned, this is what he had been told to do, and do it he did in all good faith. The moral of this anecdote is to caution the counselor not to feel he has reached his goal in working with deaf persons when he has mastered manual methods of communication. He must also master the most important prerequisite of all, and that is an understanding of the *mental activity* of his deaf client as expressed in language.

A knowledge of manual methods, however, has highly important advantages in addition to serving as a bridge over which thoughts pass between counselor and certain deaf persons. For one, it informs the deaf client that here is someone who is interested enough in his welfare to have taken the trouble to learn how to communicate with him. For a deaf individual who has spent all his life trying to master "hearing" communications abilities without success, this is a deeply moving experience. The counselor is able to gain his client's confidence and co-operation on a far deeper level than he ordinarily would.

For another, it gives a young deaf client a feeling of status to be able to manage his own interviews without the perennial need to have someone else do his talking for him. This in itself moves him a step farther along the road to maturity—a small step in many cases, but an important one. Very often it marks the first loosening of the bond of dependence between mother and client. There is no doubt that a knowledge of communications methods by a counselor of the deaf possesses distinct therapeutic as well as communications values.

Finally, a knowledge of manual communications, and especially the sign language, is the most important single aid I know in teaching *verbal language* to those young deaf adults who are particularly deficient in this area. And the single most important agent in this enterprise is the deaf teacher of the deaf. I have used both with great gratification in habilitation work. It is my personal belief that there is an important place for skilled and capable deaf persons in the habilitation of young deaf adults.

In conclusion, the habilitation of our young deaf people is in essence an extension of the education of our deaf pupils, particularly in the areas of language and psychosocial maturity. This being so, problems in habilitation are the concern of the educator as well as the counselor and warrant his deep consideration. The educator is in the best position of all to attack these problems at their points of origin. Again, I most earnestly urge that he do so through objective research, particularly in the areas of greatest moment to the ultimate welfare of deaf persons: language and the curriculum.

50. Counseling Students with Speech and Hearing Problems *

ALBERT T. MURPHY, *Assistant Professor, Special Education, Counseling Service and the Speech and Hearing Center, Boston University*

THIS PAPER considers the function and philosophy of the college or school counselor concerned with students having speech or hearing problems. There appear to be as many different conceptions of his role as there are staff members referring clients to him. Unfortunately, some speech/hearing therapists have contributed to this confusion by working within conceptual frameworks emanating from the thinking of voice teachers and other persons influential in the profession whose early academic training has been largely in fields like drama and the speech arts, such as discussion, debate, and public speaking.

As occurs in other professions, this minority group has sometimes tried to maintain the efficacy of certain pet and pat theories even though exposed to the strain of powerful antithetical evidence from other professional workers, some of whom may regard their own "system" as equally near sacrosanct. Finally, phrases like "remedial speech," "speech training," "speech drills," "corrective retraining," "breathing exercises," and "vocal techniques" found in countless textbooks, articles, school catalogues, and lectures have helped to perpetuate a stereotyped conception of speech/hearing rehabilitation as a formally directive, prescription-giving approach to these particular adjustment problems. Even in the area of stuttering, considered by modern theorists as a psychodynamic symptom of a diffuse personality disorder, the majority of speech/hearing therapists in this country still treat the symptom by augmenting the regulating and repressing forces of the organism by way of suppression or control procedures rather than investigating and clarifying the individual's underlying behavioral processes in the light of his present and past stress situations.

Other speech counselors try to adopt a more client-centered approach but—because of lack of training or experience, or due to a basic feeling of doubt concerning the client's capacity to grow and achieve better adjustment abilities if given certain emotional or expressive freedoms in an

* Reprinted by permission of the author and *Personnel and Guidance Journal,* 33:260–264; January, 1955.

atmosphere of reintegration, or because of a personal feeling of discomfort in trying to maintain a relationship they are unable to "control" according to rigidly preset attitudes, therapy structure, and goals—they gradually assume a more comfortable role of therapy *director*. In any case, such a person feels sincerely that this is the best approach to the situation; no doubt, often it is, but perhaps equally often it is just the only thing he is able to do.

A third group of speech counselors, on the basis of extensive clinical and experimental evidence from workers in clinical psychology, social anthropology, and educational psychology, assume that many speech disorders, totally or in part, are symptomatic of underlying personal-social anxieties and must be handled accordingly. If a speech symptom is psychogenically motivated, the concern must be with the constellation of these motivations rather than with control or suppression of the symptom. They feel that the greater the total emotional involvement, the greater the need for a diagnostically therapeutic process incorporating the following concepts: (1) a two-way interaction of counselor and client with focus on the patient rather than on the symptom; (2) a permissive and supportive communication atmosphere which includes a recognition, acceptance, and reflection of feelings, attitudes, and reaction patterns by the counselor in a manner structured to produce increasing insight; and (3) an assumption that in general, the lower the anxiety or the higher the frustration tolerance of the individual, the better the adjustive capacities; that is, the better the speech adjustment.

From this viewpoint, speech symptoms which are to any degree psychologically motivated are serving an adjustive aim—they are purposive—for the individual. If the philosophy of a particular speech counselor is basically client-centered in such cases, there arises the question of estimating the degree to which a symptom *is* emotionally purposive. If the disorder is not primarily of emotional origin, must the counselor disregard his basic philosophy and become more directive? If so, how much? There is the possibility of underestimating the intensity of the emotional factors and finding oneself dealing intellectually with a person whose speech problem more and more appears to be psychologically maintained. On the other hand, one can easily be nondirective when perhaps the main approach should center on questions and advice.

It appears that the therapist must play the role of a "general" speech counselor who can adapt to the presence at different intensities or to the absence of emotional signs as causal factors in speech problems. However, the term "general counselor" can include so much that it has little common meaning unless defined. If speech counseling is viewed as an omnibus activity which includes the diagnosis and rehabilitation of emotionally stable "organic" clients (e.g., cleft palate, hard of hearing, dental and other oral irregularities) in addition to the speech/voice improvement of average speakers, then it seems difficult for the speech counselor to be anything but "general" in his approach. From this viewpoint, the student who has been recommended to take a course in "Discussion Procedures in Industry" instead of "Public Speaking" experiences speech counseling just as does the anxiety-ridden Mary who stutters severely and considers leaving school because of her inability to adjust to class and social situations.

Client-centered speech counseling is regarded in this paper as a process applicable to those individuals having speech or hearing problems which are emotionally motivated or those clients in which the communication ability is disrupted primarily or in part by a "nonfunctional" factor, such as organic or intellectual deficit, or foreign language influence, but which is complicated by a psychological overlay. The aim is to develop insight concerning the nature of the emotional links with the speech dysfunction by the structuring of a communication situation in which the contributing personal and environmental forces are decreased in intensity. In a progressively adjustive process, the individual's realm of consciousness concerning the forces affecting oral communication efficiency and comfort is extended so that the anxiety level may subside until he is perceiving self, people, and situations more realistically.

Counselors in general can be reasonably sure that the majority of persons they see have personal problems of some degree. The speech counselor cannot be as certain of the presence or degree of emotional difficulties in the person about to step into his office. The convenient approach is a more or less directive one; it is not necessarily the better one. What particular type of speech behavior does our client have? Is it a mild, moderate, or severe deviation?

Are causal factors organic, educational, intellectual, environmental, personal, or a blend of these? A basic question is: How much can the speech counselor be "general" in approach and still maintain his integrity concerning the philosophy of therapy he believes in?

(Ten case studies were included in the original paper but are omitted here for lack of space.)

The client-centered counselor of individuals with speech and hearing disorders finds it necessary to function within a highly pliable framework of attitudes. The degree of emphasis on a directive or nondirective approach will vary according to his perception of the emotional comfort or discomfort of the person. Such a framework for speech counseling is workable if it includes the following modes of action.

1. Where there is no emotional subsoil basic to the speech symptom and no other important observable personality problem, a direct, informational approach is efficacious and necessary.

2. If the speech symptom is psychogenically motivated, the two-way interrelationship of supported, reflected, and integrated communication meaning is set up. The focus is not upon the symptom as such but upon the individual and the release of more effective adjustment through insight concerning the symptom behavior–dynamics relationship.

3. Individuals with speech disorders that are basically physical in cause very often experience emotional discomfort which may be a result of or quite distinct from the organic deficit. A combined therapeutic approach in which one therapist provides information and advice and another provides supportive counseling has proved highly effective.

4. When the problem is a diffuse one, there is often the question of judging which is the major problem. Is it the client's speech maladjustment, severe stuttering, or one of his general behavioral maladjustments? Obviously the function limits in the light of the counselor's training and other available therapy personnel are major considerations. Is the counselor trained as a clinical psychologist, or is his academic background one mainly of speech pathology and audiology with a sprinkling of course work having a psychodynamics content? The less the experience in psychodynamics, the sooner the need for referral in psychogenically determined behavior problems. On the other hand, the greater the organic factor in a psychosomatic disorder, the greater the need for effective treatment from the viewpoint of speech/language and hearing rehabilitation training which the general counselor may not have. This poses the problem, in many institutions, of the person who is to provide the help: the general counselor or the speech therapist. Few institutions have an individual fully trained both as a clinical counselor and as a speech pathologist/audiologist. The crucial, and possibly unanswerable, question seems to be not only "What is the function of the person counseling clients with speech/hearing disorders partially or totally motivated by psychogenic factors?" but also "Who in my particular setting is best qualified to handle such clients?"

51. Vocational and Counseling Aspects of Deafness: Counseling Needs and Services for the Adult Deaf *

HOWARD L. ROY, *Chairman, Department of Psychology, Gallaudet College*

DEAF PEOPLE are people, and what is true about the biological and social needs of hearing people is true also for deaf people. Loneliness is loneliness, no matter how it came to be. Frustration is still frustration, no matter what the cause, and a sense of achievement is still a sense of achievement, whether the individual is hearing or deaf. But to speak of the counseling needs of the deaf in that way only would beg the question, and I have no desire to do that. Instead, I will stay with the intent of the topic and discuss those counseling needs which in some way seem to characterize deaf clients rather than clients in general. However, my remarks about deaf people will be limited to those who have been counseled in the Counseling Center at Gallaudet College in the few months we have been in operation. I will try to show in what ways our clients are similar to or different from the clients of counseling centers for hearing people.

The Counseling Center is a very small organization. We have four psychologists, a part-time psychometrist, and a part-time psychiatrist.

We began operation when the school term opened in September, but we did not see any clients for several weeks. Because 25 to 30 per cent of the people we see do not speak or read lips well enough to communicate orally, we attempted to learn sign language and the manual alphabet. At first this was nearly a full-time task.

Altogether we have seen just over one hundred people, about eighty of whom are students. The kinds of problems cover a considerable range. The objectives of the Center are to provide educational, vocational, and personal counseling for clients, both student and nonstudent. It is not intended, of course, that we will engage in long-time intensive therapy of very sick persons. In the personal problems area we hope to do two things: (1) provide preventive counseling or therapy and (2) identify

* Reprinted by permission of the author and *American Annals of the Deaf*, 107:562–565; 1962.

those of the group with adjustment problems serious enough to warrant treatment which we cannot provide and help them to find adequate treatment.

We are trying to build up libraries of tests and other measures and of occupational information. We are collecting programed instructional materials to be used with students who have deficiencies in some of the learning skills.

In co-operation with the Office of Psycho-Educational Research under Dr. Schein, we are doing some research now, and have more planned, to develop objective and dependable information about our clients. Among other things, we are much concerned about the effectiveness of our predictors when we apply them to deaf people.

It seems to me that what I say about our clients will be more meaningful if it is said against a background of information obtained from hearing clients. For purposes of comparison, we will use some data recently obtained at the Counseling Bureau of the University of Minnesota and some gathered several years ago at the Student Counseling Bureau at Rochester Junior College.

Chart 1. Per cent of individuals in the total student bodies of three institutions who sought counseling.

	Demand for Counseling
Gallaudet	20
Rochester Junior College	13
University of Minnesota	12

First, do the same proportions of students in a college for the deaf seek counseling as in hearing colleges? As you see from Chart I, approximately 20 per cent of our student body has sought some kind of service at the Counseling Center in the first semester of operation. Compare that with 12.4 per cent in a year's time at Minnesota and 13 per cent in a year's time at Rochester Junior College. We appear to be doing a bit more business, but there are some things which might have affected these percentages. Minnesota has an eight-week waiting list. Perhaps many people get discouraged and do not wait. Also, we are brand new, and it may be people are just curious.

Almost equal percentages of girls and boys seek counseling in Minnesota and at Gallaudet.

What brings people to the Counseling Center? About half of our student clients are referred by faculty members, heads of departments, or deans.

The other half come of their own choice or because it was suggested by a friend.

Chart 2. Per cent of individuals giving one as the named primary reason for seeking counseling.

	Personal	Educational	Vocational	Financial	Health	Family
		Problem Area				
		(Reason for Coming as Given by the Client)				
Gallaudet	9	43	43	3	1	1
U. Minn.	8	40	48	1	1	1
Rochester J. C.	9	36	55	—	—	—

Generally speaking, whether a client is referred or comes in voluntarily, he gives one reason for coming. This may or may not be the real reason for his coming, but it is necessary to start with it. A comparison of the reasons given for seeking counseling in the two hearing schools with reasons for coming here is shown in Chart 2.

Chart 3. Per cent of individuals who sought counseling in each of the three institutions whose primary problem was judged by the counselor to be in one of the named areas.

	Personal	Educational	Vocational	Financial	Health	Family
		Problem Area				
		(As Judged by the Counselor)				
Gallaudet	17	44	28	2	3	6
U. of Minn.	18	34	44	1	1	1
Rochester J. C.	19	30	51	—	—	—

In all three schools there is the usual tendency to claim, not a personal problem, but one in a vocational or educational area. In Chart 3, however, we see that the counselors judged the primary problem to be in the personal area about twice as often as it was claimed by the client.

Notice the apparently greater concern with educational problems in Gallaudet than in the other two schools and a lesser concern with vocational problems. We think that this is more apparent than real. We believe there might even be more vocational problems among our deaf clients than among hearing clients. The severity and immediacy of the educational problem is so great that we give attention there. It is quite possible that the proportion of persons judged to have personal problems is also an underestimate. It may be that we are putting out brush fires when the forest is burning. However, the cold fact remains that if we can do nothing to help some of our clients educationally, they will not be here long enough for us to help them in any other way.

Chart 4. Examples of problems noted in the vocational area.

> Lack of Job Information and Experience
> Lack of Knowledge of Self
> Unrealistic Goals
> Dependence and Passivity
> Literal-Mindedness, No Generalization

Chart 5. Examples of problems noted in the educational area.

> Poor Study Habits
> Lack of Reading Skills
> Poor Preparation for College Work
> Overload
> No Meaningful Goal

Chart 6. Examples of problems noted in the social-emotional-personal area.

> Difficulty in Social Interaction
> Lack of Acceptance of Self and Environment
> Unwillingness to Face Difficulties
> Lack of Motivation
> Immaturity
> Dependence

As you are well aware, problems seldom come singly. Charts 4, 5 and 6 show what counselors considered to be primary problems or at least the problems of most immediate concern. Actually few of our clients who had a social-emotional-personal problem did not have some vocational or educational involvement as well. I think that needs no elaboration.

There are other needs related to the counseling process.

1. Communication is sometimes difficult. I refer to something over and beyond the means of communication, important though that is. Many concepts we think meaningful to hearing youngsters appear to pose problems for some of our deaf clients. Words which are part of the everyday conversation of hearing people may not be in the conversational vocabulary of deaf people. The need is *ours;* we need to know much more about how deaf people think, how they feel, what goals are meaningful for them, and so on.

2. There is a great need for the development of knowledge in psychometrics as they pertain to the deaf. At present we and others are finding some tests results which are hard to explain and hard to interpret for clinical application. On structured personality inventories, we get scores which by the hearing norms are decidedly deviate. Why are they deviate? Is it because the items do not mean the same things to deaf people that they meant to the hearing people on whom they were developed? Is it be-

cause the experiences of deaf people actually result in a different clustering of personality traits? We do not know.

On an interest inventory which has a validity index to warn the psychometrist if the client has not read and understood the items, *many* deaf students have validity scores outside acceptable limits.

We must not jump to the conclusion that because of these difficulties we cannot use tests with deaf people or even to the more conservative one that we need special norms for the deaf. Tests used clinically provide much useful information. The magnitude of a validity coefficient has much less significance in clinical use than when tests are used for selection.

3. We need to know more about our methods of interacting with the client. What kind of interview techniques are best? Can nondirective methods be used effectively? In what areas can we expect to find naïveté to a greater degree than among hearing clients? There are many questions.

Much research is needed—experimental, statistical, and that which is basically anthropological in approach.

52. Counseling Hearing-Handicapped Children in School *

JOSEPH S. RUDLOFF, *Teacher of Deaf and Hard-of-Hearing Children in San Diego, California*

T HE ULTIMATE AIMS of education for hearing-handicapped children are similar to those for hearing children. Although there is no unanimity concerning the goals of the public schools, a common thread is often evident in the consensus of what the goals should be. We hope that our children will develop into individuals who have well-integrated personalities and who are happy in the community, in the family, and in their vocational relations.

Some may wonder if these aims are realistic for the hearing-handicapped child, for some children will learn to speak and understand with consider-

* Reprinted by permission of the author and *Exceptional Children*, 30:251–255; February, 1964.

able accuracy and facility, while others will not. All the variables which have great bearing on the attainment of these aims seem to include implications centered around the fact that this is a hearing world. Everything is essentially tailored to the hearing person.

Since the deaf or hard-of-hearing child, possibly more than any other child, may follow a pattern initially set for him by his teacher, it is important to examine how the teacher may counsel the child in order to work toward the above-mentioned aims of education. The teacher's efforts must be deliberate and planned if effective counseling is to take place. These efforts might well be directed in two principal areas: self-knowledge and self-direction.

If the hearing-handicapped child can achieve an appropriate self-concept, he will more easily make the life adjustments required of him by society. Not only must the child be aware that he must adjust to living with hearing people; he must also eventually realize that hearing people will have certain negative attitudes toward him.

Let us examine what we do know about attitudes of hearing persons toward the hearing-handicapped. Myklebust (1950) states that the deaf and hard-of-hearing are viewed as an unhappy class. Some persons go a bit further and believe that the general opinion is that hearing-handicapped people are melancholy, narrow, selfish, and unreliable. There are mistaken evaluations of the possibilities for achievement. Hearing persons who have had limited association with the deaf and the hard-of-hearing may hold all hearing-handicapped people on a common level, not allowing for individual differences and aptitudes among them. In addition, the deaf and hard-of-hearing are viewed as a dependent class of people. Many think the deaf are peculiar and inferior. Perhaps this is because there is a tendency for an individual to be frightened by those different from himself. In any case, this is a recapitulation of opinions concerning the attitudes of hearing people.

Related Research Findings

To be more precise, let us now examine some pertinent studies. Elser (1959) studied 1,258 children having a loss in excess of 35 decibels. These children were placed in regular classrooms part of their school day. He states that the hearing-handicapped children as a group did not enjoy the reputation of the average of the class. Although the hearing-handicapped children were not identified as the most rejected in a classroom group, the study did show them to be less accepted than the average for their classmates. The five traits used as criteria were (1) popularity, (2) ability to play games, (3) rating as a good sport, (4) ability to get their lessons, (5) personality.

In 1954, ten selected fourth-grade hearing-handicapped children from a school for the deaf were integrated as a group with twenty-five hearing children in a regular public school classroom located in New York City. One of the purposes of the study was to examine the nature of social acceptance of the hearing-handicapped. In this respect, Justman and Moskowitz (1957a, 1957b) summarized their findings by stating:

No matter which one of the sociometric devices is used as a criterion, the deaf children tend to evoke little reaction, either positive or negative, from the hearing pupils. Moreover, when deaf children are chosen by hearing children, the choice is more likely to be negative, rather than positive, in tone. It would seem that the hearing children recognize the presence of the deaf children in their classes, but fail to develop any marked degree of feeling toward them.

In a more recent study concerned with attitudes about deafness, Horowitz and Rees (1962) worked with 266 hearing people divided into three groups. It is important to realize that their sample consisted of various age levels from children in the first grade of an elementary school in an economically average neighborhood to college students and PTA members. The findings show some areas of clear knowledge and other areas of great confusion. The subjects tended to perceive as deaf all people who actually had varying degrees of hearing loss. There was the general impression that hearing aids guaranteed normal hearing, and there were vague and varied opinions on the capabilities of the deaf. Children showed better understanding than college students and adults of how deafness is related to speech difficulty. Children pointed out that not only are deaf children unable to hear others; they cannot hear themselves. Younger children were more consistent in realizing that a hearing aid does not guarantee perfect hearing.

All these attitudes based on opinions and on research must be considered when the teacher is trying to lead the hearing-handicapped child to self-knowledge. Included in self-knowledge is realizing what other human beings think of them and learning to understand hearing people. The deaf and hard-of-hearing, by their attitude and manner, must eventually demonstrate that they know how hearing people feel. This is brought out briefly in the film *That the Deaf May Speak* (Lexington School for the Deaf, New York City) when the plea is made that part of what it means to be deaf is made that part of what it means to be deaf is having that extra bit of patience, that extra bit of understanding, that hearing people may not have in a given situation.

Self-Direction

Building self-direction, like building self-knowledge, should also be a calculated and deliberate effort on the part of the teacher. Successful self-direction cannot be brought about en masse. It is an individually tailored item. The hearing-handicapped population, along with the hearing population, is living in a rapidly changing world. Yet, regardless of the changes and thrusts into obsolescence around us, there are still basic needs to be satisfied.

First, the hearing-handicapped child must have a sense of individuality, a sense of self. In some respects, he already has this as he sees that he is not entirely like his hearing brother. The crucial point is how he copes with this realization we may have helped him achieve. Is he comfortable in his knowledge?

The deaf and hard-of-hearing child needs the consistency that is good training for all children. This means organization in his experiences. Regular hours for daily routines will produce a rhythm and a foundation for self-discipline. Consistency is also the guide word in discipline at home and at school.

The difficulties of the hearing-handicapped child may not be academic or in limited speech and speech reading. They may be undesirable personality characteristics. This, too, is part of his sense of individuality. The child must have the language for explaining himself or his circumstances to others. Such mannerisms as frowning and looking unpleasant when unable to understand hearing people eventually does have an effect on self-concepts. The deaf and hard-of-hearing are constantly on the receiving end of those attitudes referred to earlier.

Second, the hearing-handicapped child must develop a sense of independence and self-sufficiency. The ideal is to reach the most adequate level of adjustment within the recognized limitations. The counseling task here is to help each child (and his family) to evaluate realistically such factors as academic achievement, frustration tolerance, and personality make-up. The pupil should not be placed in situations that would result in undue stress on adjustment potential. There should be some measure of success derived which would build self-confidence. It is hoped that eventually the hearing-handicapped person will learn to set realistic goals by himself and reasonably attain them. Initiative is probably more easily fostered when this sense of independence begins to grow.

Thinking ahead to the time when vocational plans must be made, let us consider the occupational interest profiles of the deaf. Geist (1962) studied over 900 employed hearing-handicapped males. It was concluded that the interest profiles of the hearing-handicapped seem to be quite similar to the interest profiles of analogous hearing occupational groups. Perhaps such information will make our guidance of youth more positive as they show particular interests or preferences.

If the deaf and hard-of-hearing are to feel secure socially, they must acquire the ability to say and do the thing that is generally acceptable. The actual meaningful experience is one of the best training grounds. Engaging in activities with hearing people suitable to the age level would begin to build security in this area. These activities might include games, dances, trips, parties, attendance at sporting and entertainment events, and club membership. If properly managed, these learning opportunities could promote proper social behavior. The problems that might arise could be discussed at faculty meetings, and concerted action or planning for a series of lessons might evolve.

Third, the hearing-handicapped child must develop a sense of responsibility. This would include responsibility for his own actions. Consistency by parents and teachers is essential in this area. An examination of the primary aspects of responsibility reveals the assumption that the subject realizes the consequences of his behavior. If the child is eventually to direct himself with good purpose, the various implications of his actions must be considered. Responsibility is usually thought of in relation to other people, and for that reason the child must be responsive to the needs of others.

Fourth, the hearing-handicapped child must develop a sense of time perspective. This means being able to utilize past experiences (successes and failures) in order to plan ahead. The successful completion of a planned project is often dependent upon the appropriate use of the time allotted for that project. The amount of time available for a task is always a key factor in attaining any goal, and an awareness of this gives greater hope that more realistic goals will be set. The worthy use of time to meet current needs must be coupled with realizing that time is necessary to complete a future plan as well.

Fifth, the hearing-handicapped child must develop a sense of personal values and a philosophy of life in order to deal with problems. This development is partially the outgrowth of the previous four points. It is an ongoing, dynamic process as the child continues to mature.

Traditionally, a teacher is usually thought to be concerned primarily with teaching students to develop concepts about the external world, while a counselor is usually thought to be concerned with helping students to acquire and understand personal information and knowledge. Since the hearing-handicapped student's interpretation of the world about him is influenced to a large extent by the direction of his teacher, it is important that the teacher of the deaf and hard-of-hearing be aware of the guidance he may afford the student. If the hearing-handicapped can be helped to self-knowledge and self-direction, the many adjustments necessary in a lifetime in a hearing world will be more easily made.

Suggested Readings

Beasley, Jane. *Slow to Talk*. New York: Teachers College, Columbia University, 1956.

Bigman, S. K. "The Deaf in American Institutes of Higher Education," *Personnel and Guidance Journal*, 39:743–746; May, 1961. Survey of 1,857 students lists college admission and attendance policies, academic achievement, and social participation with implications for college counselors of deaf.

Blish, S. C. "Educational and Vocational Guidance of the Deaf." (Paper presented at Council for Exceptional Children Convention, Chicago, 1964.) Follow-up study of 113 Clarke School for the Deaf alumni over ten-year period shows 72 went on to secondary school, of whom 41 graduated and 29 were still in school; 9 went to trade schools; 25 went to business school, of whom 22 graduated; 7 went to junior college, of whom 5 graduated; 13 attended college, of whom 3 graduated and 5 are still in college; 12 students took on the job training, of whom all but one are at work. The range of Stanford Achievement test scores was from grade 3.8 to 11.3 with a median at 7.2. The scores of those attending secondary schools ranged from 5.3 to 11.3 with a median of 8.1. Comparative reading scores were for the whole group 3.1 to 10.4 with median at 5.9 and for the secondary group 4.0 to 10.4 with median at 6.6. The comparative Wechsler scores (of IQ) were for verbal IQ: whole group median 92, secondary school group median 96; performance IQ: whole group median 113, secondary group 115; full-scale IQ: whole group median 102, secondary group median 106.

Fitzsimmons, Ruth. "Parent Teacher Conferences and Speech Handicapped Children," *Education*, 82:222–225; December, 1961.

French, Sophia. "Doll Play: A Sociometric Device, Etc.," *Volta Review*, 62:331–334; September, 1960. Doll play recommended as a useful guidance technique for young deaf children.

Geist, H. "Occupational Interests of the Deaf," *Personnel and Guidance Journal*, 41:50–55; September, 1962. Interests of various deaf occupational groups were ascertained by using the Geist Picture Interest Inventory. "The interests of the deaf seem to be no different from those of the hearing in similar occupations."

Hall, W. A. "Return from Silence, a Personal Experience," *Journal of Speech and Hearing Disorder,* 26:230–236; August, 1961.

Irwin, Ruth B. "Group Parent Counseling in the Public Schools," *Abstracts of the 39th Annual Convention of the American Speech and Hearing Association,* 15:10; October, 1963.

——. *A Speech Pathologist Talks to Parents and Teachers.* Pittsburgh: Stanwix House, 1962.

LeVine, Edna S. *Psychology of Deafness: Techniques for Appraisal for Rehabilitation.* New York: Columbia University Press, 1960.

Lichtenstein, F. "Guidance Work with Stutterers," *High Points,* 44:44–50; January, 1962.

Lunde, A. S., and Bigman, S. K. *Occupational Conditions Among the Deaf: A Report of a National Survey.* Washington, D.C.: Gallaudet College, 1959. Comprehensive survey of 10,000 deaf adults' occupations found 400 distinct jobs with satisfaction and job stability high and greatest concentration in printing trades. There was marked emphasis on skilled and semiskilled manual jobs to the detriment of wholesale and retail selling.

McDonald, E. "Group Parent-Counseling," *Abstracts of the 39th Convention of the American Speech and Hearing Association,* 15:10; October, 1963.

Myklebust, H. R.; Neyhus, A.; and Mulholland, Ann. "Guidance and Counseling for the Deaf," *American Annals of the Deaf,* 107:370–415; 1962. This excellent article, unfortunately too long to include in full, should be read by all counselors working with the deaf. It begins by noting that there is a critical need for guidance and counseling if deaf persons are to achieve their potential. It notes that this guidance begins with the parents in the child's infancy and continues:

"At school age the educational implications of deafness come into the foreground and continue to be of importance throughout the period of school life. Problems which arise and must be viewed in terms of the need for guidance include the discrepancy between the parent's expectations and the actual abilities of their child, between poor achievement in light of good potential fo learning, including lack of success in speech and language, failure in school subjects, inadequate personal-social relationships with those of his own ag and many others. During the high school years the guidance needs chang with foremost attention directed toward the goals and objectives of adult hood. Often this period is one of frustration and anxiety for the individua with deafness as well as his parents; all concerned, for the first time mus accept, frequently, for the first time, limitations which had not been full recognized. . . . Vocational choice and training becomes a major concer one which not only requires a realistic attitude on the part of the individu and his family but also on the part of the guidance counselor. One of the primary functions of guidance is put to the test at this particular period and only those who have the necessary training and experience can fulfill the need in terms of the maximum benefits to the individual."

The authors then discuss common problem categories: the superior, the emotionally disturbed, and academically limited, the retarded, and those with other handicaps. Information to be included in the case history consists of (1) identifying information, (2) statement of the problem, (3) medical history, (4) educational history, (5) family and social history, (6) employment history. Appraisal of individual abilities is then made in the following areas: (1) sensory abilities, (2) intelligence, (3) social maturity, (4) personality and emotional adjustment, (5) motor ability, (6) ability to communicate, (7) interest pattern, and (8) special aptitudes. A listing of tests for the deaf is then given, and six case studies are presented. A lengthy bibliography is appended.

Phillips, R. M. "Vocational Guidance for Adult Deaf," *American Annals of the Deaf,* 107:566–569; 1962.

Roraback, J. B. "Special Factors in the Rehabilitation of the Deaf," *Journal of Rehabilitation,* 29:15–17; 1963.

Rosenstein, J. "Perception, Cognition and Language in Deaf Children," *Exceptional Children,* 27:276–282; January, 1961. Careful review of literature with fifty-nine references concluded that cognitive operations, such as concept formation, may not require linguistic coding, and hence deaf children may be taught in such fashion that linguistic elements are minimized. Rosenstein found no differences in conceptual performance between a group of deaf and hearing children. Prior training and experience greatly enhance the ability to conceptualize. With improvement in teaching methods, the inferior performance of the deaf child on cognitive tasks may be overcome.

Roy, H. L. "Counseling Centers for the Deaf," *Rehabilitation Record,* 6:35–36; 1960.

Spriesterbach, D. C. "Counseling Parents of Children with Cleft Lips and Palates," *Journal of Chronic Diseases,* 13:244–252; 1961. Analysis of interview data from 175 sets of parents of affected children compared with control parents result in suggestions regarding counseling in this area.

CHAPTER 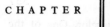 MISCELLANEOUS PHYSICALLY
HANDICAPPED

IN THIS FINAL CHAPTER have been placed miscellaneous papers on various guidance problems of handicapped persons. Other than the adjustment in self-concept, the need for effective diagnosis and early therapy, and the importance of vocational guidance, which are characteristic of guidance practices for all exceptional children, there appear no special aspects here. It would seem that guidance practices for all kinds of exceptional children continue to make headway in proportion as we identify with and regard these children as worthy of our time and attention. We conclude, therefore, with a statement with which the first paper began: "Concern for the qualities of exceptional human beings arises out of an exceptional concern for the qualities of all human beings."

Barsch and Ruddell begin the chapter with an excerpted summary of their study on reading development among CP children. Baum continues with an analysis of the family adjustment to the handicapped child. Cantoni, who has many articles on the handicapped, contributes one on the work possibilities for the cardiac. Kir-Stimon further discusses the same subject. Lerner and Martin provide a most useful article on college attendance by the handicapped. Overs and Routh contribute very practical articles on evaluating self-concept in the handicapped. Schiller does the same for CP children and youth. Tucker and Olson contribute more information on college-going for the handicapped. Williams and Canton conclude with a discussion of vocational problems of the severely disabled

53. A Study of Reading Development Among Seventy-Seven Children with Cerebral Palsy *

RAY H. BARSCH, *Jewish Vocational Guidance Service, Milwaukee*

BETH RUDDELL, *Jewish Vocational Guidance Service, Milwaukee*

Rationale for This Study

CLINICAL EXPERIENCE in evaluating the psychological functioning of cerebral-palsied children over a ten-year period by both authors suggested that a first step to viewing reading development in organic children might best be taken as a survey study of a selected organic population. The question to be investigated was simply "If a systematic clinical evaluation of present reading development of cerebral-palsied children were to be made, would results indicate significant features and would such a survey provide leads for further, detailed study?"

The hypothesis for this study might simply be stated as: a *single, systematic, developmental, clinical evaluation of reading development would reveal significant findings.*

.   .   .   .

Summary and Conclusion

This study was designed to investigate the reading development of children with cerebral palsy. Seventy-seven children between the ages of five and sixteen, who were attending school, were evaluated by the same specialist in reading development. All children were patients of the Cerebral Palsy Clinic of Milwaukee. During the period from September, 1958, to June, 1959, every new patient referred to the clinic for diagnostic evaluation or reactivated patient who returned to the clinic for medical re-evaluation was automatically scheduled for reading evaluation if attending school and within the specified age range.

The purpose of the study was simply to conduct a comprehensive individualized evaluation of the reading development among a cerebral-

* Reprinted by permission of the authors and *Cerebral Palsy Review*, 23:2:3–10; March, 1962—abridged.

palsied population. Each child was evaluated as intensively as his handicap allowed in the following areas: (1) development of basic sight vocabulary, (2) method of word attack, (3) visual discrimination, (4) auditory discrimination, (5) picture interpretation, (6) sequentialness, (7) ability to perceive simple relationships, (8) ability to name common objects, (9) auditory and visual memory, and (10) language formulation patterns.

Each child was also rated as being Articulate or Inarticulate in terms of clarity and intelligibility of oral speech. Clinical impressions of intellectual functioning were employed as intelligence classifications rather than precise intelligence test scores. The diagnostic medical classification of type of cerebral palsy, which was contained in the patient's clinic chart, was used to designate classifications on a medical basis.

Twenty-two cases were classified as spastic hemiplegic, triplegic, or diplegic and grouped together for tabulation purposes under the single heading of quadriplegic. There were 21 cases with a diagnosis of athetosis and 5 ataxics. In the 3 remaining cases, the medical summary indicated that the specific nature of the child's cerebral palsy condition had not yet been determined.

The distribution of the study group according to school placements revealed that 32 cases were attending regular elementary schools, 26 were attending orthopedic schools, 10 were in classes for the educable mentally handicapped, and 9 were placed in the classification of *Other*. This classification included children attending special classes for the deaf, visually handicapped, residential schools, etc. Fifty-two per cent of the cases were placed in the first three elementary grades which provided a pronounced emphasis upon the crucial reading development ages. When clinical impressions of intelligence were used to group the 77 cases, 19 were judged to be functioning below 70 IQ, and 23 were within the 70 to 90 IQ range. Twenty-three cases were judged to be functioning within the average range from 90 to 110 IQ, and 12 cases were found to be above average in intelligence.

Fifty-eight cases were judged to have intelligible and understandable speech, and 19 were considered to be inarticulate.

Three major classifications of reading development levels were employed after analysis of evaluation data. *Advanced* was used to designate cases achieving reading efficiency beyond that expected for chronologic age or grade placement. *At level* was employed to designate those cases whose over-all reading development was determined to be within expected efficiencies for chronologic age or grade placement. *Retarded* was applied to those cases whose over-all reading function was judged to be developmentally one or more years below chronological age or grade placement.

According to these three classifications, 6 per cent (5 cases) were found to be *advanced,* 25 per cent (18 cases) were *at* (grade) *level,* and 69 per cent (54 cases) were *retarded* in reading development.

To subject these percentages to closer inspection and analysis, a variety of comparative frequency tables were organized from the data collected. School placements, medical diagnostic categories, and clinical impressions of intelligence and articulation levels were compared to development of basic sight vocabulary and method of word attack.

The composite chart below (Table 25) includes various factors related to classifications of reading level. It will be noted that all cases who were rated as being *at* (grade) *level* had some development in basic sight vocabulary and some method of attacking new words. In the *retarded* reading group, there is an approximate 50:50 distribution on both basic sight vocabulary development and a system for attacking new words. For at least 50 per cent of the *retarded* reading group, failure to progress in either one or both of these areas is a significant factor. It is interesting to note that 22 per cent of the cases judged to be below 90 IQ had managed to achieve reading competence. At first glance, it would appear from this finding that the clinical impression of intellectual functioning had been inaccurate. However, the question of whether or not those factors measured in intelligence testing have any direct and specific relation to reading skills

TABLE 25—COMPOSITE CHART SHOWING PERCENTAGES ON VARIABLES CONSIDERED IN THIS STUDY ACCORDING TO LEVELS OF READING DEVELOPMENT

	Retarded (per cent)	Level or Advanced (per cent)
Inarticulate	89	11
Articulate	64	36
No Basic Sight Vocabulary	59	—
Developing or Adequate Basic Sight Vocabulary	41	100
No Method of Word Attack	46	—
Word Attack—Positive	54	100
Under 70 IQ	95	5
Under 90 IQ	83	17
Above 90 IQ	43	57
Hemiplegic	46	54
Quadriplegic	76	24
Athetoid	84	16
Ataxic	80	20

has not yet been sufficiently clarified in the literature. Either of these two considerations could serve as an explanation for this finding.

The athetoid group showed the highest percentage of *retarded* readers (84 per cent), while the hemiplegic group showed the lowest (46 per cent). The hemiplegic group is the only diagnostic category which reflected a higher percentage of *at level* or *advanced* readers than *retarded*.

Analysis of various comparative relationships suggests that the following summary comments are pertinent.

1. Inarticulation as a deterrent to reading development was a factor for only one-fourth of this group. The athetoid group revealed the highest incidence of cases classified as Inarticulate (45 per cent). The incidence of Inarticulate classifications diminished as intellectual estimates were higher

2. In 75 per cent of the cases, the clinical impression of intelligence was directly related to the child's reading development and could be classified as being accurately predictive. In the other 25 per cent of the cases, the child's performance in reading surpassed expectancy based on IQ or dropped far below expectancy based on IQ.

3. More than half of the total group studied were managing adequately in the development of a basic sight vocabulary.

4. More than half of the total group were also managing to acquire a system for attacking new words.

5. The frequency of good and poor readers was comparatively similar for both regular and orthopedic schools.

6. On a general basis, the hemiplegic cases were the best readers.

54. Some Dynamic Factors Affecting Family Adjustment to the Handicapped Child *

MARIAN HOOPER BAUM, *Clinical Psychologist,*
Lorain County Child Welfare Board, Elyria, Ohio

S OME YEARS AGO, one of our more perceptive humorists cartooned a reference to the central dynamic factor I shall discuss: an adult male, standing with arms laterally extended, wears, as I recall, some sort of clinical uniform. One of his sleeves merges with that on the arm of a similarly dressed small boy who dangles spread-eagled in the air beside him. The caption is something like this: "My child is an extension of myself." Kozier (1957), writing of parental reactions to children born with severe brain defects, uses virtually the same words:

In many ways, a child represents to the parent an extension of his own self. . . . When the baby is born the mother's wish to be loved is partially transferred from her own person to that of the baby. To the father, a normal child is often an affirmation, at least in part, of his own sense of success. The capacity to produce unimpaired offspring is psychologically and culturally important for the parents' sense of personal adequacy.

Jordan (1961), points out that "identification of mental retardation at birth comes at a time when parents are vulnerable physically and psychologically." In Spock and Rheinhart's appealing documentary volume, *A Baby's First Year*, the parent's sense of deep responsibility for the condition of the newborn is described: "The first glimpse . . . The old questions: 'It it a boy or girl? Has she got all her fingers and toes?' This last question seems to spring from the almost universal human doubt: 'Am I a good enough person to be blessed with a perfect baby?' " The authors may have considered and rejected adding a statement to the effect that such a doubt is rarely based in reality, and as Jordan points out, "normality" and "perfection" are not, in fact, equivalent. But when, in a particular birth, the second term of the proposition is unfulfilled—if, in fact, the parent produces an obviously defective, handicapped child—the relentless unconscious, having accepted the original proposition as true, may demand

* Reprinted by permission of the author and *Exceptional Children,* 28:387-392; April, 1962.

that the first term is therefore false. And then the painful search must begin for ways to defend against the anxiety that would be aroused by conscious awareness of this threat to this ego, particularly of this threat to its narcissistic components.

I have observed that parental reactions to the birth of a blind or ortho-pedically imperfect child differ more in degree than in kind, generally, from reactions of parents of more globally handicapped children. Parents of deaf children, too, may experience similar feelings; but in clinical practice one more often sees the child in whom deafness masquerades as retardation and/or emotional disturbance, so that these parents often react to the finally differential diagnosis of deafness with relief.

Threat to the ego can be severe when awareness comes later, as well. Hersh (1961), emphasizes parents' reactions to later diagnosis, saying,

Probably the largest number of parents feel at the time of the birth of their child that he is normal. It is only later, as his development lags, that he is seen as not normal. Still later, however, in recapitulating, many mothers admit that they suspected rather early that their child was different. Statements such as "He was just different," "He was too still," and "He was like a lump of clay," are common. . . . We have known some mothers who fought the world on behalf of their child, almost because they knew too soon that the child was different. They had a secret that acted as a bond between self and child. The invasion of the outer world and its harsh realities could be climaxed in no other way than a pitched battle in which their struggle to maintain the cherished secret was waged.

Physicians' Reactions

Professional persons are likewise threatened and anxious. Several observers' reports (Patterson, 1956; Zuk, 1960; Solnit & Stark, 1961) indicate that practitioners whose duty it is to interpret findings of mental retardation are often unnecessarily harsh and even brutal in their language and, one would also suspect, in their manner. Solnit and Stark also cite the urgency with which some physicians attempt to hurry mothers into plans for institutionalizing their defective newborns as evidence of the advisers' anxiety. I believe that our anxiety stems from sources which include, on whatever level it may exist individually, that such an interpretation is a socially rejecting act, however unavoidable it may be. None of us is culture-free; we all share to some degree our culture's attitudes of rejection toward the handicapped for practical and economic reasons, as Zuk (1960) observes. The positive aspect of our conflict likewise parallels society's: we cherish our opportunities to assist in the rehabilitation of these families and individuals as evidence of our personal affirmation of the value of the human being, the first of Wright's (1961) "basic dozen" of principles that direct rehabilitation. Some of us must work through the anticipated and realized projection of our feelings if such a diagnosis should be appended to a child of our own. Solnit and Stark also note "the physician's own feeling of helplessness and resentment that his work has failed to produce a normal child." In this connection let me call attention to the part played in unnecessarily delayed diagnosis by anxiety, fear of blame, and the altogther reasonable desire on the part of the physician to avoid parents' hostility.

Parental Grief

Solnit and Stark have recently directed attention to the mother's reaction to the birth of a mentally retarded, defective infant, describing this event, in part, as "the 'sudden' loss of the baby that was expected." They see, in the mother's reactions, an expression of grief for the "lost" child, the perfect baby, and the onset of a mourning process which must inevitably extend over a long period of time. These observers note, despite differences, certain similarities here to mothers' reactions to a dead child: "Feelings of loss; intense longings for the desired child; resentment of the cruel blow that life's experience has dealt; and the guilt that the dead or defective child may evoke by representing the consequence of unacceptable feelings or thoughts."

Although mothers seem to be involved more deeply at the time of birth of a retarded or defective child, fathers, it is agreed, have similar and related feelings. Hersh (1961) finds fathers more removed, less emotionally involved, more objective, and less expressive of their feelings and believes mothers suffer the more intense feelings, in general. He notes that fathers who have not yet achieved or are currently working through their separation from their own fathers often appear to have a particular problem with their retarded child and that "a retarded son may create a real puncture in the male ego unless the father is well established as father and husband. This problem is often expressed in aggressive and disapproving action. More subtle and difficult to help is the father who smothers and denies the boy his own manhood. Adolescence is particularly stormy, but affords some basis for confrontation and identification between father and son." He notes that fathers tend to ignore the present problems of feelings out of concern for the long-term economic and social dependency of their retarded children.

Bowlby (1960) groups psychological responses to bereavement—stages of the mourning process—as follows.

(*a*) Thought and behavior still directed toward the lost object;
(*b*) Hostility, to whomsoever directed;
(*c*) Appeals for help;
(*d*) Despair, withdrawal, regression and disorganization;
(*e*) Reorganization of behavior directed toward a new object.

Many observed parental reactions to handicaps in their children can be conceptualized within this framework. Admittedly defensive in function, these responses are necessary protections of the parental ego. It is our experience that many parents display a fluidity of response, seeming to pass back and forth among these stages, omitting some and repeating others, sometimes showing behavior appropriate to two or more stages simultaneously and unpredictably. Avoidance and denial of the problem, of the diagnosis, or of the child himself fits Bowlby's first category: that of thought and behavior directed toward the lost object.

Denial of Abnormality

Along with other observers (Hohman, 1959; Zuk, 1959), we have observed that parental needs to prove the normality of the handicapped child (another form of denial) are expressed in pressures for achievement that often produce emotional instability in the child. The fantasy of the "imprisoned knower," so often seen in the parents of athetoids, is another manifestation of denial of mental deficiency in the child. Reality often serves the cause of denial to some extent: defective, handicapped children often require much maternal energy and attention; families may be limited in size (Holt, 1958); the special one may be an only child. Thus the opportunities for comparison of development with that of normal siblings is limited. Then, too, accurate intellectual evaluation of children with severe motor and sensory deficits is admittedly difficult, even for the experienced examiner; little wonder that parents and even teachers believe whatever they need to believe about the child's "true" ability.

Consequences to the child of continued denial and avoidance used as mechanisms of defense by parents may be severe: one moderately retarded little boy whose mother has insisted, against advice, that he remain in public school has begun soiling, though previously completely trained, and has dropped significantly in functioning intelligence (20 IQ points). Another moderately retarded little girl has been pushed to strive for perfection in all areas, with the result that each year the child becomes, in the words of her teacher, "more nervous, is regressing, showing poorer school performance."

Parental Hostilities

Bowlby (1960) quotes Lindemann on grief as referring to " 'feelings of hostility,' surprising and quite inexplicable to the patients, which appeared sometimes to be 'spread out over all relationships' and at others to be channelled into 'furious hostility' against specific persons: the doctor or the surgeon are accused bitterly for neglect of duty." Bowlby further observes that in the sorrow which supplants this anger, "the bereaved either makes unreasonable demands or else hardly seems to know what he wants, and often becomes irritable and ungrateful to those who try to respond." That this picture describes the behavior of many of our parents of handicapped children, there can be no doubt. In working with these parents, one can often sense, in some, the tears so close to the surface; in others, the rage that is barely controlled; in groups (Auerbach, 1961), the doleful atmosphere which nothing seems to dispel. If these reactions are regarded as temporary or even as fixated stages of the mourning process, our professional ego functioning improves, our own reality testing is less likely to be impaired.

Whether one takes a position regarding hostile reactions of parents to interpretation of a diagnosis of a child's severe and irreversible disability as a stage in a process of mourning (Solnit and Stark), or whether one regards parents' hostility toward the adviser as a displaced reaction to frustration by the existence of the handicapped child, as does Zuk, few clinicians have escaped being the target of such feelings. Reality again contributes to parents' hostile feelings: the child *is* frustrating, the community *is* rejecting—although the climate has improved vastly in the past ten years—and professional advisers *are* sometimes harsh.

In view of all the confluences that make up these feelings in parents, it is not surprising that many parents' reports to us, even long after the fact, continue to reveal their clear, even if erroneous, focus on their rejection of the diagnosis and their resentment of the persons who have given it, implemented it, and reminded them of it. Perhaps the impact of the handicapped child on the family can be slightly less damaging if we make every effort to remove any reality basis for these hostile feelings, including our own unwittingly hostile responses to parents' hostility (Sarason, 1953).

Feelings of Guilt and Shame

Parents' anxiety, on the one hand, and their anger or hostility, on the other, evoke guilt. Guilt feelings, a function of the superego, are a partial transmutation of anxiety (Fenichel, 1945). As the parent of the handicapped child is threatened by high levels of anxiety as well as of anger, the almost universally observed guilt in these parents is overdetermined.

Hostility toward the child himself, or anger, as Zuk (1960) has suggested, evokes guilt. He believes that parental guilt arises as a consequence of the displacement of anger from the disappointing, frustrating child to the parent's own self and also as a consequence of the unacceptability of chronic anger toward one's child. He further states (article in press) that negative parental feelings exist in most parents of normal children as well. "Normal" parental ambivalence, the love-hate conflict, is as unavoidable in parents as it is in children. Almost from the time of conception the child's mere existence, one's concern for it and need to protect it, the consequences of pregnancy, both psychological (Deutsch, 1945) and physiological, to the mother and to a lesser extent to the father as well, involve frustration of many even elemental needs, evoking at least occasional resentment, discomfort, family friction, and anger. As the child is born and continues his development, the developmental process of parenthood, particularly for parents with their first child, continues to entail countless need frustrations, deferred gratifications, and endured discomforts. We believe so strongly in the importance of early life experiences of the child to his later personality development that many of these negative responses to our normal children are mild enough, and the positive responses are strong enough, to prevent outward expression of aggressive feelings toward the child. In this age of "togetherness," emphasizing the value of the child (occasionally more aptly described as the tyranny of the child), aggressive feelings toward one's own children evoke anxiety in many (but not all) social strata of American society and are not outwardly expressed. But in the case of the handicapped child, the strength of these negative feelings is more intense, for reasons of reality as well as on intrapsychic bases. Parental gratifications are fewer, opportunities for ego enhancement are rarer, and aggressive feelings reach sufficient height to evoke extreme guilt (Baily, 1961).

A related phenomenon in these parents is the frequently observed feeling of shame. Lynd (1958) distinguishes shame from guilt carefully as follows: "Guilt, or self-reproach, is based upon internalization of values, notably [one's own] parental values—in contrast with shame, which is based upon disapproval coming from outside, from other persons." The relationship between the two exists because, as Fenichel puts it,

he super-ego is derived from the introjection of a piece of the external world i.e., parental standards]. . . . The incorporation of this piece of the external world occurs relatively late; thus the super-ego remains that part of the mental apparatus closest to the outside world. Many persons remain influenced in their behavior and self-esteem not only by what they consider correct themselves but also by the consideration of what others may think.

One mother of a child in our program objected bitterly to the child's transfer from one to another class of the same level of retardates. This superficially irrational objection was refractory to administrative persuasion because, as the mother was able to confide, the new class was located in a church, the old in a public school. The mother needed to be able to say (to others as well as to herself), "My daughter goes to X School."

Shame is also apparent in sibling relationships of the retarded child. One mother of a large family engaged a sitter for the first time to play with her four-year-old mongoloid daughter, an attractive child. The sitter took the child to the park, played with her there, took her for walks down the main street of town. The sensitive and articulate mother reported that she asked herself why none of the child's siblings, who often volunteered to amuse the child, had ever appeared with her in public.

Appeals for help are seen in retarded children's parents ofttimes as an expectation that "somebody" or "the community" or "the school board" should come to their aid, should help them bear this intolerable burden. Parent associations are justifiably proud of their success in bringing the needs of their handicapped children to the attention of the community in many localities; but when one observes certain parents for whom no amount of service is ever adequate to their needs and demands, their reactions may be better understood as relevant to their progress through the work of mourning.

Withdrawal

Behavior appropriate to Bowlby's fourth stage of mourning—"Despair, withdrawal, regression, and disorganization"—is likewise observed in many parents. Jordan cites Schipper's study in which six mothers of mongoloid children "regressed to a more immature level of behavior and became more dependent on their own mothers." Kozier (1957) reports that sometimes, when babies are born with severe brain defects, the parent's initial shock

is so prolonged as to interfere with his functioning at home and in the community. The threat to him of having produced a child severely malformed may be so great that he may not be able to carry out even the most urgent of parental responsibilities. He may try to leave his baby in the hospital indefinitely; he may deny the baby's need for special treatment; he may neglect the baby physically; or he may devote himself so exclusively to the child that he is cut off from other life experiences.

Here we can see a number of mourning responses—denial and avoidance, hostility toward the defective child, hostility toward the self, or guilt—as well as disorganization of usual patterns of functioning.

Summary

The practical purpose of any attempted dynamic formulation of parental reactions to the awareness of global defect in their child is to provide insights into behavior that enable the professional adviser to help these parents "see the child as a separate human being, and his handicap as an unfortunate accident of nature" (Kozier) or, as Jordan puts it, "to help the parent . . . see issues more clearly and make necessary decisions." The parent must be assisted, through the repetitive working through of feelings, to reach the final stage of mourning, wherein his behavior is reorganized and directed toward a new object: the handicapped child as he *is,* in realistic terms. Working through the psychological process of mourning is a laborious and lengthy procedure. Assessment of and consideration for parents' progress in this working through of their reactions may enable us to help parents achieve this important goal.

55. Can Cardiacs Work? *

LOUIS J. CANTONI, *Coordinator of Rehabilitation Counselor Training, Wayne State University, Detroit*

IN 1959, according to the American Heart Association, heart and circulatory diseases took 877,000 American lives. Thus, heart and related ailments accounted for more deaths than all other causes combined.

It is estimated that at least 10,000,000 Americans have cardiac conditions, resulting in a work loss of 69 million man-days annually. This lost time represents more than a billion dollars in unearned income.

Conference Recommendations

Can cardiacs work? What can be done to conserve years of investment in educational preparation and job skills? In November, 1959, at a statewide conference of the Michigan Heart Association held at Wayne State University in Detroit, several discussion groups addressed themselves to these questions. Following are key thoughts and recommendations that came out of the day's session.

1. Vocational rehabilitation should begin at the time of diagnosis, not after a person's medical problem has been solved. This points up the need for (*a*) guidance services in schools and (*b*) rehabilitation services from employers and community agencies, both public and private.

2. Medical and vocational rehabilitation can be implemented not only in large urban rehabilitation centers where work capacity may be determined quite readily but also in general hospitals and by private physicians and school and community health and guidance personnel. Whenever feasible, the rehabilitation process should be initiated and carried out where the patient or client is. The majority of those who have heart disease can be served adequately by their family doctors if the doctors will give selective placement agencies an evaluation of patients' functional capacity.

3. People with cardiovascular disease, whether homemakers, farmers, or office or factory workers, should know the energy requirements of various tasks. They should be able to relate calorie-per-minute expenditures on various kinds of jobs to the severity of their own heart conditions. Work

* Reprinted by permission of the author and *Vocational Guidance Quarterly*, 8:239–240; Summer, 1960.

simplification units, such as that sponsored by the Michigan Heart Association at Wayne State University, help cardiac housewives to know the energy requirements of various tasks in the home. Homemaking classes, in which noncardiac husbands are also welcome, cover such topics as body mechanics, kitchen work, cleaning, and laundry.

4. A graded activity program, incorporating both physical and occupational therapy, aids the return to maximum functioning. The place for the inception of such a program is the hospital.

5. Ultimately, the best work tolerance test is a time test with opportunity to experience the demands of various assignments. Graded exercises stimulate collateral circulation so that new coronary arteries feed blood to the heart.

6. When a worker might be placed on a physically demanding job, it is useful to have an impartial estimate of his ability to work. Cardiac work classification, for the 20 per cent who should have it, calls for a team approach employing, ideally, several specialists: industrial physician, psychiatrist, industrial nurse, counseling psychologist, medical social worker, and vocational counselor. Other specialists also enter the picture. The services of a cardiologist are, of course, required. Physical and occupational therapists and other specialists may also make a contribution.

7. Counselors, as well as physicians, must remember that patients with severe heart conditions may want to work, whereas those with minimal damage may not be so motivated. No two individuals respond to chronic illness in the same way; therefore each specialist will need to contribute not only his skill but also a tempered optimism in his efforts with cardiacs.

8. Organized labor objects to waivers which remove employer responsibility in the employment of cardiacs as well as others of the physically disabled. Sometimes, however, a waiver of rights to workman's compensation may seem desirable from the standpoint of the employee. In any case, waivers should be based on findings of a team of specialists in heart disease and rehabilitation.

9. Legislation may be needed to limit employer liability when heart attacks occur on an employer's premises. The concern here is with first disablements, not second injuries. An authority should be set up to establish degrees of impairment and of concomitant liability in cardiac cases.

10. A team of interested professionals should help prepare a medical, educational, social, and vocational program for a cardiac child from the time he is known to have heart disease to the time that he has suitable job placement or is successfully habilitated. During grade and high school years, such a team should include, at least, the child's parents, physician, nurse,

teacher, and counselor. A cardiac child should be encouraged early to acquire attitudes, knowledges, and skills that ready him for jobs he can do.

The Counselor's Role

It is impossible to solve all the problems of the chronically ill. No doubt some cardiacs must settle for less. With them it is a matter of learning to live with restrictions imposed by disability. Of the 85 per cent who survive a first heart attack, however, 75 per cent return to work for their old employers, usually at the same jobs they held before their heart attack.

In a nation in which 5 per cent of the working population has heart disease and in which 400,000 people with coronary heart disease are being added to the labor market yearly, vocational counselors can play an important role by knowing and appreciating not only the physical limitations but also the personal and vocational problems of cardiac clients.

56. Rehabilitation Counseling with Cardiac Children *

WILLIAM KIR-STIMON, *Director of Personal Counseling Services, Rehabilitation Institute of Chicago*

THE REHABILITATION INSTITUTE of Chicago, the Chicago public schools, and the Chicago Heart Association recently concluded a five-year pilot study designed to serve children with rheumatic or congenital heart disease. Entitled the Vocational Guidance and Counseling Project, the program has been an attempt to assist the individual schools in their handling of cardiac cases and effort to provide for the disabled youngsters in Grades 7 to 12 the co-ordinated services of a "rehabilitation team."

Ten years ago a cardiologist, and later on a teacher-nurse were assigned to the Bureau of Health Services. Since that time, cardiac case finding and

* Reprinted by permission of the author and *Personnel and Guidance Journal,* 40:551–556; February, 1962.

reviews of cardiac children have continued to be a part of the program, with initial contacts now made by over one hundred teacher-nurses in the school system. Provision was originally made for cardiac children in the special schools, but the project was then extended to children with heart disease in the regular schools. Because of increased value placed upon the service by high school personnel, the program was expanded from the tenth to include the eleventh- and twelfth-grade students, with fewer being referred from the lower grades. The Heart Association for a while employed a social worker to co-ordinate activities and do follow-up, including such field work as was necessary. In the last half of the program, follow-up was done by the individual schools concerned and only occasionally by the Institute.

The problem of pediatric heart disease is significant in that it is estimated that nationally a half-million children of school age are affected. New York City is said to have some 5,000. In Chicago the estimate runs to approximately 2,400 cardiac children in the public schools. The Rehabilitation Institute Project saw 164 children in five years, mainly for diagnostic study and recommendations, with some short-term counseling provided. The Chicago program was liquidated at the Institute early in 1960, and the procedures used in the cardiac unit are being integrated into the local school system at this time. To our knowledge, the parochial schools have no such service available. Although the State's Division of Services For Crippled Children provides medical care in suburban areas, there is no similar rehabilitation team project outside the city proper.

Objectives

Major objectives instrumental in setting up the project remained the same during the five-year period:

1. to give the child with heart disease a sound, although perhaps in some cases tentative, basis for educational-vocational planning leading to economic self-sufficiency;

2. to help the parents understand and accept the child's potentialities as well as his limitations;

3. to assist the schools in planning programs for this group of handicapped children;

4. to serve as a resource to the physician in the care of his patient; and

5. to assess the unique guidance needs of school children with heart disease.

Project Operation

Operation of the project necessitated for each case the services of a social worker, vocational counselor, clinical psychologist, and pediatric cardiologist. In addition to the professional services enumerated, the Institute has also made available to the project as needed its departments of speech therapy, occupational therapy, physical therapy, and internal and physical medicine. Thus, a cardiac child with hemiplegia was rediagnosed as having a mild cerebral palsy; specific recommendations have been made for speech correction in a youngster with cleft palate; others with limited abilities have been evaluated in an OT prevocational exploration program; a number of visual examinations were recommended, EEG's suggested; etc. It has been computed that the evaluation and counseling process consumed some 20 man-hours per child at a total cost of approximately $160 per case. Estimated savings to the school system as a result of the findings is some $52,000. This is based on the fact that eighteen of forty-six children in special schools were referred to regular schools for an estimated period of 53 child-school years.

Population

A review of the total population seen reveals an age spread of five years, from thirteen to eighteen, with a slight preponderance of males to females (89:75), and a disproportionate percentage of nonwhites (36.5). About one-third of the children come from homes of marginal economic status, with many families receiving public assistance. More than half (56.1 per cent) had both parents in the home, with the others (43.9 per cent) showing equal instances of loss of at least one parent via divorce, death, separation, or desertion. It cannot be assumed that this has been a group statistically representative of the school population as a whole, since many of the youngsters referred to the project were referred by reason of "maladjustment" as well as for cardiac evaluation. It is also assumed that there were others, both with lesser cardiac disturbance and with more severe heart damage, who were not seen, either because the extent of their physical disability was more obvious or because they presented no overt behavior or scholastic difficulty. Hence the findings reported are largely descriptive and provocative rather than explanatory of causal relationships. The research has been supplementary to an ongoing program and not the result of a designed study per se.

Intelligence Test Data

Wherever practicable, individual tests of intelligence were administered at the Rehabilitation Institute. These included the WISC, WAIS, Wechsler-Bellevue I, or the Revised Stanford Binet. Others utilized were the Raven Matrices and the Revised Beta. Scores obtained from the school were based upon either the Kuhlman-Anderson, the Primary Mental Abilities, the California Mental Maturity, or, when the Bureau of Child Study was involved, the WISC or Binet. In view, then, of the conglomerate nature of the test data, no attempt was made to obtain a mean IQ.

Medical Findings

In a follow-up report on eighty-eight cases referred to the Institute between February, 1955, and mid-1957, 67 per cent of all the cardiac referrals were found to be able to participate in full or normal activities. It was found that one-third of the children referred from special schools for the handicapped were able to attend regular schools, and their transfers were effected. Before referral to the project, 81 per cent of all the children seen had been restricted needlessly or the supervision of their activities had been confused, unrealistic, and inconsistent. Of the sixteen congenital heart cases, corrective surgery was recommended in one and the operation was successfully performed. In a review of another seventy-six cases seen by the Institute staff in the two years preceding November, 1959, it was found that approximately half of the students in special schools could be transferred to regular schools.

Among the "cardiac children" in both groups were over a third who were found on examination to have no demonstrable heart disease. Some of these were truly iatrogenic cases. A few were actually homebound shut-ins. These were rather dramatic, with parent, child, and family physician involved, and, as was anticipated, there was some difficulty on the part of parents in accepting the fact that their children were not handicapped. In several instances, there were serious emotional sequelae. All in all, of the 164 youngsters only a third of the total group was in need of any appreciable limitation of physical activity.

Psychosocial Problems

However, not all the benefits derived from the program were of a medical nature. In the most recent consecutive sample of 76 cases, 20 were referred by the Institute to other community agencies for professional assistance with family problems. Approximately half of the 76 were found to have reading problems, many of these of such a nature that they had been considered as being subnormal in intelligence. Almost half of the group were found to have psychological problems warranting further exploration and attention. These ranged from moderate anxiety to psychopathy, brain injury, a reactive depression to sexual trauma, and incipient psychosis. A number of others were salvaged from truancy; one pregnancy was discovered and appropriate prenatal care arranged. In the last two years it was felt that approximately 44 per cent of the cases should ideally have been referred to social agencies for case-work assistance.

In the earlier analysis of eighty-eight cases, 60 per cent were found to have serious reading difficulties. Arithmetic and other basic skills were frequently lacking within the group of poor readers. Some 40 per cent of the children at that time were in need of treatment by child guidance clinics, family service, and other agencies.

Anxiety As a Factor

Hidden disabilities like cardiac disease can be more crippling emotionally than physically. Peer acceptance of the child's disability is often dubious. Symptoms and limitations are likely to be exaggerated, and constant explanation by child or parent may be necessary. There is also, on the other hand, a greater possibility of oversolicitous behavior by sympathetic teachers and parents because of their lack of understanding of the nature of the disease, their guilt feelings, or a projection of their own fears. In general, one can expect an exacerbation of previous ego deficiencies on the part of the child, whatever these may have been, with an increase in passivity and in dependency needs. This is further complicated by the typical adolescent need for testing out independence and aggressivity. But in general these children can be said to be rather depressed, defeatist in attitude, and lacking initiative. There is predominant fear of death and considerable body preoccupation, with anxiety usually covert but often evidenced when under pressure, as in psychological test situations.

Because many of these cardiac conditions were diagnosed years ago, alleviating this anxiety by bringing to the fore the precipitating stress—their cardiac status—is not a simple matter. A youngster who has been at one time led to believe that he will not live beyond the age of fifteen will not at the age of fifteen and a half or sixteen, when told he can live a fairly normal life, accept the new prognosis with equanimity and change his life style; he is likely to continue to live as though each day were his last, just as his parents are likely to accept the new medical findings with some hesitancy. Although some of the children seemed to disregard the physical restrictions placed upon them, those seen in the cardiac program tended to become for the most part observers rather than participants.

This anxiety, masked under various façades—acquiescence, blandness of affect, sullenness, or bravado—was reflected in other areas: in poor reading ability and other academic achievements; difficulty in decision making; compulsivity; inability to tolerate frustration; fear of expressing feeling; and simply regressive behavior—tears, negativism, etc. Although some of this is undoubtedly neurotic anxiety of other causation displaced in one way or another, much of this reactivity must be related to the physical trauma and its sequelae. In general, however, these youngsters tended to function like the older anxiety neurotic who works below the level of his ability and immobilizes himself by a simpler level of achievement.

Comparison with New York Study

In this sense there were considerable similarities between this group and the youngsters in the New York study of the Vocational Advisory Service. Although the income level of the Chicago group appeared to be somewhat higher than that of the eastern families, their limited social experience and cultural impoverishment was quite obvious. This may be related to shunting off of some of the developmental experiences normal for other youngsters at their age level, a result of the physical restrictions imposed upon them and by their periods of hospitalization and illness. The complicated family situations noted in the New York study were also found in the local picture.

The inadequacy of their educational background, with a preponderance of reading difficulties, was noted in the Manhattan study as well, where the reading disability presented in most cases a greater handicap than the cardiac condition itself. On the other hand, we did not observe in the Chicago group as a whole an excessive absence record to account for their educational deficiencies. This may have been hidden in unrecorded tardiness and the half-days and other occasional absences forgotten by both parents and child but which may mount up considerably. We did note, however, that many of the poor readers were having difficulty in this area even in the primary grades but kept no record of the onset of reading disability.

Although there were instances of acting-out behavior in the Chicago group, there was not a great deal of antisocial activity, as found in the New York study. Our group appeared to be rather homebound for the most part, with a consequent restriction of peer group activities and limited participation in afterschool hours activities at school. There was a similarity in the lack of experience of these children in traveling about the city and their lack of knowledge of the various means of transportation or of city areas. Seldom did we see a child who had had the experience of going off "downtown" to a movie with other youngsters, of going to one of the two big league baseball parks, or of visiting the aquarium, planetarium, museum, or beach.

Educational-Vocational Plans

What is even more significant, there did not appear on the whole to be any interest or initiative in exploring other activities. Consequently their vocational outlook, too, was quite unimaginative. Vocational interests were usually quite uncrystallized, like those of many adolescents, but they also exhibited unrealistic aspirations somewhat unexpected in older teen-agers. Typical interest inventories were fairly useless because of lack of try-out juvenile work experiences and unfamiliarity with fields of work.

We made considerable use of our occupational information files, but even this elementary material was all too frequently either uninteresting to them or too threatening. They tended to show more than the usual amount of adolescent confusion and indecision and had evidently avoided thinking of future plans because of anxiety over their physical states. In this respect, in the last two years of the project we frequently simply showed these youngsters how to use a local map, explaining the gridiron layout of the city streets and the use of transportation facilities, how to utilize the classified telephone directory, newspaper ads, etc., and referred them to the school counselor or the state employment office for part-time or summer work experience.

Educational-vocational recommendations at the time of last contact can be summarized somewhat as follows: It was felt that 81 of the 164 children, or somewhat less than 50 per cent, should continue in their same course of study at either the elementary or high school level. Among these, 25 were considered most suited for some specialized studies such as business, shop, or commercial art programs.

Other school objectives: 19 to be enrolled or continue in technical high schools and 17 in vocational high schools—the latter with specific goals such as beauty culture and hairdressing, sewing, practical nursing, millinery, printing, carpentry, auto mechanics, etc. Fourteen students would be dropping school completely because of age, lack of mental ability, or need for immediate medical care. Another 11, it was felt, should either enroll or go on with a part-time work-school "continuation" program. Of those graduating from high school, 7 were recommended for college entrance, 8 for junior college, and 2 for direct job placement through the State Employment Service. Five others needed specialized programs—summer school, EMH classes, private tutoring, etc.

Contributions of Project

What have been the major contributions of the project beyond the usual values for the client in any good counseling program? As seen by the team itself, these were as follows.

For the school: (1) It pointed the way toward the incorporation of such services into the regular administrative program of the public school system. (2) Teachers, teacher-nurses, principals, and other school counseling and administrative personnel were able to assess on the basis of individual children already known to them the value of an extensive work-up of this nature. (3) It was felt that individual personnel became cognizant of the meaning of "rehabilitation" and became active proponents rather than skeptical observers. (4) It established a method of adequate case finding in hidden disabilities such as this and preparing the family, child, and private physician for accepting referral to a special program of this nature. (5) There was a growing awareness that emotional factors involved may outlast and be more significant at times than the physical disability. (6) The program stressed the need for periodic counseling of the handicapped youngster right on home ground, so to speak, for follow-through within the framework of the school itself. (7) The cardiac program served as a model for possible future use in handling other disabilities through an interdisciplinary team approach.

For the parents: (1) Responsible family members had an opportunity to discuss freely the cardiac status of their youngster and to have questions answered in a round table family-type conference, both in a team setting and with individual members of the team. (2) They were offered professional help on other problems that concerned them about family-child relationships and frequently took advantage of this. (3) There was an opportunity to ventilate personal problems and obtain referral to an appropriate resource in the community if they so desired. A certain amount of immediate personal counseling and case work was made available. (4) They could begin to plan realistically for the future.

For the professional staff: (1) There was the demonstration that many children were needlessly restricted in their physical activity and that most could plan for a productive life. (2) Technically, there was confirmation of the value of "multiple-counseling" sessions in which more than one discipline was involved with patient and/or family. (3) The team approach was found essential in diagnostic work-ups, with all four disciplines interacting to their mutual advantage. (4) It was shown that a professional clinic of this kind could function as co-ordinator, so to speak, between private physician, school, parent, and child. (5) The need was found, for the most part, for positive constructive counseling on a pragramatic level rather than for a clinical-psychotherapeutic approach per se. It was recognized that the staff was dealing first of all with the effects of specific physical trauma, and it was essential to handle this in a rather direct manner with questions posed and answers provided. Information giving then had a prominent role concomitant with any counseling that was done.

There are many unresolved questions, continuing problems, and unmet needs evident. Our awareness of these arose not so much from any planned evaluation research as from the operational aspects of the pilot study itself. To begin with, there is the question of stimulating the private physician, who sees the child and family at the acute stage of the illness, to refer to the rehabilitation resource in the community for team work-up and recommendations. The problem, too, of the early screening of emotional problems has special pertinence for those with hidden physical disabilities and should be a concern of both the school and the medical community. Another important aspect is the need for research on the difference in essential personality dynamics and in requisite handling of children with progressive diseases, congenital conditions, and those afflicted by sudden onset.

Another question pertains to the need to retain in school more of these children who are not ready for the world outside. Then there is the matter of dovetailing a child-evaluation program such as this with community facilities for handicapped adults at the time the youngster leaves school. For the school, there is still the need to do periodic preventive counseling, especially with those from economically depressed homes where one parent is likely to be missing from the family constellation. Our experience also points up the need for special efforts to provide more work orientation and enrich life experiences.

Summary and Conclusions

In summary, 164 school-age children with cardiac disabilities were evaluated in a vocational guidance and counseling project. This entailed a five-year demonstration program at a rehabilitation center, in co-operation with a metropolitan school system and local heart association. Although the population was somewhat select, certain findings seem significant. Most of the children were found able to participate in normal activities, and of those in special schools for the handicapped one-third were transferred to regular schools. From 50 to 60 per cent had serious reading problems, and arithmetic skills were frequently lacking within the group. Approximately two-fifths of the cases seen were in need of treatment by child guidance clinics and family service or other social agencies. The psychosocial aspects in this Chicago group showed similarities to a previous New York study. Educational-vocational recommendations were made in each case, and some initial counseling was done with child and parent.

57. What Happens to the College Student with a Physical Handicap? *

RUTH S. LERNER, *Bureau of Education and Vocational Guidance, Hunter College, New York City*
MARION MARTIN, *New York State Department of Education*

THIS IS THE STORY of 59 young people with physical handicaps who attended Hunter College during the last ten years. Its focus is their vocational rehabilitation, since all of them had substantial vocational handicaps and believed that a college education was highly advisable for their successful vocational adjustment. Of this group 33 were graduated, 15 are currently in attendance, while only 11 have withdrawn. Among these were 27 orthopedic and neuromuscular disabilities, 11 cardiacs, 7

* Reprinted by permission of the authors and *Personnel and Guidance Journal*, 34:80–86; October, 1955.

hard-of-hearing, 3 visually limited, 5 with pulmonary tuberculosis, one each of multiple sclerosis, epilepsy, Still's disease, cleft palate, renal tuberculosis, and a chronic skin condition. All these students were serviced jointly by the Hunter College Bureau of Educational and Vocational Guidance and by the Division of Vocational Rehabilitation of the New York State Department of Education.

Hunter, a liberal arts college, is one of the municipal colleges of the city of New York. It is nonresidential and tuition-free. Its main center, located in Manhattan, is convenient to subway and busses; all classrooms are in one building; there is elevator service for students whose physical conditions requires it; and there is a ramp leading out to the street. The program for the physically handicapped has been jointly administered by the office of the Dean of Students and the office of the Bureau of Educational and Vocational Guidance. Health, financial, and social guidance are the responsibility of the Dean of Students; educational and vocational guidance, the responsibility of the Dean of Educational and Vocational Guidance.

Nature of Handicaps and Physical Status

An evaluation of the physical status of each of these students follows. It has been made in terms of their ability to function in daily living activities such as self-care, travel, and ability to communicate in speech and writing.

Of the 22 with orthopedic limitations of the lower extremities, 6 were dependent on wheel chairs, 13 were ambulant with crutches, 2 were ambulant with artificial limbs, and only one was completely ambulant without any prosthetic aids. Of the remaining 5 orthopedically limited, 3 had considerable limitation of function caused by absence or weakness of upper extremities and 3 were limited by extremely small stature. Of the 11 cardiacs, 3 were limited to four-hour activity, 2 to six-hour activity. All the hard-of-hearing (7) were adequate lip readers and were able to participate in classroom activities either with or without a hearing aid. Two had visual limitations in addition to the hearing loss.

Of the visually handicapped, 2 were essentially one-eyed; the third had serious restriction in both eyes. Among the tuberculous, all were cases of arrested pulmonary tuberculosis. Four were on four-hour activity, one on six-hour activity. The one case of multiple sclerosis had poor co-ordination and double vision. Both the case of chronic skin disease and that of Still's disease had limited function of all extremities. The case of nephrectomy had limited daily activity. The case of convulsive disorder was not restricted because seizures were under good control. The case of cleft palate had serious speech difficulty.

Student Background

All these students, at the time of college admission, lived at home with their families. Their major support was supplied by the family, with the exception of 2 supported by public welfare funds because of family illness. Of the remaining 57, 10 of the parents were employed in sales and clerical occupations, 10 in semiskilled occupations, 10 in service occupations; 9 were proprietors of small businesses, mainly stationery stores and restaurants. Six were in professions such as physician, pharmacist, and teacher; 6 were in skilled and 6 in unskilled occupations.

All these students received their high school education under the New York City Board of Education. Twenty-six attended regular classes; 11 attended regular classes with special bus transportation and elevator privileges; 13 received instruction through a combination of hospital, home instruction, and regular class; 9 received home instruction.

Test Findings and College Achievement

These findings have been set up in such a way as to highlight differences, if any, in any of these areas between those who succeeded in college and those who did not. For that reason, each test finding, high school average, and college index has been presented separately in a table showing results for those who graduated, for those who dropped out of college for scholarship reasons, and for current students. The figures in this table do not include all subjects. If at the time of referral the students were already achieving satisfactorily in college, no testing was done.

Table 1 shows that no scholarship dropout had an IQ above 119, that 11 of the 20 graduates for whom IQ's are available fell between 100 and 119, and that one successful student had an IQ of less than 100. There is thus considerable overlap (between 100 and 119 IQ) between those who succeeded in college and those who did not.

The American Council on Education (ACE) Test raw scores show an overlap between 60 and 99 for successful and nonsuccessful students, but no unsuccessful student had an ACE raw score above 91.

As to high school average, all dropouts had high school averages below 80, but 10 of the 33 graduates also had high school averages below 80.

TABLE 1—TEST FINDINGS AND SCHOLASTIC ACHIEVEMENT OF GRADUATES, SCHOLARSHIP DROPOUTS, AND CURRENT STUDENTS

est and holastic chievement	Graduate	Dropouts	Current Students
ST			
): *			
Below 100	1		2
100–109	6	3	3
110–119	5	2	5
120–129	7		4
130–140	1		
CE (raw score):			
Below 60	1		
60–79	3	1	1
80–99	9	3	4
100–119	11		4
120–139	5		3
CHOLASTIC ACHIEVEMENT			
igh school average:			
Below 75		1	2
75–79	10	2†	6
80–84	17		5
85–89	4		2
90–95	2		
ollege index:			
Below 1.6		4	2‡
1.6–2.5	18		9
2.6–3.4	11		3
3.5–4.0	4		1

* Otis IQs have been used except in a few cases where Wechsler-Bellevue scores ere used.
† One student withdrew voluntarily because of poor scholarship.
‡ Only freshmen are allowed to remain with this index.

hus, although 23 of the graduates had high school averages above 80, there considerable overlap of the two groups between 75 and 80 high school verage.

College achievement as measured by index shows the usual distribution, ith the largest number falling into the C group (1.6–2.5), the next rgest into the B group (2.6–3.4), and the smallest number in the A roup (3.5–4.0).

It would appear that *no single* measure available at the time of college dmission can be relied upon to predict college achievement, although igh school average is more reliable than any other single measure. Un-

doubtedly there are factors other than those measured by grades and score
which influence college success. In this connection it is worthy of note tha
2 of the graduates had high school averages and test scores so low tha
they were not admitted as freshmen to the day session. They attende
the School of General Studies as nonmatriculated (fee-paying students
until they achieved the academic requirements for admission. One of thes
students made the dean's list in her senior year.

Counseling

All these students required special opportunities for counseling. Man
of them, while still in high school, were referred by their schools o
medical or other agencies to the Division of Vocational Rehabilitatior

Of the 59, 33 were known to the Division of Vocational Rehabilitatio
prior to college admission; 26 were referred to this agency by the speci
counselor for the handicapped at Hunter College. This latter group wa
not known to any special counseling service prior to college admissior
The age of referral ranges from fourteen to twenty-nine years, with 36 c
the 59 having been referred between sixteen and nineteen years of age
On the whole, the orthopedic and cardiac were referred at an earlier ag
than the other groups. On the other hand, no hard-of-hearing, visuall
limited, or tuberculous was referred before eighteen years of age. Th
reason for this would appear to be that either the age at onset was late
as in the case of the tuberculous (sixteen to twenty years of age), or th
physical limitation did not become a serious handicap until college, as i
the case of the visually impaired and the hard-of-hearing.

There was an interchange of information, prior to admission when po
sible, between the special counselor at the college and the Division c
Vocational Rehabilitation. In cases of severe disability, there was dire
consultation. As soon as possible—prior to admission, in some cases—
a counseling relationship was set up between the special counselor an
the student.

There continued throughout the student's college career a joint respons
bility between the Division of Vocational Rehabilitation and Hunter Co
lege in regard to the total adjustment of the student. Based on need, ther
were conferences on vocational plans, college major, program load, emc
tional problems, medical rehabilitation; and prior to graduation there wa
a review of vocational goals and plans made toward immediate placeme
or graduate study.

The average number of individual counseling sessions ranges from 6 t

10, with as many as 26 at the college and 40 at the Division of Vocational Rehabilitation. The length of counseling contact extends from one through five years at the college and to as long as eight years at the Division of Vocational Rehabilitation. In some of these cases, contact was started during the convalescent stage after illness or while they were in high school. In a few cases, although the student is graduated from the college, service is still not complete and the Division of Vocational Rehabilitation will continue to work with the client until she is employed.

In addition to the counseling hours with the individual agency, there were a number of joint interviews between the student, the Division of Vocational Rehabilitation, and the Bureau of Educational and Vocational Guidance. These were held when plans were being formulated which required joint consultation.

The fact that 48 of the 59 students were referred to the Division of Vocational Rehabilitation for counseling is striking. It would seem to indicate that the services of the Division are being used by students for long-range planning rather than solely for financial or employment assistance.

Major Fields

A survey of the major fields and vocational objectives shows, on the whole, a close relationship between the two in the case of the graduates. In the case of those who dropped out of college, there is naturally a change from the student's original objective. For example, one student entered college planning to become a physiotherapist, withdrew, and then took training as a clerk-typist.

Many of these students entered college with definite vocational goals, some of which were completely realistic both in terms of the training required and the placement possibilities. In some cases, however, the student's original objective appeared to be unrealistic either because of the severity of the handicap or because of scholastic ability.

Wherever feasible, every effort was made to plan in the direction of the student's educational and vocational objective. At the same time, the college program was arranged to allow for exploration and additional training through minor and elective courses in secondary fields which could become vocationally useful if the original objective proved impossible of realization.

Of the 33 graduates, 30 have achieved their final objectives in their major field of interest. Of the remaining 3, one is working in the field of business, her minor interest; one in the accounting division of an educational institution, which was in line with her supplemental training; and one who selected a major field unsuited to her personality and scholastic ability, secured employment in a sales capacity.

Among the graduates, the social work field was chosen by 13; science (biology, chemistry) by 6, English by 3, speech therapy by 2, psychology by 2, history by 2, political science by 2, Latin and Greek by one, economics by one, and mathematics by one. While social work was selected by a majority of these students (10 orthopedics, 2 hard-of-hearing, and one visually limited), no cardiac or tuberculous selected this field. Eight of the graduates attended graduate school in the fields of social work, science, or speech. Three were awarded fellowships for graduate study, and 5 were granted tuition assistance by the Division of Vocational Rehabilitation.

Length of College Course and Age at Graduation

Twenty-four of the group—more than two-thirds—completed the college course within four and one-half years. Those who required longer (2 cardiacs, one tuberculous, and one epileptic) were out of college altogether for one or more semesters for health or financial reasons. Where there has been long hospitalization during the later high school years or many years of home instruction, students have been advised to carry reduced programs for the first year in college. It would appear, therefore, that college may be expected to require four and one-half or five years, except where the physical condition is such as to require intermittent withdrawals from the college for surgery, rest, or further rehabilitation. It is noteworthy that academic failure is not responsible for the lengthening of the college attendance.

None of these students completed college before the age of twenty-one; 7 of them completed it by twenty-one, and more than two-thirds of the group (25 of 33) completed their course by the age of twenty-three. Of the remaining 8, 4 were under twenty-five and 4 over twenty-five at the time of graduation.

Dropouts

Of the total group of 59, 11 dropped out of college for a variety of reasons. This is 18 per cent of the whole group. In the college at large, the net student mortality rate, reported in 1945, was 38.7 per cent. A more ecent study, published in 1953, reported 36 per cent as the net mortality ate at the School of Liberal Arts of the College of the City of New York. 3oth these percentages show that the student mortality of the physically ιandicapped at Hunter is only about half that of the general student population.

Of the 11 who withdrew, 27.3 per cent were dropped by the college for ιoor scholarship. This compares very favorably with the rate in the general tudent population, in which case 45.2 per cent of those who withdrew were ιfficially dropped by the college for poor scholarship. A few other students ‚27.3 per cent) withdrew voluntarily, although they met the college tandards, because they felt their scholarship was not high enough to varrant remaining at college. Of the remainder, 18.4 per cent left for a ιombination of reasons—emotional, financial, and personal; 9 per cent ιor employment; 9 per cent transferred to another type of professional tudy, and 9 per cent left for marriage.

Other Services

Included among the special services provided by the college were certain individual arrangements made by the counselor with instructional ιnd administrative officers of the college. For example, arrangements were ιade with the chairmen of several science departments for the use of pecial equipment in the science laboratories, with the librarian for special ibrary privileges, with the registrar for special programs allowing for ιttendance at treatment centers, rest periods between classes, and a miniιum of traveling between classrooms.

Among the services of the Division of Vocational Rehabilitation are ᴌiagnostic, medical, psychological, and vocational services. Hearing aids ιave been purchased, and financial assistance for college fees, lunch, ιnd transportation costs has been granted. Automobile driving instruction ιas been provided for some students confined to wheel chairs. For those vho withdrew, specialized training courses for business and other vocaιonal areas have been purchased.

Under the administration of the New York City Board of Education ιnd with funds furnished by the Division of Handicapped Children of the ᴌew York State Department of Education, students under the age of ιwenty-one who are seriously disabled and who are unable to use public ιansportation have been provided with private transportation to college ιy taxi and station wagon. In a few instances the Division of the Vocational Rehabilitation assisted in the transportation costs after the twenty-first birthday, provided that the student met the standards for college training.

Other services provided by the college and the Division of Vocational Rehabilitation were the establishment and maintenance of contacts with various medical and other community agencies working with these students.

Summary and Conclusions

1. There is a wide variety of disabilities represented in this group, and every major disability is included.

2. Of the 59 case studies, 48 may be considered academically successful since 33 graduated and 15 are currently in attendance. Of the 11 who withdrew, only 3, or 5 per cent, were dropped by the college for poor scholarship.

3. The prospect for graduation for these students is considerably better than that for the average entering freshman.

4. No single criterion can be relied upon to predict their college achievement. The high school average is better, on the whole, than any other single measure. Motivation toward college success and willingness to exert maximum effort toward that goal appears to be a highly significant factor.

5. A great variety of vocational fields has been chosen by this group, the largest number in the area of service to people. A much smaller percentage of this group than of the Hunter College population as a whole entered the field of education. Although several are engaged in scientific occupations, none have entered the field of medicine or nursing. In general the level of vocational aspirations is toward a higher level of prestige than that of their parents.

6. Most of these students received their basic preparation for entering employment during college attendance.

7. Early and close co-operation between a college guidance service with specialized counseling for the handicapped and a state rehabilitation agency appears to be of great service to the students in their educational and vocational adjustment.

In summary, it may be said that this ten-year study has been primarily a success story showing clearly that, within limits, students with major physical handicaps can be helped to achieve satisfactory college experience and employment if given suitable and adequate services.

58. Marginal, Spuriously Marginal or Handicapped? *

ROBERT P. OVERS, *Vocational Guidance and Rehabilitation Services, Cleveland*

THE SOCIOLOGIST, Parsons, notes that in order for a society to become industrialized, members of the society must place a high value on working hard and consistently. The individual worker is motivated by internalizing this value. Sanctions are employed against those who because of age and sex grouping are expected to be employed or in the labor market but are not. Even those not employable are expected to ready themselves for employment. Vocational rehabilitation is a mechanism for returning such deviants to the fold.

Vocational rehabilitation studies tend to show that if treated as individuals through selective placement and re-engineered jobs, the disabled who are hired are as productive as other workers. However, scientific management does not want to treat workers as individuals. The rationalization process calls for reducing workers to interchangeable and replaceable cogs after the machine prototype.

Handicapped workers are not to be confused with marginal workers, although the two categories may overlap frequently and considerably. By "marginal" we mean those workers who are less efficient than the employer is willing to hire and keep at work unless the demand for products and services is so great that the employer has a sufficiently wide profit margin to make it profitable for him to absorb the greater labor cost of using marginal workers. Workers may be marginal in a variety of ways. They may lack the physical, mental, emotional, or motivational ability to do the job at an appropriate rate of output. They may have too frequent absences. They may make excessive errors as a result of poor judgment, perceptual deficiencies, or lack of skill. In more intangible ways they may interfere with adequate production. Because of poor interpersonal relations they may cause friction with management or other workers, making work an uncomfortable social situation for everyone there. The

* Reprinted by permission of the author and *Rehabilitation Counseling Bulletin,* 7:1:21–27; September, 1963.

marginal worker is indeed a "worrisome thing." In the business ethos h
is a production "bug" to be avoided at all costs like a worn-out o
obsolete machine. Full employment is strenuously resisted on the groun
that "those fellows will be cluttering up our plants." During World War I
this complaint was voiced at theoretical and folk levels. The Nationa
Association of Manufacturers put it this way:

Finally, when millions of men are taken into the armed forces, this curtailmer
of the labor supply, in combination with the necessity of getting military supplie
and the willingness to pay almost any price for them, causes business to bi
for labor and accept a degree of inefficiency which at other times would b
ruinous.

Yet marginality is relative, not absolute. Expanding man power to a reall
full utilization of the labor force is seen by Likert and Seashore in
different light.

A dramatic demonstration of the adaptability and modifiability of manpowe
occurred during the months following America's entry into World War II
Millions of people changed to new occupations completely unlike those to whic
they had become accustomed. Millions of people—aged, handicapped, and non
employed—became a part of the manpower pool and acquired job skills or
technical competence. The existing estimates of the availability of manpower i
the various occupational categories became meaningless. . . . Marginal peopl
—formerly considered inappropriate for certain jobs—were successfully taugh
the necessary skills.

Wherever we wish to peg our own estimate of the relative efficiency o
the marginal worker, it is certain that he occupies a specialized place i
the labor market. It seems likely that marginal workers receive marke
competition for jobs from productive workers working overtime or workin
a second job. The productive worker is apt to produce at a greater rat
on a second job or on overtime than the rate at which the margina
worker will produce during his first 40 hours. As, spurred by automation
the work week decreases, the lot of the marginal worker in this respec
may be expected to worsen. Marginal workers also compete with eac
other. Furthermore, the kinds of jobs they are capable of doing withi
the price-profit system are, in a relative sense, decreasing.

Let us now consider the relationship of the marginal worker to th
occupationally handicapped worker. The sentimental "hire the handi
capped" approach has led many to overlook the fact that the handicappe

as a group are much more likely to be marginal than a group of non-handicapped workers. Such studies as have been done have compared handicapped workers who were actually hired with the nonhandicapped. It seems certain that these were a highly selected group. Employers rarely hire handicapped workers who are also marginal.

The acquisition of a handicap frequently converts a productive worker into a marginal worker. For instance, an individual of low intelligence and little education and with social skills appropriate to his status may have been a highly productive worker as a construction laborer. He injures his back and is no longer able to do this work. His potential for retraining is low; consequently, he is now a marginal worker in relation to any other occupation.

As we have mentioned before, not all physically, mentally, and emotionally handicapped workers are occupationally handicapped. For instance, in a great many jobs a lower-extremity amputation fitted with a prosthesis causes no difficulty. Neither are all occupationally handicapped workers marginal. Although occupationally handicapped, a worker may be motivated to stick to a job in spite of pain or fatigue and maintain a high level of productivity. Other occupationally handicapped workers are so adept in their interpersonal relations on the job that co-workers and bosses help them maintain a satisfactory rate of productivity.

In addition to marginality resulting from inferior productive capacity, other workers are relegated to a marginal status insofar as hiring preference is concerned by assumptions made about them by employment managers and employment interviewers. Intermittently subject to this unhappy attention are racial and religious minorities, older workers, young workers, and parolees, as well as the occupationally handicapped. We may call these the spuriously marginal workers. Barkin likewise reaches this conclusion.

There is the large group of unemployed in areas of declining employment for whom alternative jobs have to be developed, preferably in their own communities. But there is an even larger group who suffer from religious, educational, or mental handicaps; or prejudices against advanced age, sex, union affiliation, or other similar factors. These persons are often black-listed and relegated to the human scrap heap.

The following paradigm may help highlight the interrelation of actual marginal workers, spuriously marginal workers, and the occupationally handicapped.

PARADIGM OF INTERRELATIONSHIPS AMONG MARGINAL, SPURIOUSLY MARGINAL, AND OCCUPATIONALLY HANDICAPPED WORKERS

Marginality Resulting from Actual Productive Inferiority	Spurious Marginality
1M physically handicapped (untrained and/or incorrectly placed)	1S physically handicapped (if trained and correctly placed)
2M mentally handicapped (incorrectly placed and/or ineffectively supervised)	2S mentally handicapped (if correctly placed and effectively supervised)
3M emotionally handicapped (incorrectly placed and/or ineffectively supervised)	3S emotionally handicapped (if correctly placed and effectively supervised)
4M older workers (incorrectly placed)	4S older workers (if correctly placed)
5M alcoholics (by definition those whose symptoms resulting from alcoholic intake have resulted in adverse job performance)	
	5S women
	6S members of racial groups against whom prejudice is felt
	7S members of religious groups against whom prejudice is felt
	8S entry workers
	9S parolees

The dyads 1M-1S through 4M-4S are mutually exclusive. Aside from this, any given individual may fit into more than one group in the table above. These are, of course, ideal type categories. In actuality it is assumed that workers may be arranged in a continuum along a dimension of productivity.

The chief purpose of vocational rehabilitation counseling is to help occupationally handicapped clients move into a status of employment or at least employability. This may occur in a variety of ways.

1. Counseling may help clients make a suitable vocational choice preliminary to rehabilitation training (1M, 3M).

2. Counseling may help clients make a suitable vocational choice preliminary to job placement (1M, 2M, 3M, 4M).

3. Counseling may produce a vocational appraisal useful to a placement interviewer in effecting satisfactory placement (1M, 2M, 3M, 4M).

4. Counseling may effect an attitude change in the client so that he is in some cases able to overcome the prejudice of employers and escape from the spuriously marginal categories (1S, 3S, 4S, 5S, 6S, 7S, 8S, 9S).

5. Counseling may produce useful recommendations for effective supervision techniques (2M, 3M).

In addition, a major task of counseling is to change the client's perception about his handicap. For those clients so incapacitated as to be unable to work, counseling may help them utilize their remaining capacities in study or hobbies to substitute for the satisfactions they would ordinarily find in work. This function is shared by educational and occupational therapists, social workers, and many others.

Within the current individualistic approach to vocational rehabilitation, vocational rehabilitation training is the most effective technique for preparing an occupationally handicapped individual for a job. The marginal worker can climb out of his unemployable position by learning a skill the employer wants and not generally available on the labor market. In a sense, rehabilitation training creates a position where one did not exist.

Such a solution is available only to those who reach a fairly high skill level, and there are limits to this solution. Because of low intelligence, illiteracy, geographic and social class immobility, family responsibilities, and inflexible attitudes, not all the occupationally handicapped are amenable to vocational rehabilitation training. An additional group has the ability to reach only a minimum level even with training.

Under the tenets of one school of economic theory, as described by Galbraith, a pool of unemployed is necessary to prevent inflation. If this assumption is correct, then whenever a vocationally handicapped person is rehabilitated and put to work, an employed worker must become unemployed in order to maintain the necessary level of the pool. Our conclusion from this must be that the handicapped individual is more valued by society than the nonhandicapped and to the extent of a considerable investment in vocational counseling, training, and placement. Other paradoxes arise. Some categories of the disabled—as, for instance, war veterans with service-connected disabilities—receive a tax-free disability compensation which, given a fairly severe disability and adding allowances for dependents, approaches or even exceeds the average factory wage. From a sheerly financial point of view, these veterans are better able to weather unemployment than an able-bodied individual with a similar number of dependents. In addition, the disabled are to some extent better able to withstand the guilt associated with failure to bring home a pay check.

For a bird's-eye point of view, the federal government has at times invested a considerable sum of money in vocational rehabilitation programs, while at the same time the Federal Reserve Bank has taken fiscal steps to maintain unemployment. The net effect is that in times of cyclical unemployment and in places of regional unemployment, the occupationally handicapped are being trained to compete with the nonhandicapped for nonexistent jobs. Where there is only seasonal and frictional unemployment, the retrained occupationally handicapped person still shares with the able-bodied unemployed person the risk that he, as an individual, will be one of those remaining in the unemployed pool.

The physically, mentally, and emotionally handicapped are victims of three paradoxically interwoven threads of Judaic-Christian thought.

1. Christian medical ethics decree that people, no matter how severely disabled, shall be kept living whenever possible.

2. The rationalizational of work ethos (scientific management) decrees that the level of worker performance shall be maintained as high as possible.

3. The Protestant ethic decrees (except for the lower-lower and upper-upper groups) that for those within the labor force age bracket, even with adequate income, failure to work is slightly less than honorable.

Summarizing, the disabled are: (1) kept alive, (2) denied the opportunity to work, and (3) kept in a state of guilt.

How can the rehabilitation counselor, in his professional role, cope with these paradoxes? Is it enough to continue to apply prescribed techniques to the solution of individual case-work problems? Is it enough to seek constantly to improve these case-work techniques? I do not believe so. The measure of a profession is the degree to which, on a policy-making basis, it copes with the problem within its sphere of competence. If not able to resolve the paradoxes and conflicts thrust upon it by more powerful systems in other segments of the culture, at least it clarifies for itself as a profession and for the public at large what the areas of conflict are and why the profession is limited by forces beyond its control in solving the problems within its jurisdiction. The profession, furthermore, has the obligation to forecast for society and especially for legislators the corrective action needed to carry out the mandate assumed by the profession. An occupation is not a profession until it is autonomous in this respect.

59. Body Image in Counseling the Handicapped *

THOMAS A. ROUTH, *Counselor, Florida Council for the Blind, Tampa*

IT IS DIFFICULT for a counselor to work with any handicapped client who is not ready to accept the fact of his disability. In such a situation it is important for the counselor to realize that it is not necessary for him *personally* to do something about this matter.

Other forces are at play, such as the social, economic, and environmental background of the client. In actuality, there is a play of many such factors which affect the client relative to his acceptance of his disability.

The counselor's judgments, therefore, about a particular client's disability are necessarily influenced by the cause of the disability, time of onset, and the physical as well as the mental and emotional consequences of the disability.

In strict logic, a counselor may not assume that a handicapped client understands the true and essential meaning of his handicap, because such an understanding involves the concept of *acceptance* of the disability. The theories of *nonacceptance* of disability which may be encountered many times seem very strange to those individuals who have an intact body image.

Self-Concepts Formed Early

The concept of a body image is formed unconsciously in childhood. A person generally tends to think of himself in terms of that time in his life when he functioned best and when he was at the peak of his physical abilities. Quite naturally, then, this concept is usually associated with a certain age.

As an emotionalized concept, it has tremendous importance for any individual because it affects his integration as a "whole" person. For the handicapped client, this concept of a body image implies magical propensities of power and capability, and since the client has lost the "wholeness" of his person by acquiring a disability, he therefore—in his own mind—

* Reprinted by permission of the author and *Vocational Guidance Quarterly*, 7:127–130; Winter, 1958.

may be less of a person. This very feeling may well cause him problems in other areas of feelings, attitudes, and emotions.

Of far greater importance is the fact that the client's concept of his own body image has emotional substance and meaning for him far beyond his own motor or sensory abilities. It is a personalized concept that is not subject to logical argumentation or manipulation. No matter how well educated and intelligent a handicapped client may be, his concept of his own body image can be modified only by emotional factors because, of its very essence, it is an emotional entity. No counselor has ever been successful in trying to argue a client out of his feelings by logic.

It is almost axiomatic to state that any person incurring a disability becomes a different psychological person from his former self. His entire concept changes. Regardless of his particular disability, his inner psychological self is changed. In reality, the physical disability is the very least part of the person to be affected. The client's hopes, dreams, fears, aspirations, his interpersonal relationships, his concept of his own relationship to the world around him, his concept of himself—all of these are vastly and very materially changed.

Acceptance Is Difficult

If counseling with such a disabled person is to be effective, it should start with the major premise of first having the client recognize this change in himself.

Perhaps the greatest single factor responsible for vocational rehabilitation failures dealing with the physically handicapped can be placed under the heading of "lack of acceptance of disability" on the client's part. Undoubtedly, a great many counselors have seen intelligent men walk into a wall because they did not believe the evidence of their senses that they were blind. As a case in point, there is the example of John Q, who says, "Well, I can see that Mr. X is blind. Mr. X himself can see (know) that he is blind. Therefore, Mr. X and I accept the fact that he is blind, and we may thus proceed to deal with his blindness as a vocational handicap." Such an approach to a problem sounds logical. John Q, however, is cursorily dismissing a lifetime of psychological conditioning and emotional integration which Mr. X has built up, based upon a highly individualized concept of his own body image.

It may be necessary for a counselor to help a handicapped client develop an appropriate, acceptable, and true concept of his own body image. In the main, such clients tend to think of their "loss" rather than of their "self," whether they be blind, amputees, or otherwise disabled persons.

"Real You" Is Featured

The counselor can help a handicapped client begin to develop a true concept of his own body image by finding out about the range of personal satisfactions which the client has had. Gradually, the counselor can get the client to realize that there are many key things still remaining about his original person. To do this effectively, a counselor should try to build up positive things about the client. "What is the *real you,* your handicap or your personality?" Ideally, the counselor should first develop the idea of the *real you* and then get the idea across to the handicapped client that *"the real you is still there."*

Without an adequate knowledge of precisely what psychological acceptance of disability entails for the handicapped client and without the client's having an adequate concept of his own body image, it is very little wonder that at times a counselor may feel that he has disposed of this problem of acceptance on the part of the client because the client shows enthusiasm for preliminary plans made for him. A counselor may think that such a client's motivation is excellent. Such a conclusion may be correctly drawn *only* if the client's feelings and attitudes about his disability have been taken into consideration.

In order to help a handicapped client develop a true concept of his own body image, it is necessary that the counselor cultivate specific skills and then practice them in helping the handicapped client react to his disability. One of the more effective of these skills is the use of the permissive, nonjudgmental, client-centered approach. It is that approach whereby the client is given the opportunity of unburdening his feelings, attitudes, and emotions about himself and his handicap. It is the approach wherein the counselor assumes a passive role and allows the client complete freedom in the telling of his problem.

A handicapped client has not satisfactorily accepted his disability if he simply acknowledges the fact that he is disabled and, because of this is per se reduced to a life of vocational helplessness. Such a client is showing only a passive acceptance and is resigning himself to the inevitable course of "fate." Probably he is very fearful and apathetic, living with a constant sense of foreboding failure. Because of such attitudes, his entire psychological self is likely to slowly atrophy.

Other disabled clients may accept their handicap negatively by refusing to even recognize the fact that they are disabled. And even when confronted with definitive medical evidence of his disability, such a one may cling so adamantly to his own belief that he will defy the counselor. In other words, the client's denial of the disability is at best a compensatory device which in some manner he feels is filling one of his three emotional needs for acceptance, significance, and safety.

Counselor's Feelings Important

It is important for all counselors to realize that this problem of psychological acceptance of disability would exist in anyone who suddenly acquired a disability. For the most part, however, society remains woefully ignorant about handicapped people. If any counselor should feel that he is personally exempt from these very feelings about disability, he is indulging in a type of wishful thinking that has no place in objective counseling.

If, for example, a counselor finds that he is dreading a forthcoming interview with a handicapped client, it would be wise for him to look considerably below the surface to discover adequate and appropriate reasons for his own feelings. If he cannot discover these reasons or if he can do nothing constructive about overcoming his own emotional blocking, it would be better for him to transfer the case of the handicapped client to another counselor. Such a counselor should realize that such deep-seated reasons and motivations often are not available to his own view either; because of their essence, they are unconscious in both clients and counselors alike.

Many clients who have maladjustments which are primarily emotional acquire some superimposed physical disability. A counselor should realize that many an ostensible physical disability may be a convenient smoke screen behind which the client may try to take refuge. In such cases it is important that the counselor learn about the client's maladjustments prior to the time that he acquired his present physical disability.

Sometimes a counselor finds that the client has had previous attacks of anxiety; that in the past he has had hysterical outbursts or that his glaucoma was only the last in a long series of stress diseases. The counselor may also find that the client has exploited his disability either by wandering around from place to place or by becoming a public charge. In such cases, a counselor may save valuable time and effort in determining at an early date the possible nonfeasibility of the client for vocational rehabilitation services.

Time Lag Can Be Harmful

Sometimes a counselor may begin to work with a client after an unfortunate time lag during which the client's incentive and morale are starting to wane, and he may be retreating into the role of complete invalidism. An inexperienced counselor having such a case assigned to him may be confronted with a strange lack of progress in the case. If this is so, the counselor will not be too illogical in suspecting that the essential problem may entail the client's lack of inner psychological acceptance of his disability. This may be manifested by the client in many ways, such as excessive complaints or pain, overmedication, dissatisfaction with a series of doctors or counselors, temper tantrums at home, marital crises, or violent emotional reactions.

In cases such as these, the counselor would do well to explore the entire personality structure of the client concerned. If a counselor suspects or detects a lack of inner psychological acceptance of disability and if such a condition is of long-standing duration on the client's part, he should realize that the case requires intensified clinical counseling.

It is important, therefore, for any counselor dealing with the physically handicapped to consider the client's concept of his own body image and his acceptance or lack of acceptance of his disability. Certainly, no vocational planning as such should be undertaken until these basic problems are first cleared up.

60. Creative Habilitation of the Cerebral-Palsied Child *

EDGAR J. SCHILLER, *Executive Director, Cerebral Palsy Association of Western New York, Buffalo*

A RECENT PROGRAM offered by the Cerebral Palsy Association of Western New York, Inc., provided a unique opportunity for parents of cerebral-palsied children to find fresh approaches to their many problems by appli-

* Reprinted by permission of the author and *Journal of Rehabilitation,* 27:14–15, 39, 42; 1961.

cation of current creative problem-solving principles and procedures, including "brainstorming." Since this technique is widely used in industry and government, it was also deemed feasible for solution of problems by parents of handicapped children.

The program consisted of five two-hour sessions once a month, under the leadership of Sidney J. Parnes, director of the University of Buffalo's Creative Problem-Solving Institute and director of creative education.

Opportunity was given for selecting the most important problems of the parents and applying creative procedures to find helpful solutions. The parents, working together, learned that they had much creative ability which they could use effectively in solving their problems.

After orientation to the course, Dr. Parnes taught the participants how to overcome obstacles to creative efficacy and explained ideation techniques, which led into group brainstorming. Group brainstorming is basically an idea-finding session, covered by four simple rules. These rules, according to Dr. Alex F. Osborn's widely used textbook, *Applied Imagination,* are:

1. Criticism is ruled out until after the session.
2. The wilder the ideas, the better. It is easier to tame down than to think up.
3. The greater the number of ideas, the more likelihood of winners.
4. In addition to thinking up ideas of their own, participants should suggest improvements and combinations of others' ideas.

Parents brought up many problems, each of which called for considerable discussion and consideration before it could be crystallized into a simple statement that would serve best for creative attack. Typical problems of the cerebral-palsied child, after analysis and crystallization, were found to be:

1. Instilling in him the desire to develop the use of his hands and fingers.
2. Getting him to express himself among strangers or company.
3. Increasing his desire for accomplishment.
4. Getting him to communicate his ideas.
5. Getting him to make the fullest use of his limited mental capacity.
6. Overcoming his feeling that people do not want him around.

All participants in the group sessions were given a statement of the problem and opportunity to question the related parent concerning the particular cerebral-palsied child. After this period of briefing, the moderator gave the signal to start brainstorming. During the next thirty minutes, suggestions came thick and fast; hands waved for recognition and fingers snapped to indicate that an idea was "hitchhiked" from a previous suggestion. Some suggestions brought giggles, others outright laughter; but, for the most part, participants worked seriously—yet in an uninhibited atmosphere. The brainstorming sessions were fun, but they were not *for* fun. Suggestions were made in dead earnest by people who wanted to help.

The results were impressive. Nearly a hundred suggestions were made in each case. Some were impractical, some had already been used, others were trite or even silly; but many good ideas appeared on every checklist.

Following are two of the cases, each with its rehabilitation problem and checklist. The lists, as shown here, include only twenty of the suggestions that were developed in the group idea-finding sessions during the course. Members used the *total* list of ideas in each case as a checklist in working out solutions to their respective problems.

Several of the enrollees have reported gratifying results attained by the use of specific ideas on the checklist or adaptations of them.

Case 1

A boy, aged five, cannot hold things very well and finds it difficult to use his hands and fingers. He keeps them clenched most of the time, opening them only when he is relaxed and interested in what he's doing.

The problem: How can we instill in him the desire to develop the use of his hands and fingers?

The checklist:

1. Put him in the bath and let him play with toys of sponge material.

2. Put him outdoors in a bathing suit with a pan of water and sponge. Have him empty the pan by squeezing the water over his head.

3. Teach him to play with mud and/or clay. Show him how to make little balls by rolling the material between his palms and to shape simple figures of men, birds, and animals with toothpicks for legs. He can learn to make gifts—ash trays, vases, etc.—to be displayed and treasured.

4. Give him soft wire, pipe cleaners, aluminum foil, etc. and teach him to make Christmas tree ornaments and other items by bending and assembling the materials.

5. Teach him to use hands and fingers to make shadow pictures on the wall and to play finger games such as "pease porridge hot," "cat's cradle," etc.

6. Let him help mother by opening jars and bottles, kneading dough, wringing out and hanging the wash, turning lights on and off, adjusting window shades, etc. For his help he might be paid in pennies that *he* must put into a piggy bank.

7. Interest him in helping prepare his own meals. He can learn to stir cooky batter, roll it out, and cut it into shapes. Teach him to shell peas, shuck corn, squeeze oranges for juice, use egg beater to make his own milk shakes, mix Jell-O, open cereal boxes, break eggs, make toast, butter rolls.

8. Encourage him to pick flowers (even weeds) and arrange them in vases for the house.

9. Interest him in gardening, starting with a window tray or flowerpots in the house. Teach him to turn over the soil, plant fast-growing seeds, and water them daily. Later, let him work outdoors on a larger scale with larger tools. He might grow vegetables for family meals.

10. Provide him with finger paints, crayons, chalk, and a fountain pen with a cap that has to be unscrewed; then encourage him to draw, write, and paint.

11. Dip his fingers into paint, then press them on paper to see how far he can stretch them. Do this daily and keep a record of his progress. Set goals with small rewards for attainment.

12. Prepare surprise packages (which might be used as rewards for certain accomplishments), consisting of a small toy or coin inside many wrappings of paper or string so it would take much fingerwork to find it. Also have him prepare (with much wrapping and tying) "surprises" for his relatives and friends.

13. Interest him in knitting, weaving, crocheting, and tatting. Show him how to make washcloths, doilies, and other simple items. If he shows keen interest, he might progress to making hooked rugs.

14. Provide him with a hammer, nails, and scraps of soft wood; show him how to use them. Provide additional wood-working tools when he is ready for them.

15. Give him soft rope and teach him to tie simple knots; then progress to complicated ones. The Boy Scout handbook will provide all needed information.

16. Play cards with him. This involves shuffling and dealing the cards as well as arranging and playing his hand. He might practice simple card tricks calling for sleight of hand.

17. Provide old magazines and teach him to make scrapbooks by cutting out and pasting up selected pictures. How about starting a stamp album?

18. Teach him to string things. Start with something easy—doughnuts or pretzels—then progress through spools and big beads to buttons and little beads.

19. Get him a pet that he must brush and feed daily.

20. Get him a toy piano and teach him simple tunes.

This boy showed great interest in painting and sculpture. He began with finger paints and progressed to water colors and brushes. He has learned to grip the brush and guide it with a fair degree of accuracy to fill in predrawn pictures. Meanwhile he enjoys working with clay; his recent work shows much improvement over his early attempts. Most important, he is more relaxed and increasingly inclined to keep his hands open rather than clenched into fists.

Case 2

A boy of seven, in second grade, has trouble swallowing anything but liquids, has trouble gripping things, and finds it difficult to reach his mouth with food. He is unable to walk but is learning to use crutches. Although he can dress and feed himself, he takes forever to do it. He is fond of TV, particularly sporting events. The boy is alert and has a good sense of humor but is too willing to accept his limitations.

The problem: In what ways can we increase his desire for accomplishment?

The checklist:

1. Insist that he dress and eat breakfast without help in time to catch the school bus. To allow more time, get him up earlier. This means he'll have to go to bed proportionately earlier and miss some of his TV programs. When he speeds up his dressing and eating, permit him to sleep later, stay up later, and have more TV.

2. Let him sleep in some of his clothes to speed up dressing. Also, get him clothes that go on easily, such as loafers, instead of shoes with laces, and shirts with big buttons or pull-over sweaters without buttons. Button the lower part of his shirts when they are folded after laundering; then he can slip them over his head and have only the top buttons to do.

3. Make a contest of his dressing: "See if you can get dressed before I have your breakfast ready."

4. Interest him in firemen and make believe he *is* one. Refer to the alarm clock as a fire alarm. Stress that "firemen don't dawdle." Give him five minutes to put on his shirt, etc. Use pictures of fire engines to decorate his room.

5. Urge him to speed up eating breakfast without help. If he slops food on his shirt, suggest that he leave off the shirt until after breakfast or use a bib. You might serve a liquid breakfast that he can drink through a straw.

6. Build up handles of fork and spoon so he can get a better grip on them; then make believe the spoon is a shovel and the fork a spear. Make a game of spearing the food on his plate. You might use paper plates with targets painted on them—put the food in the "bull's-eye," and keep score. The fun of playing a game will help take his mind off swallowing difficulty.

7. Provide finger food such as chicken-in-a-basket, shoestring potatoes, and sandwiches, so he won't have to use utensils. Let him watch TV while eating.

8. Select a TV program he particularly likes and schedule dinner so he'll have to finish the meal within a given time or miss the show. Utilize his interest in sports by providing hot dogs while he watches baseball and football on TV.

9. Put your voice, or the voice of an athlete friend he admires, on a tape recorder. Let him hear, "Hurry up, Andy," "Let's go, Andy," while dressing and eating. This could be made into a chant, with music and rhythm.

10. Provide music and teach him to dress and eat in tempo. Stimulate his interest in this by telling him that the dancers he admires on TV had to start by learning their steps, one by one, in time to music. He can learn to eat in the same way.

11. Utilize his interest in sports to spur his desire to conquer the crutches by encouraging him to take an active part in athletics. Show him how to support

himself with one crutch and make use of his free hand to bowl, play shuffle-board, etc., in the basement.

12. Provide him with a football helmet for his athletic efforts so he'll have no fear of hurting himself if he falls down. Place a football on the floor and let him learn to kick it.

13. Take him to sports contests, particularly the basketball games of the "wheel-chair" league. Take him to bowling alleys and let him play, after he has learned to roll a ball at home.

14. Draw lines on the basement floor and have him follow them on his crutches. Set a goal for each day—five steps, seven steps, etc.

15. Take him to as many places as possible—the park, zoo, firehouse, museums, etc.—to increase his social awareness.

16. Establish a goal by putting up a picture and/or graph to show how you expect him to be next week or next month.

17. Provide him with a peg baseball game and other peg games that will compel him to use his fingers in handling the pegs.

18. Build up his self-respect by giving him decisioins to make: what shirt to wear, what to eat at mealtime, what to do in his playtime.

19. Reward him for each accomplishment. Rewards might include a special dessert, candy, a small toy, etc.

20. Encourage him to help around the house as much as he is able. Give him small, simple tasks to help mother, and make a big thing of what he does by telling friends and relatives about it when he is able to overhear.

Great progress was shown by the boy of Case 2. He now dresses himself without help, and his eating habits have improved. He spends time at the piano every day and can play several simple tunes. He holds his fingers up, one at a time, while counting to ten, then closes each one in turn, while continuing to count to twenty. He repeats the finger exercise while counting in Spanish, then does it again in Italian. He now walks easily with his crutches and works toward the day when he can support himself on a single crutch so he can dribble a basketball.

Several parents found helpful suggestions on other parents' checklists, which indicates that some suggestions may prove useful in solving other rehabilitation problems.

Full details on creative problem solving and group idea finding are available without charge. Free literature explaining these procedures may be obtained from the Creative Education Foundation, a nonprofit organization founded in 1954 by Dr. Alex F. Osborn. The address is 1614 Rand Building, Buffalo 3, New York.

It should be kept in mind that the suggestions on these lists were intended merely as possible leads to solutions—a stimulating guide to help in developing a plan of action.

The value of these ideas will depend largely on what is done with them. Parents of other cerebral-palsied children are urged to add to the ideas on the checklist by doing some additional brainstorming.

61. Some Experiences in Educating Physically Handicapped Students *

WILLIAM V. TUCKER, *Kansas State Teachers College*

RICHARD E. OLSON, *Kansas State Teachers College*

IN RECENT YEARS several articles have been published on various aspects of college education for physically handicapped students. Early attempts at educating paraplegics at the University of California at Los Angeles were discussed by Atkinson in 1948. Some of the opportunities for wheelchair students in the University of Tampa were described in the *Crippled Child* in 1954. The nature of the job performed by the counselor of physically handicapped students at the University of Minnesota was presented by Berdie in 1955. Condon and Lerner considered adaptations made in New York colleges for physically handicapped students in 1956. Condon, in 1957, published the results of a nationwide survey of special facilities for the handicapped in colleges and universities having enrollments of over 1,200. A special report describing modified services to accommodate physically handicapped students at Southern Illinois University was prepared by Fife in 1960. While these reports are useful in their descriptions of certain educational opportunities for disabled students, they do not supply material for the study of complete experiences in any given college. It is the purpose of this present study, therefore, to detail many of the experiences at Kansas State Teachers College obtained during eight years of providing accommodations for physically handicapped stu-

* Reprinted by permission of the junior author and *Personnel and Guidance Journal*, 41:803–807; May, 1963.

dents. By considering these experiences and reports of experiences in other institutions, one may make specific conclusions and recommendations adaptable to similar situations in other colleges and universities. The usefulness of these experiences will vary according to the needs and purposes of the investigator.

Admissions

The principal responsibility of Kansas State Teachers College is the education of eligible persons in Kansas. A particularly distinctive college mission is the provision of educational opportunity for physically handicapped students. The Kansas Division of Vocational Rehabilitation (VRS) currently sponsors sixty clients on this campus, and five additional students are sponsored by other agencies for rehabilitation. VRS provides comprehensive rehabilitation services, but the College role is limited to education and those operations ancillary to this objective.

Most physically handicapped students have enrolled either as freshmen or transfer students from two-year colleges. Each student declares his physical disabilities on a personal data form, and each is required to submit a physical examination report; but special regulations are not imposed on disabled students. Individuals reporting disabilities are informed of the facilities and services available, and occasionally a student is referred to an agency for assistance. Special insurance is not required, since all students are covered by the general student health insurance program. Severely disabled students are asked to select a local physician at the time of their enrollment in order to expedite referral in the event of illness or injury. No limitations have been placed by the administration upon the number of disabled students to be accepted, but the lack of physical facilities, such as housing, has, to some extent, limited the out-of-state enrollment.

College policy has been to accept those persons who have qualified for sponsorship by Kansas VRS. For students not provided with agency support, it has sometimes been necessary to work out arrangements in consultation with various members of the College staff, a group which usually consists of the Dean of Men or the Dean of Women and representatives from Counseling, Housing, Student Services, and the proposed major area of study.

There are set procedures governing the matter of academic probation and dismissal. Students required to withdraw for academic reasons may petition the Academic Standing Committee for reinstatement. Leniency is sometimes granted students in consideration of physically handicapping conditions.

Special Procedures

Since 1958, one person in the Division of Student Services has been assigned part-time duties of supervising rehabilitation student affairs. In 1960, responsibility for physically handicapped students was assigned to the Counseling Bureau, of which the present counselor for vocational rehabilitation is a regular member. Co-ordination of policy and procedures throughout the College is now possible.

The academic advising of all students is handled by the faculty in the various departments of the College. Rehabilitation students desiring testing and counseling services have made use of the Counseling Bureau along with able-bodied students. The Counselor for Vocational Rehabilitation has resources with which to examine many aspects of the individual. Most severely disabled students have had special counseling prior to enrollment. Psychiatric consultations are regularly scheduled, and other counseling services are available through various referral agencies.

Before modified facilities made it easier for wheel-chair students to get to classes, some classes were arranged for their benefit. Classes were also relocated in more accessible places, and schedules were planned so that classes might be attended in sequence on the same floor, or at least in the same building. Equivalent instructional facilities were often not available in the new location, and the moving of large classes was considered impractical. Therefore, arrangements were made with the athlete's "K Club" for volunteers to carry wheel-chair students to classes located on floors not accessible by elevator.

Some disabled students have been granted special assistance in enrollment as far back as this study was carried. When only a few disabled students were involved, individual arrangements were made through the Office of Student Services. With the larger numbers of disabled students currently on the campus, enrollment and book-store purchases are completed by proxy. The deadline for payment of fees has been extended and book-store credit given to those persons who are sponsored by an agency. Deferred payment was found to be necessary since agencies generally did not make payment until bills were processed for approval. Prior to a given enrollment period, representatives for the agencies supplied the book store and business office with the names of students who were eligible for deferred-payment privileges.

The first instance of attendant service was arranged for a girl who was confined to a wheel chair, and since 1955 male and female disabled students have had attendants. These attendants are locally referred to as "pushers," because the nature of their assignment includes pushing the wheel-chair students. The duties performed by these pushers vary according to the needs of the disabled person, and frequently they involve helping with personal matters and room cleanliness. Students may be pushers only if they also live in college housing, and frequently the job is filled by a classmate. A unique solution to the need for attendant service has been worked out by two disabled classmates through three years of attendance at this College. One person is confined to a wheel chair, and the other is blind. In this rather remarkable arrangement, the blind student exchanges a push for steerage. Most pushers are paid by the VRS. In some early cases, when the number of disabled students was small, payment was augmented by the College, but this practice has been discontinued.

The necessity for pusher service is determined by consultation with agency representatives or College counselors, when no agency support is involved. It has been the policy of the College to permit disabled students to have a pusher if payment can be privately arranged.

Readers and note takers have been used by blind students. Payment for this service has been made by the sponsoring agency, and many sighted students have been anxious for this opportunity to earn extra money.

Many other special procedures are arranged for disabled students on an individual basis. The counselor for vocational rehabilitation works with professors in arranging special seating for students with hearing disabilities and may inform staff members when students subject to seizures are enrolled in their classes.

Students are not exempted from generally required courses because of a physical disability. Individual Gymnastics, a special Physical Education course for men, was added to the curriculum in 1951. The subject matter of the course has been adapted to the students' disability and includes such activities as weight lifting, tumbling, swimming, and basketball. The title of the course has since been changed to Adaptive Physical Education. Disabled women enroll in a physical education class entitled Corrective Rest.

The traffic office has reserved parking spaces for disabled students in several locations convenient to buildings on campus. Where parking was diagonal, some wide spaces were required to permit loading and unloading of wheel chairs.

In the spring of 1960, several physically handicapped students expressed an interest in forming a club for students with physical disabilities. The counselor for vocational rehabilitation acted as sponsor and helped the students to organize the Rehab Club. The purposes expressed in the charter were primarily social in nature; but in the fall of 1960, the Rehab Club petitioned the Office of Student Services to install cabinets for disabled students in the main classroom building. The Rehab Club contributed locks for the doors. On another occasion, the campus was surveyed, and recommendations were made for the improvement of facilities. A large number of disabled students participated during the first few months of the club's existence, but participation currently has decreased to only a few students.

During the 1960–1961 school year, the Rehab Club sponsored two exhibition wheel-chair basketball games. Since some of the players are polio victims, one game was played for the benefit of the March of Dimes. Wheel-chair basketball has not been played on a varsity basis at this college.

The placement of physically handicapped students has been handled by the College placement office and by sponsoring agencies. The only special procedures for disabled persons are the informing of prospective employers of the candidate's physical limitations. The placement office has had little difficulty in placing disabled graduates. For example, of nine disabled graduates receiving baccalaureate degrees in May of 1961, three became teachers, two continued in graduate school, one entered personnel work in industry, another accepted a job in office management, and one girl became a housewife. The placement office has no record of placement of one of these graduates.

Some safety procedures have been developed for building evacuation of physically handicapped students. Elevators are convenient for access to upper floors but are to be avoided during evacuation because of the danger of power failure. Stair-type outside fire escapes are of little value to severely handicapped students and are generally unsuited for carrying disabled persons. Where chute-type escapes exist, some assistance may be required for severely disabled persons. In classroom buildings, the evacuation of disabled students is arranged by the professor, who assigns several able-bodied students to assist in carrying wheel-chair students down interior stairways. In order to avoid congestion in a building, it is considered that only a few disabled students should be scheduled for upper floors at a given time. In dormitories, wheel-chair students live on ground floors. Periodic practice evacuations are held in all buildings, and procedures are considered satisfactory by personnel in charge of safety.

Special Facilities

Before facilities were modified on this campus, in 1954, sixteen non-wheel-chair clients were sponsored by the Kansas VRS. The first modfications were for the convenience of these students and included the installation of handrails on several stairways and the covering of stair treads in the main classroom building with a nonskid material. By the following year, forty-one clients were sponsored by VRS.

The first modifications for wheel-chair students were made in 1955. A wooden ramp was erected at the entrance to the administration building, and several curbs were beveled at street crossings. Concrete ramps have been constructed since that time. There are now twenty-five beveled street crossings on this campus. Entrances to some buildings have been beveled by the use of either wood or concrete, but these are simply variations of ramp construction, and the experiences have been similar.

Glass panels have been installed on solid doors in many locations so that disabled persons approaching the door can be seen and are less likely to be struck by the door. This danger is considerably reduced in recently constructed buildings where entrance and exit doors are of solid glass.

Requests for the modification of facilities are sometimes made by an academic department for the convenience of disabled students enrolled in that department without co-ordinating the proposed change through the counselor for vocational rehabilitation. As a consequence, some unnecessary modifications have been made which have delayed more essential improvements at other locations.

Housing has probably been the most critical problem in accommodating physically handicapped students. Many disabled students have lived in private dwellings off-campus because of limited on-campus facilities. In some cases, students have preferred to live in private quarters. For some off-campus disabled students, the college has provided temporary wooden ramps that are installed with the permission of property owners.

Freshmen women are required to live in Morse Hall for Women. Disabled women may remain in the dormitory beyond the freshman year. Morse Hall is equipped with an elevator, and only minor modifications have been necessary to accommodate disabled students. Wheel-chair women are assigned rooms on the ground floor.

On-campus housing for men was not available until the men's dormitory was erected in 1959. No elevator was provided in this structure, but the ground floor has been reserved for students unable to climb stairs. The recreation room is located on the ground floor. Rooms are designed for two students, but College policy has been to permit only one wheel chair per room to avoid some problems that have been encountered when neither person was able to keep the room clean. Wheel-chair students have usually shared their room with a pusher or another person with a less severe disability.

Some modifications have been made in dormitory rest rooms. Both showers and tubs for women are available in Morse Hall. Chairs were used inside showers in the men's dormitory, and wheel-chair students transferred themselves to the chair by means of handrails. Handrails were installed with standard water closets, and a back rest was provided at one location in the men's dormitory.

Several people have been involved in planning modifications and new construction projects, but errors have been apparent in the design of some modifications. Ramps were installed on one building after specifications submitted by the state architect included steps at all entrances. A sink was lowered in the men's dormitory for the convenience of wheelchair students, but they could no longer maneuver their chairs under the lowered basin. As a consequence of such mistakes, to make certain that proposed buildings will be accessible to wheel-chair students, the counselor for vocational rehabilitation is assigned responsibility for making recommendations on this aspect of all building specifications.

An elevator was requested in 1955 for the four-storied administration building on the basis of the need of physically handicapped students. When the elevator was installed, operating controls were placed at a convenient height for students seated in wheel chairs. In the beginning, a student employee operated the elevator between classes, and for the remainder of the time it was locked. Later, the elevator was left unsupervised, but operating instructions and a priority list of passengers was posted. Top priority has always been reserved for disabled students.

Two major construction projects are currently under way in the center of the campus. It has been necessary to close off a large area and to direct traffic over much longer routes. The new routes are inadequate for severely disabled students, and some access ways have been made in new locations.

Many other special facilities have been provided for the convenience of physically handicapped students. Tape recorders have been available for students unable to record lecture notes. A spare wheel chair and crutches were available for loan to students when their own appliances were out of order. Wheel-chair student spectators at football games have been provided a ramped platform for their convenience and safety. The improvement of existing facilities and the provision of new facilities has been a continuing responsibility at this College.

62. Vocational Rehabilitation of the Severely Disabled *

ELSA H. WILLIAMS, *Field Agent, North Wayne County Office, Division of Vocational Rehabilitation, Detroit*

DURING THE PERIOD from March, 1955, through June, 1956, the Michigan Division of Vocational Rehabilitation and the Rehabilitation Institute of Metropolitan Detroit provided a special program of rehabilitative services to 116 severely disabled clients. Most of the funds to underwrite the program came from two federal projects, one under Section 3 and the other under Section 4a2 of Public Law 565, the Vocational Rehabilitation Act of 1954.

A major provision of the special program was the location, from March, 1955, through June, 1956, of a full-time DVR counselor at RIMD. During these years RIMD was housed in a pavilion of Herman Kiefer Hospital in Detroit. Thus the vocational rehabilitation counselor was in a position to co-ordinate medical rehabilitative services with prevocational and vocational services available at various schools in the Detroit metropolitan community and at such agencies as The Detroit League for the Handicapped, Jewish Vocational Service, and Goodwill Industries.

A report on the two federal projects was submitted in July, 1956, both to the State Supervisor of DVR and to the Director of RIMD. The present report represents a follow-up through February, 1958, of the 116 clients originally picked up for project services between March, 1955, and June, 1956.

* Reprinted by permission of the junior author and *Vocational Guidance Quarterly*, 7:68–69; Winter, 1959.

Client Population

Eighty-four of the 116 clients were men and 32 were women. Their ages ranged from seventeen to seventy, with the average age thirty-eight. Of the 116, the majority had two or more extremities disabled from traumatic spinal cord injuries or from cerebrovascular accidents. Others were disabled as the result of limb amputations, poliomyelitis, tuberculosis, diabetes mellitus, arthritis, Buerger's disease, cerebral palsy, and multiple sclerosis. Also represented in this group of clients were speech problems, hearing losses, visual handicaps, emotional disorders, and mental retardation.

Upon being evaluated in the course of the special program, 18 of the 116 clients were considered to have no employment potential and were therefore denied services. Of the 18, seven were hemiplegics because of cerebrovascular accidents; two had multiple sclerosis with all four limbs uncoordinated and limited in function; two were quadriplegics from traumatic spinal cord injury; and two had four extremities disabled by poliomyelitis and other complications.

Another of the 18 was disabled by arthritis; still another had cerebral palsy with four uncoordinated extremities; one was an above-knee amputee who moved so frequently that contact was broken; another was an arteriosclerotic bilateral below-knee amputee; yet another was hemiplegic from a gunshot wound inflicted during a suicide attempt.

Practically all of the 18 had either low intelligence or emotional problems or both. In fact, it was not the severity of physical disability alone that determined that these people had no vocational rehabilitation potential. It was usually the combination of low physical and mental capacity for employment.

Four of those who had been accepted for service died before completing the program. Four others accepted for service became unavailable because of conflicts with the law. Thus, the number of clients who actually received vocational rehabilitation services under the provisions of the special programs was 90.

Rehabilitation Results

As determined in the follow-up through February, 1958, 61 of the 90 clients accepted for service have been "vocationally rehabilitated," meaning that they have jobs or have in some other way attained economic independence. Thus, 49 clients were remuneratively employed. Three men were rehabilitated to self-care, freeing their wives to become wage earners and keep their families off relief rolls. Five housewives were functionally improved. And four students returned to school.

Following are listed the kinds of work in which the 49 remuneratively employed clients were engaged. (Job classifications approximate those of the *Dictionary of Occupational Titles.*) Five were employed in professional or managerial occupations; 12 were in clerical or sales; 12 on maintenance, personal service, or domestic jobs; 4 in skilled and 11 in semiskilled jobs; 4 in packaging or processing work of an unskilled nature; and one was in an unskilled job not elsewhere classified.

Findings in Perspective

Of the 90 clients accepted for service, then, 61 were rehabilitated vocationally and 29 were not. If the 90 clients were selected because, despite severe physical disabilities, they had vocational potential, why did a third of them not find placement in some form of employment?

First of all, it must be pointed out that the 29 were comparable with the larger group of 61 in extent of physical disability. The sad truth of the matter is that these 29, like the 18 screened out of the program at the beginning, could not overcome the obstacles imposed by their own personality maladjustments. Beyond this, with a few of the 29, as was also true with some of the 18 originally denied service, there was a problem of limited intelligence.

Probably the most important single thought that comes out of this study is that vocational counseling with the severely physically disabled cannot have its full effect unless clients have the benefit of personal counseling as well. The staff limitations that existed during the period of this study are in the process of being remedied. In RIMD's new facility adjoining Harper Hospital in Detroit, the work that one vocational rehabilitation counselor did in 1955–1956 will soon be done by three.

One of the three counselors will do psychological testing to determine the clients' emotional adjustments, intelligence levels, academic and other achievements, interests, and aptitudes. A second counselor will conduct a prevocational testing unit in which clients' vocational potentials can be found out through practical tryouts in a simulated work situation. The third counselor will have extensive knowledge of community resources and will serve primarily as a referral and placement specialist.

But the point is that each of these three counselors should be first personal counselors and then specialists, one in psychological testing, another in prevocational tryout, and the third in referral and placement. For it is how a client feels about what he is doing, or hopes to do, that determines the success or failure of his own efforts and the efforts of others in his behalf. If a client is to overcome the emotional difficulties that stand in the way of his vocational adjustment, he needs the help of counselors who are qualified to work not only with his vocational problems but also with his personal problems.

Suggested Readings

Allen, R. M., and Jefferson, T. W. *Psychological Evaluation of the Cerebral Palsied Person: Intellectual, Personality and Vocational Applications.* Springfield, Ill.: Charles C Thomas, 1962. 86 pp. A detailed evaluation of testing techniques for the cerebral-palsied individual based on the assumption that he must be evaluated in terms of the nonhandicapped. Tests on intellectual, personality, and vocational assessment are reviewed. Intelligence tests are considered from the standpoint of whether they are directly administrable or whether they depend upon an informant. The need for understanding sensori-motor limitations is stressed. A brief illustrative account of research findings with the various personality tests is given. The role of self-concept in vocational choice and problems with vocation are also noted.

Angers, "Job Counseling of the Epileptic," *Journal of Psychology,* 49:123–132; January, 1960.

Auerbach, Alice B. "Group Education for Parents of the Handicapped," *Children,* 8:135; July, 1961.

Brayton, Margaret R. *The Problems, Worries, Fears, and Anxieties of Physically Handicapped Junior and Senior High School Students,* Ed.D. Thesis, Boston University, 1957.

Bringhurst, Nancy. *Educational and Vocational Adjustment of Orthopedically Handicapped Children,* Ed.D. Thesis, University of Houston, Texas, 1959.

Cantoni, L. J. "Forty-Eight Handicapped College Students," *Vocational Guidance Quarterly,* 9:268–270; Summer, 1961. Survey of problems of handicapped students at Wayne University.

Christman, D.; Flynn, A.; Gardner, M.; Houch, Dorothy; and Mahood, Eloise. "Counseling Problems," *Cerebral Palsy Review,* 17:130–131; 1956. A Temple cerebral palsy workshop group describe very briefly problems in counseling and in the psychometric evaluation of the individual with cerebral palsy.

Cohen, A. "Personality Aspects of Multiple Sclerosis," *Journal of Rehabilitation,* 28:18–20, 50–51; 1962. Review of the literature on the personality aspects of multiple sclerosis for the decade 1950–1961. The twenty-nine references reported appear to indicate that there is no distinctive personality complex associated specifically with multiple sclerosis, atlhough certain characteristics such as high dependency needs, depression, anxiety, preoccupation with self, and insecurity are frequently found in this disease, as they are in other catastrophic disability. Some indication of the influence of emotional factors and tension-producing events in inducing exacerbations of physical symptoms or remissions is indicated.

Condon, Margaret. "Extra Curricular Activities of Physically Handicapped Students," *Personnel and Guidance Journal*, 37:53–54; September, 1958. Lists various extracurricular activities by type of disability.

——. "A Ten Year Survey of Physically Handicapped Students in the City College of New York," *Personnel and Guidance Journal*, 36:268–271; December, 1957. Follow-up study of 150 handicapped students reveals that with proper training they can compete vocationally.

Condon, Margaret, and Lerner, Ruth. "Program Adjustments for the Physically Handicapped at the College Level," *Personnel and Guidance Journal*, 35:41–42; September, 1956. Details various kinds of administrative, transportation, and operating adjustments made in New York colleges.

Feintuch, A. "Contributions of the Sheltered Workshop to the Habilitation of the Cerebral Palsied," *Cerebral Palsy Review*, 22:25–26; 1961. The more seriously involved individuals benefit from such facilities by virtue of the psychological and social effects of paid work experience and positive contacts with a need to develop work habits and proper work attitudes, through the acquisition of simple skills which may increase their employability, and by receiving counseling as an integral part of the program.

Helfand, A. "Vocational Counseling in Work Evaluation of the Cerebral Palsied," *Journal of Rehabilitation*, 26:5–6, 46–50; 1960. Based upon a study of methods for the determination of the work capacities of those with cerebral palsy, the article describes the use of the work sample technique in co-operation with short-term vocational counseling as an effective procedure in the vocational rehabilitation of these clients.

Keith, R. C., and Bax, M. C. O. "Assessment, Training and Employment of Adolescents and Young Adults with Cerebral Palsy: What Facilities Are Needed," *Cerebral Palsy Bulletin*, 3:135–138; 1961. Discusses the implications, with respect to the better facilities needed for the adolescent cerebral-palsied, of the postschool unsolved problems of earlier evaluation, training, and supervision and employment.

Laird, J. T. "Emotional Disturbances among the Physically Handicapped," *Personnel and Guidance Journal*, 36:190–191; November, 1957. Of 125 physically handicapped clients, 76 per cent had elevations over 70 t-score on clinical scales of the MMPI. Of 40 who were interviewed and tested with projective tests, 45 per cent were emotionally disturbed. Concludes personal counseling is most important in vocational rehabilitation work.

Lenard, H. M. "Vocational Implications for the Cerebral Palsied," *Cerebral Palsy Review*, 23:2:13–17; March, 1962. A very good discussion of vocational rehabilitation of the cerebral-palsied individual. Points out that we should start early to give the child the "edge of time." Detailed discussion of

(1) vocational choice, (2) counseling with parents, (3) summer work experience, and other pertinent matters; sixteen references.

Linde, T. "Accent on Assets: Two Problems in Psychology and Cerebral Palsy: I, Individual Personality," *Cerebral Palsy Review*, 23:3–4, 11; 1962. Part I is concerned with problems of individual adjustment: frustration, guilt, inferiority, and idolization.

———. "Accent on Assets: Two Problems in Psychology and Cerebral Palsy: II, Social Interaction," *Cerebral Palsy Review*, 23:5–6, 19; 1962. Part II develops the point that, along with the cultivation of desirable insights and self-perceptions in cerebral-palsied persons, "the public needs help in learning to be rationally discriminant in its responses to the multitudinous stimuli presented by individuals with disability."

Lubin, B., and Slominski, Anita. "A Counseling Program with Adult, Male Cerebral Palsied Patients," *Cerebral Palsy Review*, 21:3–5, 11; 1960. Experiences attending a four-month period of individual counseling sessions followed by a three-month period of group counseling sessions are reported. There appeared to be a "need for concurrent counseling sessions with parents of cerebral palsied patients in order to provide some support for the parents through the . . . periods of change in the patients' behavior."

Morgan, M. R. "Assessment, Training and Employment of Adolescents and Young Adults with Cerebral Palsy: Facilities Now Available," *Cerebral Palsy Bulletin*, 3:139–144; 1961. A youth employment officer provides liaison between the school and postschool facilities. The National Spastic Society's employment department, along with the government training centers which are run by the Ministry of Labor, provides training and placement opportunities through sheltered workshop facilities, local day centers, and home-work programs.

———. "Vocational Guidance for the Handicapped," *Cerebral Palsy Bulletin*, 3:174–179; 1961. Reports on an international seminar held in Jerusalem.

Nadler, E. B. "Prediction of the Sheltered Shopwork Performance of Individuals with Severe Physical Disability," *Personnel and Guidance Journal*, 36:95–98; October, 1957. A study of the predictive validity of WAIS and Bender-Gestalt scores concerning the sheltered workshop performance of older severely handicapped persons showed that intellectual factors accounted for 25 per cent of the variance. Age factor unimportant.

Rosenberg, B., and Usdane, W. M. "The TOWER System: Vocational Evaluation of the Severely Handicapped for Training and Placement," *Personnel and Guidance Journal*, 42:149–151; October, 1963. TOWER (testing, orientation, and work evaluation in rehabilitation) contains an assembly of tests in thirteen occupational areas, scoring aids, response sheets, and other materials. Paper suggests practical aspects of system.

Rusalem, H. *Guiding the Physically Handicapped College Student*. New York: Bureau of Publications, Teachers College, Columbia University, 1962. 151 pp.

Schiller, E. J. "Organizing a Vocational Program for a Cerebral Palsy Agency,"

Cerebral Palsy Review, 19:2; March–April, 1958. Director of Cerebral Palsy Association of Western New York discusses process of setting up vocational training.

Schoggen, Phil. Department of Psychology, University of Oregon, Eugene, Oregon. (Research in process.) In the process of making a large number of observations on the behavior of matched pairs of disabled and nondisabled children in ordinary everyday activities at school and home.

Stephen, Elspeth. "Assessment, Training and Employment of Adolescents and Young Adults with Cerebral Palsy: An Introductory Review," *Cerebral Palsy Bulletin,* 3:127–134; 1961. The British and Scottish data on the adult cerebral-palsied indicate (1) a prevalence of approximately 0.5/1,000 adult population; (2) about 25 per cent in open employment; (3) an order of employment from monoplegics and hemiplegics (most frequent) through paraplegics to quadriplegics and athetoids; and (4) little published evidence regarding the results of vocational guidance and training (to compare with the American and Danish efficiency of 50 per cent or less).

Wolfson, R. G. "Counseling the Epileptic," *Vocational Guidance Quarterly,* 8:35–37; 1960. Vocational counseling of epileptics discussed with reference to occupational acceptability. Agency efforts are increasing this.

Worden, D. K. "The Intelligence of Boys with Muscular Dystrophy," *Journal of Consulting Psychology,* 25:369; April, 1961. MD group children had a mean IQ of 83, whereas their sibling controls had a mean IQ of 110. The MD group differs significantly.

Wright, Beatrice A. *Physical Disability—A Psychological Approach.* New York: Harper and Brothers, 1960. 408 pp.

Author Index to Reading in Guidance of Exceptional Children

(Names appearing in capitals refer to the principal authors of articles, with the article beginning on the page followed by an asterisk. Names with initials refer to annotated bibliographic citations at the end of chapters. Names without initials refer to sources cited in the readings. Names of junior authors are followed by reference to the senior author of the article.)